A Spectacular Journey

Astrology of the Famed is a gripping tour de force through the fascinating lives of Cleopatra, St. Francis of Assisi, Dracula, Leonardo da Vinci, and Beethoven—five of the most startling people in history.

Each of these extraordinary people takes on exciting new dimensions as their lives unfold in this masterful blend of astrology and historical fact. Delivered in a charming and engaging style, *Astrology of the Famed* is a fast-paced narrative, sweeping you up in the passion and adventure lived by these phenomenal people, each of whom has shaped the world.

Noel Tyl skillfully uses astrology to flesh-out the lives and times of these legendary people, filling in the gaps in each of their histories. With keen insight into the psychology and personality of these remarkable individuals, Tyl reconstructs their lives and uncovers the astrological influences behind their motivations, mind-sets, and circumstances—establishing their birth charts at last.

Find yourself transported back in time to experience the unique drama that shaped the lives of five people who changed the world. The author guides you through the ages, bringing the facts of history to life to reveal the hidden influences that made each of these people the stuff of legend.

Relive the greatest lives of all in this exciting book that blends the detective work of a mystery with the wealth of detail found only in a tell-all biography—there's never before been an astrology book like this!

About the Author

For over twenty years, Noel Tyl has been one of the most prominent astrologers in the western world. His seventeen textbooks, built around the twelve-volume *Principles and Practice of Astrology*, were extraordinaily popular throughout the 1970s. He also founded and edited *Astrology Now* magazine.

He is one of astrology's most sought-after lecturers in the United States, and internationally in Denmark, Norway, Germany, South Africa, and Switzerland, where for the first three World Congresses of Astrology he was a keynote speaker.

Noel wrote *Prediction in Astrology* (Llewellyn Publications), a master volume of technique and practice, and edited Books 9 through 16 of the Llewellyn New World Astrology Series, *How to Use Vocational Astrology*, *How to Personalize the Outer Planets*, *How to Manage the Astrology of Crisis*, *Exploring Consciousness in the Horoscope*, *Astrology's Special Measurements*, *Sexuality in the Horoscope*, *Communicating the Horoscope*, and *Astrology Looks at History*. In the spring of 1994, his master opus, *Synthesis and Counseling in Astrology—The Professional Manual* (almost 1,000 pages of analytical technique in practice), was published. Noel is a graduate of Harvard University in psychology and lives in Fountain Hills, Arizona.

To Write to the Author

If you wish to contact the author or would like more information about this book, please write to the author in care of Llewellyn Worldwide, and we will forward your request. Both the author and publisher appreciate hearing from you and learning of your enjoyment of this book and how it has helped you. Llewellyn Worldwide cannot guarantee that every letter written to the author can be answered, but all will be forwarded. Please write to:

Llewellyn's New Worlds of Mind and Spirit
P.O. Box 64383-K735, St. Paul, MN 55164-0383, U.S.A.
Please enclose a self-addressed, stamped envelope for reply, or $1.00 to cover costs. If outside U.S.A., enclose international postal reply coupon.

Free Catalog from Llewellyn

For more than ninety years Llewellyn has brought its readers knowledge in the fields of metaphysics and human potential. Learn about the newest books in spiritual guidance, natural healing, astrology, occult philosophy, and more. Enjoy book reviews, New Age articles, a calendar of events, plus current advertised products and services. To get your free copy of *Llewellyn's New Worlds*, send your name and address to:

Llewellyn's New Worlds of Mind and Spirit
P.O. Box 64383-K735, St. Paul, MN 55164-0383, U.S.A.

Llewellyn's Modern Astrology Library

ASTROLOGY
OF THE FAMED

✦ **Noel Tyl** ✦

1996
Llewellyn Publications
St. Paul, Minnesota, 55164-0383, U.S.A.

Astrology of the Famed. Copyright © 1996 by Noel Tyl. All rights reserved. Printed in the United States of America. No part of this book may be used or reproduced in any manner whatsoever without written permission from Llewellyn Publications, except in the case of brief quotations embodied in critical articles or reviews.

FIRST EDITION, 1996
First Printing

Cover Design by Maria Mazzara
Editing and Interior Design by Connie Hill

Library of Congress Cataloging-in-Publication Data
Astrology of the famed /Noel Tyl. — 1st ed.
      p.   cm. — (Llewellyn's modern astrology library series)
   Includes bibliographical references.
   ISBN 1-56718-735-8 (alk. paper)
    1. Gifted persons—Miscellanea. 2. Horoscopes. 3. Astrology.
 I. Tyl, Noel, 1936–   . II. Series.
 BF1728.2.G54A88   1996
 133.5—dc20   96-0000
                                                          CIP

Llewellyn Publications
A Division of Llewellyn Worldwide, Ltd.
St. Paul, Minnesota 55164-0383, U.S.A.

Llewellyn's Modern Astrology Library

This series contains books for the *Leading Edge* of practical and applied astrology, as we move toward the culmination of the twentieth century.

This is not speculative astrology, nor astrology so esoteric as to have little practical application in meeting the needs of people in these critical times. Yet, these books go far beyond the meaning of "practicality" as seen prior to the 1990s. Our needs are spiritual as well as mundane, planetary as well as particular, evolutionary as well as progressive. Astrology grows with the times, and our times make heavy demands upon Intelligence and Wisdom.

The authors are all professional astrologers drawing from their own practice and knowledge of historical persons and events, demonstrating proof of their conclusions with the horoscopes of real people in real situations.

Modern astrology relates the individual person to the Universe in which he/she lives, not as a passive victim of alien forces but as an active participant in an environment expanded to the breadth *and depth* of the Cosmos. We are not alone, and our responsibilities are infinite.

The horoscope is both a measure and a guide to personal movement—seeing every act undertaken, every decision made, every event, as *time dynamic:* with effects that move through the many dimensions of space and levels of consciousness in fulfillment of Will and Purpose. Every act becomes an act of Will, for we extend our awareness to consequences reaching to the ends of time and space.

This is astrology supremely important to this unique period in human history, as Pluto transits Sagittarius, and Neptune and Uranus move out of Capricorn into Aquarius. The books in this series are intended to provide insight into the critical needs and the critical decisions that must be made.

These books, too, are "active agents," bringing to the reader knowledge that will liberate the higher forces inside each person, to the end that we may fulfill that for which we were intended.

Carl Llewellyn Weschcke

Other Books by the Author

The Horoscope as Identity

The Principles and Practice of Astrology
   I. *Horoscope Construction*
  II. *The Houses: Their Signs and Planets*
 III. *The Planets: Their Signs and Aspects*
 IV. *Aspects and Houses in Analysis*
  V. *Astrology and Personality*
 VI. *The Expanded Present*
VII. *Integrated Transits*
VIII. *Analysis and Prediction*
 IX. *Special Horoscope Dimensions: Success, Sex and Illness*
  X. *Astrological Counsel*
 XI. *Astrology: Mundane, Astral and Occult*
XII. *Times to Come*

Teaching Guide to the Principles and Practice of Astrology

The Missing Moon

Holistic Astrology—the Analysis of Inner and Outer Environments

Prediction in Astrology

Synthesis & Counseling in Astrology: The Professional Manual

Edited by the Author

How to Use Vocational Astrology for Success in the Workplace

How to Personalize the Outer Planets:
* The Astrology of Uranus, Neptune and Pluto*

How to Manage the Astrology of Crisis:
* Resolution through Astrology*

Exploring Consciousness in the Horoscope

Astrology's Special Measurements

Sexuality in the Horoscope

Communicating the Horoscope

Astrology Looks at History

Forthcoming by the Author

Predictions for a New Millennium

Contents

Rectification
Finding the Correct Fit

I n this engrossing book, Noel Tyl merges the technique of rectification with the adventure, genius, drama, pomp, and circumstance of five of the most unique and interesting lives in all of history. There never has been a book like this in all our astrological literature!

Introduction by Basil T. Fearrington

♦

Cleopatra, Dracula, St. Francis of Assisi, Beethoven, and Leonardo da Vinci were all distinct and different individuals who impressed themselves upon our history emphatically. Tyl's work details, through astrology, the personal development of each unique life. You'll find definite stylistic differences in the treatment given to each chapter, adding to the fresh excitement and adventure of learning you will get from reading about each personage.

Rectification in astrology is a rigorous technique and an art form of detail. It demands and requires facility with many astrological measurement techniques, an ability to translate characterological dimensions into the astrological language, and a sharp sense of intuition. The process is the opposite of astrology as it is normally practiced: instead of using full data as a starting point for analysis, we work backward and allow life events to determine the time of birth. We make the assumption that we can define the occurrence of events in a person's life through astrological measurements and so we work to find the right "fit" through an endless series of "what if" statements, experiments, and personality characterizations. In the hands of a master like Tyl, the process works like magic. He finds the perfect fit and he shows us all how it's done.

The degree of difficulty within the rectification process is defined by the information that the astrologer has to work with. For example, if your subject were born between 10 A.M. and 10:30 A.M., it will not be very difficult to pinpoint a time of birth within the span of that thirty minutes. Much of the work will already have been done. However, if the time of birth is unknown, the challenge is quite formidable, sometimes to the point of mental exhaustion.

The degree of difficulty that the author faced in the rectification of these famous people's lives was as tough as can be. There is obviously the complication of not having a birth time, but in many cases here, the *year* of birth was also in question; and in order to even begin working with this problem (using individuals in history), an enormous amount of history must be learned and absorbed. For example, in "Cleopatra—The Queen of Kings," you will read that historians are basically in agreement with the year of Cleopatra's birth, but that the month of birth is only approximated. In order to find the right fit, Tyl had to transport himself back to the time period in which Cleopatra lived and walk in her footsteps with the perspective of the eyes of a master astrologer. He had to see what she saw, think what she thought, anticipate behavior through her history first, and then translate this into a horoscope that symbolizes her life's events and her character. To make it all fit right is a harrowing task of grand proportions. Noel does it to perfection in his inimitable "Moon in Leo in the 3rd House" dramatic fashion.

If you have any sensitivities at all, you will weep at his religious intensity when you read the life story of the very humble St. Francis of Assisi. I have never had an emotional impact from an astrological text in the way I did when reading the portion of St. Francis' story called, "The Seraph, The Stigmata, and Death." You will marvel at the genius of Leonardo da Vinci, for which chapter I provided the rectification of Cesare Borgia's horoscope. Noel uncovers an amazing measurement in relationship to the date that the Mona Lisa was stolen. You will learn the origin of the legend of Dracula and you will come face to face with the madness of Beethoven. Each chapter in the book paints a vivid historical picture with rich imagery, depth, and intrigue, all explained masterfully through Tyl's astrology. You will not only learn about astrology but will also gain in your knowledge of history.

There will be a time in future centuries when an astrologer will write a book, perhaps similar to this one, and he or she will focus upon an eccentric genius of the twentieth century in the same way that Leonardo and Beethoven come to light in these pages during our times now. Michael Jackson would definitely qualify as such a famed person with artistic/entertainment genius and eccentricities. It is easy and reasonable to visualize him being the subject of an astrologer's book on famed people centuries from now; his contribution to popular music is just that important. His is one of the most recognizable faces and names on the entire planet and he single-handedly opened the MTV age for all African/American recording artists. He is definitely a person among the famed.

In order to familiarize you with Noel's rectification style, I have selected Michael Jackson as a model to rectify in quick, concise, short steps, with logic that is easy to follow. It serves as a quick preview of what's ahead for you in this book.

Michael Joseph Jackson was born on August 29, 1958 in Gary, Indiana. The time of birth is unknown.[1] Of his birth, Michael states,[2] "I was born in Gary, Indiana, on a late summer night in 1958 ...." It is my opinion that "on a late summer night" means after 10:30 P.M. Since we know for sure that he was born on August 29 and that the birth took place late in the night, we can be comfortable with this ninety-minute span of time from 10:30 to midnight. The trick now is to define an Ascendant so that we can test angularity. Measurements to the angles are the most important consideration in the rectification process.

Figure 1 (page xii) shows a horoscope set for 10:30 P.M. There is a Taurus Ascendant with Mars rising upon the Ascendant. Venus is the chart ruler and is in conjunction with Uranus. The 5th House is very strong with the Sun-Pluto conjunction, symbolic of his entertainment prowess, talent, and creativity. It would be very easy, without the test of measurements, to accept this horoscope as a starting point, working forward to refine the Ascendant degree in Taurus. The Taurean symbolization linking the throat to singing is an easy deduction to begin and end with. But does Mars rising in Taurus fit the image that Michael Jackson projects?

---

1 The state of Indiana will not release birth certificate information. That is why we have yet to see a published horoscope of Michael Jackson or David Letterman, for example.

2 Michael Jackson and Jackie Onassis, *Moonwalk* (New York: Doubleday, 1988), 6.

Taurean energy strives to keep things as they are. A person with Mars rising in Taurus needs to project himself ideally in terms of structure and organization; energy works for the securing of the status quo and perhaps lacks innovation in the process. That is *not* who Michael Jackson is. If anything, as an artist, he has striven to buck the organization of others by not having control factors placed on his need to innovate and stay ahead of current trends. Michael led the parade against Motown Records when he and his

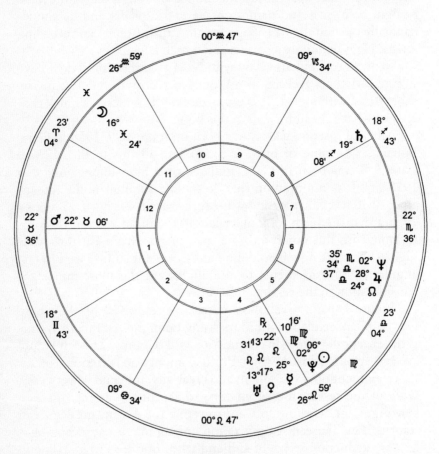

Figure 1
Michael Jackson
Aug. 29, 1958, 10:30 P.M. CDT
Gary, Indiana
87W20   41N36
Placidus Houses

brothers decided that they wanted to leave the company (during the mid-70s). This is definitely a quality of a 12th House Mars, bucking the organization, but not necessarily a Taurus Ascendent.

Think about it. You never really know what Michael is going to look like, do you? He seems constantly to retool and change his image like a chameleon. The same can be said of his music. Interviews abound where people talk about Michael's insatiable curiosity and untiring desire to learn new things. For those of us like

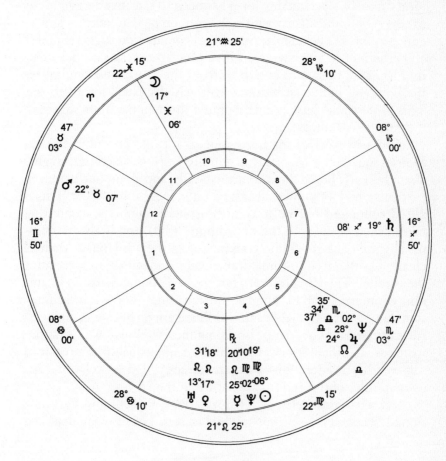

Figure 2
Michael Jackson
Aug. 29, 1958, 11:53 P.M. CDT
Gary, Indiana
87W20   41N36
Placidus Houses

me,[3] who have been close enough to observe him, the wit and quickness of mind are easily seen. Those who know him well speak of him as a prankster. All of these things, as well as his diversity as an artist, suggest a *Gemini* Ascendant, not a Taurus Ascendant.

Figure 2 (page xiii) shows another orientation horoscope set for 11:53 P.M. CDT in Gary, Indiana. It has 16 degrees Gemini upon the Ascendant. The Sun/Moon blend suggests that the mind is used to fuel idealism. There is great sensitivity here; a dedication to ideals. Jackson's personality form has been so sensitive and gentle as to suggest homosexuality within the stereotype that links those several attributes. The angular Sun-Pluto conjunction suggests power and prominence.[4] The very sensitive Moon permeates his personality form and, in square to Saturn from the 7th House symbolizes the powerful public ambition, sensitively displayed for all to see. This professional push is corroborated through the Mars square to the changed Midheaven.

Mercury, ruler of the horoscope, is retrograde and in the 4th House, squared by Mars. He is definitely preoccupied in thoughts about his early home life, about the family, and about one parent in particular, and we know that this parental focus is his father. This is all corroborated by the lower hemisphere emphasis, suggesting "unfinished business in the early home" (Tyl), and is also symbolized by the tight Sun/Pluto conjunction in the 4th House. Michael clearly has the need to think dramatically and with a king complex (he is called The King of Pop), but the early home situation is running counterpoint in his mind at the same time. There is little question that his early homelife and childhood are on his mind, and with Mercury (squared by Mars) also ruling the 5th House, we can anticipate sexual difficulties in giving of the Self, probably as a result of self-worth considerations that are directly tied to relationships (Moon, ruler of the 2nd square Saturn in the 7th).

Jackson's latest release, "History—Past, Present and Future—Book I,"[5] contains a self-portrait by Jackson. The drawing depicts a

---

3 I have been a professional musician for twenty-three years and once toured with an act that opened for The Jacksons. I had many opportunities to observe Michael in action, but could not get close enough to him to ask him about his time of birth.

4 Please see Noel Tyl's study of the Profile of Prominence in Tyl, *Synthesis & Counseling In Astrology*, Llewellyn Publications, 1994.

5 Released on June 20, 1995.

young child sitting in a corner, clutching his microphone under-neath him and looking very sad. The caption with it says:

> Before you judge me
> Try hard to love me
> Look within your heart
> Then ask have you seen my childhood

There is simply no doubt that his childhood and early homelife tensions are on his mind constantly, working in counterpoint to the need to think and communicate dramatically.

Saturn in Sagittarius in the 7th House suggests a delay in rela-tionship fulfillment, probably because of late emotional maturation. It is also symbolic of his innate caution with others, as well as an ethical idealism in relationships. These capsule descriptions let us know that the overall orientation seems to fit. It is workable. It makes sense. We are headed in the right direction!

These initial deductions must now be confirmed by angular transits, Solar Arcs, and Secondary Progressions, with tight refine-ments made through tertiary progressions. We never trust person-ality and character dynamics alone because they are based upon subjective dimensions, like one's opinion of a photograph. That is why you must confirm the rectification with *measurements*, not per-sonality factors.

The first major event in the life of Michael Jackson was in October of 1969. It was the release of the debut record of the Jack-son 5 entitled, "I Want You Back." We do not know the actual date of release in October. I am using October 15. Solar Arc Midheaven is in exact opposition to Pluto (Figure 3, page xvi), suggesting recognition and publicity. This song sold two million copies within six weeks of its release, paving the way for a succession of million sellers. The Jackson 5 had #1 smash records in 1970, 1971, and 1972, and it is easy to anticipate the Solar Arc Midheaven moving toward glory in the opposition with the Sun within all of this early success. The group's sales outdistanced The Beatles! This is a good start for us in the rectification.

Michael's first solo album, titled "Got To Be There," was released in January of 1972, followed by his motion picture ode to a rodent in the film, "Ben." Transiting Saturn was upon his Ascen-dant throughout the year, establishing a peak for him.

In November 1978, Jackson made his acting debut as a scarecrow in "The Wiz." In Figure 4 (page xvii) we see the Secondary Progressed Moon, a superb timing device in astrology, exactly upon the Descendant, with transiting Neptune upon the Descendant as well! He showed a new face to the public and began his extremely successful creative partnership with Quincy Jones.

In August 1979, the Jones/Jackson collaboration produced the first of Michael's two best albums. It was called "Off The Wall,"and was released *on the exact day that Jupiter transited in exact opposition with to his Midheaven*. It went on to sell eight million copies!

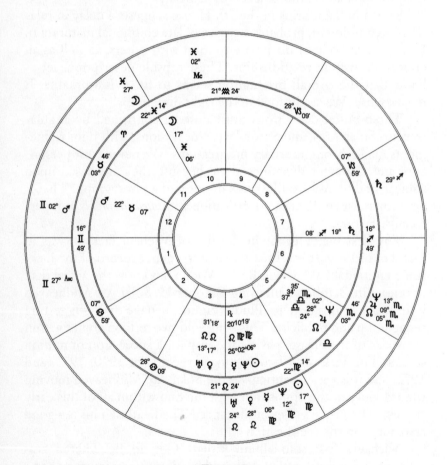

Figure 3
Solar Arc—Debut Record
Oct. 15, 1969

The album "Thriller" was released on December 1, 1982. It was followed by two years of the most amazing success that any performer in the music business has ever had. This album has sold close to fifty million copies to date and was initiated, not so much by its actual release, but by a Michael Jackson appearance on a television show called "Motown 25," celebrating the twenty-fifth anniversary of Motown Records. The show aired on May 16, 1983 with a viewing audience of forty-seven million people around the world. Michael unveiled a new dance called "The Moonwalk" and from that point on, his career and "Thriller" skyrocketed. On May

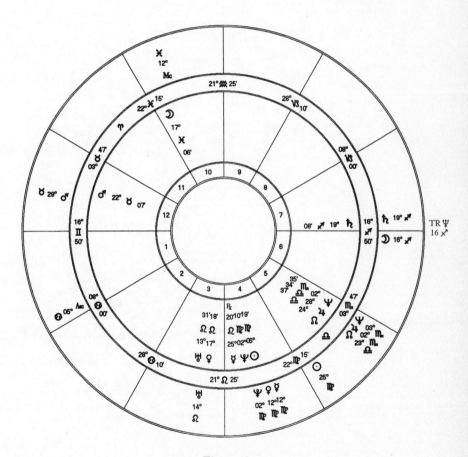

Figure 4
Secondary—"The Wiz"
Nov. 15, 1978

21, 1982, Jackson had Solar Arc Sun=Jupiter/Pluto (and SP MC conjunct Moon), which is very significant in his horoscope because of the natal picture Aries Point=Jupiter/Pluto! This is mega-success for someone with Jackson's potential. The SP Moon crossed his Midheaven in October 1983. Jackson was at a peak!

Tertiary progressions enable the astrologer to make predictions that are often exact to the date, often-times amazingly so. In Figure 5 (below) we see the day of his marriage. Please note the exact conjunctions of TP Jupiter with the Descendant, TP Moon to Pluto, and TP Pluto to the Sun! TP Uranus is less than one degree of arc from exact conjunction with the nadir, and will correspond to the

Figure 5
Tertiary—Marriage
May 26, 1994

next years of Michael's life, promising many new starts, breaks, upsets, and innovative developments. And please note: *transiting* Uranus in late Capricorn is approaching the square to Michael's Jupiter, ruler of his Descendant (December 1995, January 1996).

Jackson experienced the most trying time of his life in 1993 as the Los Angeles police department opened a criminal investigation of him based on charges that he sexually abused a thirteen-year-old boy. A civil suit was filed on September 14, 1993. The publicity and

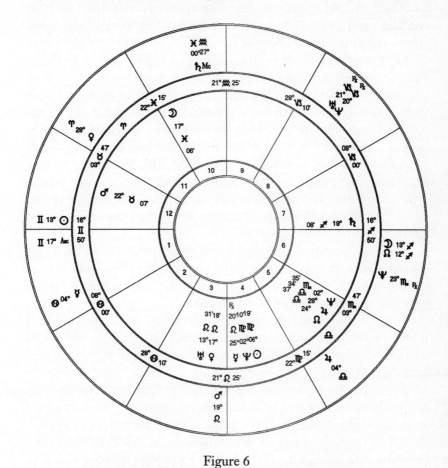

Figure 6

Inner Chart	Outer Chart
Michael Jackson	**Lunar Eclipse**
Aug. 29, 1958, 11:53 P.M. CDT	June 4, 1993, 6:00 A.M. PDT
Gary, Indiana	Los Angeles, California
87W20 41N36	118W15 34N04

Placidus Houses

stress of the charge reached their apex in November of 1993 *with transiting Neptune square Michael's MC/Asc midpoint.* Jackson canceled a tour to seek treatment for pain killers. There was a Lunar Eclipse on June 4 of that year at 14 Sagittarius (see Figure 6, page xix), conjunct Jackson's horizon (with his SP Moon crossing the Ascendant)! Eclipse Mars opposed his Midheaven; the eclipse Ascendant in Los Angeles was less than one degree from partile with his *natal* Ascendant!

Over and over again through the many years of Michael Jackson's life, we can see repeated confirmation of these rectified angles. There is just no doubt about it!

These are the kinds of things that you expect to see when the time of birth is accurate. As you read this book, you will grow to appreciate the details of the rectification technique displayed at its finest, and I want to share a personal note of gratitude to the author. I met Noel in 1976 when I went to him as a client. I was just beyond the novice level as an astrologer and had been completely turned around by his twelve-volume series, *The Principles & Practice of Astrology.* At the time, I had just come back from a music tour of Japan and China and needed to talk to him about my career and its direction. Our relationship since then has become one of the most cherished in my life.

Now, as a professional astrologer myself, that I have come far enough from that September in 1976 to be the first person ever invited to write an introduction to a Noel Tyl book is a testimony to him and all that he has shared with me.

One of the strongest synastric bonds in astrology is when a planet or angle of one chart is in conjunction or square the nodal axis of the other chart. Noel's Sun is in conjunction with my nodal axis! My Mars is in conjunction with his nodal axis, and every planet and angle in my horoscope makes a close synastric tie with his, perhaps highlighted by his Moon (conjunct my Pluto) exactly at my Sun/Moon midpoint! I can think of no higher honor for me at this time in my career than to have been asked to write this introduction. Noel, how I thank you! You are an *Astrologer Among the Famed.*

Basil T. Fearrington
Philadelphia, Pennsylvania
August, 1995

Cleopatra
The Queen of Kings

Cleopatra is the most famous woman the world has ever known. She was a Ptolemy, a Macedonian, tracing her monarchy directly to Alexander the Great who established his rule of Egypt after conquering the Persians there in 332 B.C. The city he founded—one of seventy Alexandrias he founded throughout his realms of conquest—was to become within a century the greatest city in the

An astrological rectification of the birth date and time of Cleopatra VII, Queen of Egypt

✦

known world, with gleaming white buildings reflecting the light of a burning god, with magnificent study centers preserving the arts and sciences, with the three-tiered 400-foot tall, wonder-of-the-world, Pharos lighthouse, presiding over a harbor that could host 1,200 ships at one time. Alexandria headed a sweeping desert plain that sustained over twelve million people inspired by the longest and, to them, holiest river on earth.[1]

Alexander died in 323, on June 10,[2] and gave over rule of Egypt to one of his staff-officers, Ptolemy, who declared himself king in 304 B.C. This first Ptolemy took the Egyptian title of Soter

---

1 Grant, *The Ancient Mediterranean*, 214–216.
2 Green, 475; Tyl rectification of Alexander's birth: July 22, 356 B.C. at 7:27 P.M. LMT in Pella Macedonia (21E45, 42N00); see Tyl: *Prediction in Astrology*.

I (*Saviour*), and the deified line began. Twelve more Ptolemies followed until Cleopatra ended the line and ended all Egyptian dynastic history at the close of her reign in 30 B.C.

It seems somehow appropriate that all the monumental history of dynastic Egypt from its first pharaoh, Menes, early in the fourth millennium B.C.—the Archaic Period beginning approximately 3168—was protectively enshrined in the secrecy of hieroglyphs. The achievements were wondrous, ancient, and arcane. It is somehow appropriate as well that these hieroglyphic records, when they were finally unlocked between 1822–1829, revealed first the very letters that spelled the names *Cleopatra* and *Ptolemy*.

Thomas Young and Jean-François Champollion, masters of ancient languages, studied the famed Rosetta Stone in parallel for fourteen years.[3] The Englishman isolated the *cartouche*, the oval pictogram organization of rulers' names in hieroglyphic practice; and the Frenchman, who garnered most of the credit, discovered the names that were to be Cleopatra and Ptolemy. He aligned a "Cleopatra" cartouche on an obelisk in London with a "Ptolemy" cartouche, the only name on the Rosetta stone, and decoded the key letters P, O, and L shared between them. Extending this technique to the names of other Pharaohs, like Ramesses, the name given to eleven monarchs, Champillion began to establish the phonetic symbols and meanings of the glyphs, the written form of a real, working language.

We see Egypt, all of Egypt, through Cleopatra. She *is* Egypt. She is our key to that enormous era. Besides the pyramids and Sphinx (which were 2,000 years or more old in Cleopatra's time), most of us know no more about this extraordinary epoch. Cleopatra is herself a monument.

The queen's tentacled outreach to foreign lands through the most powerful Roman leaders of history (Julius Caesar and Mark

---

3 After Napoleon's forces began their expedition to Egypt in the Summer of 1798, the study of Egyptian monuments and their hieroglyphics (Greek: *sacred glyphs*) was intense among numerous scholars in Europe. In the summer of 1799, an engineer-officer working near the Rosetta fortification some forty miles from Alexandria, found a "tabletop"-sized (the fragment measures 3'9" x 2'4" x 11") basalt stone with three obviously "copied" sections of text engraved on it in different languages: the top portion was in enigmatic hieroglyphics, the middle was demotic Egyptian (the cursive text of the priests and court), and the bottom was readable Greek.

The inscription communicated a decree of the priesthood assembled at Memphis in honor of Ptolemy V, Epiphanes (Manifestation), reigning 205–181 B.C. The black stone is now in the British Museum.

Antony, and through Antony, dealings with Octavian who would become Caesar Augustus, as we shall see) rebuilt Egypt to its greatest glory. Her rule eventually included almost the entire known world, and her treasury became the richest on earth. In every way, she was the "Queen of Kings."

Eventually, Rome stood up to her directly; actually declared war against her—and we will study the deciding battle at Actium in detail. In Roman perspective, to be foreign was to be unrefined and inferior. To be female as well, and powerful, and fabulously rich, and, specifically, Greek, comprised the ultimate profile of the ultimate enemy. That Cleopatra was favored by Julius Caesar and, indeed, bore his son (Caesarion, "little Caesar," who would become Ptolemy Caesar) made her politically tolerable at first, before her international power began to accumulate, but then her involvement with Antony in his division of the world with Octavian, Caesar's successor, was simply too much to face. In one sense, she compromised Antony and the plans of Rome; in another, Antony himself turned his back on Rome for this despised foreigner. Rome had to regain its honor and its lands. Octavian would win over Antony, and through him Rome would conquer Cleopatra.

All of this was then shaped into historical detail through extraordinary, vilifying propaganda created by Rome—its politicians, warriors, poets, and historians—against their inscrutable, intolerably female, foreign enemy. The image created was one of ambition, debauch, and power the likes of which history has not known again. Of course, the greater the demonic dimension, the threatening force, the greater then would be/was the victory over it by Rome.

The retelling of all this into countless histories, plays, operas, ballets, the classic dramas by Shakespeare and Shaw, classical paintings, and several Hollywood film extravaganzas has established Cleopatra as the archetype of the sexual temptress, the omnipotent female force that put Eve to shame, the wanton seductress who did in the world's greatest men, the murderess of brother and sister and countless others, the epitome of alluring danger, and an incomparable magnetic presence.

And then there is the nose. Ptolemy I Soter, the father of the dynasty, had the nose; undeniable, carved prominently into the face of coins; a monarch unflattered by engraver's grace; a genetic trait that could not be chiseled away. Ptolemy XII Auletes (the *Flute*

Player or *Piper*) had it too, and he fathered Cleopatra, early in 69 B.C. She too had the nose.[4]

Coinages in honor of Cleopatra (and others in the line throughout Ptolemaic history) all show the pronounced nose. Pascal, the seventeenth-century French mathematician and philosopher, is quoted as observing wryly, "Cleopatra's nose, if it had been shorter, the face of the whole world would have been changed!"[5] Yes, the nose was there, and we start almost begrudgingly to separate in our imaginations the reality of Cleopatra's appearance from the lush rumor about it.

Frequent intermarrying among all Pharaonic dynasties tended to stagnate the genetic pool. Certain traits became pronounced: bony facial structures, sometimes obesity, complexion, hair quality, vulnerability to certain diseases, dementia, and perhaps even the propensity to unique ways of thinking, even to the murder of family in the name of personal ascendancy. Born and living as a god rationalized extremes of concept and behavior. Each progenitor established a dramatic example for successive generations.

For Cleopatra, the nose was such an inheritance, and perhaps so was her murdering way throughout her reign:[6] her sister Arsinoe IV (exiled first and then executed at Cleopatra's insistence, by order of Antony); the poisoning of her brother and child-husband, Ptolemy

---

4 Auletes was formally Ptolemy XII Theos Philopater Philadelphus Neos Dionysos (respectively, the God, Lover of his Father, Lover of his Sister (or brother), the New Dionysus). These names tell a story for every Pharaoh: Ptolemy XII was a god, he got along well with his father (there was no murderous intrigue between son and father in succession), he married his sister, and he was the incarnation of another god, Dionysus. Dionysus was the Roman Bacchus, but also the god of a great wave of religious emotion, of mystical, escapist themes, that practically eclipsed the old Olympian cult. This Ptolemy wanted Dionysus to be "the unifying force of his whole empire, the heavenly representative and guarantor of the Ptolemaic house" (see Grant, *Cleopatra*, 24–25).
   It is not determined who Cleopatra's mother was, but Grant deduces very carefully that it was Cleopatra V, Auletes' sister-wife: she birthed Cleopatra and died or vanished shortly thereafter. Auletes remarried a woman unknown who birthed two sons, brothers of Cleopatra, both of whom were to co-rule with Cleopatra, one of whom *she* married and murdered, as we shall see.

5 Quoted in Seldes anthology, page 323; from Pascal's *Pensees* (London 1950). Pascal was talking about the intangible power of love, its absurdity and danger, its influence upon world change. He could not have known of the coins depicting Cleopatra's profile; he stumbled onto a truth and unknowingly and ironically twisted it to suggest that love was an enormous part of Cleopatra's success, but if her nose [of all things!] had been shorter she would have been even more successful! The ridiculousness of truth.

6 Cleopatra's grandfather, Ptolemy XI was forced by Rome (Sulla) to marry his own elderly stepmother (who was also his cousin!); nineteen days later he killed her, the people rose up and murdered him. His son Auletes (Ptolemy XII) gained the throne (named *Philopater*: he loved his father; he didn't do the killing).

XIV (this act proved by astrology, as we shall see); the former governor of Cyprus (Serapion) executed; a Phoenician pretender to a brother-relationship with Cleopatra; and the plan to murder others, including Herod of Judea, which was aborted by entreaty or wiser political strategy. The murders were always part of strategic gambits, most of them done after Cleopatra and Mark Antony became lovers; Antony wanted Egypt's money and navy, and Cleopatra extracted land dominion and enemy removal in return. This is how she negotiated. And all of this was bewitchingly beautiful? The power-demands, the strongly hooked nose, the bony face, the swarthy complexion?[7]

The Roman historian Plutarch describes Cleopatra (writing around A.D. 100, i.e., about 160–170 years after Cleopatra's time) this way: "For her actual beauty, it is said, was not in itself so remarkable that none could be compared with her, or that no one could see her without being struck by it, but the contact of her presence, if you lived with her, was irresistible; the attraction of her person, joining with the charm of her conversation, and the character that attended all she said or did, was something bewitching. It was a pleasure merely to hear the sound of her voice, with which, like an instrument of many strings, she could pass from one language to another."[8]

The study presented in the *Oxford Classical Dictionary* agrees: Cleopatra was attractive rather than beautiful, of lively temperament and great charm of speech. She was well-educated and could speak Egyptian and numerous other languages.

Harper's *Dictionary of Classical Literature and Antiquities* also echoes these descriptions: even at twenty, "Cleopatra was distinguished by extraordinary personal charms and surrounded with all the graces which give to those charms their greatest power. Her voice was extremely sweet, and she spoke a variety of languages with propriety and ease. She could, it is said, assume all characters at will, while all alike became her, and the impression that was made by her beauty was confirmed by the fascinating brilliance of her conversation."

---

7   Grant quotes a Robert Greene source, *Ciceronis Amor*, 1589, VII, 142, ed. Grosart: "Cleopatra was a black Egyptian." We know that "Egyptian" is wrong, because Cleopatra was Macedonian, Greek. Perhaps "black" is overstated. Perhaps "swarthy" is best. Shakespeare makes reference to this theme in *Romeo and Juliet* (II, 4), describing Cleopatra as a "gipsy."

8   Plutarch, *Antony*, 497.

Cleopatra had style. Poet and love-historian Diane Ackerman describes Cleopatra as "a one-woman pageant." Indeed, the dramatic packaging of this monarch was formidable, and it all had a purpose. In all the descriptions of her public presentations, we see grandeur, opulence, splendor, and over-kill, excess beyond belief. We read depictions of her receiving Antony in a room the floor of which was strewn knee-deep with roses; of dinner served with gold and bejeweled goblets, all given to the dinner guests as gifts. Pearls were inextricably linked with Cleopatra; they were the symbol of ultra-opulence to the Romans. She was always with an Amethyst; white was her favorite color.[9]

At the same time, biographer Hughes-Hallett is careful to establish that Cleopatra was a tactful and efficient ruler. She overcame the enormous financial debts incurred by her father, suffered depressed times in her own reign (when the Nile was uncooperative), but successfully rebuilt Egypt to a grandeur that commanded world attention.[10] She was able financially and in deployment of resources to support Antony's wars of conquest throughout many lands as far off as Parthia (Persia) and in his east-west empire showdown with Octavian. She consciously designed her image as the goddess Isis to arouse loyalty among her people, to whom religion was everything. Isis was the Moon goddess, the mother goddess of remarkable magical powers who was closely identified with the royal throne. She was "the mistress of every land ... taught by Hermes, and with Hermes I devised letters, both the sacred (hieroglyphs) and the demotic."[11]

Plutarch also tells us that Cleopatra was extremely skilled with languages. She spoke Egyptian, Ethiopian, Trogodyte, Hebrew, Aramaic, Syriac, Median, and Parthian. This might be open to doubt, but many sources concur (as we have seen). Language skill was definitely a dimension of Cleopatra's style that was well known. It reinforced her international poise and effectiveness considerably, especially since her Greek predecessors rarely even bothered to learn Egyptian!

---

9   According to the Latin author, Pliny, "the two pearls, the largest of all time both belonged to Cleopatra." Hughes-Hallett, 66–68, 97.

10 One of her management maneuvers was to manipulate the silver and bronze content in national coinage to create treasury savings. Grant attributes this to her great financial acumen (Grant, *Cleopatra*, 40).

11 Meyer, 158, 173 (see the fifty-seven-line identity statement inscribed on a stele in Memphis, before the temple of Hephaistos).

Additionally, all historical sources mention that Cleopatra wrote treatises on cosmetics, gynecology, weights and measures, and alchemy, and was very active with Alexandria's Medical School. Al-Masudi, a tenth-century historian, wrote that she was "well versed in the sciences, disposed to the study of philosophy and counted scholars among her intimate friends. She was the author of works on medicine, charms, and other divisions of the natural sciences. These books bear her name and are well known among men conversant with art and medicine."[12]

The Latin poet Cicero—who disliked Cleopatra and her arrogance intensely ("I hate the queen!" *Letters to Atticus* XV, 15, 2)—deigned to recognize her bookish interests. In the first century A.D., it was said that the sage Comarius had taught Cleopatra the mysteries of the philosopher's stone; and an unknown author then created the fictitious *Dialogue Between Cleopatra and the Philosophers*, and Flavius Philostratus described her as "deriving a positively sensuous pleasure from literature."[13]

Every inference about Cleopatra's sense of style suggests her genius as a propagandist. She was elegant and cultivated, extremely poised and powerful. She was most serious and anything but capricious, Bernard Shaw's recreation of her not withstanding. In every plan, we can not doubt that she was decidedly international in orientation: in the outreach of her ambition, through her interests and language skills, and in her monarchical instincts. She was deeply caught up with ritual and religion and claimed to be the incarnation of Isis, the Moon goddess, which she thoroughly and continuously exploited—with Antony as Osiris, with their twin children (Alexander and Cleopatra) as re-reincarnations of the gods as well. We see Isis as the mother goddess of all, depicted in sculpture and on coins as a suckling mother seated on a throne, promising new life and royal continuity. This spiritual (theological) dimension was very important: it fulfilled the needs of the Egyptian people for Divine attention and identified Cleopatra with the energies that controlled life and death and life again.[14]

---

12 Ackerman, 5–6; Grant, 40: her alchemy text concluded "with a boast that she could even manufacture gold."

13 Hughes-Hallett, 73; Grant, *Cleopatra*, 181; Flavius Philostratus (b. ca. A.D. 170), *Lives of the Sophists*, I, 4. 486.

14 Grant opines that "if the worship of Jesus Christ had not eventually dominated the Mediterranean, then Isis was the only divinity who might have done the same." *Cleopatra*, 118.

Cleopatra was an epic. She defined an era with immense impact and she established its end.

The Astrology

I can find no exception to the historical statement that Cleopatra was born in 69 B.C. I have searched every book I can and consulted with three renowned Egyptologists and one Hellenic scholar. The birth year is 69 B.C. However, the eminent classical scholar Michael Grant begins his engrossing biography of Cleopatra with one extra sliver of information: "Cleopatra was born *at the end of 70 or the beginning of 69 B.C.*" This gives us tighter focus indeed.

In correspondence with Professor Grant, I learned his frustration with not knowing exactly, but it is clear that his thorough study of her life suggests early 69 B.C. rather than any other time as prime for our consideration. He's right, and astrology proves it exactly.

Let us review the concepts and details of Cleopatra's historical profile as we have seen them developed so far:

✦ Cleopatra was born to an insecure throne. Her father's father, Ptolemy XI Lathyrus incurred an enormous debt with financiers in Rome. After he was murdered by his people, his son Auletes, Cleopatra's father, incurred still more debt to Rome for its support for his tottering throne. In her reign, in her personality, Cleopatra would *need security above all, at any price.* She would need to collect, hoard, and be sure of possessions and power.

✦ From a very early age, Cleopatra was privy to Auletes' difficult negotiations in Rome. She could not have helped but learn an *international* view of the world very early on: her *vast language study;* the history of the kingdom that was her birthright, taught to her at every turn; her kingdom that was pressing for growth again to enormous proportions.[15]

---

15 The people were in a revolt about paying back so much money to Rome. Auletes went again to Rome to lobby for support and, in exchange, incurred still *more* debt. History does not specifically record that the twelve–thirteen-year old Cleopatra accompanied Auletes to Rome (Astrology will prove that she did!), but, because of his enemies, it would have been unwise for him to leave her behind in Egypt with his other two daughters, i.e., the other immediate heirs to the throne. As it happened, in his absence, the people gave the throne over to the eldest daughter (Cleopatra's half-sister), Cleopatra VI Tryphaena, to co-rule with her father in absentia for a short time. In certain circles, Cleopatra's second sister Berenice IV, was regarded as queen. It was an unstable time. Grant, *Cleopatra*, 15–16.

✦ After a transitional co-rule period with her father and after his death in March 51 B.C., the young Queen, Cleopatra VII, had to fight ingeniously against a revolt engineered by Pothinus the high-priest on behalf of her co-ruler brother, Ptolemy XIII. When Cleopatra was hiding in southern Palestine, Caesar came to Alexandria to demand payments of Egypt's debt. She bravely and secretly returned, stole back into the palace to meet mighty Caesar and persuade him to arbitrate between her and her thirteen-year old brother. Caesar was dazzled by Cleopatra, and craftily helped reinstall her as sole ruler. (As we shall see, this brother drowned in the Nile in full battle armor, fleeing Caesar's forces.)[16]

✦ Cleopatra became known as a *purposeful, persuasive communicator, a propagandist.* Her *voice* was beautiful. She *wrote books and adored philosophy.* She had *style and charisma.* She was an *extremely efficient and resourceful administrator.* She engineered the murder of her sister and a very young brother (Ptolemy XIV) and others. Cleopatra *meant business!*

✦ Cleopatra *never shied from a fight:* she supported Antony in excursions throughout Asia Minor to the borders of Parthia (Persia) and, of course, in the historic final battle with Octavian of Rome. She understood *the deployment of force and the assertion of power.*

✦ Cleopatra *indulged her personal presence lavishly, purposefully, strategically.* She created sexual-emotional ties with Julius Caesar (he was fifty-two and she was twenty-one) and later with Mark Antony (he was forty-one and she was twenty-eight). The young Queen was dealing with the most powerful men in the world. She went to the singularly most extravagant lengths to impress them and shape them to her bidding for personal glory and Egypt's growth.

✦ Cleopatra identified with *sacred ritual and theological self-animation.* She portrayed herself as *Isis, the mother archetype,* suckling Horus. Cleopatra, Julius Caesar, Mark Antony (and Octavian Caesar too, Antony's rival), all had personalities split

---

16 Egyptian law did not permit a female monarch to rule alone, except in very special circumstances. Ptolemy XIII, co-ruler with her, was pushed into ascendancy over Cleopatra gradually and carefully by Pothinus, his high-priest regent, but Caesar obviously saw a better future with the courageous, captivating Cleopatra than with the young boy.

into self-proclaimed godliness. The psychodynamic gambits within world politics and on the battlefield were simply formidable. Cleopatra's armor was her indomitable self-confidence, and her chief weapons were her alluring personality and creative resourcefulness.

✦ *Pearls* cover her image; the *Amethyst* is always present.

✦ Cleopatra appears in history as the agent *to change an epoch*, to define the end of one era and the beginning of a new one.

The sense of Capricorn (administrative power) and Cancer (the need for security, for self-protection and stabilization of her rule and family line) dominate. The feeling is reinforced by the suggestions of her saturnine strategies, her self-imaging as Isis, the Moon goddess, the mother-goddess, the emphasis on pearls, the color white, and the struggle between administration and emotions or their exploitation, one negotiating for the other.

The sense of internationalism is undeniable: Jupiter and Mercury and the 9th House must be in high relief in her horoscope; reinforced by language study and a beautiful voice, and extraordinary communication power: the 3rd House. And, as well, the tremendous emphasis on brothers and sisters: all of this indeed emphasizing the 3rd–9th House axis dramatically. In Cleopatra's horoscope, this axis must be key.

The sense of ritual and religion, the capacity to make hard or harsh or passionate judgments all bring Scorpio to the foreground, as well as another echo of 9th House significances, even the 8th.

The sensual, the self-indulgent, the lush persona all suggest a powerfully positioned Venus. Her boundless imagination for pageantry and lethal subtlety suggests a reinforced Neptune dimension.

— ✦ —

Now, look at the ephemeris (opposite) for January 69 B.C. Of course, we find the Sun in Capricorn for most of the month, separating from a square with Mars early in January. In late Capricorn and into Aquarius beginning December 23, the Sun is conjunct Saturn for the rest of the month. Our expectations of Capricorn strength will be corroborated. If she were born in mid-January 69 B.C., her Sun probably would be *unaspected*, peregrine (no dignity in Capricorn):

+ 0:00 UT				Geocentric Tropical Longitudes for JAN 069 BC								
Date	Sid.Time	Sun	Moon	Node	Mercury	Venus	Nars	Jupiter	Saturn	Uranus	Neptune	Pluto
1	6:28:35	08ℑ07 30	26≈44	13♍13	13♐40	05≈31	03♎18	05♐43	29ℑ02	28♉23℞	17♊19℞	00♊04℞
2	6:32:31	09 08 24	08✕42	13 10	14 22	06 46	03 44	05 56	29 09	28 21	17 17	00 04
3	6:36:28	10 09 20	20 32	13 07	15 08	08 00	04 09	06 08	29 16	28 20	17 16	00 03
4	6:40:24	11 10 16	02♈20	13 04	15 58	09 14	04 35	06 21	29 23	28 18	17 14	00 02
5	6:44:21	12 11 10	14 10	13 00	16 51	10 28	05 00	06 33	29 30	28 16	17 13	00 01
6	6:48:17	13 12 02	26 09	12 57	17 48	11 42	05 25	06 46	29 37	28 15	17 11	00 00
7	6:52:14	14 12 53	08♉21	12 54	18 48	12 56	05 50	06 58	29 45	28 13	17 10	29♉59
8	6:56:11	15 13 42	20 50	12 51	19 50	14 10	06 14	07 10	29 52	28 11	17 08	29 58
9	7:00:07	16 14 30	03♊42	12 48	20 55	15 24	06 38	07 23	29 59	28 10	17 07	29 58
10	7:04:04	17 15 16	16 56	12 44	22 02	16 38	07 02	07 35	00≈06	28 08	17 05	29 57
11	7:08:00	18 16 01	00♋34	12 41	23 11	17 52	07 26	07 47	00 13	28 07	17 04	29 56
12	7:11:57	19 16 44	14 33	12 38	24 22	19 05	07 49	07 59	00 21	28 06	17 02	29 55
13	7:15:53	20 17 25	28 48	12 35	25 35	20 19	08 12	08 11	00 28	28 04	17 01	29 55
14	7:19:50	21 18 05	13♌15	12 32	26 49	21 33	08 35	08 23	00 35	28 03	17 00	29 54
15	7:23:46	22 18 44	27 46	12 29	28 06	22 46	08 57	08 34	00 42	28 02	16 58	29 53
16	7:27:43	23 19 21	12♍16	12 25	29 23	24 00	09 20	08 46	00 50	28 01	16 57	29 53
17	7:31:40	24 19 57	26 41	12 22	00♑42	25 14	09 41	08 58	00 57	28 00	16 56	29 52
18	7:35:36	25 20 31	10♎57	12 19	02 03	26 27	10 03	09 09	01 04	27 59	16 54	29 51
19	7:39:33	26 21 04	25 03	12 16	03 25	27 40	10 24	09 21	01 11	27 58	16 53	29 51
20	7:43:29	27 21 36	08♏57	12 13	04 48	28 54	10 45	09 32	01 19	27 57	16 52	29 50
21	7:47:26	28 22 06	22 40	12 10	06 12	00✕07	11 05	09 44	01 26	27 56	16 51	29 50
22	7:51:22	29 22 35	06♐10	12 06	07 37	01 20	11 25	09 55	01 33	27 55	16 50	29 49
23	7:55:19	00≈23 03	19 29	12 03	09 04	02 34	11 45	10 06	01 41	27 54	16 48	29 49
24	7:59:15	01 23 29	02ℑ35	12 00	10 31	03 47	12 04	10 17	01 48	27 53	16 47	29 48
25	8:03:12	02 23 53	15 28	11 57	12 00	05 00	12 23	10 28	01 55	27 52	16 46	29 48
26	8:07:09	03 24 15	28 07	11 54	13 30	06 13	12 42	10 39	02 03	27 52	16 45	29 47
27	8:11:05	04 24 36	10≈33	11 50	15 00	07 26	13 00	10 50	02 10	27 51	16 44	29 47
28	8:15:02	05 24 55	22 47	11 47	16 32	08 39	13 18	11 00	02 17	27 51	16 43	29 46
29	8:18:58	06 25 12	04✕50	11 44	18 05	09 52	13 35	11 11	02 25	27 50	16 42	29 46
30	8:22:55	07 25 26	16 44	11 41	19 39	11 04	13 52	11 21	02 32	27 50	16 41	29 45
31	8:26:51	08 25 39	28 32	11 38	21 14	12 17	14 08	11 32	02 39	27 49	16 40	29 45

Copyright (C) 1987 Matrix Software, Big Rapids MI 49307

Ephemeris for January 69 B.C.

its Capricorn essence would dominate the horoscope, run away with behaviors, unless there were mitigating, controlling circumstances.[17]

The pronounced need for security and the other Cancerian dimensions should be shown clearly, but no planet—Mercury through Pluto—is in Cancer during January. However, *the Moon itself is in Cancer(!)* during the period December 11 to just past midnight UT on December 13. It is the perfect symbolism to depict Isis, the suckling mother goddess![18]

Note the positions of Uranus and Pluto. Here could be a clincher for our search: *Uranus and Pluto are almost in exact conjunction in Taurus*, which suggests extraordinary power, upset, enforcement,

---

17 Please see Tyl, *Synthesis & Counseling in Astrology*, "Peregrination," 155–190.

18 The Ephemeris time is for Midnight UT. Alexandria, Egypt is at 29 East 54, about two hours of time eastward, later.

and individuation when/if it is integrated into the rest of an individual's horoscope. Here the conjunction is disposed of by Venus in Aquarius (which itself makes *a trine with Neptune*, and then a square with Uranus, and a square with Pluto). The big conjunction is trine Saturn in its own sign, 00 Aquarius (the Sign linked with the Amethyst), with the Sun nearby.

Reading the ephemeris line across the page for January 13, in the heart of these measurements we are bringing into focus, we see that *Saturn would be opposing the Moon in Cancer*, the extreme consciousness of the father—for a queen, the patrilineal line of inheritance—discipline, organization, seriousness. The Moon and Saturn are in their own sign, at their best, in full awareness of each other, a control-conditioning that affects personal thrusts for recognition. There's a seriousness of purpose, a mature, determined approach to things mingled with a potentially depressive, self-isolating, even plotting strategic thrust. The peregrine Sun in Capricorn floods the axis as well and may even be brought into the Saturn-Moon opposition, transcending the wide orb.

It is not difficult to picture a birth *just after midnight* on the 13th, with the Sun in 20 Capricorn positioned with Saturn in the *3rd House* (Capricorn on the third cusp, Aquarius on the fourth; picture it in your mind's eye), opposed the Moon in Cancer in the *9th*, ruling the 9th! This would fit so much of our growing profile for Cleopatra.

We can picture as well, then, that with Capricorn on the 3rd, Aquarius would be on the 4th, ruled by Saturn (and Uranus); and Leo would be on the Midheaven. What would be on the Ascendant? Probably *Scorpio*, with Pluto, its ruler, conjunct Uranus in Taurus, in the 7th House of the public. Undeniably, this is an exciting set of deductions!

We can see all of these deduced positions in our mind's eye from just the midnight positions noted on the ephemeris page. All of our profile-keys listed above have been taken care of! Our next step will be to use Arcs, Progressions, and Transits to test the *angles* of the conjectured horoscope. The Ascendant and the Midheaven specify the place and time of birth and the base for the major developments within life time. We may be very, very close now to determining through astrology a missing part of Cleopatra's history!

Special Note

The conjunction of Uranus and Pluto (Figure 1, page 14) is extremely rare. It occurs in an alternating cycle of approximately 112–114 years and then 140–144 years, then 112+, 140+, 112, etc. Such conjunctions signal a new epoch, a change in the course of human history and in conditions of a living earth. With Uranus as the archetype of rebellion, invention, and change, and Pluto the archetype of empowerment and perspective, their conjunction signifies epic alteration of perspective, the arousal of new powers, and innovation that changes the status quo most significantly.[19] The chart drawn for the first exact conjunction of the two planets from the perspective of any national capital speaks for the times to come for that nation, that area (see page 22). The quake of history gains specific reference most strongly through nations whose capital city is located so that the moment of first conjunction is directly overhead or upon the eastern horizon (conventionally, a 5-degree orb is used), and/or through a particular generation sub-group or individual leader *who assimilates the conjunction sharply within the aspect structure of his (or her) identifying horoscope*.[20]

The Uranus-Pluto conjunction of June 26, A.D. 1850 occurred at 2:40 A.M. UT in 29 Aries 40 (not over or on the horizon of any capital city, so no single country can be singled out as the core-focus of the significances). The world began to change powerfully during the following five years: there was the massive Taiping rebellion in China, killing over twenty million people; war between

---

19 It is established archaeological fact that the known world underwent colossal change, quite suddenly, circa 1200 B.C., the end of the Bronze Age. (See Drews, 48–55; Aldred, 151–155; Grant, *Mediterranean*, 78–80.) There were severe climatic changes, imbalancing migrations, and the application of new schemes of warfare, so that whole cities and national areas were defeated, erased, or changed forever. The Uranus-Pluto conjunction of December 2, 1205 B.C. occurred in 21 Scorpio 58 at about noon *directly overhead in the Middle East*. At the same time—most rare—there was a conjunction of Saturn and Neptune still in orb, exact on July 9, 1205 B.C., just five months earlier. Catastrophe. It is an exception duly noted that Egypt, under its powerful, war-Pharaoh Merenptah, was least affected by this epochal change: the king just barely staved off the onslaught of "The Sea Peoples" (hordes of migrant mercenary tribes from Shekelesh, Shardana, and Tursha (probably Sicily, Sardinia, and the Tyrrhenian west coast of Italy, with Lybians and with Phillistines from southwest Caanan). There is confusion among historians as well about this period; it was chaotic.

20 Of course this applies to the occurrence of *all* major conjunctions. History is dramatically etched into time by occurrences of the Mars-Saturn conjunction that forms approximately every twenty-two months, the Jupiter-Saturn conjunction that forms every twenty to twenty-one years (See Tyl, *Prediction*), Saturn-Pluto (thirty-three to thirty-four years), Saturn-Neptune, etc.

Turkey and Russia leading to the Crimean War with French and British involvement; the "Great War" in Uruguay; Louis Napoleon managed a coup d'état and was crown Emperor Napoleon III; the Republic of South Africa was formed out of great rebellion; there was war in Burma, slave revolts in the United States Midwest, a new constitution for New Zealand, etc., all actions of rebellion and change and empowerment of the underprivileged.

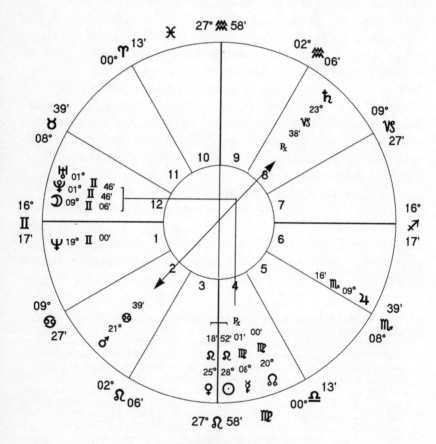

Figure 1
Uranus-Pluto Conjunction
Aug. 26, 70 B.C., 00:58 A.M. UT
Alexandria, Egypt
29E54 31N12
Placidus Houses

The next Uranus-Pluto conjunction occurred 115 years later on October 9, 1965 at 8:27 P.M. UT at 17 Virgo 10.[21] The world concertedly went into change: the Vietnam explosion began; the beginning of the cultural revolution in China was proclaimed; India and Pakistan began war; there was the eruption of Israel's six-day War with Arab nations; there was a revolt in the Dominican Republic, a coup in Algeria; the great reforms of Vatican Council II took place, dealing with prejudice and human rights; the "Hippie Revolution" left its mark upon the mores of the United States and much of the western world. There was the first walk in space and enormous leaps of technology—and, one month after the conjunction occurred, the most extensive technological breakdown and power failure in history struck much of the northeastern United States and Ontario Canada, affecting 80,000 square miles and some thirty million people for over thirteen hours.

The Uranus-Pluto conjunction we see on the ephemeris for 69 B.C. (page 11), which could be in Cleopatra's horoscope, had formed for the first time five months earlier on August 26, 70 B.C. at 00:58 A.M. UT at 1 Gemini 46. The planets then became retrograde, and Uranus, retrograding more quickly, passed Pluto to present the ephemeris listing we see for January 69.

The horoscope drawn for the moment when this "Cleopatra Conjunction" formed for the first time, perceived from Alexandria, the capital of Egypt, is shown in Figure 1 (page 14).[22]

The conjunction was in the 12th House in Gemini (to divide and conquer, to split up for reorganization), *square* the Sun-Venus conjunction in Leo and Mercury (ruler of the Ascendant and dispositor of the Conjunction) in the 4th, signifying lands, the homeland (and, through the Sun's presence, the monarch). Uranus rules the Midheaven. The signal for the years ahead suggests great tension within the monarchy, the break up of lands, and subterfugal rebellion (12th House). Note that Neptune, rising at the Ascendant, is peregrine and will threaten to invade the entire horoscope.

---

21 A personal note: This conjunction occurred exactly upon my natal Neptune, ruler of my 10th: my career changed from advertising and public relations to opera, as a singer, and, within two years of this occurrence, also to the study of astrology.

22 B.C. dates require a special turn of mind that is essential for correct computation: since there is no zero year, 69 B.C. is actually -68, which is the date we enter into the computer. In reading any table of time data for the past, it is important to ascertain the exact reference of notation: "minus" is always 1 unit-year less than the "B.C." calendar reference; the "minus 1" date-difference is key to the mechanics of computation.

Uranus is also ruler of the international 9th, i.e., Egypt's international relations. With the Conjunction's pressure on the Moon, also in the 12th, ruling the financial 2nd, the synthesis is developed easily that there will be extreme power-tension (Uranus-Pluto square with Sun-Venus) with foreign countries with regard to monies, to debts. The Sun always symbolizes the ruler, the head of government, and with the presence of Venus with the Sun and the prominent position of the Moon we can begin to expect the feminine element, a queen.

Saturn is in its own sign and is opposed by Mars, accentuating the financial/values axis (Houses 2 and 8). Saturn *also* rules the Midheaven, and this opposition from Mars echoes the Uranus-Pluto square with the Sun and Mercury. Additionally, Saturn is retrograde: forces financial and military can devastate the rule of Egypt, drive Egypt into withdrawal to an inferior position.

Overall, we see an enormous amount of tension and haggling, of coming to blows, of behind-the-scenes intrigue, Egypt and other countries. Note that the Sun rules the communications 3rd and Uranus rules the international diplomacy 9th. These are the signs of scandals and wars. The epochal rifts between Egypt (its queen: the Moon and Venus positions in the 12th and 4th Houses, respectively) and other countries will involve violent communications and warring travels or wars elsewhere as well as at home.

Central to all is that the massive conjunction of Uranus and Pluto *attacks the monarch of Egypt:* through Pluto "on" Uranus, their square to the Sun and the Midheaven, and the Mars attack on Saturn.

Mercury is in its own sign but *retrograde*, ruling the Ascendant and Virgo in the 4th, the people and the homeland. It is the dispositor of the Cleopatra Conjunction and of Neptune rising. Mercury is reinforced by the sextile with Jupiter and cramped through the sesquiquadrate with Saturn. The people are left behind, abandoned within the siege on the monarchy. The counterpoint (retrogradation of Mercury and Saturn) within this analysis could also suggest a pervasive desertion factor that undoes national force.[23]

---

23 It is astounding then to read the history: that the armies of Antony and the navy of Cleopatra suffered enormous desertions when things got tough. To the embarrassment of many historians, Antony and Cleopatra even planned their own desertion from the massive battle of Actium, as we shall see. At the very end, under siege in Alexandria, Antony would tie bribery notes to the shafts of arrows and have them shot from inside the palace over the walls to Octavian's troops to entice them to desert!

Jupiter in Scorpio always carries with it an intense sense of mission and religious rationale. Here it links that sense to Egypt's public presentation, conceivably through the relationships of the monarch on a personal level, especially through the sextile with the Sun and Jupiter's rulership of the 7th. There is an apparently contradictory grandness about relationships, personal ones and those with other countries. There is prosperity and solid gain, also a contradiction within the overall analysis, but possibly it tells us about

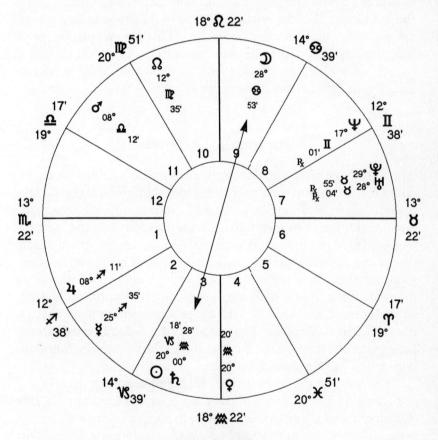

Figure 2
Cleopatra VII
Jan. 13, 69 B.C., 2:08 A.M. LMT
Alexandria, Egypt
29E54 31N12
Placidus Houses

great prosperity and then the fall through international financial problems and wars, of blind rationalization of losing programs.

This mundane reading of this phenomenological conjunction chart fits history extraordinarily well as we are uncovering it. Now we must see how this conjunction could have been tied in to Cleopatra's horoscope—personalized—so that its signal, epochal energy could be focused within the life of Egypt's Queen. The tie is clear: Uranus and Pluto can be trine to Saturn and sextile to the Moon, early in the morning of January 13. If the birth *is* in the very first hours of the morning, the Sun (and Saturn) will indeed be in the 3rd House, the Moon will indeed be in the 9th, and Scorpio will almost assuredly be on the Ascendant. This fits our profile, as we have developed it. The test horoscope for Cleopatra VII (Figure 2, page 17) is set for January 13, 69 B.C., at 2:08 A.M. LMT in Alexandria, Egypt. [Please reread footnote 22 on page 15.]

Personality Analysis

The horoscope picture makes dramatically clear what we have visualized from the ephemeris page: the 3rd and 9th House axis is highly emphasized with the Sun's presence there along with Saturn, the Sun's dispositor, in its own sign of Aquarius and ruling the 3rd; Saturn is in strong opposition with the Moon, also in its own sign, placed in and ruling the international 9th! This is a dramatic statement of skills in communications and polemics, all within an international purview, with dimensions of philosophy, publishing, and religion all fed strongly into the process. Additionally, there is the emphasis on brothers and sisters in the 3rd, all related to the focal point of the ambition, Saturn, and to the throne, the Sun symbolism and its rulership of the 10th.

The Sun and the Moon in a blend together are the heart of any horoscope. Here in Capricorn and Cancer we can expect practicality (Capricorn) and the emotions (Cancer) to compete constantly for the center of the stage, so to speak. Cleopatra's ambition and needs for emotional security are inextricably intertwined. The gambits to administer security into the life (into the kingdom; Sun rules the 10th) are always edgy, risky, precarious. We can infer that Cleopatra was dominated in her life expression by the need to establish *personal* security upon the throne and *national* security through her reign.

The Scorpio Ascendant reinforces the depth of this drive for security and authority; it adds tenacity. It also brings into consideration dimensions of a deep religious sense, power through it, the ritualization of it, the sense of mission, and the determinedness of the personal position (Fixed signs on all angles). There is a depth given to all the 9th House spiritual dimensions keyed by the Moon's position.

The Scorpio Ascendant keys us through its ruler Pluto to the epochal Uranus-Pluto conjunction in the 7th, the "Cleopatra Conjunction" now retrograded over the sign-line into Taurus. This is power, rebellion, and enormous change potential to be achieved through ambitious and international relations. This is clearly tied in to Cleopatra's core motivations through the trine with Saturn and the sextile with the Moon.

The *retrogradation* here is an important signal: such powerfully accented retrogradation in the 7th sets up an anticipation that Cleopatra was somehow a clearly identifiable loner. We can see this observation easily as an echo of the demanding Moon-Saturn opposition. There is emotional hurt, withdrawal, fear, and insecurity here, which are extraordinarily overcompensated by epically embellished public presentation: Venus is the dispositor of the conjunction, rules the 7th and is strongly conjunct the fourth cusp, angular, and opposed the Leo Midheaven. Additionally, and very importantly, Venus is trine Neptune and in mutual reception with Uranus!

Here was this Queen without a king (with brother Ptolemy XIII, a child-puppet who drowned and then, as her child-husband, another brother, Ptolemy XIV, whom she poisoned), placed upon an insecure throne over a country with a shaky, debt-ridden economy, surrounded by high-priest intrigue designed to unseat her. The threat to security personally and nationally was enormous. Not unusually, Cleopatra's personal needs became inextricably tied to the needs of her country. Who she was became who Egypt was.[24]

---

24 An aphorism in Mundane Astrology is that there is a tendency for the president or king of a country to lose his identity to the country in terms of its horoscope. In other words, the country's horoscope may take the place of the leader's horoscope. Renowned British astrologer C. E. O. Carter called this the "Law of Subsumption." I see the *reciprocal* of this law as valid as well: the nation loses its identity, so to speak, to its leader, *the leader's horoscope standing for the identity of the country.* There are extraordinary corroborations for this hypothesis throughout history, involving Roosevelt and Hitler during World War II, for example, and many tyrannical regimes throughout history. In short, leader and nation, nation and leader become each other. See Carter, 12–13.

Cleopatra wielded her strategies to fulfill her personal needs in the guise of forwarding her country. The retrogradation dimension, the withdrawal and aloneness, and contrasting showiness and pomp seen through Venus and its mutual reception with Uranus all show her double agenda.

Process—a particularly apt Capricorn trait—probably ruled Cleopatra's life: how to improve security, how to exploit international resources, how to have persuasive impact, how to fulfill her mission. There is no mention of feelings or emotional caring in any of the histories about Cleopatra. She made things happen, apparently coldly and dispassionately, to establish national security; she proceeded to cover over her weaknesses, her aloneness, her emotional world, her fears, by relating to established monarchs who would benefit her throne, her nation, and herself. The seasoned Caesar and then the ambitious Antony became her "kings." We may say that the Queen was her country and that Cleopatra—the human being—got caught up and lost in the process.

The Venus factor in Aquarius probably clarifies that Cleopatra was a people-orientated ruler. She learned her people's language, she identified herself with their religion, and there is no record of her hurting her citizenry. Hughes-Hallett cites several sources that establish Cleopatra as a public benefactor, designing and commissioning many of the great engineering projects which had enabled Alexandria to prosper. (Saturn in *Aquarius:* humanitarian/social orientation for ambition.)[25]

Venus makes the rare sextile with Mercury, in Sagittarius, adding the dimension of beauty and social effectiveness to Cleopatra's communications, specifically to her voice. With the Capricorn and Saturn focus in the 3rd, it is perfectly reasonable to assume that Cleopatra's voice was dark, low in pitch, and lustrous.

But this Venus is also the target of enemy propaganda about her public image (Venus rules the 7th): all histories depict her from the Roman point of view as the wanton sensualist, the opportunistic whore, the depraved animal, who destroyed men's lives to appease her personal lust, having her sexual partners killed after coitus, etc. This international propaganda was established by Octavian's Rome to define Cleopatra as an enemy. It was anti-monarch, anti-foreigner (barbarian, animalistic), and, very importantly here, anti-woman.

25 Hughes-Hallett, 73–74.

While the Greeks' experience with Helen of Troy could be remembered, when was the last time that mighty Rome faced a world ruler who was a woman? When would be the next time? As Hughes-Hallett points out, this enemy *chose* her sexual partners, rather than commandeering them with the sword as was the way in those days. The more vile she was made out to be, the more necessary was the campaign to defeat her.

After Caesar's assassination, Octavian and Antony and a high Minister named Lepidus formed a Triumvirate. They divided among them (Uranus-Pluto Conjunction in Gemini; see page 14) most of the known world. Through her relationship with Antony, Cleopatra would come to be seen as upsetting to this three-way rule, the balance of world leadership power.

Cleopatra's Venus was sesquiquadrate her Mars, which itself is in Libra (in its fall, disposed by Venus) receiving a supportive sextile with Jupiter in its own sign. This Mars is weak, less than strident, tending to blandness, seeing both sides of every issue. But this Mars is extraordinarily positioned in midpoint pictures linking Saturn, Uranus, Neptune, Pluto, the Midheaven, and Venus in powerful structures of behavior, as we shall see. And, of course, Mars is drive: for power and for sexuality; one fueling the other.

Was Cleopatra a sensualist? She probably was, with Venus trine Neptune retrograde (imagination), with Neptune ruling the 5th and placed in the 8th, the Houses relating to sexuality. This dimension was surely reinforced by the Scorpio Ascendant, dramatized spiritually and ritualistically. It is not hard to see all of this swooning, innovative (Venus-Uranus mutual reception, Aquarius) dimension of her personality piped directly into the pageantry of her rule and self-presentation. Venus is the most angularly placed planet and dramatically opposes the Leo Midheaven and rules the 7th.

We can feel the young woman within the Queen facing such enormous responsibilities, with no one to whom to turn; the high-priest did not have her best interests at heart, her brothers were children, her sister Arsinoe was a threat. There was the tradition and the record among the princesses of the house of the Ptolemies that had "always apparently been very much averse to taking casual lovers, especially from outside the royal house. They were not, like later Roman imperial ladies, both murderous and adulterous. They were murderous and chaste. The same extreme pride in their families which caused these royal Ptolemaic women to enter into brother-and-sister marriages deterred them from promiscuous associations."[26]

As we will see corroborated by Mars within midpoint structures, this Venus contact with Neptune, the latter's rulership and placement, and the Scorpio Ascendant do define a strong, sensuous, and passionate sexual profile, but there is also the suggestion of sublimation here, of these sexual energies being put second in her life after administrative concerns. Or, we could say that the sexual energies became part of the way she did business, so dominating are the Sun and the Moon-Saturn opposition.

The Neptune dimension is very important: it signifies her vulnerability to the covert motives ascribed to her by enemy (and historical) propaganda and, probably to a lesser extent, it signifies her penchant for the covert processes in international negotiations and intrigue, her use of her wily ways as tools for administration. For example, beyond the negotiation with Antony to have her sister and others murdered, when Antony drew the line with eliminating Herod in Judea, she did her best to stir up an underground, separatist, anti-Jewish movement in Idumaea, in the South of his country. It failed, and Antony ignored it; Cleopatra was "doing her thing."

Cleopatra was alone, starkly alone in terms of personal interaction, private or not, for most of her life. She was together with Caesar for perhaps one year in Alexandria, fresh from hiding out against the high-priest insurrection, when she got Caesar to support her over her co-ruling brother. She became pregnant, and then Caesar returned to Rome when things were relatively secure in Alexandria.

Cleopatra then went to Rome a year later.[27] Caesar feted her but kept her at a distance. Three months after her arrival (with Caesarion, their son), Caesar went off to Spain. When he returned months later, he was ailing and busy for seven months before he was assassinated. They could not have had much time together, *nor much more reason to.*

Three years later, Cleopatra teamed up with Antony, for the same motives as had fired her relationship with Caesar: Antony needed her money, and Cleopatra needed his support and the

---

26 Grant, *Cleopatra*, 84.

27 There is no record of letters between Caesar and Cleopatra. Caesar was married and had many mistresses. Their relationship appears very much the "deal," his and hers: to get Alexandria settled to pay its debt and not cause any more trouble; to get Rome on her side, regain and build the security of her rule.

expansion of her realm as he promised her. They were together one year, in which she became pregnant with twins (Alexander and Cleopatra); he went off then for *almost four years*, waging a disastrous campaign with far-off Parthia and facing up to extremely problematic affairs with Octavian in Rome. He then re-summoned her for financial help. They were together for one year, she became pregnant again with Ptolemy Philadelphus, and then they met on-again off-again (the war campaigns taking place in the Spring and Summer; with planning and funding accomplished during the Fall and Winter) they were together at different locations until their deaths in Alexandria in 30 B.C.

The point is that from age seventeen when she became queen until her death at almost thirty-nine, she is known to have been with only two men: Caesar, basically for one year, and Antony for one year and then for a span of seven years with frequent interruptions.

We can be sure that, if there had been any other man in her life, he would have made news, so to speak. This liaison would have entered the propaganda mill to sully Cleopatra's image even more, quite specifically with names, definitely to embarrass Antony. Birth control was extremely unreliable, and Cleopatra appears to have been most fertile; it is probable that another child would have been conceived and become part of the royal record. And, finally, I think we must remember that other men undoubtedly came to fear Cleopatra. In image and in person, Cleopatra was almost certainly unapproachable, stand-offish. This is borne out astrologically with our analysis of her aloneness, her preoccupation with strategy, and the withdrawal from relationships (the retrogradation of the 7th House structure) into wily inveiglement (the Neptune retrograde complex; Venus ruling the 12th) to fulfill *her* needs, her *nation's* needs.

Cleopatra's extreme identification with Isis, the fertility goddess of Egypt, meant a profile of "the Great Virgin," as Isis is hailed in the ancient Hymn to Osiris. The Greeks associated her with Artemis, the chaste goddess of childbirth. Hughes-Hallett points out how figures of Isis (Cleopatra) seated on a bench or small throne suckling the babe Horus are indistinguishable in content from representations of the Madonna and child.[28]

---

28 Hughes-Hallett, 83. Additionally, *Oxford Classical* states without attribution that "Cleopatra was ruthless toward her family in true Ptolemaic tradition. She was not sexually lax," 251–252.

I believe that the historical record and the horoscope do indeed suggest that Cleopatra was a virgin queen of twenty-one when she worked her way out of the take-over plan engineered on her co-ruler brother's behalf (aged twelve–thirteen). I think the virginity factor was a point of captivation for the world-wise and weary Caesar at fifty-two, and for Antony to know that he was indeed only her second man, following the great Caesar, the beguilement again would have been extraordinary and effective. Cleopatra undoubtedly relished the international rumors—they gave her stature and power—and she reinforced them knowingly with her exorbitant, sensual pageantry. But for this lone lady of power, *arch-discrimination* was part of her earliest strategy and it would have been continued. Her pride, her tradition, and her success could not have let her relate to anyone less than a monarch.[29]

Midpoint Pictures

Midpoint pictures depict another level of synthesis: three planets—symbols of needs, of behavioral faculties—are brought together and blended. Using the fourth harmonic within Midpoint pictures, we can glean reinforcement for the classical measurements made in initial analysis.[30]

Key to zodiacal conceptualization is the point of zero-Aries, of course, but this awareness relates as well to 0 Libra by opposition

---

29 The usually circumspect and objective historian Josephus (Jewish-born general, favored by Vespacian, privileged in Rome) was caught up with anti-Cleopatra propaganda. In *The Antiquities of the Jews*, XV, 4, he vilifies Cleopatra, and specifically in 4, 2, he tells how she endeavored to entrap Herod (whom she despised and wanted dead so she could rule Judea) through "criminal conversation with the king," that she tried to lay a "treacherous snare for him by aiming to obtain such adulterous conversation from him." He adds: "however, upon the whole, she seemed overcome with love to him." Herod thought of having her killed but decided better of it, for fear of Antony. Grant says this story can not be true (*Cleopatra*, 159–160), that it came from Herod's personal diary/memoirs. Herod hated Cleopatra, feared Antony, and diabolically was aggrandizing his own position within the swirl of propaganda.

30 The family of fourth harmonic aspects is based upon the square (90 degrees; 360 divided by 4), its subset (45 degrees, the semisquare, really the 8th harmonic), the sesquiquadrate (135 degrees; a square plus a semisquare), the conjunction and opposition. These so-called "hard aspects" suggest action and change, that which propels life development. Midpoint pictures show one planet or point in fourth harmonic relationship (any of the hard aspects) to the *midpoint* axis of any other two planets (and/or points). The equals sign (=) denotes the synthesis: Mercury=Mars/Uranus means that natal (or arced) Mercury is at (or has come to) a fourth harmonic aspect position in relation to the midpoint axis between Mars and Uranus (you can just feel that tension!). See Tyl: *Synthesis & Counseling*, Section Two C.

CLEOPATRA VII JAN 13,-0068 (69 B.C.)

Midpoint Sort: 90° Dial

♄/♇	000°11'	☿/♄	013°01'	♆/☊	029°48'	Mc	048°22'	☽/♂	063°33'	☽/Asc	081°07'
Mc/Asc	000°52'	♃/Mc	013°17'	♄	030°28'	♀/Mc	049°21'	♃/♇	064°03'	☿/♆	081°18'
♀/Asc	001°51'	♀/♃	014°15'	♂/♅	033°08'	♀	050°20'	♂/♄	064°20'	♄/Asc	081°55'
☽/♃	003°32'	♆/Mc	017°42'	♂/♇	034°04'	♅/Asc	050°43'	☿/Asc	064°28'	☉/♅	084°11'
☉/♆	003°39'	♀/♆	018°40'	☿/☊	034°05'	☽/☊	050°44'	♅/♆	067°33'	☉/♇	085°06'
♃/♄	004°19'	☉	020°18'	☉/Mc	034°20'	♄/☊	051°31'	♃	068°11'	♂/☊	085°24'
☉/☿	007°56'	♅/☊	020°20'	☉/♀	035°19'	♇/Asc	051°38'	♆/♇	068°28'	☿	085°35'
☽/♆	007°57'	♇/☊	021°15'	♂/♃	038°12'	♃/Asc	055°46'	☿/♅	071°50'	☽/♅	088°29'
♂	008°12'	☿/Mc	021°59'	☽/Mc	038°38'	♅	058°04'	☊	072°35'	☉/♃	089°14'
♅/Mc	008°13'	☿/♀	022°57'	♄/Mc	039°25'	♅/♇	059°00'	♃/♆	072°36'	♄/♅	089°16'
♄/♆	008°44'	☽/☉	024°36'	☽/♀	039°36'	☉/♂	059°15'	☿/♇	072°45'	☽/♇	089°24'
♇/Mc	009°08'	☉/♄	025°23'	♀/♄	040°24'	♇	059°55'	♂/Mc	073°17'		
♀/♅	009°12'	♃/☊	025°23'	♂/♆	042°37'	♆/Asc	060°11'	♀/♂	074°16'		
♀/♇	010°07'	♂/Asc	025°47'	Asc	043°21'	☊/Mc	060°29'	☉/Asc	076°50'		
☽/☿	012°14'	☽	028°53'	☉/☊	046°26'	♀/☊	061°27'	☿/♃	076°53'		
☊/Asc	012°58'	☽/♄	029°41'	☿/♂	046°54'	♃/♅	063°08'	♆	077°01'		

Figure 3
Cleopatra's Midpoint Structure

(the same axis) and to 0 Cancer and 0 Capricorn by square. In short, "0-Cardinals" is our orientation to the world around us. Any natal planet or point at 0 degree of any Cardinal sign is by definition configurated with "the Aries Point;" the planet's or point's symbolism will be given a push out into the world, a public boost, exposure.

Cleopatra's midpoint structure is shown in Figure 3 (above).[31] We see that her midpoints Sun/Jupiter (at 89 Mutable 14, which is 29 Mutable, within 1 degree orb of "90", which is 0 Cardinal, the square of the Aries Point), Saturn/Uranus, Moon/Pluto, Saturn/Pluto, and MC/Asc *are all* in touch with the Aries Point! This is extraordinary public projection. The pictures suggest good fortune and, for her, internationalism through AP=Sun/Jupiter; and, respectively thereafter, being known for rebellious ways, for zealous plans, the use of great force and/or the threat of public self-destruction, and her keen self-awareness of her public image through the midpoint of both her angular axes configurated with the Aries Point.

Cleopatra's Pluto (59 degrees 55, i.e., 29 Fixed 55) on this conjectured birthdate and time was at the midpoint of her Sun/Mars, which suggests a ruthless application of energy and a warring way

31 In the Table, 0 degrees = the beginning of Cardinal sign positions; 30+=0 of Fixed signs and further; 60=0 Mutable and further.

in relationships. Pluto=Neptune/Asc: the apprehension of an oppressive or threatening environment; and Node/MC, leadership and success.

The Sun=Uranus/Node: High tension with others, intense leadership style. Node=Jupiter/Neptune and Mercury/Pluto: group-spirited activity and recognition by others for persuasiveness and communication skills!

Mercury=Mars/Node and Sun/Pluto: promotion through partnership and publicity; extraordinary mental projections, "lording it over" others, great salesmanship!

Mental Profile

With all the indications of personal power and public exposure, with language skills and international point of view, with salesmanship, and enormous persuasiveness, we must assume that Cleopatra had the mental capacities to back it all up, to seize opportunities, innovate, and make conspicuous gains. She had to be very, very smart. The horoscope tells us much about this.

I have found that the diurnal speed of the Moon on the day of birth correlates strongly with observable intelligence: the faster the Moon's speed, over 13 degrees 45, for example (my arbitrary benchmark), is toward conspicuous brightness and below that is toward the average.[32] Cleopatra's Moon speed on the day of her birth was 14 degrees 27 minutes. If something didn't short-circuit her mental capacities—and the horoscope suggests just the opposite, i.e., a bright freedom, through the sextile with Venus and no other aspect, though a distant influence from Neptune—I feel that she would appear very bright, inventive, quick, thrusting with opinion, sharp.[33]

Mercury with its sextile from Venus of course suggests a beautiful voice, as we have seen. In Sagittarius, we know Mercury has the need to express opinions, make verbal thrusts, dart in and out of concepts, and that it needs an anchor. Jupiter, as well, in its own sign of Sagittarius, increases this opinionation dimension very

---

32 The fastest diurnal speed for the Moon is just in excess of 15 degrees, and the slowest is just above 11 degrees. Of course, the condition of Mercury is very important within this profile as well, but the Moon's diurnal speed is a signal that shouldn't be overlooked.

33 The opposition with Saturn is not a labor for the mind here, since Saturn and the Moon rule the sign each is in, i.e., have utmost dignity, and the Moon is well supported by the Uranus-Pluto sextile.

strongly, especially with the support from Mars. Cleopatra was impressively bright, highly opinionated, exceedingly articulate, and, I think, quite capable of seeing the other side to every issue (Mars in Libra) and could strategize according to her needs and plans, very effectively. With all her awareness of other tongues, other lands, philosophies, and histories, she certainly had a world view of things.

Cleopatra probably had a superb memory, suggested by Moon in Cancer (hoarding, retaining) and a strong anchor to perceptions (and wisdom) denoted by Saturn. All of this is reinforced so strongly by this major axis occurring in the the 3rd–9th House mental axis.

The Mercury midpoint pictures (see page 25) suggest that she knew how bright she was. She let people around her know too.

The midpoint picture of Saturn=Neptune/Node suggests emotional hurt, fear of deception, and jealousy. Here is a reminder of the lone position we have seen for the private Cleopatra.

As we have noted, Mars is not obviously in the power position we would expect for Cleopatra's aggressiveness. But, through six midpoint structures, linking Mars to all planets except Jupiter, this Mars becomes titanic, linking together all the key concepts of her power profile: Mars=Sun/Mercury, excitement, nervous energy, and drive; Moon/Neptune, personal magic; Uranus/MC, temperamental rash action for ego recognition; preoccupation with and the fear of attack; Pluto/MC, striving for power, a drive for dominance; and Venus/Uranus, strong love excitement and creativity!

And finally: Neptune=Mercury/Jupiter, beguiling fantasy and magnetism.[34]

These midpoint pictures synthesize every observation we have made about Cleopatra's personality. As a final note, we must recognize that classically, Mars is the planet denoting sexual energy and its application as well as aggressive behavior (for a monarch: armed force). This sense is certainly captured within the insight that power is sexual; as strategy and conquest, power is an aphrodisiac.

Now, we must take Cleopatra's horoscope and test it carefully through time and history within her life. Her story will be told and her horoscope will be rectified simultaneously. Our attention must be chiefly directed to the *angles* of the horoscope and to the *Moon*,

---

34 These phrases describing the midpoint pictures are almost verbatim from the midpoint directory presented in both Tyl, *Prediction* and *Synthesis & Counseling*.

the measurement references that are most sensitively affected by a change of birth time, even within the span of four minutes.[35]

Seven event-periods of vital significance marked Cleopatra's life. They will test the horoscope we have created for her at many levels. The first is her father's death and her assumption of the throne of Egypt on March 13, 51 B.C.

This time period begins significantly six years before, when she was just twelve. We can presume that Cleopatra was deeply influenced by her father, Auletes, since her Capricorn Sun, symbolizing her father (ruler of the 10th) and his/her monarchy, is all-pervasive in her horoscope. Cleopatra had already seen much that would found her own administrative posture, structured through her personal predispositions, her personal "style."

Rome's imperialism was focused within its "First Triumvirate" of rulers (Julius Caesar, the great military hero and world conqueror Pompey, and Marcus Licinius Crassus). She saw her father Auletes seek help from the Triumvir to restore and ensure his tottering throne. The price for Rome's support was six thousand talents, equivalent to seventeen million dollars, or to the entire revenues of Egypt for six months, or perhaps even for a whole year.[36]

When the Egyptians began to revolt at being entirely subjected to the will of Rome and at paying so much extra to replenish the royal treasury, Auletes again fled to Rome for help, in the late Spring 57 B.C. History is not sure, but astrology shows that it was most probable that *Cleopatra went with him:* transiting Uranus was exactly conjunct her Moon in the 9th for the extremely important international trip, and transiting Saturn was not far behind. This would be a critical time for her personality development. Additionally, Solar Arc (SA) Mercury was exactly square her Mars, ruler of the 6th, her father's ninth! They traveled together. She absorbed it all. She began her intensive study of languages. Her intrigue with international outreach and political strategy was awakened to dominate her life.

In Rome, the twelve-year-old saw Auletes wheel and deal. When his enemies from Alexandria sent a group of 100 men to

---

35 Normally, one degree of the zodiac passes overhead at the *Medius Coeli* (MC, Midheaven) every four minutes of clock time. Indeed, this one degree can represent a change of *one year* in timing projections made through Solar Arcs or *one month* through the Secondary Progressed Moon or one Lunar month through Tertiary movement of the Sun and Midheaven (and usually Ascendant).

36 Grant, *Cleopatra*, 13.

Rome to confront Auletes with their charges, Auletes had their leaders murdered as their ships landed. He distributed huge bribes throughout Rome to enlist support. Rome made another demand for payment in return for re-enstating Auletes on his throne. This time the amount was almost *twice* what had been asked before— now the cost was 10,000 talents! It was a shaming and frightening burden, but it did mean that Rome and its businessmen had a powerful vested interest to preserve a secure Egyptian monarchy.[37]

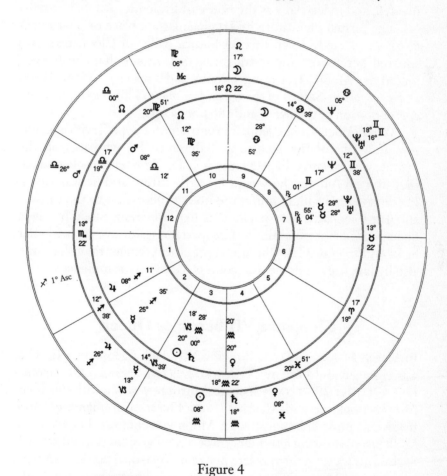

Figure 4

Inner Chart
Cleopatra VII
Jan. 13, 68 B.C.

Outer Chart
SA Father's Death
Mar. 13, 51 B.C.

37 Ibid., 16–17.

In Cleopatra's horoscope at that time as well (see page 17), SA Saturn was at 13 Aquarius (add 12 years/degrees of arc to natal Saturn as Solar Arc abbreviation) and 4 months (20'; average rate per month is 5') just 34' away from exact square to her Ascendant. We can see this as a warning sign, and it certainly was in order: in Auletes' absence, the Egyptians gave the throne over to Cleopatra's elder sister, Cleopatra VI Tryphaena. Fighting her for that honor was another sister, Berenice IV. Loyalties in the kingdom were divided, and indeed so was the house of Ptolemy.

The formal investiture of Tryphaena took place on December 5, 57 B.C. Exactly when this SA Saturn (ruler of Cleopatra's 3rd) squared her Ascendant as transiting Saturn simultaneously conjoined her Moon. Transiting Uranus had advanced off the Moon *and was opposing Saturn in the 3rd and ruling it!* This is extraordinary corroboration of the event and the horoscope.

When Auletes and Cleopatra returned to Egypt, Tryphaena was somehow out of the picture and Berenice IV, who was on the throne, was executed by her father's order. The tensions had taken their toll on Auletes; he was in his early fifties, and he was ailing. He dictated his will, defining the line of succession to the throne, and our Cleopatra was specified as heir-apparent. Since by law a queen could not rule alone, Cleopatra was to co-rule with her brother, Ptolemy XIII, who was eight years younger than she. And, also by law, she would be in second place to his prominence.

Cleopatra VII becomes Queen

In March 51 B.C., Auletes, Ptolemy XII, died. Cleopatra VII, who was eighteen and Ptolemy XIII, who was ten, assumed the throne. Figure 4 (page 29) shows Cleopatra's birth horoscope with the Solar Arc positions for mid-March 51 B.C. The measurements capture the events most dramatically: SA Moon was conjunct her rectified Midheaven, showing a tremendous career focus; SA Ascendant at 1 Sagittarius was exactly opposite her Pluto (personal power), SA Saturn was just 23 minutes of arc past precise opposition to her Midheaven ("major change in the family or in the profession; possible death concerns within the extended family; the father figure; an extremely important time of life development"[38]), and the mighty

---

38 See Solar Arc Directory, Tyl, *Prediction* or *Synthesis & Counseling*, Appendices.

Uranus-Pluto conjunction itself—the signal of her age, of her fate—*had arced to conjunction with her Neptune in the 8th House.*

Additionally, Secondary Progressed (SP) Venus (not shown here) was exactly upon the Nodal axis (popularity) and her SP Ascendant was at 28 Scorpio, *exactly opposed Uranus,* an extraordinary happening to recognize her being!

Cleopatra VII and Ptolemy XIII took to themselves as well the title of Philopater, lover of the father, to respect the memory of Auletes and acknowledge the proper transition. Cleopatra's own name meant "glory to the father" in Greek. Indeed, Cleopatra's Sun in Capricorn belonged symbolically to her father as well.

Josephus gives us an acid glimpse into the Roman analysis of Cleopatra's administrative drive: "... for if there were but any hopes of getting money, she would violate both temples and sepulchres. Nor was there any holy place that was esteemed the most inviolable, from which she would not fetch the ornaments it had in it; nor any place so profane ... if it could but contribute somewhat to the covetous humor of this wicked creature."[39] He continues in this vein and begins to betray the propagandist thrusts to show Cleopatra enslaved by extravagance and lusts.

Certainly Cleopatra was extremely ambitious. The astrology has revealed so much of that to us, and as she got older and grander and more involved with intrigues and power plays in the world, her strengths became more pronounced and more vilified by those who feared her. But upon assumption of the throne, Cleopatra was carrying the enormous burden of her father's debts to Rome and a critical food shortage, since the Nile had failed to rise high enough to flood the banks and support crop growth and harvest.[40]

Additionally, Cleopatra agreed to send troops to help the Roman governor of Syria against the Parthians (Persia). Her soldiers mutinied and refused to go—recalling the promise we saw in the Uranus-Pluto conjunction chart. This mutiny was an eruption of nationalist feelings against being vassal to Rome. These feelings

---

39 Josephus, *Antiquities,* XV, 4, 1 (90).

40 The farming economy of Egypt was totally dependent upon hydraulic engineering to provide water in a rainless land. The regular seasonal flooding of the Nile was close to a life and death matter. It entered the consciousness and religion of the people deeply. The Pharaoh was thought to command the Nile in league with the heliacal rising of the star Sirius. This was how the world began. This was how one of Egypt's three calendars was established. See Aldred, 69–72; Whitrow, 24–29; Grant, *The Ancient Mediterranean,* 38–43; all sources of ancient Egypt.

were everywhere in Egypt, and they played into the hands of a eunuch named Pothinus who had become Cleopatra's brother's counsel, Ptolemy XIII's Regent. Pothinus was completely hostile to things Roman.[41]

Two and one-half years into her co-rule, all these pressures threatened Cleopatra crucially. The press was on, and the young queen left Alexandria—or was ousted—into exile between June and September 49 B.C. It is thought she went south into the hinterlands of Upper Egypt (South); it is thought that she went just across Egypt's borders into southern Palestine, over which Egypt had had relations from war to peace for over 1,500 years, and while strongly under Roman rule at the time was not threatening to her.[42]

We can see this oppressive time in the "Father's Death" horoscope (Figure 4, page 29) for her assumption of the throne, by just moving the Solar Arc positions forward a little more than one degree (March 50 B.C. to June 49). Most significantly we see SA Saturn conjoining Cleopatra's Venus, which opposes her Midheaven and rules her 7th, the House of the Public. Additionally, seeing the queen's horoscope as the horoscope of the people, this Saturn depression of the Venus symbolism corresponds to the bad times in the kingdom, in the farmlands, the dryness. As well, the 4th House in the horoscope of a country or a monarch *represents the opposition party*, those against one's rule; here is the clear suggestion of the high priest pushing forward the best interests of Ptolemy XIII, her brother (Venus in the 4th is Venus in the second of her brother's derived Ascendant, which is Cleopatra's 3rd).[43]

We can see that the SA MC nearing 8 Virgo at the time of exile is entering the square with natal Jupiter: this is a marvelous time for

---

41 Hughes-Hallett, 17.

42 Celebrated Egyptian campaigns into Canaan, well up to Syria, are commemorated in the names of Thutmose III (the Battle of Megiddo in northwest Palestine) ca. 1460, Ramesses II (the Battle of Kadesh just northwest of the Dead Sea) ca. 1275, Merenptha ca. 1208, and Ramesses III ca. 1182 (one of the latter two against the Sea Peoples, involving Phillistines). Egypt long maintained fortified bases in Gaza on the southwest coast. See Drews, 120–121, 129; Grant, *The Ancient Mediterranean*, 72.

43 Derivative Houses is the adjustment of a new Ascendant to any House of focus in any horoscope and then seeing the Houses issuing in conventional symbolism from that new starting point. For example, here the 4th House is the second of Cleopatra's 3rd, her brothers and sisters. The 9th House is the 12th House derived from the 10th, as another example, suggesting here that international concerns, on the one hand important for Egypt's security with the Moon in its own sign there, but on the other hand the potential source for her undoing, the twelfth dynamic and the opposition from Saturn.

success, professional gains, internationalism, and legal issues. This is the silver lining within the cloud, which will mature with the arrival of Caesar from Rome!

Studying this period of time in Cleopatra's life extremely closely, astrology is able to suggest to history that Cleopatra left Alexandria in response to the pressure from the people throughout Egypt, the economy that was affected by Nile conditions and near-famine, and to the ambitious collusion within the Palace. We can suggest strongly that she left on May 20, 49 B.C.[44]

The Siege, Caesar, and Security

Cnaius Pompeius Magnus (106–48 B.C.) was a great Roman general and statesman, part of the first Triumvir with Caesar and Crassus. This three-way rule of the Roman world broke down into civil war [recall the "Cleopatra Conjunction" in Gemini, page 15], just as we shall see happen within the second Triumvir involving Octavian, Antony, and Lepidus, to be created upon the assassination of Caesar.

In the warring among them, Pompey and Caesar clashed at Pharsalus in central Greece, and Pompey, in defeat, fled to Egypt for protection. Pothinus, young Ptolemy's Regent, did not want to receive Pompey and have it appear to Caesar's Rome that Egypt was allying itself with the losing side in the Roman strife, so he contrived to have Pompey the Great murdered. This is one of the most celebrated assassinations in history. It was accomplished in the sight of his wife, Cornelia, as Pompey was being helped from the small boat that had brought him from his ship in Alexandria harbor to the shore. He was alone, defeated, and hoping for rescue by Egypt. The date was September 28, 48 B.C. Pompey was stabbed and beheaded, and his body was thrown into the sea.[45]

Grant opines that, in the view of much of Rome, "the murder of Pompey earned the fifteen-year-old Ptolemy XIII a place in Dante's Inferno, in company with Judas and Cain. Cicero, on the other

---

44 Transiting Pluto was exactly opposed her Mercury during this time and transiting Uranus was exactly opposed her Saturn. Then, Mars as trigger was transiting late Gemini conjoining her Neptune and opposing her Mercury. Finally, the Tertiary Progressed Ascendant was precisely conjunct her rectified natal Midheaven and, simultaneously, the Tertiary Midheaven was precisely upon her rectified Descendant!

45 This murder is vividly recounted by Plutarch in "Pompey," 132–135.

hand, although he had been one of Pompey's supporters, remarked that after the defeat at Pharsalus such a conclusion, at some time or other, was inevitable."[46]

The times in Egypt had been terrible that year of 48 B.C., due to the Nile. Its rise was the smallest on record according to Roman historians, who were watching the situation carefully indeed, and Julius Caesar himself, for his expeditions, needed money. He set off to Egypt with ten warships (brought down from Roman installations in Rhodes) and a medium-sized force of 3,200 infantry and 800 calvary. He went to collect what he could from Egypt's treasury against the horrendous debts owed to Rome. He needed money for his civil wars during the break up of the Triumvir.

Caesar arrived in an anxious and rioting country just four days after the murder of his onetime friend and recent enemy, Pompey. It was October 2, 48. When Ptolemy's "foster-father," a philosopher in the court named Theodotus, came to Caesar's ship to greet him and assist him to shore, he presented Caesar with Pompey's signet ring ... *and* the general's severed head, which had been embalmed.[47]

Plutarch records this event with horror and poignancy: "when he [Caesar[came to Alexandria, where Pompey was already murdered, he would not look upon Theodotus, who presented him with his head, but taking only his signet, he shed tears."[48]

With no real accompanying force in terms of numbers, Caesar had walked into a terribly dangerous situation: the riots in Alexandria had taken the lives of several of his soldiers, he was not organized or strong enough to retaliate against and quell a general rebellion, the threat of an escalation of hostilities was very real, and he was confined to the palace for safety. Here was mighty Caesar, come to Egypt to talk about world issues to an adolescent pharaoh— who was not even there, who was with his army on the eastern frontier—and all of this was standing in Caesar's way to get the money he desperately needed! We can allow ourselves the editorialization that Caesar was fuming, frustrated, fiercely angry! He knew Pothinus was running everything, that he was ill-feeding the Roman forces, inciting the people to mayhem, and, as Plutarch continues: "the eunuch Pothinus, who was the chief favorite and had lately killed Pompey, who had banished Cleopatra, [and] was now secret-

---

46 Grant, *Cleopatra*, 58.
47 Ibid., 61.
48 Plutarch, *Caesar*, 230.

ly plotting Caesar's destruction (to prevent which, Caesar from that time began to sit up whole nights, under the pretense of drinking, for the security of his person)." And Caesar could not just forget his money mission and leave, to return stronger later, since the prevailing winds at the time trapped his ships in the harbor.[49]

Caesar hatched a plan which Pothinus perhaps had not anticipated: Plutarch wrote, "Caesar did not want Egyptians to be his counselors [push him around, tell him what to do], and soon after privately sent for Cleopatra from her retirement."[50] He sent for young Ptolemy too.

How Cleopatra arrived back in Alexandria, into the palace, to meet Caesar is told by Plutarch, as he continues: "She was at a loss how to get in undiscovered, till she thought of putting herself into the coverlet of a bed and lying at length, whilst Apollodorus [a Sicilian confidant] tied up the bedding and carried it on his back through the gates to Caesar's apartment. Caesar was first captivated by this proof of Cleopatra's bold wit, and was afterwards so overcome by the charm of her society that he made a reconciliation between her and her brother, on the condition that she should rule as his colleague in the kingdom."

Cleopatra was twenty-one. Caesar was world-wise and fifty-two. Obviously, her daring, her poise, her extraordinary mind and, undoubtedly, her sensual way, magnetically virginal as well, captivated him. We can also never forget that in Caesar's awareness also was the fact that Cleopatra was the crest of a most royal wave that had begun 400 years earlier with Alexander the Great, the world's first unquestioned, famous god-hero. Their liaison developed. Cleopatra became pregnant with Caesar's child, to be named Caesarion.

Here's how Caesar solved the problems of the palace, Cleopatra, and his troops being under siege:

✦ Caesar soothed the crowd, promising a suitable settlement to their national interests and his financial business there.

✦ Caesar negotiated to give over Cyprus from Roman rule to the Ptolemies, specifically to Cleopatra's sister Arsinoe and the much younger brother who will become Ptolemy XIV. This would get *them* out of the palace, out of Cleopatra's (and his) way.

---

49 Hughes-Hallett, 18.
50 Plutarch, *Caesar*, 231.

✦ Outnumbered five to one (Pothinus had called back from the eastern front 20,000 Egyptian soldiers, headed by Achillas), Caesar went into action: he put Ptolemy XIII under arrest in the palace, staved off Achillas' first attack, and then himself attacked by firing all the Egyptian ships, seizing the Pharos lighthouse, and gaining complete control of the harbor.

Arsinoe got free from the palace and went as turncoat to Achillas who, with the army, declared *her* Queen of Egypt! We know that Cleopatra will remember this and have her executed for this act seven years later.

✦ Pothinus tried to join Arsinoe and Achillas. Caesar learned of the plan and had Pothinus murdered.

✦ Caesar was almost killed in a turn of the siege battle, and conceived of the final phase of the plan that would save them: he sent the young Ptolemy XIII, the teenager in his golden armor, out of the palace and over to Ganymedes (who had killed Achillas and was now leading the armies). Grant points out that Caesar's reasoning was that Ptolemy was "highly motivated" not to have Arsinoe gain the upper hand, let alone Ganymedes and the army, i.e., without him!

For months, the siege raged, September–December 48 and further. In early March 47, rescue troops started to arrive, including a considerable number of troops from Judea.[51] This influx awakened the loyalties of many, many Egyptian Jews, an enormous number of whom had populated Alexandria as descendants from Jacob (Israel) and his extended family (including his son, Joseph, who came the earliest and rose to administrative power in Egypt) who arrived in Egypt around 1876 B.C. to escape famine in ancient Canaan.[52]

---

51 Josephus, *Antiquities*, XIV, 8, 1.

52 Free, 74. The number of Jews increased enormously over the centuries. There was the return to Canaan through the mass Exodus or through many smaller migrations, probably between the mid-fifteenth and mid-thirteenth centuries. Two centuries before Cleopatra, seventy-two Jewish translators were organized by Ptolemy II Philadelphus to translate the Pentateuch (the first five books of the Hebrew Bible; the Pentateuch *(pen'-ta-took)*. This important Greek translation is known to this day as the Septuagint *(sep-too'-uh-jint)*.

Everything shifted to Caesar's and Cleopatra's favor. Young Ptolemy XIII retreated to the Nile, boarded a boat with his aides, the boat sank, and, weighed down by his armor, Ptolemy drowned.[53]

It was May 47, eight months after Pompey's murder and Caesar's arrival in Egypt. Caesar—and Cleopatra—had prevailed. Caesar left Egypt in July, leaving the country to its own rule in the hands of Cleopatra, forgiving an enormous portion of Auletes' debt. Cleopatra was twenty-two and seven months pregnant with Caesar's child. To fulfill the law, Caesar had Cleopatra marry her youngest brother, Ptolemy XIV, aged twelve.[54]

Figure 5 (page 38) is Cleopatra's horoscope brought forward to October 13, 48 B.C., within a few days surely of Cleopatra's incognito return to the palace and Ptolemy XIII's return from the field. It was the time that both monarchs met Caesar for the first time. It was the time of the siege. It was the time of Cleopatra's liaison with Caesar and her impregnation. It was the time that her co-ruling brother drowned. It was the time within the year of her secure return to the throne and her marriage to her youngest brother.

Cleopatra came of age.

Again, the astrological correspondence to Cleopatra's historical reality is extraordinary, reinforcing again and again the confidence we should have in her birth date and time.

The *preceding* Lunar Eclipse takes a position within this chart also: it occurred on July 15, 48 B.C. at 4:09 A.M. UT, at 19 Cancer/ Capricorn 2 *conjunct Cleopatra's Sun at 20 Capricorn!* This is extraordinary emphasis. It is a statement of illumination, of full awareness (Full Moon), of change (eclipse) affecting everything she stands for. The focus would be triggered in December 48—probably when she discovered she was pregnant with Caesar's child—by transiting Jupiter square the natal Sun, the point of the preceding eclipse. The accentuation of the Lunar phenomenon is inescapably the accentuation of female and male, fecundation, Isis and Osiris.

---

53 Herodotus points out that to drown in the Nile gained the blessing of Osiris, conferring god status on the victim. To offset this, Caesar located the body and paraded the golden armor before the people to emphasize the mortal death. Grant, *Cleopatra*, 77.

54 Intermarriage was not a Greek way, it was an Egyptian tradition. The gods Osiris and Isis were husband and wife and also brother and sister. This was a rationale, a blessing, if you will, for many Pharaohs to marry their sisters. They would keep the blood-line pure, and, Grant adds, intermarriage would diminish the number of pretenders to the throne outside the family. Grant, *Cleopatra*, 26.

Would this child, this tie with Caesar, extend the house of Ptolemy to Rome, to the realm of other gods as well?

The Solar Arc of the Moon opposed Venus is exact. it speaks of gentle things: love relationship (Venus rules the 7th) with a foreigner (Moon rules the 9th), impregnation, heir apparent to the monarchy.

In parallel, this Moon=Venus arc describes the political relationship with her brother, the *marriage* that was necessary by law.

SA Neptune square to Mars echoes this coming of age through liaison with Caesar as well: Neptune rules the 5th and is in the 8th

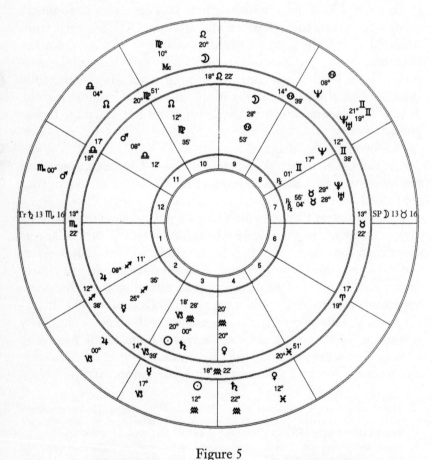

Figure 5

Inner Chart	Outer Chart
Cleopatra VII	**SA Meet Caesar**
	Oct. 13, 48 B.C.

natally (children, sexuality, speculation, values) and it brings its symbolism forward in the arc of time to a high-tension relationship with Mars in Libra, relationship. This arc also suggests a change of course of action through something unusual, secretive, sensual, incredible.

The hard aspect of SA Mars square to natal Saturn is clearly the combative tension with her brother Ptolemy XIII, his death, and with her sister Arsinoe and her exile. It is the end of the line (fourth dynamic) for this brother and this sister; Mars rules Aries on the 6th, the fourth house of Cleopatra's sibling 3rd.[55]

The transits invigorated these powerfully delineated background measurements: transiting Pluto was exactly opposed Cleopatra's Mercury, and transiting Uranus was exactly opposed/conjunct her Nodal axis during the entire period: a tremendous adjustment of her life perception, her perspective for development, public acceptance, her image, her impact through her plans and communication skills.

Two measurements cap all of these into a time capsule of meaning for history: in the period January through April 47, when the siege was ended, when Cleopatra rose up again and ascended the throne with her brother, Ptolemy XIV, *transiting Saturn (ambition, symbol of her brother through rulership of the 3rd) was exactly conjunct the Ascendant we have divined for the queen!*

And finally, the Secondary Progressed Moon—a most telling measurement in its time sensitivity—on October 13, the beginning of Cleopatra's adult life, the beginning of her tested and matured relationship with her people, with Caesar, with her brother-husband, the SP Moon was at 13 Taurus 16, *precisely upon her horizon at the 7th cusp!*

---

55 In the analysis of Solar Arc aspects with natal planets and points, the arcing planet very often brings into the directed relationship the significance of the natal House the arcing planet rules; this is combined with the significance of the House holding the natal planet and the House it rules. The Arcs then effect synthesis. Tyl, *Prediction in Astrology*.

The Ides of March and Caesar's Death

With one more look at Figure 5 (page 38), we see the pro-
gressed/directed Sun arcing at 12 Aquarius 11 applying to a square
with her Ascendant, precise in November 47. This augurs well for
her reign in its new start and for the birth of Caesar Ptolemy (Caesarion), which occurred in early September 47.[56] Coins were issued
to commemorate his birth and show Cleopatra suckling the infant
in the image of Isis suckling Horus.

We have noted the transit of Saturn over the Ascendant during
the culmination of the exacting time with Caesar in Alexandria. It
signalled so strongly the sense of coming of age, a critical focus of
development, involving two brothers and one sister. That transiting
Saturn would now move on and very soon oppose the powerful
Uranus-Pluto conjunction in the 7th. Cleopatra would face up
again to an extraordinary developmental period, undoubtedly
involving her "partner," her husband/brother co-ruler or Caesar
once again and/or the general public. We can estimate that transit
time for Saturn to be 16 degrees, half a sign (normally two and one-
half years per sign, some thirty months) to be about fifteen months
after October 48. This would be January–February–March 46.

Additionally, we see the SA Midheaven applying to conjunction
with the Nodal axis, an indication of grand public exposure for a
monarch, working with others about a year away as well.

The SP Moon rising over the seventh cusp exactly in October
48 (normally at a rate of 1 degree per month) should conjoin
Uranus and Pluto in 15 or 16 months, January 46, *the same time
span as transiting Saturn's opposition with this same place.* An important time indeed.

This was certainly the time when Cleopatra was motivated to
go to Rome, to meet again with Caesar, to bring the year-old Caesar Ptolemy out into the open to clarify the child's mighty parentage. In addition, Grant says, "the main purpose of her visit,
however, was to continue her close personal relations with Caesar,
since it was on him, treaty or no treaty, that her whole position
depended. This was a matter about which she had reason to feel
anxious, because Caesar had other mistresses besides Cleopatra."[57]

---

56 Grant, *Cleopatra*, 83–84.
57 Grant, *Cleopatra*, 86.

Here we see Cleopatra's personal fears coming to the fore-ground: the jealousy, the insecurity—there had been no letters exchanged between her and Caesar—and her need to have a partner to help her with her responsibilities and her ambition. These dimensions of Cleopatra spoke eloquently from her birth horo-scope, as we have seen. These dimensions were now clearly and dramatically emphasized by the transit of Saturn and the progres-sion of the Moon.

Preparations were made, and, with Caesarion and Ptolemy XIV (now thirteen) and a grand entourage, Cleopatra and her ships arrived at Rome in November 46 as the progressed Moon came to 9 Gemini, *precisely opposed her Jupiter in Sagittarius!*.

When Caesar had left Alexandria, he had gone directly into other battles, so heated still were Rome's civil wars. In the year before being able to settle down in his own capital, he established three more victories after Alexandria. In October 46, just before Cleopatra's arrival, he mounted an extraordinary public pageant in Rome, complete with floats and parades, to celebrate his four Tri-umphs. The highlight of the pageant was the parade of Egyptian prisoner-soldiers from the siege in Alexandria. This parade was led by Arsinoe IV, in total disgrace.

Caesar seems to have kept Cleopatra in splendid lodgings, but at a distance. He was immensely busy and his health was failing clearly. Grant reports that Caesar "appears to have become liable to attacks of epilepsy, and he suffered from headaches and fainting fits."[58]

In January 45, Caesar left to do battle again, in Spain. He returned eight months later, and again was ailing. He made his will on September 13, 45, *adopting as his son his grand-nephew Gaius Octavius*, who would become known as Octavian and then as Augus-tus Caesar. It will be Octavian, after Caesar's death, who will be in league with Mark Antony and another Roman noble in the Second Triumvirate. It will be Octavian who will defeat Antony and Cleopatra at Actium and precipitate their deaths.—Roman law for-bade recognizing foreigners in a will as heirs. Therefore, *Cleopatra and their son Caesarion were not mentioned.*

This must have jarred Cleopatra deeply into insecurity. Undoubtedly she knew this stipulation of Roman law, but she also knew well that anything was possible by the proclamation of Cae-sar—that was a monarch's way; it was the experience of her history.

---

58 Grant, *Cleopatra*, 91.

Did she feel abandoned? Did she feel that, after all that had happened, there would be no dream of world power through a marriage between Egypt and Rome, through Caesarion? Why should she even be in Rome? Even though Caesar surely negotiated some respite from her anxiety, she certainly became aware of troubled times ahead, once again.

Two months later, on November 7, 45 B.C. at 1:31 A.M. UT, there was an eclipse of the Moon precisely on Cleopatra's *Ascendant-Descendant axis*, 13 Scorpio-Taurus.

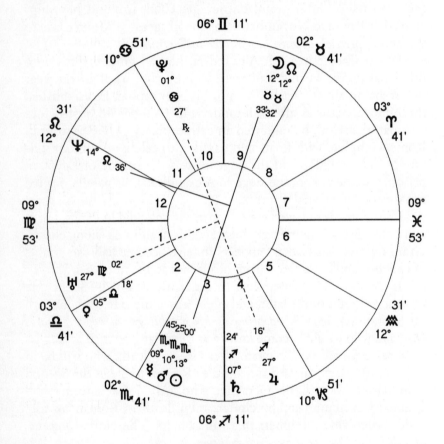

Figure 6
Lunar Eclipse — Rome
Nov. 7, 45 B.C., 1:22 A.M. LMT
Rome, Italy
12E29 41N54
Placidus Houses

Figure 6 (page 42) shows this Lunar Eclipse from the vantage point of Rome. The eclipse axis was tightly squared by Neptune, ruler of the 7th House in the mundane chart. This chart becomes exceedingly personalized, of course, if it ties in to an individual's natal horoscope, just as any transit picture does. This chart applies powerfully to Cleopatra through her Ascendant, i.e., *the axis of the transit eclipse is exactly on her horizon*, and transiting Neptune is square the eclipse axis *and* her Ascendant. With this transiting Neptune in 14 Leo, it will now apply to Cleopatra's Midheaven in 18 Leo, usually a time of confusion, dissolution, vagueness, loss.

An eclipse is a powerful point of emphasis wherever it falls. Its significance is triggered, if you will, by a transit—so often, Mars—when it later comes to square, conjunct, or opposed the eclipse point; in Cleopatra's case, when Mars is between 11 and 15 degrees of a Fixed sign. This would happen in the time period ahead for Cleopatra, *at the beginning of the second week of March 44 B.C.*

In the mundane chart for the eclipse, the power of its accentuation of Cleopatra's life is increased greatly by the Mars-Mercury conjunction with the Sun (with her Ascendant at the time of the eclipse). I feel that it is significant—especially in a monarch's horoscope—that the epochal conjunction of Uranus and Pluto which we studied in the heavens, in history, and in Cleopatra's horoscope at the outset of this rectification is now *developed into a very close square relationship*. This configuration is actually a second T-Square, an angular one of great power (Uranus=Jupiter/Pluto) suggesting a major upset in the way things go, a time when the tables are turned. Jupiter here joins Neptune as co-ruler of Pisces on the 7th. This chart warns of a tremendous change of direction, a twist of fate that will involve Cleopatra's relationship with someone, her brother/husband co-ruler, or indeed, Caesar.

Caesar planned another campaign. He was to leave Rome on March 17, 44. His aim was to conquer the East, to emulate Alexander. A meeting of the Senate was called for March 15, the Ides of March.[59]

---

59 The Ides in the ancient Roman calendar were the 15th days of March, May, July, and October, and the 13th days of all the other months. The Ides occurred eight days after the "Nones." The complicated Roman system for dividing the month had "Calends" on the first, the days of new moon, with the Ides marked by the days of full moon. The counting of days was extremely complicated and pivoted upon the Ides, which were reckoned as days before the Calends of the succeeding months. This cumbersome (and inaccurate) system was still in use in western Europe as late as the sixteenth century A.D.! See Whitrow, 68.

Plutarch vividly sets the scene and tells the tale: "Many strange prodigies and apparitions are said to have been observed shortly before this event. As to the lights in the heavens, the noises heard in the night, and the wild birds which perched in the forum ... As Caesar was sacrificing [an animal propitiation], the victim's heart was missing, a very bad omen ... One finds it also related by many that a soothsayer bade him prepare for some great danger on the Ides of March ... As he went to the senate, [Caesar] met this soothsayer, and said to him by way of raillery, 'The Ides of March are come,' who answered him calmly, 'Yes, they are come, but they are not past.'"[60]

Plutarch tells us of other omens, about curious turns in Caesar's dinner conversation the evening before regarding what sort of death would be the best. [Caesar's reply was, "A sudden one."] About how during that night, all the doors and windows of his house had flown open together. In an enormous start, he awoke to brilliant moonlight and saw his wife, Calpurnia, fast asleep but groaning indistinct words.

When it was day, Calpurnia—whom he had never seen superstitious or so alarmed—begged Caesar not to go to the senate. He agreed, and sought to send Antony to dismiss the senate, but a close confidant (whom Caesar had made a second heir) who was himself involved in the real conspiracy to kill Caesar, "spoke scoffingly and in mockery of the diviners." He told Caesar that the senate was primed "to vote unanimously that he should be declared king of all the provinces out of Italy." What would they say, then, if Caesar cancelled *this* meeting?!

As Caesar entered the anteroom to the senate, a known philosopher and teacher who had got wind of the plot approached Caesar and gave him a note: "Read this, Caesar, alone, and quickly, for it contains a matter of great importance which dearly concerns you." Caesar tried to read it, but he was jostled and hindered by the crowd of those who had come to speak with him, who were vying for his attention.

Plutarch continues: "All these things might happen by chance. But the place which was destined for the scene of this murder, in which the senate met that day, was the same in which Pompey's statue stood ... showing that there was something of a supernatural influence which guided the action and ordered it to that particular

---

60 Plutarch, *Caesar*, 239–242.

place ... Cassius, just before the act, is said to have looked towards Pompey's statue, and silently implored his [Ptolemy's] assistance."

When Caesar entered the senate chamber, the senate rose to greet him. The conspirators gathered closely around Caesar as he sat down on his bench, which was probably specially large in size and slightly elevated. One Tillius laid hold of Caesar's robe with both his hands and pulled it down from the neck to lower Caesar's head and torso. This was the signal.

Casca gave the first cut into Caesar's neck. Caesar grabbed the dagger, screamed in surprise, called for help. The astonishment among the senators not included in the conspiracy (Grant says there were sixty conspirators and that that was why the secret surely got out to some) froze them in place. The attackers stabbed Caesar repeatedly as he still clutched the warning note that had been given him, using it as well to fend off the blows. "It had been agreed that they should each of them make a thrust at him, and flesh themselves with his blood; for which reason Brutus also gave him one stab in the groin ... when he [Caesar] saw Brutus's sword drawn, he covered his face with his robe and submitted, letting himself fall." Caesar had been stabbed twenty-three times, and in the hysteria of the moment, many of the conspirators had themselves been wounded by each other. When it was done, Brutus stood forth to give a reason for the assassination, but the senate would not hear him.

With swords drawn, the conspirators roared out into the streets to stir up a popular revolt, but the city withdrew in horror and stillness. Ptolemy says, strangely, that the people respected Brutus and pitied Caesar. The senate seized control of the situation and calmed things. They ordered that Caesar should be worshipped as a divinity and that not one detail of what he had ruled during his tenure could be revoked. At his cremation, there was much emotion, and some citizens took flaming brands from the pyre and rushed to fire the homes of the assassins, but they were gone. The senate had given them duties out of the country.

Cleopatra was alone.

Figure 7 (page 46) shows Cleopatra's SA directions to the time of Caesar's death. There is the sensitive horizon line we have established, which absorbed the Lunar Eclipse four months earlier. *Transiting* Neptune was applying *to conjunction with her Midheaven.*

SA Pluto in the 8th House (matters of death, inheritances) exactly opposed Mercury in the 2nd (which is the eighth house of the 7th, i.e., Caesar's eighth). While this arc usually intensifies communication, discernment, and persuasion abilities, it also *demands an adjustment of perspective.* The House placements here definitely bring matters of death into consideration.

This deduction is strongly corroborated by SA Mercury exactly conjunct Cleopatra's Sun in the 3rd House. This is the press to think about one's ego position, to make new plans, to adjust perspective.

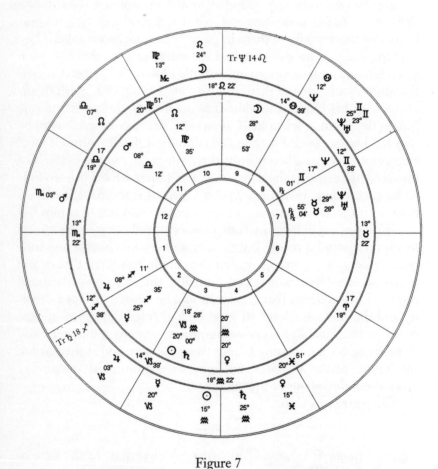

Figure 7

Inner Chart
Cleopatra VII

Outer Chart
SA Caesar's Death
Mar. 15, 44 B.C.

In that second week of March, transiting Saturn was in 18 Sagittarius opposed Cleopatra's Neptune in the 8th House. Transiting Mars had just squared the Lunar eclipse axis and was at 19 Aquarius 14 opposed her Midheaven and within 9 minutes of arc at the midpoint of Venus/Midheaven, with Venus ruling her 7th and 12th. The midpoint of SA Sun/Sat, obvious to the eye at 20 Aquarius was exactly upon her Venus, giving the midpoint picture of SA Sun/Saturn=Venus, potential victimization in relationship (or love), suppressed feelings.

What a shock this event must have been for her. She must have felt such ominous anticipation for months ahead of time, alone, stationed to the side of Caesar's life, her child husband and the baby about her as well, a country to rule in absentia, dreams to strategize ... and then the assassination of her key to security. The Tertiary Progression horoscope—an extreme test of her birth time—for that historical day is shown in Figure 8 (page 48).[61]

It is extraordinary to see TP Moon (which advances in Tertiary Progression about 13–14 degrees per month of life) conjunct TP Mercury and both tightly opposed the epic Uranus (and Pluto conjunction)! Here was Cleopatra's specific power-experience in relation to her partner, the man in whom she trusted for her security. It was crucial on that day and for the week thereafter (TP Moon advances about 3 degrees per week of life). TP Venus is exactly square to the Midheaven, a strong contact with a key angle, echoing her natal Venus opposition to her Midheaven. In other words, TP Venus is square its natal position and the Midheaven, calling tremendous attention to all things signified by Cleopatra's Venus: her partner, the 7th House, particularly.

And finally, remarkably, we see TP Midheaven (a key angle) exactly opposed Cleopatra's natal Sun!

And there is more: in this event analysis we have seen repeated reference to the 7th House as representing her partner, Caesar. Initially, we included reference to her marriage and governing

---

61 Tertiary Progressions are similar in principle to Secondary Progressions (one day for one year) but equate the ephemeris listing of each day after birth to one Lunar month of life. Tertiaries develop approximately twelve times faster than Secondaries. The key considerations are the positions of the Sun, Moon, Ascendant, and Midheaven—and then the planets—in relation to the natal positions. There is importance as well to the day (month) when the Sun changes sign. Computers now make the computation of Tertiaries lightning fast and accurate. They are powerful tools for specific time analysis in astrology and in rectification. Contacts with angles are vitally important.

partner, her brother/husband, Ptolemy XIV, and we must not forget this.

Cleopatra is shaken to her depths. She concludes her business (treaty, reaffirmation, etc.), gathers her entourage and returns to Alexandria in late June 44. She surely thought constantly with all her capacity and resourcefulness about how to secure her future, her country's future, the extension of the House of Ptolemy. With Caesar gone, would Ptolemy XIV, now fourteen and one-half, be advised in Alexandria to push his prerogatives as the male ruler to

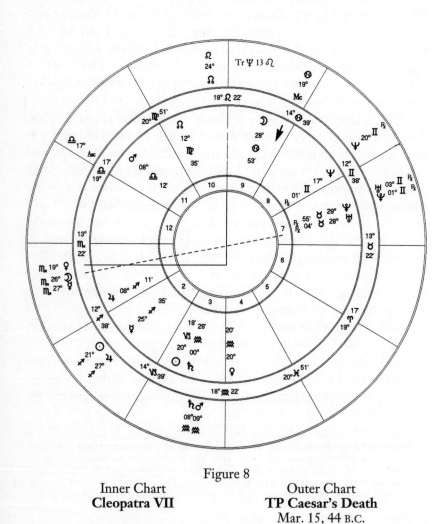

Figure 8

Inner Chart
Cleopatra VII

Outer Chart
TP Caesar's Death
Mar. 15, 44 B.C.

usurp Cleopatra's power; would her position be threatened? She had no one to help her now.

Ptolemy XIV died suddenly six to eight weeks later in August 44.

Josephus tells us twice that "she had her brother slain by private treachery; that she had already poisoned her brother, because she knew that he was to be king of Egypt."[62] Hughes-Hallett suggests that there is no proof of this but that Cleopatra "can not be cleared of suspicion."[63] Grant writes that "There is no reason to believe that the accusation was untrue. If Cleopatra could demand the death of her half-sister (as she did three years later), she was also capable of murdering her half-brother. And his death was too opportune to be accidental."[64]

The astrology adds conviction to the charge: Cleopatra surely murdered her husband/brother/co-ruler. Her history was filled with this kind of intrigue. She had seen it first hand through the actions of her father Auletes. She had been continuously privy to his example of self-preservation strategies. Cleopatra meant business. Every fear of insecurity was revived within her. Ptolemy XIII had been the same age when he was pushed by Pothinus to demand power, forcing Cleopatra's exile, instigating the siege. Ptolemy XIV now was a similar threat. She was alone, but she had Caesarion Ptolemy. Kill Ptolemy, long live Ptolemy. She poisoned her brother and elevated her son to co-ruler, at age three, as Ptolemy XV.

Here is the astrology: In August 44, transiting Neptune was still squaring her Ascendant exactly and applying to conjunction with her Midheaven. On July 2, with TP Moon having advanced to conjoin her Saturn *in the 3rd*, she probably determined her plan. She then had the murder executed when the TP Moon crossed the fourth cusp (opposed the Midheaven) and went on to conjoin Venus, August 18–23, with transiting Mars opposed her Jupiter in the 2nd, i.e., looking out for her best interests. *Neptune, behind it all, rules subterfuge and poison.*

Neptune also rules Cleopatra's 5th and, after she is freed of the treacherous activity, becomes the symbol for the coronation of her

62 Josephus, *Against Apion*, II, 5 (58); *Antiquities*, XV, 4, 1 (89).

63 Hughes-Hallett, 20.

64 Grant, *Cleopatra*, 97–98.

baby as co-ruler: Ptolemy XV Caesar ascended to the monarchy (10th House) through nefarious means.

With all of this, at the beginning of the new reign, Cleopatra adjusted her titles and entitled her son/co-ruler. She eliminated her title "Philadelphus (Brother-Loving) but kept the designations Thea Philopator (Goddess who Loves her Father). To her son, Ptolemy XV Caesar, was given the title Theos Philopator Philometor (God who Loves his Father and Mother). She had these names proclaimed everywhere and engraved on temple walls. She was the sole ruler and the goddess Isis. Grant sees these titlings, especially the child's, as Cleopatra's way of confirming that he was the sole son of Julius Caesar and to imply that he was Caesar's only true heir, diluting Octavian's—Caesar's adopted son's—claim to the power of lineage.[65]

Everything was in its Capricorn place. Cleopatra was restructured if not secure. For the next three years, Cleopatra ruled strongly and well, working her way through demanding concerns, through the continued poor performance by the Nile and the effect that that had on the people's spirit and the nation's productivity. She was not in the limelight as before and certainly not as she would be in her future. Out of the murky transit of Neptune over her Midheaven, the Solar Arc development of her Sun to opposition with her Midheaven in 41–40 would strengthen her monarchy (see Figure 7, page 46). The SA/SP Sun would then apply to conjunction with her Venus—a new partnership, a new association—all when she was twenty-eight to twenty-nine years old, as SA Moon (add 3 degrees for 3 years to the position in Figure 7 for abbreviation) would square the mighty conjunction in her 7th House. It would also be the time of her Saturn return and Saturn's subsequent transit over her fourth cusp. Definitely, a dramatic, life-changing, new level of development was soon to come.

---

65 Ibid., 98–99.

Antony Enters Cleopatra's Life

Upon the death of Caesar, Rome was confused. The highly experienced and successful general, Mark Antony, was at odds with Caesar's heir, Gaius Octavius (Octavian), about rulership, almost to the point of civil war. Eventually they joined forces with Marcus Lepidus, a prominent statesman and soldier: the Second Triumvirate was established. They were a strong front against Brutus and Cassius, the prime murderers of Caesar.[66]

Both Cassius and Brutus, warring against Rome from separate locales, solicited Cleopatra's aid. In the light of what appears to be callous exploitation—soliciting allegiance from the queen-mistress of the god-leader they had just assassinated—we can wonder if Cassius and Brutus thought that Cleopatra was indeed pure guile and ambition, that she would "understand" the political stratagem of their having killed Caesar. Did Cleopatra in her late middle-twenties give that impression, inviting the overture? Is this the all-pervasive Capricorn Sun? Or is this the way monarchs did things then, and Cleopatra would follow suit?

In 42 B.C., Cassius and Brutus both committed suicide. The Triumvir was master of the world. Antony and Octavian divided the world between them: Antony took the East (including Egypt); Octavian took the West. Antony was forty and in age and experience had clearly a superior edge over Octavian who was just twenty.

To recognize Antony's rule, the Ephesians—keepers of the Temple to Artemis, the Moon Goddess—recognized him as the New Dionysus. Antony was now a god. Octavian was the adopted son of a god. All of this was most serious. From the start, Octavian was certainly intimidated by everything Antony represented. The competition between them was extraordinary.

Antony was planning a major conquest of Parthia. He was stationed in Tarsus. He needed support and money. He summoned Cleopatra to come to meet with him in Tarsus, on the river Cydnus.[67]

---

66 It was agreed that Antony's step-daughter would marry Octavian, ratifying their accord and placing Antony and Octavian closer together within the Triumvir than either one of them was with Lepidus.

67 Tarsus was a major city of the world, located at the extreme northwestern point of the Mediterranean, just across the water northeast of Cyprus, in south central Turkey. It was the meeting place of West and East, of the Greek culture and its oriental counterpart. It had been under Persian control until Alexander took it over in 333 B.C. Antony gave Tarsus the status of a free city. Shortly after the lives of Antony and Cleopatra, under the rule of Octavian (who becomes Augustus Caesar), Tarsus became the intellectual center of the world, surpassing even Alexandria and Athens.

Cleopatra had met the swash-buckling, bearded, very popular, burly Antony when she was last in Rome. It is presumed she knew him reasonably well and liked him. She knew he was married to a very powerful woman, Fulvia, who herself was a public figure, a great heiress, previously married to other famous men, and was the first woman to be on Roman coinage. And Cleopatra knew that Antony was an unabashed philanderer.[68]

Knowing his reputation and background so well, Cleopatra had every reason to plan her grand entrance into Tarsus strategically, for specific effects. This entrance and her entire stay at Tarsus was a pageant staged in a style of luxury that approached the unbelievable. Plutarch's account of her sailing down the Cydnus river has entered fiction, drama, and cinema and become legend:

> She made great preparation for her journey, of money, gifts, and ornaments of value, such as so wealthy a kingdom might afford, but she brought with her her surest hopes in her own magic arts and charms ... She came sailing up the river Cydnus, in a barge with gilded stern and outspread sails of purple, while oars of silver beat time to the music of flutes and fifes and harps. She herself lay all along under a canopy of cloth of gold, dressed as Venus in a picture; and beautiful young boys, like painted Cupids, stood on each side to fan her. Her maids were dressed like sea nymphs and graces, some steering at the rudder, some working at the ropes. The perfumes diffused themselves from the vessel to the shore, which was covered with multitudes, part following the galley up the river on either bank, part running out of the city to see the sight ... The word went through all the multitude, that Venus was come to feast with Bacchus [Dionysus, Antony], for the common good of Asia.[69]

And so had "The Goddess of Ten thousand Names, Shelter and Heaven to all Mankind, the House of Life, the Word of God, the Great Mother of all the Gods and of Nature, the whole of Wisdom and Philosophy. Her magical powers were incomparable. She was Victorius over Fate."[70]

The people—and Antony—comprehended what Cleopatra intended: there was to be an alliance, the beginning of a sacred

---

68 Grant, *Cleopatra*, 114.
69 Plutarch, *Antony*, 496.
70 Grant, *Cleopatra*, 118; Meyer, 173.

marriage between two great gods. We see that beginning as well in her horoscope (Figure 9, page 54).

Shown here are the Secondary Progressed positions, *with the Moon conjunct the Midheaven, and the Sun conjunct the fourth cusp, for Cleopatra's arrival in Tarsus!* This is a Progressed Full Moon at the time of her meeting with Antony to capture the world.[71]

The Solar Arc Moon had advanced to 28 Leo in the 10th House, ruling the 9th, exactly square her natal Uranus-Pluto conjunction in the 7th: *all her personal needs were awakened to the power of partnership with someone foreign in a foreign land!*

Transiting Neptune had left her Midheaven behind and was exactly opposite Cleopatra's spectacular Venus, suggesting a swoon of luxury, imagination, pageantry, and sensuality; transiting Jupiter at 18 Taurus was square that Venus, augmenting it greatly, and transiting Uranus was at 8 Libra intensifying to an extreme every consideration of Cleopatra's Mars and its powerful mid-point structures!

This is simply an epic explosion of potentials. It is fireworks fired for gods. And for the entire period of her arrival and negotiations and romance with Antony, *transiting Saturn was conjunct Cleopatra's Sun*, crystallizing her life focus of ambition.

Antony asked for Cleopatra's and Egypt's personal, material, and financial support in his grand campaigns. He got that support in exchange for serving her demands: among them, the execution of her sister, Arsinoe IV, whom Cleopatra had never forgiven for establishing a force against her in 48; the execution of the high priest of Artemis in Ephesus, because he had sided with Arsinoe (an entreaty on his behalf spared him); the execution of the former governor of Cyprus (which Caesar had given over to the Ptolomys); and the execution of a Phoenician youth who was a brother-pretender to her throne.

Her future had begun. And so had her end.[72]

— ✦ —

71 The preceding Lunar Eclipse occurred on March 2, 41 B.C. at 3:06 UT in 9 Pisces/Virgo 35, accentuating her 4th and 10th Houses. The Saturn in that chart, at that moment was at 20 Capricorn 53 exactly conjunct Cleopatra's Sun.

72 Look back to Figure 7 (page 46) with the Solar Arc positions set for March 15, 44 B.C. Note Mars on its way to Cleopatra's Ascendant, in 10 degrees, almost 10 years, 35 B.C. Measure SA Neptune advancing to oppose Cleopatra's Sun in 8 degrees, 8 years, 36 B.C. This will be a very difficult time for Cleopatra, through the Armed Forces (Mars rules the 6th), in foreign lands (Neptune in the 9th), through her lover and their military gambles together (Neptune rules the 5th). We can anticipate much confrontation and upset. We shall see.

Cleopatra and Antony returned together to Egypt in October 41. Four months later, Cleopatra realized that she was pregnant with Antony's child.

In March 40, they learned that the powerful and dangerous Parthians had taken the attack to Antony's lands on two fronts at the same time, and Antony's wife, undoubtedly jealous of Cleopatra's role in her husband's life, used her power to mount a military attack on Octavian in Italy, clearly to set Octavian against Antony, perhaps as well to get Antony's attention back to the homefront. The fighting was savage and Fluvia and her forces were defeated.

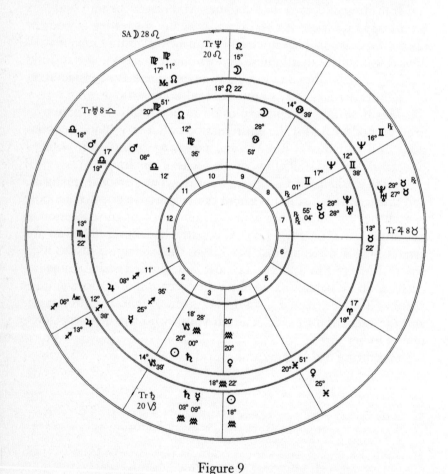

Figure 9

Inner Chart
Cleopatra VII

Outer Chart
SP Antony at Tarsus
Aug. 1, 41 B.C.

Antony had to leave Alexandria and Cleopatra to regain control of his military positions and his marriage. He punished Fluvia severely. She became ill and died. He reconciled with Octavian and married Octavian's very young and beautiful sister, Octavia, who had recently (and conveniently) been widowed.[73]

Antony stayed away for three and one-half years, from early 40 until the Autumn of 37. Grant observes, "Obviously, this separation weakened her [Cleopatra's] influence over his action."

The First Defeat and The Donations

In November–December 40, *with transiting Saturn precisely on the fourth cusp*—new beginning, new start, childbirth—of the horoscope we have created for her, Cleopatra gave birth to twins: Alexander and Cleopatra. Here were Osiris and Isis reborn of Isis.

Grant makes an interesting note: "Were Antony and Cleopatra—mother of his recently-born children—writing to each other at this period, apart from official communications? Did the Egyptian court feel obliged to send him a congratulatory message on his wedding? All we know is that Cleopatra kept herself informed of Antony's doings through an Egyptian astrologer attached to his entourage. And she gave this man the additional task of hinting to Antony from time to time that he should win free play for his own noble personality by detaching himself as far as possible from Octavian."[74]

During this long hiatus, Antony's new wife became pregnant, twice. During her second term, he sent her back to Rome *and again summoned Cleopatra* to meet him in Antioch (just to the southeast across the Gulf from Tarsus). He again needed support and money. Cleopatra joined him. It was around October 37 (transiting Uranus was exactly square her Saturn, an enormous reintensification of ambition; SP Ascendant was exactly conjunct her Jupiter in Sagittarius). They wintered together; Cleopatra promised Antony all her

---

73 All histories. Grant, *Cleopatra*, 123–124.

74 Grant, *Cleopatra*, 127. Stories about high-priest astrologers of ancient Egypt are surely apochryphal. Whitrow, page 28: "the twelve signs of the zodiac did not appear in Egypt until the Hellenistic period, nor is there any trace of astrological ideas there before then." This Hellenic period began in 332 B.C. with Alexander the Great and the House of Ptolemy that followed. Cleopatra's informant used Greek knowledge. Astrology's Claudius Ptolemy, the astrologer, lived in the early second century A.D. and was not of the earlier royal line.

support to rebuild his fleet and to protect his interests in the Mediterranean, but she struck a hard bargain: she in turn wanted extensive territories in what is now Lebanon, Syria, Jordan, and southern Turkey.[75]

The next years 36–35 B.C., the years we anticipated (see above to footnote 72) came quickly. Cleopatra was again pregnant. Antony left in May 36, mightily fortified to fight the huge, high-risk campaign with Parthia, which had been building for years. This campaign would be his greatest endeavor ... and begin the failures of his life.

Antony's rear-guard and supply column of 7,000 men was ambushed by a horde of some 50,000 horse-archers led by turncoat allies en route to Parthia. He had to turn back, fighting all the way. In total, he lost 20,000 men, almost half his soldiers. It was October 36. The snows began in Armenia.[76]

Figure 10 (page 57) is our horoscope for Cleopatra directed to October 30, 36 B.C., Antony's and her time of defeat. As we anticipated "several years ago" (footnote 72), SA Mars came to her Ascendant, the fighting spirit, military assertion, being in the midst of challenge and attack. SA Neptune came to exact opposition with her Sun, loss, disillusionment (as well as another childbirth, with Neptune ruling the 5th). The loss of a battle or part of a kingdom is strongly indicated as well through the Sun's rulership of the 10th, the House of Cleopatra's reign, authority, and queenship. She was allied with Antony; her reputation—under extreme attack throughout the known world—was at stake. A victory would have stopped the propaganda. The defeat intensified it. She was to blame for Antony's defeat; she distracted him; she caused him to get a late start to the East.

The SP Moon was at 0–2 Scorpio tightly square to Cleopatra's Saturn. These were trying times.

Antony again sent for Cleopatra to meet him. She was slow in coming because she was giving birth to their third child, Ptolemy Philadelphus, and she needed time to put together the huge sums of money and materiel that were required. She arrived to resurrect Antony in Syria in January 35. The remnants of army reorganized, reinforcements being gathered, Antony and Cleopatra returned together to Alexandria in the spring.

---

75 Hughes-Hallett, 25.
76 Grant, *Cleopatra*, 147–148.

Antony was planning yet a new offensive on Parthia but he was diverted by Sextus Pompey, the younger son of the great dead general, who was launching pirate attacks from his base on Sicily and was also negotiating with the Parthians, threatening to turn with them and with his legions against Antony. Antony sent men to pursue Sextus and kill him March–August 35. The good weather was over, and he had lost much time in this diversion.

Recuperation and refurbishment in Alexandria seem to have taken an entire year.

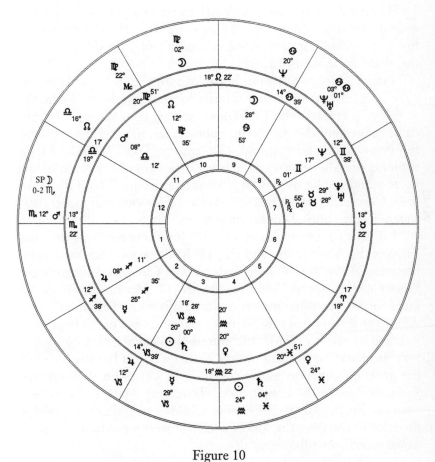

Figure 10

Inner Chart
Cleopatra VII

Outer Chart
SA Parthia Defeat
Oct. 30, 36 B.C.

In Spring 34, Antony launched a new campaign against Armenia. Cleopatra accompanied him half way. He went on and won easily. Antony plundered much. It was a major success against a second-class foe.

In September 34, Antony returned to Alexandria, this time hollowly victorious. The score to settle with the Parthians pervaded all plans. But, in late September, there was a grand Triumphal procession, parading his prisoners before the public. (The histories tell of the king of Armenia shackled in gold refusing to bow before Cleopatra.) Cleopatra and Antony gave the occasion a particularly religious tone. Antony was dressed as the god Dionysus, in a saffron robe of gold.[77]

Then a few days later, probably October 1, 34 B.C., there occurred one of the great days of Cleopatra's life: the Celebration of the "Donations." Antony awarded himself and his goddess much of the world to be theirs forever.

Figure 11 (page 59) is our horoscope for Cleopatra and the *Tertiary* Progressions and major transits for this grand day. Again, the astrology is remarkable: TP Venus is exactly conjunct her Descendant, suggesting the wonderful public reception and the apparent fulfillment of her partnership with Antony. The TP Nodal Axis is conjunct the Midheaven axis, another major angular contact, telling us of grand public display in professional terms. The TP Ascendant, Cleopatra's developed and projected persona that month, was square to the epochal conjunction in the 7th!

It is simply extraordinary that TP Jupiter is conjunct the Sun, ruler of the Midheaven, and the TP Midheaven—her monarchy, her place in the Sun—is precisely conjunct Cleopatra's magnificent Jupiter in Sagittarius. Additionally, her TP Moon is exactly conjunct Saturn, the illumination and crystallization of ambition!

At the level of real time, transiting Uranus, out of the huge conjunction in her 7th House, had transited to *conjunction with Cleopatra's Ascendant!* Transiting Jupiter in that week of her life opposed the great conjunction exactly! Transiting Venus on that day was precisely square the conjunction! Transiting Mars was precisely conjunct the Nodal axis! At exactly mid-day in Alexandria, perhaps the time of the gala, the Moon in transit was in the first degree of Aquarius conjunct her Saturn!!

---

77 Grant, *Cleopatra*, 161.

We are not understating the fact that the astrology we have developed here defines most accurately the essence of Cleopatra the person, the timed steps of her development, and the dimensions of her destiny. In this way, astrology can help archeology and ancient history by providing vital information that is missing in the records or material finds. There can be no doubt with the evidence we have developed that Cleopatra was indeed born January 13, 69 B.C. at 2:08 hours in the morning.

Let's celebrate with Cleopatra and Antony—there will be the deciding battle soon, and then shortly thereafter they will be dead.

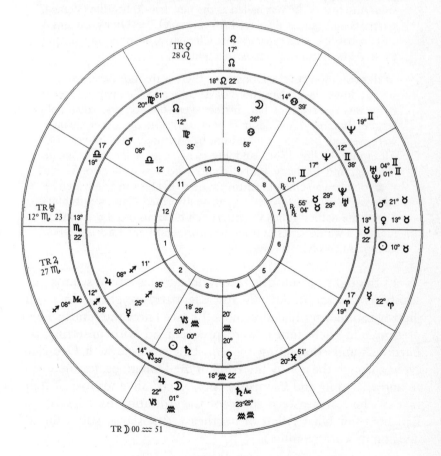

Figure 11

Inner Chart
Cleopatra VII

Outer Chart
TP Donations
Oct. 1, 34 B.C.

In a ceremony of spectacular magnificence he [Antony] declared Cleopatra 'Queen of Kings' and Caesarion, her official co-ruler, 'King of Kings'. His own children by her, the six-year-old twins and two-year-old Ptolemy Philadelphus, were proclaimed kings and queen. To each of these juvenile monarchs Antony granted vast realms.[78]

There, in the Gymnasium, he and Cleopatra took their places high above the crowd, upon golden thrones set side by side on a platform shining with silver. It was surely not the first time that Cleopatra had worn the robes of Isis, but the identification was particularly noted upon [by Plutarch, see below] upon this occasion. And just as she was hailed as the new Isis-Aphrodite [Venus], portraits and statues displayed Antony as Osiris-Dionysus, and it was probably in this capacity that Cleopatra, at some time during these years, honoured him with a temple.

At this ceremony of the Donations, there were four other thrones set at a lower level than those of Antony and Cleopatra. One of them was reserved for her thirteen-year-old son and royal colleague Ptolemy XV Caesar (Caesarion). On the other thrones were seated her three children by Antony, the six-year-old Alexander Helios [Sun] and his twin sister Cleopatra Selene [Moon], and Ptolemy Philadlephus who was only two. When everyone had assembled, Antony rose to his feet and delivered an address. What he proposed to say, he informed them, was in honour of the deified Julius Caesar. Then he announced the conferment of a whole series of titles, territories and overlordships upon Cleopatra and her children.[79]

In the light of Antony's recent defeat, this would seem a self-satisfying ceremony, Antony and Cleopatra caught up in a religiously ratified, rarified aloneness. But we know the future. Their present and their future were preoccupied with upsetting the Parthians and completing the constant struggle with Octavian. Now, through the epic delineation of the Donations, for the world to know, Antony and Cleopatra "possessed" all lands east of Italy, east of the northeastern shore of the Adriatic, the edge of the Balkans (now what is left of northeast Yugoslavia, still a line of division in world conflict).

---

78 Hughes-Hallett, 26
79 Grant, *Cleopatra*, 162–163. See also Hughes-Hallett, 26; Plutarch, *Antony*, 515.

War with Rome

The Donations of October 1, 34 B.C. was a ceremonial attack upon Octavian. It had an infuriating impact. Octavian openly criticized Antony. Antony sent replies. A private one—a fragment of it—has come down to us through Suetonius (Augustus):

> Antony writes, "What's come over you? Is it because I go to bed with the queen? But she isn't my wife, is she. And it isn't as if it's something new, is it? Haven't I been doing it for nine years now? And what about you, is Livia the only woman you go to bed with? I congratulate you, if at the time you read this letter you haven't also had Tertulla or Terentilla or Rufilla or Salvia Titisenia or the whole lot of them. Does it really matter where you get a stand—or who the woman is?"[80]

The real understanding of Octavian's pique came down to the significance Octavian put upon Cleopatra's child by Caesar, that which had threatened him for eight or nine years: with that holy name, Cleopatra certainly had designs on Rome, and, with Antony, she now had extraordinary force at her disposal.

In addition, there were the Sibylline Books, a collection of oracles of mysterious origin, preserved in ancient Rome and consulted by the Senate in times of emergency or disaster.[81] These Books had the position and impact as would be had by the quatrains of Nostradamus actually used by the National Security Agency on Capitol Hill in Washington D.C. The verses were basically anti-Roman,

---

80 This is man-talk, obviously, but from a very experienced veteran of forty-eight to a very young leader of twenty-eight. Philandering was accepted practice among men in Italy and in Greece. Wives were kept alone and subservient. The women allowed (accepted) to be high-spirited and extravertedly expressive were courtesans.

　　Sex was an exchange of admired resources. The Romans saw promiscuity as virility, homosexuality among men as role-assertion and status reinforcement (among women, reinforcement within loneliness). Men dallied with servants and slaves of either gender. For the Greek mind "innate goodness had to express itself as beauty. When men loved men, they adored flesh and virtue simultaneously." See Ackerman, 20, 22. There are many, many detailed references to Octavian's bi-sexuality, insults and challenges about his record, determinations of how much he charged to take the passive role. And much is recorded similarly about the great Julius Caesar. Here, in Antony's note to Octavian, Octavian knew of what and from where Antony wrote. See Cantarella, 158–159.

81 According to Livy, there were originally nine of these books; the remaining three were preserved in a stone chest underground in the temple of Jupiter Capitolinus and committed to the high priests. Octavian, later as Augustus, was to destroy most of the verses and put the remaining ones in gilt cases under the base of the statue of Apollo. All were lost in the fire under Nero.

pro-Greek. They spoke of a *woman* who would bring salvation, about the Day of Judgment, the glorious Millennium being at hand. Details about current battles and politics fit. Cleopatra fit.[82]

Octavian communicated earnestly with Antony afterward about how to defuse the situation. There was an enormous amount of political intrigue with Antony trying to keep groups of senators on his side during debate in far-off Rome.

Antony and Cleopatra went eastward to stay in Ephesus and then in Athens, there throughout the summer of 32 B.C. The rebuilding had placed all the sea-power of the East under Antony's control. Grant reports that there were 300 merchant vessels, 500 warships and in addition, 75,000 legionnaires, 25,000 light-armed infantry, and 12,000 calvary.[83] Antony divorced his wife Octavia, and except for his hidden political ties—which were loosening quickly—Antony was severed from Rome.

Grant reports that Cleopatra was constantly beside Antony in all meetings and war plans. There were delays, almost as if they didn't know when enough was enough; or was it insecurity and fear about what lay ahead; or perhaps it was Cleopatra's inexperience undermining Antony's characteristic sureness and driving capacity for leadership.

They appeared ready finally to seize the initiative and invade Rome, but it was May 32. With all the war force, they could not have reached Italy in that same summer. Antony had *missed* the best time! He held up and reinforced his *political* machinery, instead, having his bribe money minted in his own mint in Italy and spread on his behalf among the influential.

In December 32, Octavian severed the Triumval tie with Antony. This meant that, Antony was just a "private citizen, an ex-official." And Octavian "formally and ceremoniously—"with all possible solemnity"—declared war against Cleopatra. "She was the ideal national foe, the oriental woman who had ensnared the Roman leader in her evil lucury, the harlot who had seized Roman territories, until even Rome itself was not safe from her degenerate alien hordes."[84]

---

82 See Grant, *Cleopatra*, 172.

83 Grant, *Cleopatra*, 193–194.

84 Grant points out that Octavian did this (war against Cleopatra instead of Antony) to give Antony's supporters in Rome a chance to change their mind about their allegiance. He was trying to discharge the tensions with Antony into the vile personage of Cleopatra. See *Cleopatra*, 201.

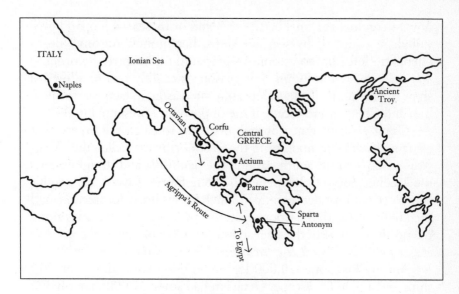

Actium: The Final Battle

In September–October 32, Antony and Cleopatra moved to the west to Patrae, which is on the north-northwest coastline of the Pelopponesian peninsula (see map). They expected Octavian's naval force, under the brilliant admiralship of the great Agrippa, to come directly from the West. Instead, Agrippa brought the fleet far to the south, to Antonym, and then started to the north, clearing out Antony's outpost installations along the western Pelopponesian coastline, which cut off his supply lines from Egypt in the south. At the same time, Octavian crossed the Ionian Sea and landed much to the north at Corfu and began his advance south. Antony and Cleopatra at Patrae were now between Agrippa and Octavian.

Octavian reached Actium, and so did Antony. They were across the narrow strait from each other. Agrippa had taken over Patrae and was on the sea to the west.

Many of Antony's men began to desert. He executed several of them to dramatize a deterrent. A dysentery epidemic broke out. His troops were sorely weakened. Antony crossed over to Octavian's land side, offered to do battle, but Octavian refused. More men deserted.

Early in August 31, the campaign was seriously threatened. Antony's two tries to get out to freedom had been put down. Health and supplies were terrible. In a war strategy meeting, to determine how to conduct the final battle—by land or by sea—Cleopatra prevailed: it would be by sea; her ships, her money. Antony's tie to Cleopatra left him no option. In preparation, he gave the order *to take sails on board the craft*. His reason ostensibly was to allow his ships to pursue the Roman ships, but the reason, in fact, was to allow him and Cleopatra to escape if the opportunity presented itself.

Grant explains that Antony's plan was to catch the breeze that came up in the afternoon from the west northwest (called the "Maestro"), ride it to the south, around the peninsula and straight across the Mediterranean to Egypt (a trip of ten–fourteen days). He told his land force commander secretly to watch for his break for freedom and then to retreat with the troops eastward by land, continuing up along the north coastline of the Aegean into Asia Minor. *One of the members of Antony's War Council deserted and told Octavian the entire plan.*[85]

Antony had some 20,000 legionnaires—many ailing—on 230 ships and a plan for escape. Octavian had some 37,000 men on 400 ships and full knowledge of what to expect.

Figure 12 (page 65) is Cleopatra's horoscope with the Solar Arc positions for September 2, 31 B.C., the day of the Battle of Actium. Her chart has now developed signs of terror—with more to come: SA Pluto, with Uranus, is exactly square her Mars, delineating extreme force, attack, effort, both hers in application and *upon her* in attack (Pluto rules Ascendant, Mars rules her Armed forces). This violence is to the loss for her Antony (partner) with Mars ruling the 6th and the 6th being the twelfth House derived from the 7th.

Solar Arc Neptune is applying to her Moon—*and would increase its position even after the battle*. This is her position within duplicity and desertion; it is bewilderment, fear, the most intense state of insecurity. It affects her in terms of her lover and her plans for her children since Neptune rules the 5th; indeed, it affects every grand thought she has ever had about herself as goddess (in the 9th). Cleopatra is distraught. She sees the end.

SA Saturn has just squared Jupiter, normally a conviction of what is right. She had been/would be dogmatic about it, the issues and strategies. It was her decision to mount this entire campaign, now in its seventeenth month. It was her decision to meet Octavian on the sea instead of on land.

---

85 Grant, *Cleopatra*, Chapter 12. (Desertion and duplicity color so much of this saga, promised by the Uranus-Pluto conjunction chart analysis; recall pages 13–14.).

Cleopatra's Tertiary Progressions (not shown here) on this day of battle place her Sun precisely upon her Neptune, a severely specific echo of her sense of ego loss at this moment, the dimensions of deception surrounding her, and her awareness within her spirit that all was lost—but *not all* would be: TP Jupiter was retrograde upon her natal Sun. Here was *out-and-out luck*. On this day, she *would* escape.

The battle plan was for the ships to come side by side to one another, with the infantry men marauding over the deck.

Antony's entire fleet came out from the little gulf and formed a crescent arc along the west coast. Octavian's ships lined up similarly facing them a mile or so off shore in the west!

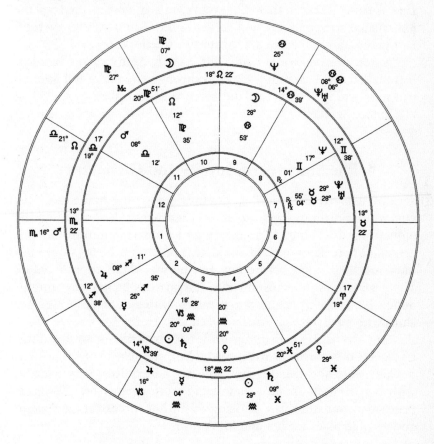

Figure 12

Inner Chart
Cleopatra VII

Outer Chart
SA Actium
Sept. 2, 31 B.C.

Agrippa held back, wanting to bring Antony's ships out into the sea so that he could outflank them, squeeze them in, board and conquer. It was "about mid-day" when Antony attacked [remember the rescue wind expected in the late afternoon]. With great patience, Agrippa pulled back, luring Antony further out. They met. The battle raged.

Imagine all those ships, all the noise, the passion, the fear, the intense summer heat. As Octavian and Agrippa surrounded Antony and Cleopatra—her ship laden with jewels and gold, all that was left of the support funds—there was a break in the middle of the collapsing arc-lines of ships. Cleopatra's "squadron" passed through first Antony's center then Octavian's, raised sails, picked up the anticipated strong breeze and veered south. Antony followed right behind her, and they had a head start to freedom.

Antony's naval force could not escape. Many surrendered or were taken; the remaining suffered through the night and gave up in the morning. His great land force was overtaken by Octavian and surrendered.[86]

The Suicides of Antony and Cleopatra

Antony delayed his arrival at Alexandria by going first to a Greek enclave in northern Egypt to allow Cleopatra to enter Alexandria alone, to calm things if necessary and prepare politically for his arrival. Their defeat meant the defeat of Egypt. News would not have reached Egypt before her, but he was thinking well ahead. Here we get another insight into Cleopatra's penetrating intelligence, her sense of image, and creative strategy: she decorated her ships with garlands as if she had been victorious!

As soon as she had things under control, the news did arrive and, according to historical record (Dio), she slew many important personages who, disliking her and her adventures, were pleased with her disaster—before they could work against her. She then proceeded to gather vast funds to outfit her forces yet once again and to align allies for her and for Antony.

86　Grant points out that Antony fought the battle not to win but to escape, *Cleopatra*, 212. He still had sixty ships out of 230, with him and elsewhere, and there would be another day to fight.

Antony arrived deeply depressed and brooding. He isolated himself. The sense of death was in the air; it was in his talk; in the next battle, they might not be so fortunate to escape. Cleopatra took charge. She sent her co-ruler son, the King of Kings, Ptolemy XV Caesar, off to India to study.[87] She prepared her own escape to India, to found a new oriental kingdom. She was not quite thirty-nine years old. It was probably mid-November 31.

Octavian calmed upheavals in Rome stirred by veteran soldiers who wanted their pay. Octavian's treasury was very low because of the uprisings and Actium, and he determinedly coveted the treasury of Egypt, the last horde of fortune remaining in the Mediterranean not under Rome's control.

Octavian left Italy in January 30 B.C. and went to Syria. Herod in Judea and many others all turned sides (they were part of Antony's "East") and joined with Octavian. His way was now clear to the very gates of Egypt.

Cleopatra tried to deal with Octavian. She told him she would abdicate if her children could inherit the throne. Antony offered a huge sum of money. A bribe was sent. There was no reaction from Octavian.[88]

Octavian advanced to an eastern suburb of Alexandria. There was a skirmish with an advanced cavalry force, and Antony won. He rewarded one of the soldier heroes, and that night, that hero defected to Octavian! Antony sent bribes tied to arrowshafts shot over the palace walls into the encampment of Octavian's men. Antony even offered to settle everything through single hand-to-hand combat with Octavian!

On July 26, 30 B.C. at 11:31 A.M. UT there was a Lunar Eclipse. The eclipse took place at 29 Cancer-Capricorn 35, almost precisely conjunct Cleopatra's natal Moon-Saturn axis; *her Moon at 28 Cancer 53 and her Saturn at 0 Aquarius. Cleopatra would be dead in seventeen days.*

---

87 Plutarch tells us that, on the way to India through Aethiopia, Ptolemy XV Caesar was persuaded by a turncoat tutor (named Rhodon) to turn back, since Octavian planned to make him king! When the boy returned to Alexandria, Octavian was advised, "Too many Caesars are not well." So afterward, when Cleopatra was dead, Ptolemy XV was killed. No Caesar's son threatened any more the new Caesar to be. *Antony*, 531.

88 Grant, *Cleopatra*, Chapter 13.

On August 1, 30 B.C., Antony sent his fleet out to take on Octavian's. Antony's men deserted.

Antony sent his ground troops out. Antony's men deserted.

Octavian occupied the palace and all of Egypt. This was the "great month," the holiday Rome would observe in times to come for having been rid of its grimmest peril, the madness created by Cleopatra's whoring strategies. Josephus and all historians after him report Octavian's commemoration of this victory through his choice of this month's name for his imperial title: Augustus Caesar.

Cleopatra barricaded herself in her mausoleum with her treasure, hoping against reality that she still could negotiate her freedom.[89]

Grant records:

A report came to Antony that she had committed suicide. She was said to have sent the news herself in order to persuade him to do likewise, but perhaps she had dispatched some other incoherent message which was misunderstood. At all events Antony believed that she was dead, and ordered his servant Eros to kill him too. But Eros turned the blade upon himself: so Antony took another sword and plunged it into his own body.

Antony's stomach wound was not immediately mortal. Plutarch continues:

"... and the flow of blood ceasing when he lay down, presently he came to himself, and entreated those that were about him to put him out of his pain; but they all fled out of the chamber, and left him crying and struggling, until Diomede, Cleopatra's secretary, came to him, having orders from her to bring him into the monument [where Cleopatra was]."

Antony was transported to the mausoleum and had to be hoisted with "ropes and cords" up to the higher floor since the door was heavily barricaded.

"Those that were present say that nothing was ever more sad than this spectacle, to see Antony, covered all over with blood and just expiring, thus drawn up, still holding up his hands to her, and lifting up his body with the little force he had left.

---

89 With her were her lady-in-waiting Charmion, Iras her hairdresser, and a eunuch. All histories.

"When she [and her attendants] had got him up, she laid him on the bed, tearing all her clothes which she spread upon him; and, beating her breast with her hands, lacerating herself, and disfiguring her own face with the blood from his wounds, she called him her lord, her husband, her emperor." (*Antony*, 529.)

Antony was dead.

Octavian's men entered the mausoleum as Antony had been lifted, using their own ropes, and captured Cleopatra. Plutarch tells us that Cleopatra was ill with fever from the self-inflicted beating and scratches incurred during her hysterical agony over the dying Antony. Octavian went to meet with her to assess the treasury. [Imagine that meeting, all the currents of anxiety, rumor, lust, death, money!] She asked for her freedom, her last negotiation; he said little in return. It is thought he did not know quite how to end the situation and that he hoped she would kill herself.

On August 12, probably in mid-morning, Cleopatra was given permission to visit Antony's tomb. It would surely have taken three or four hours to make herself presentable, to restore a semblance of the queen, let alone the poise of Isis, to get her thinking straight about what she would do that day. The visit to Antony's tomb would have been heart wrenching, with oglers studying her every move and listening to the lamentation of her oratory over his sepulchre, which Plutarch quotes at length. And, "having made these lamentations, crowning the tomb with garlands and kissing it," perhaps two hours later, Cleopatra repaired to her quarters.

Plutarch records that she bathed and had a sumptuous meal. We can imagine that meal taking place between 6 and 7 P.M. She then prepared a letter for Octavian, asking to be buried "in the same tomb" with Antony. She dispatched the sealed letter to Octavian. When he read it, he knew the situation was soon to end itself.

We can imagine Cleopatra then, shortly after 9 P.M., retrieving the vial of poison that almost assuredly was part of her toilette, a monarch's safeguard against capture at any time, certainly a threat at all times within her last two years of constant fear and exposure. She had poisoned her brother Ptolemy XIV and perhaps others. She anticipated poison every time she began a meal. Poison was a woman's way. Poison is Neptune.

We can imagine her last warm discussions with Iras and Charmion. Resigned, less fearful, probably sure in her mind that she was going into an eternal time of hymns and light. We can imagine the loving acknowledgment that her faithful attendants were preparing to accompany her in death. We can imagine her last attentive assessment of how she would appear when she would be found, lying on a bed of gold, dressed in a flowing gossamer evening veil, arranged among her most precious jewels, with her ladies dead at her feet.

Probably some fifteen minutes after ten o'clock that night, Cleopatra ended an era of 300 years and the House of Ptolemy. Cleopatra departed history and entered legend.

Figure 13 (page 71) is the chart for the probable time of Cleopatra's suicide on the established date of August 12, 30 B.C. With all the astrology study we have made in parallel with the major events of her life, we have seen time and time and time again exactness that is extraordinary, especially involving the Sun, Moon, the angles, Saturn and Neptune, at levels of Directions, Progressions, and Transits. This chart is similarly startling.

Transiting Moon at 20 Virgo is exactly squaring transiting Saturn, which is conjunct Cleopatra's natal Neptune. This transiting Moon has just begun to separate from a conjunction with Neptune about 14 hours earlier at the beginning of Cleopatra's final day.

It is intriguing to note that transiting Pluto in this death chart at 23 Cancer is exactly opposed Saturn in the "Cleopatra Conjunction" chart, the signal of an epoch, analyzed on page 15. Transiting Pluto is in the 12th of that chart, and Saturn in that chart is in the 8th. And now at the moment of the end, the significators show the loss of all.

Figure 14 (page 72) is our final chart, Cleopatra's horoscope with the Solar Arc positions to her last day. One final time, the symbols speak a validity that challenges belief: her SA SP Sun, within 1 minute of arc(!) is exactly square the dominantly all-powerful Pluto of the "Cleopatra Conjunction." SA Neptune, the disappointment, the lamentations, the martyrdom of suicide, the poison of it all, is conjunct her all-consuming Moon, her reigning need for personal and national security.

The Secondary Progressed Moon was at 19 Capricorn 43 *conjunct her natal Sun.*

And in her Tertiary chart for this moment, the TP Moon is exactly opposed her *Neptune,* and her TP Midheaven—her place in the sun upon that last day—is exactly opposed her Moon!

— ✦ —

Grant believes Cleopatra poisoned herself. He points out that she and her doctor, named Olympus, were close to the Alexandria School of Medicine and were well informed about poisons of every kind.

It is recorded everywhere that the only marks on her body were two little pricks on her arm. In the light of Plutarch's extensive detailing of Cleopatra's wailing and self-flagellation over Antony's body and a tantrum struggle with Octavian, it is interesting that no other marks were recorded. Perhaps they were but have become

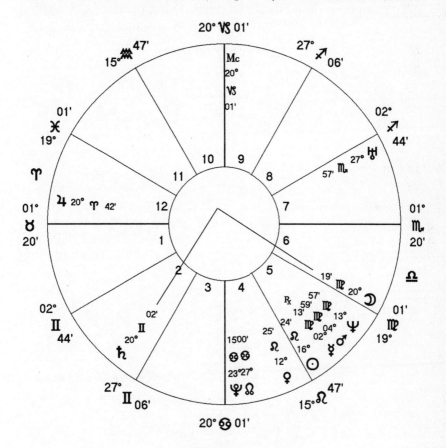

Figure 13
Cleopatra's Suicide
Aug. 12, 30 B.C., 10:14 P.M. LMT
Alexandria, Egypt
29E54 31N12
Placidus Houses

lost in the surrealism that took over portrayal of her death, isolating the smallish snake (which Isis is sometimes portrayed with, coiled about her arm) as the tool of her death, ravishing Cleopatra's languid body in an opulent boudoir, the final tryst.

While the bite of the Nile asp (a small cobra) was sometimes used for capital punishment in Alexandria—most painless and humane—we must appreciate that the archetypal phallic symbolism of the snake fit in well with the sordid propaganda about Cleopatra that had become extreme by her death and has continued to this day throughout dramatists' and poets' fancy, painters' canvas, and

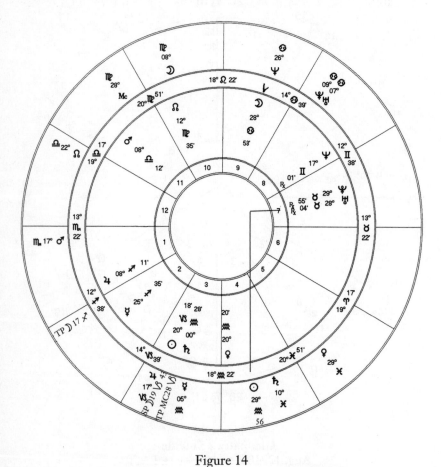

Figure 14

Inner Chart	Outer Chart
Cleopatra VII	**SA Suicide**
	Aug. 12, 30 B.C.

movie-makers' marketing concepts. A story was created about how the snake was smuggled to her in a basket of figs; but there was no snake to be found when she was discovered dead.

When Octavian had read her note, he knew what was happening. He sent messengers to her to see. They arrived just as the deed had been done. And Plutarch now ends our search for, our study and discovery of Cleopatra: "but on opening the doors they saw her stone-dead ... and Charmion, just ready to fall, scarce able to hold up her head, was adjusting her mistress's diadem. And when one that came in said angrily, 'Was this well done of your lady, Charmion?' 'Extremely well,' she answered, 'and as became the descendant of so many kings;' and as she said this, she fell down dead by the bedside."

Bibliography

Ackerman, Diane. *A Natural History of Love*. New York: Random House, 1994.

Aldred, Cyril. *The Egyptians*. London: Thames and Hudson, 1987.

Bao-Lin Liu and Fiala, Alan D. *Canon of Lunar Eclipses 1500 B.C.–A.D. 3000*. Richmond, VA: Willmann-Bell, Inc., 1992.

Budge, E. A. Wallis. *The Mummy*. New Jersey: Wings Books/Random House, 1989.

Cantarella, Eva. *Bisexuality in the Ancient World*. New Haven, CN: Yale University Press, 1992.

Carter, C. E. O. *An Introduction to Political Astrology*. London: Camelot Press, 1951 (1969).

Drews, Robert. *The End of the Bronze Age: Changes in Warfare and the Catastrophe CA. 1200 B.C.* Princeton: Princeton University Press, 1993.

Free, Joseph P. *Archaeology and Bible History*. Grand Rapids, MI: Zondervan Publishing House, 1969.

Grant, Michael. *Cleopatra*. New York: Simon and Schuster, 1972.

_____. *The Ancient Mediterranean*. New York: Meridian/Penguin, 1969.

Green, Peter. *Alexander of Macedon*. Berkeley, CA: University of California Press, 1991.

Guerber, H. A. *Greece and Rome: Myths and Legends*. London: Studio Editions Ltd., 1994

Holroyd, Stuart and Lambert, David. *Mysteries of the Past*. London: Bloomsbury Books, 1992.

Hughes-Hallett, Lucy. *Cleopatra—Histories, Dreams and Distortions*. New York: Harper Perennial, 1991.

Josephus, The Works, translated by William Whiston. Hendrickson Publishers, 1944.

Meyer, Marvin W. Editor. *The Ancient Mysteries—A Sourcebook*. HarperSanFrancisco, 1987.

Michelsen, Neil F. *The Tables of Planetary Phenomena*. San Diego: ACS Publications, 1990.

Oxford Classical Dictionary, Second Edition. Oxford: Oxford University Press, 1970.

Peck. Editor. *Harper's Dictionary of Classical Literature and Antiquities.* New York: Cooper Square Publishing Inc, 1955.

Plutarch. *The Lives of the Noble Grecians and Romans,* Vol II. New York: The Modern Library, 1992.

Seldes, George, Editor. *The Great Thoughts.* New York: Ballantine, 1989.

Tyl, Noel. *Synthesis & Counseling in Astrology.* St. Paul, MN: Llewellyn Publications, 1994.

_____ *Prediction in Astrology.* St. Paul, MN: Llewellyn Publications, 1991.

Whitrow, G. J. *Time in History.* Oxford: Oxford University Press, 1991.

Personal correspondence and conversation with the eminent historian Michael Grant; Hellenic History Professor Robert A. Hadley; distinguished Egyptologist Robert Bianchi; Amid Nuby-Moussa with the Egyptian Embassy in Washington D.C.; and Dr. Andrea McDowell of Johns Hopkins University, Middle East Studies.

Specialized references at the Oriental Institute of the University of Chicago, the Mullen Library at Catholic University, and the Woodstock Library at Georgetown University in Washington, D.C.

Index

Francis of Assisi
Most Humbled of Men

I n early biographical accounts of Francis, there is an insistent comparison made between his birthplace, Assisi, 150 miles north of Rome, and ancient Babylon. Both cities were corrupt, politically fractured, and war-torn. In Assisi, let alone throughout Italy, the Church did not help matters: it was a shell of neglected ideals. The papacy had risen to its apogee of self-indulgent material splendor, and its priests, for the most part, were heretical, self-serving, drunken revelers, and conniving, commercial opportunists.

An astrological rectification of the birth year, date, and time of Saint Francis of Assisi

✦

Assisi was a small hill town in Umbria. It was older than Rome and, for hundreds of years into the early thirteenth century, certainly due to its central geographic position within the shinbone of Italy's bootleg, was continuously at the center of bloodily exploiting feudalism. War was a condition of life in every city of Italy, and especially in Umbria and Tuscany where each hill fortress and municipal fiefdom competed for dominance of trade routes and for the favors of Rome. Perversely, war was "a sign of liberty, a joy of living. Even faith in God could not be sustained without military skill."[1]

---

1   Fortini, 253–255, 244, 53.

Francis was born into such times. War was all about him. He was rich and privileged through his father's position as a successful cloth merchant; he had everything he could want, and he was "proud of spirit, in accordance with the vanity of the world."[2] As a young man, Francis had a great confidence, a broad, uninhibited swagger. He spent his money recklessly. He was very popular with his peers: his social poise, musical talents, and persistent cheerfulness charmed everyone. He loved revelry and song. His youth was golden; he was the life of everyone's party, an inspired troubadour, a seductive romantic; and he dreamed of becoming a Knight. *He* would survive the socio-political oppression; *he* would be free to make life meaningful, *he* would be personally significant. His clothes would be beautiful and his sword would be noble. In his own words, "the whole world will someday bow before me and pay me homage!"[3]

Knighthood—which we associate historically in its pure, chivalric form with France—did not develop significantly in Italy. It remained an intriguing but foreign ideal. While there were few damsels in distress in Italy, as it were, there were instead treaties being violated, populations tortured and mutilated, cities sacked and burned. Abbots of the Church were also caught up in the feudal pattern; they were more often warriors for conquest than saviors of the spirit. For Francis, then, his hero of all heroes was the French Knight Gautier de Brienne, the conqueror of a kingdom, the rescuer of a widowed queen and her daughter from a dark prison, the courageous and ardent lover of a beautiful lady—the complete heroic ideal. He, Francis, would become such a man of adventure: "He would leave one day and go forth to find his love in a far-off land. He would put an all-white ensign on a fine ship. He would become a Crusader. He would scale mountains covered with

---

2 Celano, I, #1. Brother Thomas of Celano was an eyewitness of much of Francis' life, having become a Brother in the Franciscan Order some seven years after it began. Thomas was the first biographer of Francis, by commission from Pope Gregory IX upon canonization of Francis on July 16, 1228, two years after his death. Thomas' actual descriptions of Francis in his youth are harsh, quite possibly in hyperbole that was part of biographers' style in that day, especially by/of the spiritually aware. Yet, all histories make the point that Francis was exceedingly cheerful, generous, kindly, creatively poetic, and musical, and indeed lived clearly in the direction of hedonism. Fortini called Francis "Lord of the Merrymakers," 129–137.

3 Cristiani, 24. Such pompous statements by Francis—so full of himself, if you will—are recorded by all biographers of Francis but are excused as tongue-in-cheek, as "a daydream of Francis' poetic soul." The biographers see these statements as *prophetic* of his life to come, when Francis becomes the holiest of men.

perpetual ice, go through seas beyond every known limit. He would conquer a splendid kingdom."[4]

After his military service in Assisi's war with Perugia and his painful imprisonment,[5] Francis and a companion who shared the dream of valor began their journey to enlist themselves into the service of Count Gautier de Brienne, to win their knighthood within his ideal. Francis' "eyes shone with joy ... 'I know that I'm going to become a great prince.'"[6]

Not far along on their trip to France, Francis was stricken with a severe fever and had a vision, and he began to learn that there was possibly a different path to fulfillment of his dreams for personal significance. He turned back to Assisi. Coincidentally, at about the same time, the good Count Gautier's own knightly career came to an end in a besieged castle; he was "transfixed by an incredible number of arrows." The dream was gone; a different knighthood would now present itself to Francis.

Ecco il Santo! Ecco il Santo!! "There's the saint! Here comes the saint!!" Children squealed with carnival excitement; their parents craned their necks out of windows; people scurried out of their homes to watch, to ogle, to listen, with rapt attention, to the poorest, dirtiest, most dreadful beggar they had ever seen. This Francis owned nothing. He spent long times alone in caves. He was known to pray constantly—for hours or days on end—talking intimately with God. His joys were deprivation and rebuke. He acknowledged and demonstrated time and time again that he was more lowly than a leper.[7]

---

4   Fortini, 144–145. Francis heard this grand tale about Count Gautier from his merchant father, Bernardone (big Bernard), who traveled often on the Via Francesca to France to do business. From the gathering of merchants there, Bernardone learned news of the world and brought it home to Assisi.

5   This particular bloody clash between Assisi and Perugia (a much larger hill town, seventy miles to the north), two cities continuously at war, lasted approximately eighty-nine years beginning in approximately 1200, when Francis was nineteen or twenty years old. Francis was imprisoned by the Pergugini in the Autumn of 1202. The Grand Crusade to which he had aspired, the Fourth Crusade (1202–04), was taking place at this same time: the Knights Templar, fighting to recover Christian holy places from the Moslems, laid bizarre siege upon Constantinople, a city allied to the cause. Out of these many Crusades from 1095–1290 issued a spiritual insanity that eventually brought about mass suicides among people walking across Europe, desperately lost, fighting pilgrimage battles, seeking through martyrdom some significance for their lives and a link with the Christ. See Goodrich, 179.

6   Cristiani, 26.

7   Cristiani, 31, and all histories.

Francis' strong, beautiful voice was so often raised in song; his melodies in praise of God would bring people to surround him. Birds would still their own songs and listen from the rooftops and from the fountain in the *piazza*.

Francis wore no sandals, he had no staff; only a miserable gray-cloth sack-covering cordoned with a piece of rope covered his slight body, his lean, delicate, pained flesh.[8]

Francis degraded and humiliated himself and practiced pitiable self-sacrifice to extremes that defy belief. In the beginning of his private crusade, Francis was indeed thought insane. He was aberrant. He had suddenly become the antithesis of what he had been. Assisi's most popular, shining youth was now a madman on the very streets and among the very friends he had known all his life. He was an untouchable—*until* he was endorsed extraordinarily by Pope Innocent III, the greatest prelate of the Middle Ages, *until* he successfully rebuilt churches stone by stone, *until* his miracles of loving, faith, and healing became known everywhere, *until* his following grew to number many thousands in many lands.

Drawn by Francis' captivating words, his sermons that promised God's eternal love, people gave away all trappings of their material life to live with Francis, according to his Rule, only for God and Godliness. They gave up on their miserable mundane life. They abandoned war. They became embarrassing examples for the wanton priesthood. The public's jeers turned to respect and awe. Francis' famous greeting of *Pax et Bonum*, "[May God give you] Peace and Goodness," ceased to be laughable, outrageous, or absurd. People gradually began to understand, to re-find the forgotten principles and ideals of the life of Jesus. Spirits rose again, and, through Francis, the Church was revived. And then ... Assisi was called the new Jerusalem, "clothed in light."[9]

These are two portraits of the same man. One is an identification with rich, ribald freedom achieved through Knightly might; the other is an identification with surreal, spiritual freedom through

---

8 Thomas of Celano, a writer of great artistry, portrays with words Francis' appearance in sharp detail, as vividly as if by painter's brush. All descriptions of Francis throughout this study come from Brother Thomas' portraiture. See Celano, I, #83 particularly; quoted by Fortini, 325.

9 Fortini, 87, note k. The reference is made from Isaiah 60, *Song of Triumph for Zion*. Dante and other authors made these references to Francis' Assisi. The imagery of the "light," the sun, is pervasive in Francis' life, and culminated in the composition of his *Canticle to the Sun* during the days preceding his death.

ascetic humility. Each state is entirely antithetical to the other. And as we shall see, the change in Francis—the conversion—was "so incredibly sudden."

As we have noted, the era into which Francis was born was a time of arch-suffering, which was given neither explanation, nor meaning, nor hope by the Church. For the people, their sense of self was lost. Loneliness, frustration, and supplication were poured into the records of religious art as the agonies of the spirit embodied in the crucified *Corpus Christi*. Jesus, the Son of God, had indeed been sacrificed by God the Father to atone for all the sins of mankind. In acknowledgment of their suffering and His sacrifice, mankind identified poignantly with Jesus. Mankind *could* find meaning within life. Through the crucified Jesus, mankind *could* find salvation with the Father.[10]

Francis would pray most of his lifetime for this complete empathy with Christ. His identification with suffering would go to the ultimate degree, to manifesting (receiving) the wounds of Christ on the Cross upon his own body, the *stigmata*, during an ecstatic vision two years before his death.

The duality of Francis' identity—the confusion and change—is evident even in relation to his birth date. There is unanimous agreement among the hundreds of biographers of Francis that he was born late in the month of September but no one knows if the year was 1182 or 1181. Some authors begin their work with one year and slip into the other in later references.

Francis was born while his hot-headed, hard-working father, Bernardone Moriconi, was off on his seasonal buying trip to Champagne in France. Francis' mother, Pica, portrayed as pious and "fully attuned to the things of God," had her newborn son baptized as Giovanni, in homage to John the Baptist, establishing a powerful, conscious link between her son and the life of Jesus.[11]

---

10 Paul Tillich (1886–1965), the eminent German-born theologian, made a strong premise for the fact that, in times of great terror, such as Francis' time in the Middle Ages, which endured the Crusades and so many dynastic wars like the ones between Assisi and Perugia, great religious myths would come to the foreground to suggest something beyond suffering, something possible through suffering. It was a sur-reality "beyond the stress of battle, corpses, death, hatred, and cold revenge." Tillich's most famous work, *Courage to Be*, puts forth that the anxieties of death, meaninglessness, and guilt are the great concerns of all individuals. Goodrich, xxi, and personal study with Tillich at Harvard.

11 Fortini reports that all biographers are in agreement about Pica's piety. As well, "the people of the city believed that Pica had the God-given grace of being able to foretell the future." (Page 87.)

When Bernardone returned on the Via Francesca from France, he objected to his son being named after an ascetic, a man of the desert, this madman John the Baptist. His son was to be a powerful businessman in his father's footsteps! He changed Giovanni's name away from the ascetic's image to a name representing all things good, refined, and profitable: the boy would be called Francesco (the Frenchman), and he would learn French as a second language.[12]

What can we anticipate astrologically to capture the extraordinary, mystical division that emerged in Francis' identity? In studies of the stigmata from Francis to present times (much more about this later), the disposition to multiple personality is apparently so very closely linked with the empathic suffering "that they could be two different aspects of the same phenomenon."[13]

Is there an extreme alteration of consciousness triggered by the harsh life of Francis' times, i.e., in Jung's terms, a dynamic existence or effect *not* caused by an arbitrary act of will?[14] Do the incessant praying for empathy with Christ's suffering, the protracted fasting, the mortification of the flesh, and the self-inflicted torture of such a severe religious life create, perpetuate, and enhance an ecstatic state of divine grace in the mind? What might suggest this in the horoscope?

Is there a pathological state of self-hate present, bent on ultimate self-destruction, rationalized en route as a religious experience of the highest order? What would be the tensions that suggest such personality implosion and destruction?

Is there something here that is truly mystical experience extreme in personal manifestation, caused by highly specialized reaction to highly personalized pressures? Astrologically, what would the *disposition* to such reaction be?

The division of personality could lead us to look for emphasized double-bodied signs in Francis' astrology, a psychodynamic interplay of different directions or levels within conflicting need

---

12 Fortini, 88–89. In the Middle Ages, it was thought that one's name influenced one's life. Rather than every mention of his son's name recalling a desert-hermit who had dressed in sackcloth and eaten locusts and wild honey, the new name would create an image of fortune made through French wares, wools, and silks.

13 Harrison, quoting Ian Wilson, *The Bleeding Mind*, 18.

14 Jung, 4. Relating his discussion to Rudolf Otto's term, "numinosum," that which is external in orientation and seizes control of the subject as its victim.

pressures and behavioral resources; perhaps a conspicuous ret-rogradation pattern could portray a counterpoint to the chief line of life development. The alteration of consciousness, the self-devaluation/hate/punishment, the mystical escape could all rest on a conspicuously aspected *point of vulnerability and confusion* estab-lished symbolically in the horoscope.

This vulnerability to pressures to adopt a different life—suddenly—the state of confusion that would allow or *even invite* such a shift would certainly suggest a horoscopic *preparedness* for dramatic adjustment, for rescue or escape.

All these considerations speak of Neptune and Pisces (and of Jupiter, Pisces' co-ruler: religion; the ministry; and, perhaps with Mars, knighthood). Neptune always presents something that is other than it seems. There *is* confusion connected with Neptune; there *is* hypersensitivity; there *is* creativity, aesthetics, the mystical; there *is* the vulnerability and the preparedness to accept the power of new stimulus, ranging from drugs to dreams, to visions, to spiri-tual experience.

Additionally, conspicuous within the symbolism of Neptune, there is the theme of *sacrifice:* something must be given up for something else to be fulfilled. Something must be deduced, changed, adjusted, got out of the way to make room for something newly revealed, something newly understood. As well, there is always the potential that *idealism* will grace (or complicate) the posi-tion of Neptune in the horoscope, i.e., manifest in life behavior through Neptune. Idealism is the signal of what *should* be, what *can* emerge and reward the life.

When human beings feel high anxiety in reaction to criticism of themselves and their world, and when they recognize personal lim-itations, especially within the threatened state of only a brief exis-tence in a troubled world, *they look for a new life structure and meaning.* They can imagine a life infinitely better than what actual-ly is. Fantasy can dominate as an escape mechanism; people can entrust themselves totally to God's forgiving love and ultimate power which is above criticism and beyond death. This is the phe-nomenon of religious revival, of being "saved" and "born again." It is a dedication of personal perspective to God. Personal responsi-bility is turned over to the Divine.

In astrology, Pluto is the planet of perspective, the most of what we can expect from experience, feeling, and vision. It is the concept of empowerment through knowing. For Francis, we should anticipate dramatic focus on Pluto and Neptune through horoscopic synthesis at the core of his life.

The Astrology

Without question, biographer Arnaldo Fortini's work in service to the life of Francis is overwhelming in scope, replete with details, and sensitive in style. His research brings forward the date of September 26 for Francis' birth. He quotes a reference in the General History Records of the Franciscan Order, but he is quick to add that there is no concrete evidence for that date or any other.

This September date also appeared in the seventeenth century—and persists now—as the date upon which Assisi celebrates Francis' birth. Our astrological study will suggest that September 26 is indeed the correct date.[15]

For the year of Francis' birth, Fortini and most biographers and compendia of historical dates always mention two years, 1182 and 1181—in that order—as possibilities. For no apparent reason, most show preference for 1182. Our astrological study will present conclusively that 1182 is *not* correct; that 1181 is indeed the birth year for St. Francis, on the date September 26, in Assisi.[16]

Both orientation horoscopes shown on the opposite page (Figures 1A & 1B) are set for noon on September 26 in 1182 (1A) and in 1181 (1B).

---

15 Fortini, 86, note f. This birth date should not be confused with the Church Feast Day of St. Francis which is celebrated on October 4, the date of Francis' funeral and burial, the day after his death.

16 The reason there is no apparent ground for choosing between the two year-dates is undoubtedly complicated by the fact that event-dating throughout Francis' life, except for dates linked to formal Church actions, Feast Days, and his later activities when he was very famous, are also vague, with, at best, occasional references to seasons of the year rather than exact months or days. So ideas like "in the Summer or Fall of 1201, when Francis was nineteen or twenty" are very confusing for astrology but good enough for medieval history. In September of 1201, born in 1181 or 1182, Francis could be nineteen or twenty, depending on when in the year or in the month the reference is made.

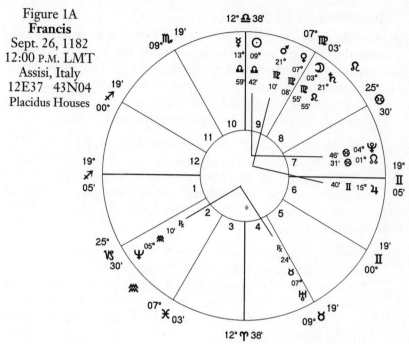

Figure 1A
Francis
Sept. 26, 1182
12:00 P.M. LMT
Assisi, Italy
12E37   43N04
Placidus Houses

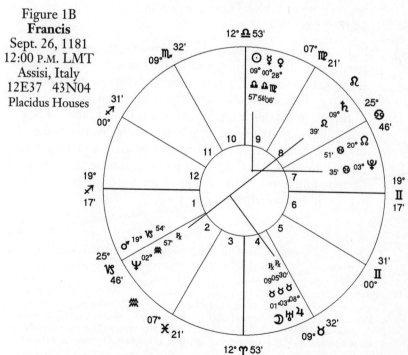

Figure 1B
Francis
Sept. 26, 1181
12:00 P.M. LMT
Assisi, Italy
12E37   43N04
Placidus Houses

Observations for Chart 1182

✦ In the 1182 chart, the Sun-in-Libra emphasis establishes the strong base for social energies working through the personality to please others and gain appreciation. The Virgo Moon in conjunction with Venus echoes these Libran energies within a reigning need (Moon) focused on being correct, exact, "right," fastidious, and insightfully discriminating.[17]

✦ The Moon would never be in Libra that day, but it could be in Leo, in a 6-degree orb separating conjunction with Saturn, for a few minutes just after midnight. This would add not only the severity and reform which were part of Francis' humiliation before Christ but also the need to show it all dramatically (Leo).

✦ There are conspicuous references to the Fire-sign flare and self-dramatization throughout Francis' life documentation. For example: "The gossipers said that he was a cocky fellow who thought himself better than his position warranted. In truth, he never in the world would tolerate being second to anyone in anything."[18] There was also Francis' reputation for bravery, reported by Thomas of Celano as "impulsive and not a little rash."

✦ Pluto is square the Sun, a very important corroboration of part of our initial anticipations. This aspect always promises some kind of reform, a revolutionary change from one perspective of life to another, and the reliance on a subtle control of others to establish one's power position. Francis' life certainly adjusted its perspective as dramatically as can possibly be conceived, and in the process of that adjustment and change he touched the ways of life of thousands during his lifetime and many millions since then throughout the world. He did indeed establish a new Order of being.[19]

---

17 The Sun-Moon blends discussed here come from the work of Grant Lewi some fifty years ago and my own research presented in Tyl, *Synthesis & Counseling*, I, D, especially beginning on page 76.

18 Fortini, 112.

19 Pat Nixon (March 16, 1912, close to 11:45 P.M., PST in Ely, NV); Greta Garbo (September 18, 1905, close to 7:30 P.M., CET in Stockholm, Sweden); Marlon Brando (April 3, 1924, close to 11:00 P.M., CST in Omaha, NE); and Prince Charles (November 14, 1948, at 9:14 P.M., GMT in London), all have the Sun-square-Pluto aspect natally.

✦Jupiter in Gemini, a double-bodied sign, ruling Sagittarius and Pisces, two other double-bodied signs, is squared by Mars in Virgo: opportunistic energies always working ahead of everyone else. Francis was inventive and persuasive to a fault; he would regale bishops and the Pope himself with irrefutable arguments about the validity of his work.

✦Uranus and Neptune are square, another strong corroboration of our anticipation. Uranus—which Alan Leo cast as "The Awakener"—intensifies all that we expect from Neptune, which, in turn here, is trine to the Sun. Both Pluto and Neptune touch the Sun, a strong orientation argument for this date in 1182.

Additionally in this chart, Mercury and Venus are in mutual reception, reinforcing the constant references in the historical literature to Francis' beautiful voice, his persuasiveness, his creativity with song, his sweetness and social poise. For example: during a battle in the war with Perugia, "And in the midst of it, Francis' voice, which seemed so melodious to those who usually listened to it, thundered out, loud enough to rise over the deafening noise"... at the final Christmas, and at the outdoor creche scene that he created for a torchlighted mass in a cave, "His voice rings out like heavenly music that none of those present could ever forget: 'a strong voice, a sweet voice, a clear voice, a sonorous voice'... his voice seems to resemble the sound of a lamb."[20]

Mars is oriental, the last planet to rise before the Sun, suggesting the spirit of promotion of a cause.[21]

Observations for Chart 1181

✦The Sun-in-Libra component is reinforced and expanded conspicuously by the conjunction of Mercury and Venus. Mercury and Venus are still in mutual reception, but their conjunction now brings to the foreground a very strong idealism.[22]

---

20 Fortini, quoting Thomas of Celano, the earwitness: 156, 533, and many other references. Even on his deathbed, his body wracked with pain from two decades of mortification, Francis raised his voice in song: "Francis became a troubadour again, as he had been when he was twenty. Songs poured out of him," Fortini, 581.

21 See Tyl, *Synthesis & Counseling*, beginning page 497.

22 Ibid., 105–112.

Additionally, Mercury is conjunct the Aries Point, putting the behavioral faculties of Mercury strongly into public view: Francis' public speaking, his preaching.[23]

✦ Most dramatically, *the Moon is in tight conjunction with Uranus and Jupiter*—a tremendous, explosive emphasis of identity, intensified in terms of all things Taurean.

We shall see that Francis became a "builder," not just metaphorically, i.e., a builder of faith or a new way to God, but *literally*, as a rebuilder of dilapidated, neglected churches. Pope Innocent III's powerful dream—which we shall review later—saw Francis as holding up, symbolically rebuilding, the stones of the Church that was near collapse. Francis' actual conversion in the San Damiano chapel was crowned by God's own voice: "Go Francis, and rebuild My house, for it is about to fall into ruins!"[24]

This is a critical observation between the two charts: in Figure 1A, the Moon in Virgo, ever so possibly in Leo, or in Figure 1B, emphatically accentuated in Taurus, ever so possibly in Aries earlier in the day (but beginning to lose the triple conjunction with Uranus and Jupiter). The overtones of building, the overwhelming focus on possessions as the value fulcrum of life development—the overturning of the status quo, so decidedly, revolutionarily Uranian—the putting right what should be right: all of this is strongly suggested by this powerful cluster.[25]

The Sun-Moon blend in the two signs ruled by Venus strongly reinforces the social outlook of Francis' life energy. The personality becomes the major asset. There would be strong aesthetic inclinations. Everything would be expressed in terms of human interest and welfare; popularity would be guaranteed.

✦ In the 1181 chart, the Sun-Pluto square is also present, AND the Neptune component, also square Uranus and the Moon

---

23 Ibid.,. beginning page 312.

24 All histories; see Cristiani, 36.

25 I have long observed and described the Moon in Taurus as a need to keep things as they are, a resistance to change. Companion to this observation always is the consideration of putting things right, rearranging things as they should be. In this powerful cluster, the conjunction with Uranus and Jupiter intensifies the capacity to set things right and reinforces Francis' missionary zeal.

and Jupiter, *is now opposed by Saturn*—mortified, i.e., subjected to humiliation and shame. That Saturn-Neptune axis is tightly *squared* by the triple conjunction of Moon-Uranus-Jupiter in Taurus; in Fixed signs, an anchored focus of behaviors that can dramatically shape the entire personality, a *dimentia praecox*—a fixated hysteria operating independently of all else. Jupiter-Saturn contact always "proves a point."

In summation, the triple conjunction of Sun in Libra, with Mercury and Venus (social sense, aesthetics, creativity, idealism) squared (empowered) by Pluto with the extraordinary identity formation of Saturn-Neptune (ambition, sacrifice, altered consciousness) squared by Moon-Uranus-Jupiter says it all. Mars in Capricorn is exalted and makes no aspect with any planet: it can run away with the horoscope in terms of emphatic, definitive, coercive self-application. This would be Francis' swagger, his bravura and bravery, his blind conviction, his early liberalism. All of this would be graced by the Sun's cluster and anchored in the awesome Saturn-Neptune T-Square, which itself is tied to the triple conjunction of Sun-Mercury-Venus by sextile and trine, respectively. *All of this would be sublimated, as we shall see.*

When Saturn opposes (squares or conjoins) Neptune there is confusion and doubt in any life, in relation to where these planets are placed and the Houses they rule. A choice of some kind is almost invariably enforced during life. Without preparedness, ambition can disappear, but *with* preparedness (Taurus structure), *with* energy (Mars exalted, unaspected), *with* enthusiasm (Jupiter conjunction), *with* intensification for awakening and reform (Uranus), a complete change in the direction of life is not only possible, *it is invited.*

The Fire-sign flare (intensity) is spoken for in a different way, by the almost exact conjunction of the Moon with Uranus.

Neptune—confusion, vision, sacrifice—is the conspicuously aspected point of vulnerability and confusion established symbolically in the horoscope.

Additionally, Mars is brought to conjunction with the Lunar Nodal Axis, keying a strong maternal influence, which is suggested in Francis' early life and public outreach which we shall see later.[26]

---

26 Tyl, *Synthesis & Counseling*, 49–63.

Both charts share the Libra social-public focus, but 1181 is stronger through the tighter organization of Mercury and Venus with the Sun. Both charts have a tenable Moon position, but the 1181 Moon organization is imposingly conceived. Both charts have the Sun-Pluto relationship. Both charts have a Neptune focus, but 1181 is dramatically stronger through the opposition with Saturn. Summarily, between the two charts, the portrait in 1181, in its extremism, is undeniably more appropriate.

What Time was Francis Born?

Above all in the life of Francis, two characteristics stand out repeatedly in all descriptions of his ways. First, upon his conversion, which we will share in detail later as one of our time-tests of the horoscope, there is the absolutely *obsessive denial of all possessions*, including money, even if money were given to him. Poverty was everything to Francis. Even academic learning was incompatible with the humble life; he thought it simply a formalization of frivolous curiosity. For over twenty years, Francis lived the metaphor *that he was married to "Lady Poverty."*[27]

Lady Poverty became the beautiful damsel of distress for Francis the Knight. Early in his crusade, he composed a love song: "Have mercy, sweet Jesus, have mercy on me and on our Lady Poverty. For her I languish, because of her I have no peace, and you know, Jesus, that you love me because of her ... When your disciples abandoned you, when they denied your name, she stayed always at your side ... High, so very high was the cross and Mary could not ascend it. But she, Poverty, our Lady, was there. More strongly than ever up there she united herself to you ... Grant that for her I shall live, that in her and with her I can die."[28]

Another example: "With all zeal, with all solicitude, he guarded holy Lady Poverty, not permitting any vessel of any kind to be in

---

27 Cristiani, 33. On the point of education, it is presented repeatedly in the histories that Francis was no ignorant, uncultured man deprived of intellectual accomplishments. His knowledge of theology "was so profound that many thought it a gift from God." But for the gifted Francis, learning could never intrude upon prayer and must never weaken humility. Fortini, 450.

28 This ballad is quite long; it was written by Francis in French. These excerpts show the beginning of Francis' extraordinary identification with Jesus, the crucified Christ. They share the ever faithful spouse, Lady Poverty; it is she who represents the most faithful ideal. Fortini, 232–233.

the house [at best a cave], lest it lead to superfluous things ... For, he used to say, it is impossible to satisfy necessity and not give in to pleasure." Francis rarely even allowed himself to eat donated food that was cooked. If he relented even the slightest, he would mix the morsel of food with ashes or destroy its taste with cold water.[29] "At times the saint would repeat: 'In as far as the brothers depart from poverty, in so much will the world depart from them, and they will seek,' he said, 'and not find. But if they embrace my Lady Poverty, the world will provide for them, because they have been given to the world unto its salvation.'"[30]

And at his death, "The saint rejoiced and was glad out of the gladness of his heart, for he saw that he had kept faith with Lady Poverty to the end. For he had done all these things out of zeal for poverty, so that he would not have at the end even a habit that was his own, but, as it were, lent to him by another."[31]

The second most outstanding characteristic of Francis' life was *humiliation*, his wounding himself in every way possible by neglect of anything that would make his life easier. Mortification *is* the appropriate word here, extensive debasement and humiliation, the eradication of any sense of self-worth except that which he gained through identification with Christ on the Cross.

After his trip to Gauthier de Brienne was aborted, after the debilitation of prolonged relapse to fever left over from his horrible imprisonment by the Perugini, we see Francis once again with his ribald companions at dinner. He was strangely preoccupied and separated from reality. One of his friends had sport with him in his uncharacteristic aloof state: "Tell me, Francis," he asked, "is it the thought of a forthcoming marriage that makes you stand there like a man of stone?"

---

29 Celano, I, #52.

30 Ibid., II, #70.

31 Ibid., II, #215. And Thomas adds here an apology on Francis' behalf that, at the very end, he did wear a "little cap of sackcloth" to cover the wounds he had endured in the barbarous cauterization treatments given to him for his failing eyes.

   Additionally: within two years after Francis' death, an anonymous book called *The Sacred Romance of Blessed Francis and Lady Poverty* appeared. It was clearly inspiration for Dante in his tribute to the saint and Lady Poverty in *The Divine Comedy*: in Canto XI of "Paradiso," Dante says that Lady Poverty had been deprived of a spouse for over a millennium, i.e., since the time of Christ, but St. Francis was to be her new lover. Dante echoes the close identification between poverty and the Passion of Christ. Stock and Cunningham, 59.

"Yes," Francis replied, "I am seriously thinking of getting married, and the bride I have chosen is the noblest, richest, and most beautiful of all the women you know!"

...These words, [and then] "the peals of laughter, completely upset Francis and destroyed all the joy he had had in his past pleasures. From that very hour, he began to despise himself."[32]

The marriage to Lady Poverty was forming in his mind and one of his vows to her was to be self-mortification: the more Francis tested his resolve, denuding himself of all things, protecting himself from nothing in his life, the more he found joy.

The domain of possessions and the psychodynamic experience of self-worth both focus themselves within the 2nd House.

In one sermon, after a long illness, Francis stood on the public stone where prisoners were regularly placed to be mocked, and addressed the crowd of people: "You think I am a holy man, as do those who, on the basis of my example, leave the world and enter the order and lead the life of the brothers. Well, I confess to God and to you that during my illness I ate meat and some stew." Thomas of Celano reports that many who heard Francis were deeply stirred by his bizarre admission and his obviously sincere contrition. They heard Francis passionately accusing himself of doing wrong by taking care of his health under threat of dying! "Where then does that leave us, we who live so easily according to our desires and indulgence of the flesh?"[33]

In response to public enthusiasm for him, his strong effect on others, Francis would command one of the brothers to drag him through the streets on a rope, shouting to all: "Look at this glutton, this worthless fellow, who ate chicken meat without telling you!"

When the crowds admired Francis more and more for his humility, he would command another brother to shout insults at him. This went on and on in Francis' life every day, and then he would retreat to solitary, long fasts alone in a cave, praying constantly.[34]

---

32 Cristiani, 29. Report of this happening in Francis' life is attributed to "The Three Companions," mysterious witnesses to Francis' life. Thomas of Celano names them as Brothers Leo, Ruffino, and Angelo, humble brothers close to Francis from the very beginning.

33 Fortini, 461.

34 Cristiani, 87–88; all histories.

For Francis, the utmost possible degradation was perfect joy. It tested his resolve, his dedication to the suffering experienced by the Christ and it defined his crusade. Francis had meaning not only for others who gradually came to understand his example but for himself as well, alone in a world which only Jesus had experienced.

Astrologically, this inter-relationship between Poverty and Humiliation, Sacrifice and Mortification, is symbolized by the Saturn-Neptune opposition. By rulership and tenancy, the placement of this key concept *must involve the Ascendant and the 2nd House dramatically*. The archetype must be personalized to the deepest.

A Pisces Ascendant would bring the vision and aberrant bliss of Neptunian symbolism to Francis' core. A Pisces Ascendant would place the triple conjunction in Taurus into the 2nd House.

Figure 2 (page 96) is the horoscope for Francis of Assisi, September 26, 1181 at 4:41 P.M., LMT in Assisi. The Ascendant in the 16th degree of Pisces was set by testing transits, arcs, and progression to angles against the events in Francis' life. For example, the Solar Arc projection of Neptune—the focal point of our appreciation of Francis' identity—comes to conjunction with the Ascendant at the time when Francis received the vision of all visions and received the wounds of the crucified Christ upon his own body. This miraculous event, the first stigmata, occurred on September 14, 1224, almost exactly forty-three years after his birth. Forty-three years may be abbreviated as 43 degrees and added to natal Neptune to approximate the actual Arc: 2 Aquarius 57 + 43 = 45 Aquarius 57, which is 15 Pisces 57).[35]

The Divided Identity

The Uranus-Moon-Jupiter conjunction in Taurus, the Moon exalted in Taurus, by itself suggests *intense identity development through possessions*. The ruler of the 2nd, Venus, the dispositor of the triple conjunction, is in broad, excessive square with Pluto, is angular, and is led into conjunction with the Sun through its conjunction and mutual reception with Mercury. This is one level of the 2nd House manifestation potential: intensified, expanded, rich possessions, a strong, ebullient, and forthright self-worth profile.

---

35 The exact arc, as we shall see, brings SA Neptune to 16 Pisces 5. For approximation techniques and exact measurement management in Solar Arc theory, please see Tyl, *Synthesis & Counseling*, 204, 289, 383.

Another level is the modification of the triple conjunction in Taurus by the involvement with the Saturn-Neptune opposition. The opposition axis squaring the triple conjunction depresses, cuts off, mortifies the 2nd. And the *retrogradation* of Uranus and Jupiter there—with Jupiter ruling the 10th and the 9th, obviously the hope for international glory hand in hand with religious ideals in his life—suggests ever so clearly the contrapuntal concept within concerns of possessions and self-worth. There is bound to be a drastic

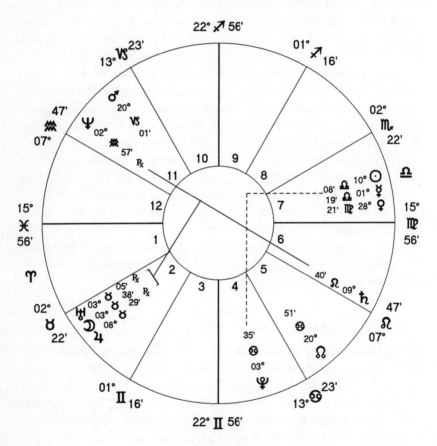

Figure 2
Francis of Assisi
Sept. 26, 1181, 4:41 P.M. LMT
Assisi, Italy
12E37 43N04
Placidus Houses

shift, an imbalancing development of change that will alter Francis' life in terms of the 2nd House.

Neptune rules the Ascendant, and so does unaspected, exalted Mars, ruler of Aries. Here again we have the two personal projections: the swaggering libertine, the warring knight, and the

+ 0:00 UT				Geocentric Tropical Longitudes for SEP 1181								
Date	Sid.Time	Sun	Moon	Node	Mercury	Venus	Mars	Jupiter	Saturn	Uranus	Neptune	Pluto
20	0:21:59	03♎32 59	04≈01	21☋12	19♍53	20♏02	16♑10	09♉08R	09♌05	03♉20R	03≈00R	03☋34
21	0:25:54	04 32 02	17 56	21 08	21 33	21 16	16 44	09 03	09 10	03 17	02 59	03 34
22	0:29:51	05 31 24	01✕45	21 05	23 15	22 31	17 18	08 57	09 16	03 15	02 59	03 34
23	0:33:47	06 30 47	15 26	21 02	24 58	23 46	17 53	08 51	09 21	03 13	02 58	03 34
24	0:37:44	07 30 13	28 56	20 59	26 42	25 01	18 28	08 46	09 26	03 11	02 58	03 34
25	0:41:40	08 29 40	12♈12	20 56	28 26	26 16	19 02	08 40	09 31	03 09	02 57	03 35
26	0:45:37	09 29 10	25 12	20 53	00♎10	27 31	19 38	08 33	09 36	03 06	02 57	03 35
27	0:49:33	10 28 41	07♉55	20 49	01 54	28 46	20 13	08 27	09 41	03 04	02 57	03 35
28	0:53:30	11 28 15	20 22	20 46	03 38	00♎01	20 49	08 21	09 46	03 02	02 56	03 35
29	0:57:26	12 27 51	02♊33	20 43	05 22	01 16	21 24	08 14	09 51	03 00	02 56	03 35
30	1:01:23	13 27 30	14 33	20 40	07 05	02 31	22 00	08 07	09 56	02 57	02 56	03 35

+ 0:00 UT				Geocentric Tropical Longitudes for OCT 1181								
Date	Sid.Time	Sun	Moon	Node	Mercury	Venus	Mars	Jupiter	Saturn	Uranus	Neptune	Pluto
1	1:05:20	14♎27 10	26♊24	20☋37	08♎48	03♎46	22♑37	08♉01R	10♌01	02♉55R	02≈55R	03☋34R
2	1:09:16	15 26 53	08☋12	20 34	10 31	05 01	23 13	07 54	10 05	02 53	02 55	03 34
3	1:13:13	16 26 39	20 02	20 30	12 13	06 17	23 50	07 47	10 10	02 50	02 55	03 34
4	1:17:09	17 26 26	01♌59	20 27	13 55	07 32	24 26	07 39	10 14	02 48	02 55	03 34
5	1:21:06	18 26 16	14 09	20 24	15 37	08 47	25 03	07 32	10 19	02 46	02 55	03 34
6	1:25:02	19 26 08	26 37	20 21	17 17	10 02	25 40	07 25	10 23	02 43	02 55	03 34
7	1:28:59	20 26 02	09♍27	20 18	18 58	11 17	26 18	07 17	10 27	02 41	02 55	03 33
8	1:32:55	21 25 59	22 41	20 14	20 37	12 33	26 55	07 10	10 31	02 39	02 55	03 33
9	1:36:52	22 25 57	06♎20	20 11	22 17	13 48	27 33	07 02	10 35	02 36	02 55D	03 33
10	1:40:49	23 25 58	20 20	20 08	23 55	15 03	28 11	06 54	10 39	02 34	02 55	03 33
11	1:44:45	24 26 00	04♏38	20 05	25 33	16 18	28 48	06 47	10 43	02 31	02 55	03 32
12	1:48:42	25 26 05	19 08	20 02	27 11	17 34	29 27	06 39	10 47	02 29	02 55	03 32
13	1:52:38	26 26 11	03♐41	19 59	28 48	18 49	00♏05	06 31	10 51	02 26	02 55	03 32
14	1:56:35	27 26 19	18 13	19 55	00♏25	20 04	00 43	06 23	10 54	02 24	02 55	03 31
15	2:00:31	28 26 28	02♑37	19 52	02 01	21 20	01 22	06 15	10 58	02 21	02 55	03 31
16	2:04:28	29 26 40	16 52	19 49	03 37	22 35	02 00	06 07	11 01	02 19	02 56	03 30
17	2:08:24	00♏26 52	00≈54	19 46	05 13	23 50	02 39	05 59	11 04	02 16	02 56	03 30
18	2:12:21	01 27 06	14 45	19 43	06 48	25 06	03 18	05 51	11 07	02 14	02 56	03 30
19	2:16:18	02 27 22	28 24	19 40	08 22	26 21	03 57	05 42	11 10	02 11	02 57	03 29
20	2:20:14	03 27 39	11✕52	19 36	09 57	27 36	04 36	05 34	11 13	02 09	02 57	03 29
21	2:24:11	04 27 58	25 08	19 33	11 31	28 52	05 16	05 26	11 16	02 06	02 57	03 28
22	2:28:07	05 28 18	08♈14	19 30	13 04	00♏07	05 55	05 18	11 19	02 04	02 58	03 27
23	2:32:04	06 28 40	21 10	19 27	14 37	01 23	06 35	05 10	11 22	02 01	02 58	03 27
24	2:36:00	07 29 03	03♉50	19 24	16 10	02 38	07 14	05 02	11 24	01 59	02 59	03 26
25	2:39:57	08 29 28	16 19	19 20	17 43	03 53	07 54	04 53	11 27	01 57	02 59	03 26
26	2:43:53	09 29 55	28 35	19 17	19 15	05 09	08 34	04 45	11 29	01 54	03 00	03 25
27	2:47:50	10 30 23	10♊40	19 14	20 47	06 24	09 14	04 37	11 31	01 52	03 01	03 24
28	2:51:47	11 30 54	22 35	19 11	22 19	07 40	09 54	04 29	11 33	01 49	03 01	03 24
29	2:55:43	12 31 26	04☋24	19 08	23 51	08 55	10 34	04 21	11 36	01 47	03 02	03 23
30	2:59:40	13 32 00	16 11	19 05	25 22	10 11	11 14	04 13	11 37	01 44	03 03	03 22
31	3:03:36	14 32 35	27 59	19 01	26 53	11 26	11 54	04 05	11 39	01 42	03 03	03 21

Copyright (C) 1987 Matrix Software, Big Rapids MI 49307

+ 0:00 UT				Geocentric Tropical Longitudes for NOV 1181								
Date	Sid.Time	Sun	Moon	Node	Mercury	Venus	Mars	Jupiter	Saturn	Uranus	Neptune	Pluto
1	3:07:33	15♏33 12	09♌54	18☋58	28♏23	12♏42	12♐34	03♉57℞	11♌41	01♉40℞	03≈04	03☋21℞
2	3:11:29	16 33 52	22 02	18 55	29 54	13 57	13 15	03 50	11 43	01 37	03 05	03 20
3	3:15:26	17 34 32	04♍28	18 52	01♐24	15 13	13 55	03 42	11 44	01 35	03 06	03 19
4	3:19:22	18 35 15	17 17	18 49	02 54	16 28	14 36	03 34	11 46	01 32	03 07	03 18
5	3:23:19	19 35 59	00♎32	18 46	04 23	17 43	15 16	03 27	11 47	01 30	03 08	03 17
6	3:27:16	20 36 45	14 15	18 42	05 52	18 59	15 57	03 19	11 48	01 28	03 09	03 17
7	3:31:12	21 37 32	28 26	18 39	07 21	20 14	16 38	03 12	11 49	01 25	03 10	03 16
8	3:35:09	22 38 20	13♏00	18 36	08 49	21 30	17 19	03 04	11 50	01 23	03 11	03 15
9	3:39:05	23 39 11	27 50	18 33	10 17	22 46	18 00	02 57	11 51	01 21	03 12	03 14
10	3:43:02	24 40 02	12♐48	18 30	11 44	24 01	18 41	02 50	11 52	01 19	03 13	03 13
11	3:46:58	25 40 54	27 45	18 26	13 10	25 17	19 22	02 43	11 52	01 17	03 14	03 12
12	3:50:55	26 41 48	12♑33	18 23	14 36	26 32	20 03	02 36	11 53	01 14	03 15	03 11
13	3:54:51	27 42 42	27 06	18 20	16 00	27 48	20 44	02 30	11 53	01 12	03 16	03 10
14	3:58:48	28 43 38	11≈20	18 17	17 24	29 03	21 25	02 23	11 53	01 10	03 17	03 09
15	4:02:45	29 44 34	25 15	18 14	18 46	00♐19	22 07	02 17	11 53	01 08	03 18	03 08

Copyright (C) 1987 Matrix Software, Big Rapids MI 49307

suffering scapegoat, the bleeding beggar. This duality—like a hot poker immersed into cool water—is signaled perfectly through double-bodied Pisces and the retrogradation of both Neptune and Jupiter, its rulers.

The potential change of life perspective is also suggested by the Pluto square with the Sun, as we have seen. Pluto rules the 8th, the concerns of death matters, of the martyrdom of values and the body of Christ.[36]

Saturn rules the 11th, love hoped for, anticipated, received; love in terms of or in spite of or through discipline, debasement, pain, confinement, solitude. What is idealized through Neptune is sacrificed through Saturn's involvement. Within the T-Square, Saturn relates powerfully with the Moon, ruler of the 5th, the House of love given. Francis' life epitomized the giving of love through all he had in order to receive back the ideal love of Jesus.

And through it all—as testified by all histories, by all witnesses, by all biographers—Francis was cheerful and joyous to a fault! Sun-Mercury-Venus are focused within Libra, Mercury and Venus are in Mutual reception, both ruling the 7th: idealized relationship with the world at one level and then another.

---

36 The 8th is always the twelfth dynamic of the 9th in Derivative House readings. So much of theology, to explain life, is founded on explanation and assimilation of concerns about death.

FRANCIS OF ASSISI SEP 26, 1181

Midpoint Sort: 90° Dial					
☿ 001°19'	☿/♅ 017°12'	♆ 032°57'	♂/Asc 047°58'	♅/♇ 063°20'	♃/♆ 080°43'
♇ 003°35'	☽/☿ 017°28'	♅ 033°05'	☊/Asc 048°23'	☽/♇ 063°36'	♄/♅ 081°22'
☉/♀ 004°15'	♆/♇ 018°16'	☽/♅ 033°21'	☉/♇ 051°52'	♀/♄ 064°00'	☽/♄ 081°39'
☉/☿ 005°44'	♀/♃ 018°25'	☽ 033°38'	♀/♂ 054°11'	☿/♄ 065°29'	♀/Asc 082°08'
♂/Mc 006°28'	☿/♃ 019°54'	Mc/Asc 034°26'	♆/Asc 054°26'	♃/♇ 066°02'	Mc 082°56'
☊/Mc 006°53'	♂ 020°01'	♃/♅ 035°47'	♀/☊ 054°36'	☉/♆ 066°33'	☿/Asc 083°37'
♅/Asc 009°30'	♂/☊ 020°26'	☽/♃ 036°03'	☿/♂ 055°40'	☉/♄ 069°54'	♃/♄ 084°04'
☽/Asc 009°47'	☊ 020°51'	♄/♆ 036°18'	☿/☊ 056°05'	♂/♅ 071°33'	☉/Asc 088°02'
☉ 010°08'	☉/♅ 021°37'	♃ 038°29'	♄/Asc 057°48'	☽/♂ 071°49'	♇/Mc 088°15'
♂/♇ 011°48'	♄/♇ 021°37'	♄ 039°40'	♅/Mc 058°00'	♅/☊ 071°58'	♀ 088°21'
♃/Asc 012°12'	☽/☉ 021°53'	♇/Asc 039°45'	☽/Mc 058°17'	☽/☊ 072°14'	☿/♀ 089°50'
♇/☊ 012°13'	☉/♃ 024°19'	♀/Mc 040°38'	☉/♂ 060°05'	♂/♃ 074°15'	
♆/Mc 012°56'	♂/♆ 026°29'	☿/Mc 042°07'	☉/☊ 060°29'	♃/☊ 074°40'	
♀/♅ 015°43'	♆/☊ 026°54'	♀/♇ 045°58'	♀/♆ 060°39'	Asc 075°56'	
☽/♀ 015°59'	♂/♄ 029°50'	☉/Mc 046°32'	♃/Mc 060°42'	♅/♆ 078°01'	
♄/Mc 016°18'	♄/☊ 030°15'	☿/♇ 047°27'	☿/♆ 062°08'	☽/♆ 078°17'	

The Mercury/Venus midpoint at 89 Mutable 50, i.e., 29 Mutable 50, just at the "Aries Point" of 0 Cardinal, brings idealization, joy, and public awareness *out into the open*, keeps them there to establish Francis in the eyes of the world. MC=Venus/Asc suggests "a sense of beauty, a recognized romantic."[37]

Saturn=Pluto/Asc (Saturn square the midpoint of Pluto-Ascendant) shows the utmost power used for personal advancement and fulfillment. In other words, for Francis, his quest was *a life and death matter*, a fixation, a projection for eternal life with God, through the live suffering of Christ's death.

Venus=Pluto/MC, Sun/Asc is a picture of emotional charisma and social appeal. Time and time again in the histories, we read that Francis had an hypnotic effect on others through his voice, his words, his sincerity, his joy, and his love.

Additionally, the symbolic location of poverty, penance, solitude, and even wild birds (which are part of a miracle we shall see later) is the 12th House. Here ruled by Uranus which brings these concerns to the Moon in the 2nd. The arc of Neptune will carry with it the opposition from Saturn throughout the 12th House for the entire second half of Francis' life.

We locate humility in the 6th House, and there we see this powerful, dramatic show of ambition, Saturn in Leo. the House is ruled

---

37 All Midpoint pictures are derived almost verbatim from Tyl, *Prediction in Astrology* or *Synthesis & Counseling*, Appendices.

by the Sun which is beautifully bright in the 7th. Again, we see the double identity formations presenting themselves everywhere.

Even the definite preoccupation with singing and song is a manifestation of Taurus and the enormous concentration there in the 2nd House. The dispositor, Venus, is reinforced further through the mutual reception with Mercury in the 7th.[38]

Brother Thomas of Celano's description of Francis as he saw him with his own eyes, as he lived and worked with him for years in the Order, animates this extraordinary horoscope even more. The description is a veritable catalogue of astrological keywords that fits perfectly this horoscope we have just discovered:

> O how beautiful, how splendid, how glorious did he appear in the innocence of his life, in the simplicity of his words, in the purity of his heart, in his love for God, in his fraternal charity, in his ardent obedience, in his peaceful submission, in his angelic countenance!

> He was charming in his manners, serene by nature, affable in his conversation, most opportune in his exhortations, most faithful in what was entrusted to him, cautious in his counsel, effective in business, gracious in all things. He was serene of mind, sweet of disposition, sober in spirit, raised up in contemplation, zealous in prayer, and in all things fervent.

> He was constant in purpose, stable in virtue, persevering in grace, and unchanging in all things. He was quick to pardon, slow to become angry, ready of wit, tenacious of memory, subtle in discussion, circumspect in choosing, and in all things simple. He was unbending with himself, understanding toward others, and discreet in all things.

> He was a most eloquent man, a man of cheerful countenance, of kindly aspect; he was immune to cowardice, free of insolence. He was of medium height, closer to shortness; his head was moderate in size and round, his face a bit long and prominent, his forehead smooth and low; his eyes were of moderate size, black and sound; his hair was black, his eyebrows straight, his nose symmetrical, thin and straight; his ears were upright, but small; his temples smooth.

> His speech was peaceable, fiery and sharp; his voice was strong, sweet, clear, and sonorous. His teeth were set close together, even, and white; his lips were small and thin; his beard black, but

---

38 See Munkasey for detailed rulership concepts among the Houses.

not bushy. His neck was slender, his shoulders straight, his arms short, his hands slender, his fingers long, his nails extended; his legs were thin, his feet small.

His skin was delicate, his flesh very spare. He wore rough garments, he slept but briefly, he gave most generously. And because he was very humble, he showed *all mildness to all men*, adapting himself usefully to the behavior of all."[39]

We now see vividly the modifications of Pisces through Saturn's opposition with Neptune. We see the pervasive public show of Sun-Mercury-Venus. We hear the strengths of Mars in Capricorn (with the redness darkened), and the deep self-empowerment of Pluto. We feel the uplift of Jupiter as ruler of the Midheaven and the 9th. We feel the dramatic confrontation of Aquarius and Leo channeled through the Saturn-Neptune opposition and then through the suffering of the 12th to the wounded presence of the 1st, taking over the energies of youthful swagger yet remaining in Aries. We see the denunciation of what is real in favor of what can be. We see the obsession with the ideal that changed the direction and level of life, establishing self-sacrifice once again—for redemption of the world.

War, Imprisonment, New Ideals

The division of Francis' identity, the alteration of his ideals begins with the dreadful war between Assisi and Perugia. This particular war began slowly with the defection of a powerful Assisian to Perugia. Beyond the symbolisms of loyalty and pride, there was a commercial loss through estate taxes and commerce for Assisi and a commensurate gain for Perugia. For some two years, there were raids and skirmishes between the two cities, the razing of crops, ambushes, and disputations. Other Assisian leaders jumped city-allegiances. The consuls of Assisi raced to assemble an army.

The long-awaited battle that would decide the issues finally took place in November 1202, the Battle of Collestrada (some sources say the Battle of St. John's Bridge). Francis was thoroughly swept up in the preparations and knightly overtones of the battle. "Perhaps the hand of some noble lady reached out to give him a

---

39 Celano, I, #83.

white scarf. Perhaps some of those who had predicted a heroic life for him saluted him now, calling him by name."[40]

The assembled armies came face to face 800 yards apart along the Tiber just outside Perugia. The Perugino army, with standards flapping above their hoisted swords, attacked the outnumbered Assisians. The battle was ferocious. Nothing was spared, not even the lepers' hospital. It was a massacre "beyond every measure." The river was swollen with bodies and blood. The stragglers were hunted down like wild animals.

> Oh, how disfigured are the bodies on the field of battle, and how mutilated and broken are their members! The hand is not to be found with the foot, nor the entrails joined to the chest; on the forehead horrible windows open out instead of eyes. That no prophet, interrogated before the battle could have seen such omens! Oh, you of Assisi, what a sad day and what a dark hour was this![41]

Francis was taken prisoner.

Figure 3 (page 103) shows the Secondary Progression for early November 1202 in the ring around Francis' natal horoscope. The important transits of the time and the Tertiary Progressed (TP) Sun position are noted as well. The SP Moon—very time-sensitive and telling in astrology—is in the 12th House and opposed natal Saturn at the time of the battle, reinforced by the exact opposition with SP Saturn.

Transiting Saturn had been exactly opposed Francis' Sun a month before the battle, and transiting Pluto at 2 Leo was beginning its critical square to the 2nd House group. Transiting Uranus at 7 Leo was squaring Francis' Jupiter, ruler of his 9th and 10th, intensifying the dreams of international conquests, the potential fortunes of crusading, the professional ideals for himself.

Indeed, Francis' horoscope shows critical times of change upon him. Note the SP-SA Sun at 1 Scorpio. Within two years (degrees), the Sun will oppose Uranus and the Moon; we can certainly expect an extraordinary new development, a "new Francis," if you will. As well, *the SP Moon will be crossing the Ascendant* in

---

40 Fortini, 153.

41 Fortini, 155, quoting Bonifazio da Verona, a poet and "master of astrology," commissioned by Perugia to write a grand poem to glorify the city and its conquests. This work would build upon Bonifazio's ode about the descendants of Ulysses, the legendary founder of Perugia. Fortini, 56, 154.

almost three years (11 Aquarius to 15 Pisces, 1 degree per month projection for the SP Moon).

Francis is in prison. His "happy-go-lucky" youth is gone for ever. Once again life's pain became more real to him than his fascinating dreams, his heroic enthusiasms and hopes of glory, more real than stirring fanfares, waving banners, and flashing blades, more real than even great courage.

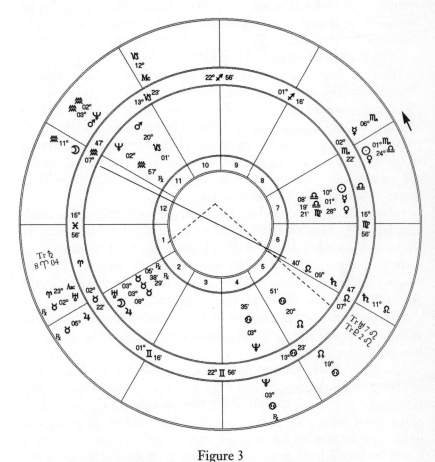

Figure 3

Inner Chart	Outer Chart
Francis of Assisi	**SP War/Prison**
Sept. 26, 1181, 4:41 P.M. LMT	Nov. 10, 1202
Assisi, Italy	
12E37 43N04	

Placidus Houses

Even though Francis was imprisoned with the nobles, conditions were squalid and miserable. This time in prison brought to Francis his first experiences of humiliation and suffering. But, following his instinctive way of giving, of living life with joy, *he took responsibility for the other prisoners.* This revealed his courage, "but offended the sensibilities of his companions, who reproached him and called him crazy. One day, one of them told him that his joy was an insult to their common misfortune. Francis answered, "Of course, your bad luck grieves me. But I cannot help being happy, because even though my body is imprisoned in these walls, my spirit is free."[42]

The change of ideals had begun.

Francis himself became very ill after one year in the dungeons. Though weak and exhausted, his irrepressible joy endured. "Thrown down on his bundle of straw, burning with fever, his eyes shone as if lit by a supernatural light." He was delirious. He spoke of winning the greatest liberty the world had ever known, that he would soon be revered by all men. His fever rose and stayed. And so did his obsession ... as the Sun began to oppose and transiting Pluto began to square Uranus and the Moon.

Bernardone negotiated his extremely ill son's release, probably very late in December 1203. [Tr Mars was exactly opposed Francis' Pluto on December 30 in the 4th House, a bid for freedom and an activation of paternal force. Tr Venus was exactly conjunct Francis' Midheaven at 23 Sagittarius, Tr Saturn was Stationary Direct trine the Midheaven, and SP Moon was sextile the Midheaven.]

Francis remained in a trance-like state during his convalescence at home. He was deeply preoccupied with the sense of an empty life. Nothing excited him.

Early in 1205, Francis did come around (the SP Moon was applying to his Ascendant; see Figure 4, page 106). With his first returned energies, he devoured the tales of Count Gautier de Brienne about whom all of Assisi spoke. He tried to be as he was before, projecting his future again in terms of knighthood. With a noble Assisian friend, Francis made plans to make the long journey to enlist in the services of de Brienne and win knighthood through arms. Fortini observes that Francis must have had a conspicuous skill in and love of weaponry (exalted Mars; Aries intercepted in the

---

42 Fortini, 161–62.

Ascendant) to persist, in the wake of his horrid war experience, to fulfill his life through conquest.[43]

At that time, de Brienne was on a mission against Sicily and was headquartered in Lecce, far south in the Apulia region in the very heel of Italy, some 700 miles from Assisi. Francis and his noble friend, their eyes afire, set out for their noble futures.

In Figure 4 (page 106), working with the chart we have created for Francis, we see just what we anticipated when he was captured during the war:[44] SA-SP Sun has come *exactly to opposition with his Uranus,* suggesting always an independent, even revolutionary spirit, a new project.[45]

At the same time, the SP Ascendant was approaching conjunction with Uranus, and, so very important as we anticipated, *the SP Moon was conjoining Francis' Ascendant!* This signaled a whole new thrust in his life, a thrust for personal ambition and glory. It was decidedly high-minded and international in scope: transiting Saturn at 8–9 Taurus was *exactly conjunct natal Jupiter,* ruler of the 10th and 9th Houses, co-ruler of the Ascendant!

We know Francis did not complete this trip to Apuila. He barely reached Spoleto, just twenty-five miles from Assisi! He became feverish again, a clear relapse into his illness of the dungeon. [A counter-message through transiting Saturn?] In his languid state he had a vision; a voice questioned him about his goals and sent him back to Assisi: "there you will be told what you must do, because what you have seen must be understood differently from the way you have understood it." Again, we see the divided organization of Francis' awareness and life experience.[46]

It appears as if Francis lived an uneventful year in Assisi after this experience. His companion had gone on to glory, and Francis had returned to bewilderment. He was waiting. He could not reclaim his old ways. At a banquet, his friends jeered at him when he spoke of strange ideas of a different life. His mother, however, seemed to know what was happening to him and kept up supportively with his

---

43 Fortini, note l, 177.

44 The exact time of the beginning of this trip is not known. It is almost surely early 1205; probably March, when the weather had cleared for easier travel, when nature lured beauty from the countryside and romance from the hearts of young knights-to-be.

45 Being one's self and getting away with it.

46 All histories; see Cristiani, 26–27; Fortini, 188.

transformation. His only joy was in prayer and in sharing all extra food with the poor.

He began to give to the poor more and more and more, everything he would have with him at any time of meeting. He longed to be one of the unimportant, the humble, the poor, to sit with them at a church door and beg for charity.[47]

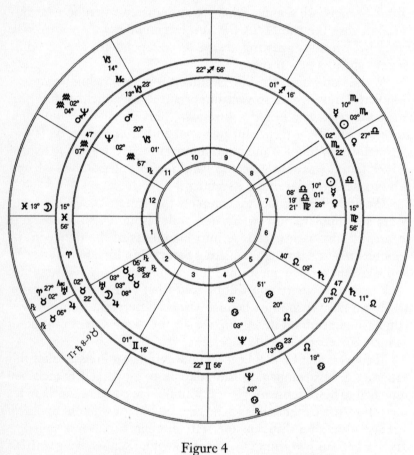

Figure 4

Inner Chart	Outer Chart
Francis of Assisi	**SP Apulia/Spoleto**
	Mar. 21, 1205

47 Fortini, 203.

1206: To Rome, The Leper, and The Cross

In the Spring of 1206, Francis announced he was going to Rome, "to fulfill a visit to the thresholds of the saints Peter and Paul." He dressed as a pilgrim, with a short cloak and a staff, in a group making their way on foot slowly and joyously to the City of God.

Figure 5 (page 108), with the Solar Arc positions in the outer ring, is set for June 1206. We see that the SA Ascendant has come 25 degrees (Francis is almost twenty-five years old) to exact opposition with his Sun. This is another step in his conversion transformation that began with his imprisonment, was punctuated by the vision in Spoleto, and now would be completely confirmed within five months. Francis would have his answer. He would know what to do.

In Rome, in front of St. Peter's, Francis exchanged his clothes with a beggar and blended in with a sea of the poor. "Some of them suffered from the most repugnant infirmities—monstrous sores, maimed and crippled bodies, blindness, paralysis." He begged for alms, in French. "Speaking French seemed to take him out of his original milieu. He felt he was changing his life-style. (Besides, he spoke French only when he was happy.)"[48]

On his way home to Assisi—he wished to stay among the poor, but he was anxious about the other Assisians with him—it is said that Francis had his remarkable experience with the Leper. The experience *did* occur in his life, but probably *after* Francis returned to Assisi, enriched by his experience in Rome.[49]

One day, Francis was riding down the road that led past the leper hospital, deeply absorbed as usual in his amorphous thoughts. His horse reared up suddenly. "To Francis' horror," a leper stood in the middle of the road, immobile, just staring at him. The leper did not move. His gaze was described as penetrating.

"An instant that seemed an eternity passed. Slowly Francis dismounted, went to the man, and took his hand. It was a poor emaciated hand, bloodstained, twisted, inert and cold like that of a corpse. He put a mite of charity in it, pressed it, carried it to his lips. And suddenly, as he kissed the lacerated flesh of the creature who was the most abject, the most hated, the most scorned of all human beings, he

---

48 Cristiani, 33–34.

49 The recounting of Francis' dramatic experience with the leper has Francis on horseback when they meet. When he made his pilgrimage to Rome and back, Francis was on foot.

was flooded with a wave of emotion, one that shut out everything around him, one that he would remember even on his death bed.

"As the leper withdrew his hand, Francis raised his head to look at him again. He was no longer there."[50]

At the end of his life, Francis dictated several impassioned personal statements as part of his *Testament*. He recorded what the exact turning point for him was in the extraordinary change of his

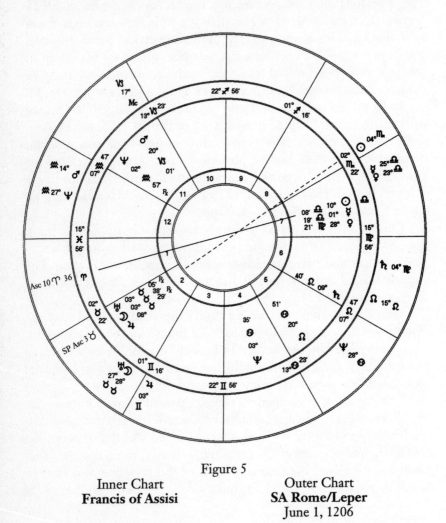

Figure 5

Inner Chart
Francis of Assisi

Outer Chart
SA Rome/Leper
June 1, 1206

50 All histories, but especially Fortini, 211. We must note that St. Bonaventure thought that the leper was Christ himself.

identity and the path of his life. He said: "This is how God inspired me, Brother Francis, to embark upon a life of penance. When I was in sin, the sight of lepers nauseated me beyond measure; but then God himself led me into their company, and I had pity on them. When I had once become acquainted with them, what had previously nauseated me became a source of spiritual and physical consolation for me."[51]

This life-significant experience quite possibly took place on October 7 or 8, 1206. Nineteen days earlier, on September 18, 1206, a Lunar Eclipse of great importance within Francis' horoscope took place. It is shown here as Figure 6 (page 110).

The Eclipse occurred at 2 Libra, *with Neptune conjunct the Moon and opposed the Sun conjuncted by Mercury*, the axis squared broadly by Jupiter. This Eclipse is within orb of the Aries Point, especially with the Mercury and Neptune components lagging just over the sign line in Virgo/Pisces. The strongly magnified Eclipse axis is square the Ascendant at Assisi, *and falls directly upon Francis' Mercury at 1 Libra 19, squared by his Pluto at 3 Cancer.*

This emphasizes Francis' mental process, his need to know how to relate to his world. This Eclipse emphasis invites new ideas, new vision. Normally, such an eclipse construct waits for a transit trigger to be manifested in life experience: this occurred on October 7, when transiting Mercury, having just made its station turning Direct at 2 Libra, was precisely upon the Eclipse position axis and upon Francis' own Mercury. Additionally, on that day, transiting Mars and Pluto were exactly upon his Saturn, ruler of the 11th.

The final step in Francis' complete dedication to Jesus and his knowing what Jesus meant for him to do took place in the tiny church of San Damiano, a third-century center for Assisi's earliest Christians and a place of many reputed miracles.[52]

---

51 Fortini, 212. Additionally: we can say that the saintliness of Francis was measured in great part by his ability to love those who were by nature, by convention, by circumstance unlovable.

52 "By the grace of God, there were many miracles in that place. Those possessed by demons who begged for peace were liberated. Lepers were rid of their terrible sores. Farmers who prayed for the salvation of their crops from the threat of storm saw the cloud melt away." Fortini, 214.

The San Damiano Chapel could have identified itself some hundreds of years later with the bishop St. Damiano who died in Pavia in 715, St. Peter Damian who was born in Ravenna in 1007 and died in 1072 in Faenza, or—least likely—Cosmas and Damian, brothers martyred early in church history. In modern times, Father Damien de Veuster (1840–1889) was a Belgian Roman Catholic missionary working with lepers on the Hawaiian Island of Molokai.

Early in October 1206, so very probably on the 14th—still within the scope of the recent Lunar Eclipse and the leper experience—Francis entered the abandoned church to pray. It was in great ruin; no lamp burned before the altar; the walls were cracked and crumbling; the beams were worm-eaten, the paintings faded; grass and weeds invaded the sanctuary. Yet a painted, wooden, Byzantine image of the Crucified Lord that hung by the altar had survived all the decay: "an image of goodness and

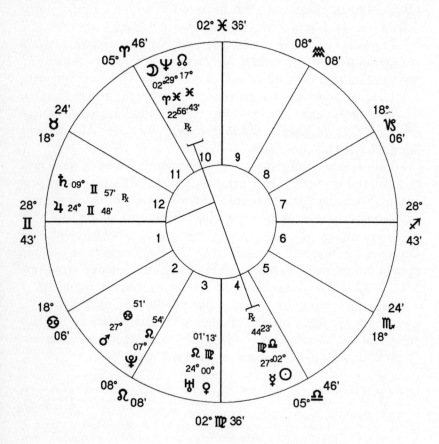

Figure 6
Lunar Eclipse
Sept. 18, 1206, 10:01 P.M. LMT
Assisi, Italy
12E37   43N04
Placidus Houses

suffering, expressing with extraordinary vividness both martyrdom and love."[53]

Francis asked again for guidance, surely remembering his vision and the instruction in Spoleto just a few months before. As all biographers report, the gaze of Jesus from the cross was suddenly fixed upon Francis. The eyes became animated, and there was a whispered voice, like a sigh: "Francis, go and repair my house, which, as you see, is falling into ruin." This instruction was repeated three times.

Francis was frightened. He rushed to the old priest who had custody of the crumbling chapel and gave him all the money he had and then went as fast as he could into Assisi to begin his mission of rebuilding San Damiano.

Figure 7 (page 112) is the Tertiary Progression for October 14, 1206, the highly probable date of Francis' completed conversion. Tertiary measurements are extremely birth-time sensitive: one year of life equates to one lunar month after birth. Here, for Francis, we see his TP Moon—the most critical Tertiary measure—on this day precisely opposed his extraordinarily focalized Neptune. At the same time, TP Jupiter was squaring Francis' Ascendant axis, and transiting Jupiter had just crossed Francis' fourth cusp.

Francis ran to his father's shop, gathered up the most expensive fabrics he could and raced to a nearby town where he wasn't known, and there he sold the wares. He returned to Assisi with the money and turned it over to the priest of San Damiano. He was given refuge in this little church. Francis was now an "oblate," a layman living under protection of the Church, and his mission was launched.

When Bernardone learned what Francis had done, he was outraged. The town came abuzz with gossip about the renegade son. Bernardo thought "he must have been taking poppy juice or maybe dogs' brain and hemlock juice. Nothing but drugs could have made him change like this, all that craze for glory gone. Now he won't have anything to do with that sort of thing ... Obviously, he is possessed by a demon."[54]

---

53 This cross was later preserved for seven hundred years by the Poor Clares [female Franciscan followers under the direction of St. Clare, as we shall see] inside the cloistered monastery of St. Giorgio in Assisi. It is there today on view for the public.

54 Fortini, 218. Note the Neptune imagery.

Francis had to hide from his father, beyond the little church. Four months later, in March 1207, Francis came out of hiding to confront his father. The SP Moon was now opposed his Sun.[55]

Townspeople could not believe the transformation. He was drawn and pale, and his clothes were in shreds. He appeared deranged. This was the shining youth who was to be a great prince,

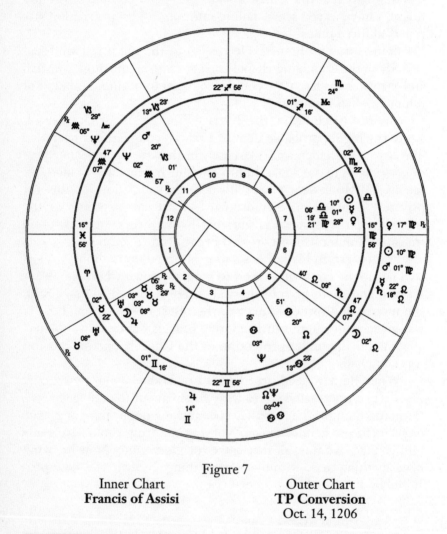

Figure 7

Inner Chart	Outer Chart
Francis of Assisi	**TP Conversion**
	Oct. 14, 1206

---

55 See Figure 4 (page 106): the SP Moon is at 13 Pisces in March 1205. In March 1207, two years later (24–26 months/degrees average) its position will be close to 39 Pisces or 9 Aries, opposite the Sun.

a knight in the Crusades, the lover of the most beautiful woman in the world? He was jeered and pelted with garbage and mud. He was stoned. "The violence that the statutes permitted the people to use against lepers were turned against the madman who had allied himself with lepers in a a monstrous familiarity." His father seized him and imprisoned Francis in his house, underground, in chains.[56]

Bernardone could not prevail upon the converted Francis to return to his sensibilities. The father left on one of his trade trips, and Pica, Francis' ever loving, faithful, and pious mother freed him. Francis left his home never to return again.

Bernardone returned from his trip and brought criminal charges against Francis (rebellion and squandering, Uranus). The harshest punishment could be banishment, even excommunication. Francis was ordered to stand before the bishop's court in the bishop's palace, in the piazza of Santa Maria Maggiore. It was February 24, 1207. The bishop was in his finery, the people were agape at Francis' dreadful appearance. The bells rang to start proceedings.

Figure 8 (page 114) is the Tertiary Progressed chart for the moment the trial began; it has advanced from the chart of Francis' conversion (Figure 7, page 112) to bring the Sun to conjunction with the seventh cusp, the Ascendant to conjunction with natal Neptune, and most importantly the Moon to exact conjunction with Mercury, that degree area so powerfully excited just five months earlier by the Lunar Eclipse. These measurements clearly say that this is the turning point of Francis' freedom, his becoming his own man, as it were, someone clearly of his own mind, and it again reinforces the validity of the birth year, date, and time we have created for Francis.

The bishop demanded that Francis return the monies to his father, adding that the church would be restored in other ways.

Francis replied, "Lord Bishop, not only this money that I took from him do I wish to restore to him, with all good will, but even the clothes that he has given me." Francis stunned the gathering with his reply; he ran into a room off the piazza and, before anyone could react, he reappeared naked with his tattered body-cloth bundled in front of him. "It was his great act of renunciation that freed him from all servitude to earthly things."[57]

---

56 All histories; see Fortini, 219–221.
57 Fortini, 228–229.

The Path To Evangelism

Francis worked hard and long begging for stones to rebuild San Damiano. Many people laughed at him, and many had pity. His work throughout two years restored three churches. When work on the third one, the little tenth-century chapel at Porziuncola (also Portiuncula), was finished, another life-changing illumination occurred for Francis, establishing the formal Order and Rule for his mission.

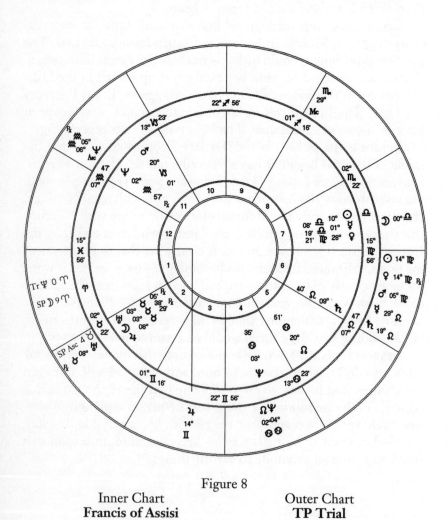

Figure 8

Inner Chart
Francis of Assisi

Outer Chart
TP Trial
Feb. 24, 1207

It was two years to the day from the renunciation of his father and all worldly goods: the feast of St. Matthew, February 24, 1209. Francis was attending Mass in the early morning. The celebrant read from Matthew 10:7–14:

> As you go, proclaim the good news, "The kingdom of heaven has come near." Cure the sick, raise the dead, cleanse the lepers, cast out demons. You received without payment; give without payment. Take no gold, or silver, or copper in your belts, no bag for your journey, or two tunics, or sandals, or a staff; for laborers deserve their good. Whatever town or village you enter, find out who in it is worthy, and stay there until you leave. As you enter the house, greet it. If the house is worthy, let your peace come upon it; but if it is not worthy, let your peace return to you. If anyone will not welcome you or listen to your words, shake off the dust from your feet as you leave that house or town.[58]

Francis listened in astonishment. These were the instructions Christ had given to his disciples on the eve of their going out to preach to the world. Here in the words of Christ were *his* instructions as well, and Francis resolved to obey every letter of their meaning. He discarded his shoes and his stick, and he changed his belt for a cord.

These instructions became the first Rule of the Order of the Friars Minor. Their uniform was now set. Francis was established before God and the world. He indeed had become a knight, and he would win souls for his Lord.

It is simply astonishing to check the Lunar Eclipse before this moment of inspiration and conviction, the Eclipse that presaged this additional focus of mission in Francis' life. Figure 9 (page 116) shows this eclipse of January 22, 1209, thirty-three days before the feast of St. Matthew. Pluto—perspective, empowerment—is precisely conjunct the Eclipse axis, and so is Venus with the Sun in Aquarius. This massive statement falls *on Francis' Saturn, within his awesome T-Square.*

We can see as well that Mars in the Eclipse chart is precisely conjunct Francis' Sun: further empowerment. The Ascendant-Descendant axis of the Eclipse chart at Assisi is congruent with Francis' natal Ascendant. The chart's close Saturn-Neptune square

---

58 HarperCollins Study Bible, New Revised Standard Version.

relates to Francis as well through his Mercury at 1 Libra. This astrology is undeniably prophetic.

In even further corroboration of this time, Figure 10 (page 117) shows the Secondary Progressions for the day of this solidifying inspiration: SA-SP MC is precisely conjunct Francis' Mars, his SA-SP Sun is opposed his Jupiter, ruler of the 9th and 10th; the SP Ascendant is precisely conjunct natal Jupiter; and, finally, SP Moon is exactly conjunct natal Uranus-Moon. Again, we have verification of Francis' birth year, date, and time.

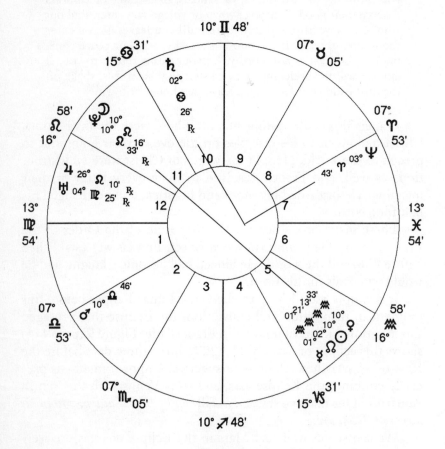

Figure 9
Lunar Eclipse
Jan. 22, 1209, 8:01 P.M. LMT
Assisi, Italy
12E37   43N04
Placidus Houses

The Tertiary Progressions for that very day (not shown) are also astounding: the TP MC is exactly conjunct the natal MC we have captured for Francis, and the TP Ascendant has returned to its natal position as well! And if the Mass that morning had started at 6:30 or 7:00 (just after dawn), transiting Moon and Mars at 10 Libra would be exactly conjunct Francis' Sun, with transiting Pluto in 9 Leo 29, precisely conjunct his Saturn.

Astrology speaks eloquently of awareness, purpose, and, indeed, miracles as well.

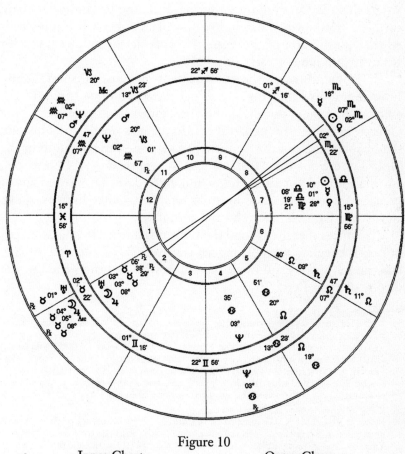

Figure 10

Inner Chart
Francis of Assisi

Outer Chart
SP Evangelism
Feb. 24, 1209

The Growing Order — Pope Innocent III

Several followers joined the Friars Minor. The first one is nameless to history but the second, ironically, was named Bernardo, as was Francis' estranged father (Bernardone, "big Bernard"). The small group begged and suffered together. Francis continued to set a daunting example of self-mortification, humility, and prayer. The Knights of Lady Poverty were most solicitous of one another, suffering hunger and discomfort almost beyond imagining. More and more people took them seriously. The totality of their poverty and humiliation went beyond derangement: it *had* to be sincere, genuine ... inspired.

Francis had written into a formal Rule the teachings he heard through Matthew that day in Porziuncola. He knew his Rule needed the approbation of the Pope. He and eleven followers left for Rome in late June or early July 1210.[59]

In Rome, through the endorsement of Assisi's Bishop Guido, Francis and his Friars quickly gained access to Pope Innocent III, who was the most powerful and strategically skilled leader of the Church in the entire medieval era. Innocent's major goals beyond the establishment of the political papacy were the liberation of the Holy Land from the Moslems and the repression of heresy, i.e., anyone who did not accept Jesus, and, indeed, the lay movements of preachers like Francis and his followers who, unlike Francis, spoke against the Church hierarchy and authority.[60]

"So it was that they found themselves facing each other, the fool of Assisi, kneeling with his ragged companions on the rich mosaic, and the most powerful of all the popes who had succeeded to the throne of Saint Peter."[61]

---

59 In Oxford, there is strong critical observation about Francis: "It is hard to imagine any more improbable founder of an order, for Francis had a talent for disorganization and was reluctant to produce a rule." These "Rules" were very important: they qualified the Order for Church approval and they guided behavior of the constituents of the Order. Francis' first Rule from the Gospel of Matthew was simple but bureaucratically crude. A second Rule followed when the Order grew larger, but it was deemed too strict and was never used. A final Rule would be approved by Pope Honorius III in 1223, three years before Francis' death.

60 Innocent III (c. 1161–1216), installed 1198. Under his reign, the papacy reached the peak of its power and influence. He forced King John of England to become his vassal and had Emperor Otto of Germany deposed in favor of Frederick II. He initiated the Crusade of 1202 and supported the Crusade of 1208. He presided over the fourth Lateran Council (1215) and planned the fifth Crusade, the culmination of the medieval papacy.

61 Fortini, 294.

The date of the meeting was probably August 17, 1210, judging from the astrology of that time: TP Moon was precisely on the fourth cusp, transiting Jupiter was precisely conjunct Francis' Mercury, and transiting Mars at 3 Leo was precisely square Uranus-Moon. One other measurement was to become a key to Francis' victory in Rome: just one month before his twenty-ninth birthday, *natal Pluto at 3 Cancer 35 had arced to exact opposition with Francis' "signature" Neptune.* Something supernatural—as had been with him for sometime—could inspire his mission once again.

With greatest poise and utter humility, Francis spoke to the Pope of his mission and his Rule of sacrifice and poverty. The Pope replied that he thought the life that Francis and his penitents proposed to follow was too rigid and harsh. He did not doubt their fortitude, but "would those who came after them have the same ardor?"

Francis replied at once "that ability to make a total renunciation comes as a gift from Jesus Christ."[62]

The discussion took clever semantic turns to each side in turn and was suspended in a polite stand-off. The Pope and Francis agreed to pray for guidance and meet again, and that night, the supernatural did occur once more: the Pope had a dream [some sources say "vision"]. He found himself in a grand Basilica with an array of relics that encompassed all of Christian history. A great rumble thundered through the temple. The pillars and columns were teetering, they were cracking and about to collapse. He closed his eyes and heard the terrible noise of crashing. But when he reopened his eyes, he saw that all had been saved, that a "gigantic man" had supported the Basilica on one shoulder alone. He saw that this man was the beggar of Assisi.[63]

With his advisors, the Pope anchored the argument that if Francis and his followers *were* prohibited to live according to the Gospels—to conform to the life of Jesus—it would be a vilification of Jesus who inspired the Gospels. The Pope then listened to Francis' eloquence and studied his countenance. He saw clearly the man of his vision. He rose, and turning to the cardinals surrounding

---

62 All histories. See Fortini, 297; Cristiani, 55; Celano, I, #32–33.
63 The same vision has been found in the records relating to the approbations of the Rule of Saint Dominic (of Spain), an Order parallel and contemporaneous with Francis' Friars Minor. Most histories credit the vision to the Pope's dealings with Francis. The astrology suggests that this is so as well.

them, said solemnly, "this is truly the man who, with example and doctrine, will uphold the church of Christ."

Francis and the Friars Minor brothers had their Rule approved and were granted the privilege of preaching. The Pope even promised his help into the future.

Clare: The Feminine Among the Friars

Throughout history, women have had great difficulty getting close to God: they lived under the crude criticism of Eve, the unalterable edict that Church clergy must be male, and a cultural positioning away from the benefits of education. The exceptions who transcended the traditional role expectations of women stand out in history.

One of these is Clare [Chiara], born of a noble family living just outside Assisi. The family was extremely religious, Clare's mother having made the grand and dangerous Pilgrimage to Jerusalem.[64]

All histories state emphatically that Clare was beautiful, opulent, and dramatically self-aware. Her courageous, pious, noble mother worked constantly to arrange a proper marriage for Clare to extend the noble family. Clare resisted adamantly.[65]

Clare had been drawn to the "crazy man," Francis, "whom the street boys attacked with mud and stones. His remarkable humility fascinated her more than any great deed in war or in knightly tournaments." A secret meeting was arranged between this daughter of the powerful feudal lord of San Rufino and the mortified, humble Francis.

Here was the grand and beautiful damsel, ideal for the earlier Francis, the Knight of Assisi. That thought must have gone through Francis' mind during his year of secret indoctrination

---

64 The trip to the Holy Land began with the crossing of the Mediterranean from the ports in southern Italy to Damietta on the Egypt coast, just East of Alexandria and North of (modern) Cairo. Then there was the two-week trek to the desert of the Sinai peninsula and then the two-week crossing of the sands, guided by nomadic, dangerous Arabs, to the Gaza region in southwest Judea. Thirst, wild animals, and robber bands threatened constantly. Then there was the two-week journey 250 miles north-northeast through Judea to Jerusalem.

A second route was from ports on the south-southeast coast of Italy, in the Apulia region, maintained by the Crusaders; across the Adriatic to Constantinople (Istanbul) and then across Greece and down through Turkey, a very long, rough overland way as well.

65 Fortini, 337.

meetings with Clare. Clare decided to dedicate her life to the way of Francis; Francis was freeing the way a woman could do this.[66]

On Palm Sunday, March 27, 1211,[67] Clare wore "her richest clothes and all her jewels, like a bride," to the public church service in the piazza. This was the first Palm Sunday celebration after the ten years of war with Perugia. "It was a glorious, happy morning, a morning of exultation and adoration."

As the faithful walked to the altar to receive the symbolic olive branches, Clare remained in her seat—undoubtedly creating a commanding spectacle for all. Bishop Guido—the friend of Francis—added to the drama: he carried the last olive branch into the congregation and solemnly gave it to Clare, "as if this were a part of the rite."

Clare remained alone in the piazza and in a trance-state most of the day. At dark, she found her way to the tiny chapel at Porziuncola. She went to the altar and, one by one, she took off her jewels, the ornaments of the life she was leaving behind her. She loosened her golden hair and it was cut off, and she received from Francis' own hands the poor habit of a Friar Minor. She received honor from the assembled "ragged knights" and, with Francis, went on foot two miles to the Benedictine Monastery of San Paulo delle Ancelle di Dio, into the dark of her new world, to lead the eventual Order of the "Poor Clares," women living the life of Christ.[68]

Figure 11 (page 123) is the horoscope for Clare's birth, which I have *rectified* to 12:00 noon. There is no escaping this golden hour: her noble birth and dramatic charisma (Sun-Venus conjunction in Aquarius in the 10th, Mars-Neptune exact conjunction opposed the *Moon in Leo* also in the parental axis, the opposition axis squared by the Ascendant); her beauty (Venus ruler of the Ascendant conjunct

---

66 Psychoanalyst Nitzah Yarom, in her Freudian study of Francis (see Bibliography), suggests that the spiritual fire that engulfed Clare and Francis (according to the accounts of The Three Brothers) was indeed sexual. Francis knew a scandal would develop if a woman were in the Order. He cloistered Clare in a series of nunneries, keeping her from the mission of serving the poor as he did. This was his denial of sexuality once again, and/yet (in my opinion) keeping his trophy near. Clare and Francis were close all his life. See Yarom, 39.

　　Thomas of Celano (I, #18) points out several times in his description of Clare her chastity, her virginity, and aligns those virtues with Francis' virginity as well. The older historians make a great deal of this observation.

67 A traditional chronology dates this conversion and acceptance event in the year 1212, but recent research establishes the year as 1211. See Cristiani, 66; Fortini, 338, note f. Astrologically, the year 1211 is overwhelmingly confirmed, see text and chart.

the Sun and Midheaven); and the pronouncedly obvious capacity to change her way of life from the conventional to the avant garde, from noble heritage to fringe rebellion (always the case in the contact between Saturn and Uranus, here in opposition, with Uranus ruling the Midheaven); the ego presence and individualistic reward needs (Moon in Leo and Jupiter in Aries); her adamant refusal (obstinate resolve, Fixed Angles) to consider marriage, but to pursue a new way to relate to the world, a new life perspective (Pluto, ruler of the 7th, is peregrine); and her contrapuntal mindset allied with a higher way of giving love (Mercury retrograde in the 9th, ruling the 5th House of love given, also peregrine).

The time test of Clare's horoscope confirms date and time conclusively: at her conversion at age eighteen, SA Pluto=MC and SA Asc=Uranus; SA Sun=Neptune; and, during her study period with Francis, the Secondary Progressed Moon at 19 Aries was squaring her natal Pluto; and *Tertiary* Moon at 16 Cancer was *exactly* conjunct natal Pluto on the day of her conversion, the TP Sun was *precisely* opposed her Jupiter, and the TP MC was at 00 Libra, conjunct the "public" Aries Point axis.

Clare was consecrated an Abbess by act of the Lateran Council in November 1215 (discussed later): at that time, the transiting Saturn-Uranus conjunction in 5 Libra was precisely opposed Clare's Jupiter in Aries, i.e., her need for ego recognition, her individualistic religiousness.

Clare would be canonized in 1255.

Clare is important in our appreciation of Francis as a manifestation of his *anima*, that part of him sensitive to things feminine, to nurturing, caring, archetypal loving. This Jungian concept (with the parallel *animus* in women, their awareness of things masculine) explains the significance of Clare's pleasure in calling herself the "little plant of her Holy Father, Francis."[69] She considered him her "nurse," because "from him she had drunk sweet milk at the time she had been reborn to life."

---

68 The same arguments about the harshness of the life style that Pope Innocent III gave to Francis were registered by the Church with Clare. Her argument was as eloquent as Francis' had been: "Holy Father, release me from my sins, but not from the obligation to follow our Lord Jesus Christ!"

At Francis' canonization ceremony in 1228, two years after his death, Pope Gregory IX acknowledged Clare's personal privilege to follow the rigorous Rule but made it an obligation for the Poor Clares—under pain of excommunication—to accept the legacies and gifts made to them, and forbade them to give any of them away. Christiani, 73.

Clare had a most telling dream, reported by her companion, Sister Filippa: She brought to Francis a basin of hot water and a linen towel to dry his hands. She was happy in her submission and abasement, this humbling of herself for love. "And when she had come up to Saint Francis, he bared his breast and said to the virgin Clare: 'Come, take and drink.' And when she had done so, the Saint admonished her to drink again; and that which she drank was so sweet and delightful that she could in no way describe it. When she

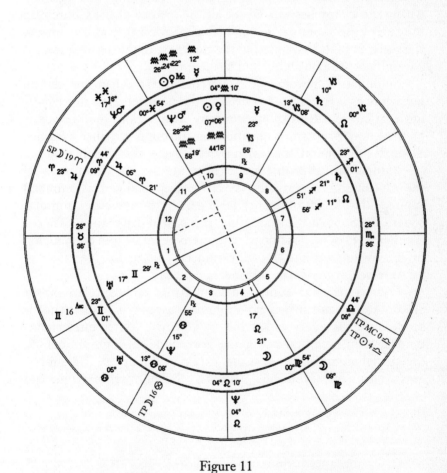

Figure 11

Inner Chart	Outer Chart
St. Clare	**SA Conversion**
Jan. 20, 1193, 12:00 P.M. LMT	Mar. 27, 1211
Assisi, Italy	
12E37 43N04	

had finished, the nipple remained between the lips of the blessed Clare, and taking in her hand that which remained in her mouth, it seemed to her of such pure and shining gold that she could see in it her own reflection, as in a mirror.'"

Psychological studies attest to the thin line between religiousness and sexuality, the ecstatic feelings, the idealized goals, the dynamics of relationship that include identification, projection, conversion, and most importantly, submission. Nuns are "married" to Jesus; all Orders wore wedding rings.[70] The sexual underground within the clergy has existed for all the history of the Church. In the face of the unnatural demand of celibacy for men and women in the service of God, conquering the weakness of the flesh represents a formidable responsibility and challenge.

Sublimation becomes the key defense mechanism: certain behaviors to serve one set of needs are renounced for a supposedly more noble self-dedication elsewhere. In religion, sublimation is part of the process of purification through sacrifice. Ideally, through sublimation, the sexual hysteric becomes sexually frigid.

Francis' sexual profile was clearly intense: his Moon, ruler of the 5th (love given, sexuality) is exactly conjoined with Uranus and Jupiter; Pluto, ruler of the 8th (also part of the sexuality profile) is square the Sun. At the same time, this sexual drive was poised for another level of management: with the powerful triple conjunction in Taurus squaring the "mortification axis" of Saturn-Neptune, *we see repression, renunciation, sacrifice, sublimation.*[71]

Francis' Mars is exalted in Capricorn—adding to its power symbolically—and makes no Ptolemaic aspect in Francis' horoscope (perhaps a very wide trine with Venus). Mars must be contended with; it can take over the horoscope through militarism, dictatorial administration, sexual excess. While these Mars energies are ripe for dominance, with the scheme of self-sacrifice and

---

69 In Latin, the words are beautiful: *Parva plantula sancti patris Francisci*. Fortini, 357.

70 St. Bernard (1090–1153, two generations before Francis) was a French abbot (Cistercian) and preacher of great fame and prestige. He was close to popes and King Louis VII and organized support for the Second Crusade. He introduced the concept of erotic unity with Christ, the spiritual marriage through love, into Christian mysticism. See Yarom, 23.

71 The historian John Holland Smith, writes, 89: "Chiara [Clare] found Francis irresistible ... Having impressionable girls fall in love with them is one of the earliest perils that would-be mystics and ascetics have to learn to deal with. The indications are that Francis nearly failed this test. There are hints and stories enough in the *Lives* [Celano] and the *Mirror of Perfection* [*Speculum Perfectionis S. Francisci*, ed. Sabatier, Paris, 1898] to show that he always found celibacy difficult.

ecstatic mysticism, they are also ready for sublimation. These were the energies that Francis had to deal with in giving up his dreams of knighthood and his libertine ways. Throughout his life, the symbolism of Mars seems to disappear in his horoscope and in his life, except in his preoccupation with fire (as we shall see).

In any extreme case like this (like *these*, including Clare, and indeed, the other Friars and Poor Clares), one asks where the energy goes, how well managed is it in its transferral to something non-libidinal.

It is obvious—as psychologist Nitza Yarom points out—that sexuality for Francis (and most of the other stigmatics who followed through the centuries) was turned into "preoccupation with the body, by the use of the defense mechanism of conversion."[72] Chronic weakness or illness is very much part of the stigmatic's life profile as we shall see, and Francis himself observed that from the day of his conversion on he was continuously sick.[73] The stigmata, while a complete identification with the suffering of Christ, was also a total identification with the Highest Love and, it follows, the ultimate—depleting and exhausting—fulfillment of body-mind-spirit outreach.

It is also obvious in Francis' life that his sense of aesthetics, creativity, and love of beauty—the Venus focus through Libra and Taurus—reinforced by contrast by his revulsion initially felt for and long remembered about lepers, were also clear manifestations of his very strong *anima*. Jung averred that the *anima* projection was not an invention of the conscious mind but was a spontaneous product of the unconscious.[74]

Francis could project all this upon Clare, spontaneously, instinctively, while her cloistered position helped his sublimation process do its work. Symbolically then, the victory over the body was won once again.

Figure 12 (page 126) shows the synastry between Francis and Clare. Most dramatically, we see her Sun-Venus-MC cluster conjunct Francis' all-pervasive Neptune, the fulcrum of his vision, idealization, sacrifice, and sublimation. Clare's Jupiter is opposed Francis' Sun-Mercury. Her Ascendant trines his Venus and her

---

72 Yarom, 60.
73 Green, 84.
74 Campbell—Ed., 151.

Moon trines his Midheaven. Finally, her Uranus squares his Ascendant and her Saturn crowns his Midheaven.

This is an extraordinary interrelationship of identities. Each of these individuals, in the rarified realm of developing sainthood, needed the other to fulfill the coupling of man and woman in the service and love of God.

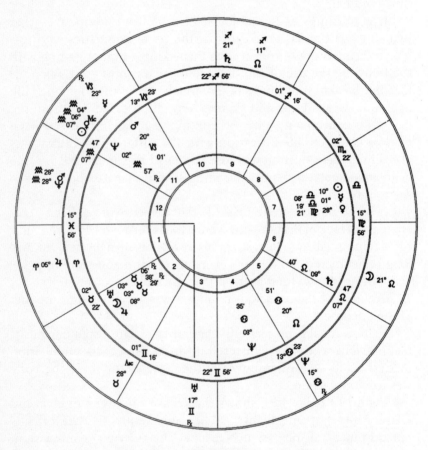

Figure 12

Inner Chart	Outer Chart
Francis of Assisi	**St. Clare**
Sept. 26, 1181, 4:41 P.M. LMT	Jan. 20, 1193, 12:00 P.M. LMT
Assisi, Italy	Assisi, Italy
12E37 43N04	12E37 43N04

Placidus Houses

Growth of the Order — The Lateran Council

The number of brothers following Francis continued to grow rapidly. Groups of brothers traveled and preached in many different areas and began to take stations in other countries. Organization and quality control of the mission became important concerns. A date for convening was established for the Order, to take place every Pentecost—to celebrate the gathering together of the Apostles after Christ's Death and Ascension—at the Chapel of Porziuncola. This schedule was difficult to keep, but the brothers did convene in 1212, 1214, 1217, 1219, and 1221.[75]

The main thrust of the Franciscan mission became to go beyond Italy to preach to the infidels. This is what Innocent III wanted as well. The entire Christian world was aghast at the Saracen takeover of the Holy Land.[76]

Francis planned a mission to the Middle East, but did not get out of the harbor. He tried a second time, setting sail for Damascus, only to have a storm cast his ship ashore in Slovenia. He stowed away on a ship back to Italy and then set off for Spain. Of this trip, we do not know any further details and can only assume that this journey was a failure also. Although the Order was growing very quickly, this time must have been most frustrating for Francis personally, and, indeed, we can assume that the aborting of his trips abroad was assimilated as even deeper humiliation, keeping him in his place, as it were.

---

75 By 1282, fifty-six years after Francis death, the Order's growth had been so rapid that it maintained 1,583 houses in Europe. Having a "house," of course, was against Francis' earliest Rule which allowed no safety, no stronghold, no cloister, no possessions, no privileges, i.e., those chains to the affairs of the world. His Order was to be defenseless and exposed. It is remarked in many realistic studies of his life that, toward the end of his days, Francis did lose control of the Order organizationally. Cunningham, 15, and others.

76 Saracen was the name most popularly used in the thirteenth century to describe the Moslems, "the nomadic people of the deserts between Syria and Egypt." However, this is a very broad and imprecise label of geography. The Moslems were centralized in Constantinople (Istanbul) and North Africa. The takeover of Jerusalem was accomplished in 638 by the Moslem conqueror 'Umar (in power 634–644), second successor of Muhammad. There was nothing on the Temple site at the takeover (since Vespasian had overthrown Jerusalem, July 1, 70, and razed Herod's expansion of the rebuilt remains (by Zerubbabel, c. 530 B.C.) of Solomon's original Temple, c. 1000 B.C.). By the early thirteenth century, some six mosques had been built and rebuilt on the Temple Mount. The Crusades were planned repeatedly throughout Europe to attack and recover for the Christians this holy place in Jerusalem. The Dome of the Rock, one of Islam's holiest shrines built over the rock from which Muhammad ascended to heaven, still dominates Jerusalem.

At this time, Francis was living through his "Saturn Return," transiting Saturn's return to its birth position, which usually "announces" itself some six months before exactness, and with retrogradation periods can be extended over one and one-half years. For Francis, the Return was shorter, June–December 1211. But, at the same time, he absorbed Tr Uranus conjunct his 7th cusp, certainly a get-up-and-get-moving aspect, a new-look-for-the-Order pressure from mid-1211 to mid-1212; and most importantly, *Tr Neptune was opposed his Sun from June 1210 through the middle of 1212*, a protracted period of frustration, delay, bewilderment. Immediately after the Saturn Return, Tr Saturn pressed upon the seventh cusp from mid-1213 through mid-1214, and his tactical frustrations cleared up gradually as Neptune eased away.

There is a beautiful, miraculous aspect to this time during Francis' mission that has been portrayed countless, countless times throughout history and religious art: Francis' sermons to the birds. This miracle certainly fits the relation between transiting Neptune and the Sun at this time, and the beautiful words of Thomas of Celano are most fitting to describe it:

> While many were joining the brothers, as we said, the most blessed father Francis was making a trip through the Spoleto valley. He came to a certain place near Bevagna where a very great number of birds of various kinds had congregated, namely, doves, crows, and some others popularly called daws. When the most blessed servant of God, Francis, saw them, being a man of very great fervor and great tenderness toward lower and irrational creatures, he left his companions in the road and ran eagerly toward the birds.

> When he was close enough to them, seeing that they were waiting expectantly for him, he greeted them in his usual way. But, not a little surprised that the birds did not rise in flight, as they usually do, he was filled with great joy and humbly begged them to listen to the word of God. Among the many things he spoke to them were these words that he added: "My brothers, birds, you should praise your Creator very much and always love him; he gave you feathers to clothe you, wings so that you can fly, and whatever else was necessary for you. God made you noble among his creatures, and he gave you a home in the purity of the air; though you neither sow nor reap, he nevertheless protects and governs you without any solicitude on your part."

At these words, as Francis himself used to say and those too who were with him, the birds, rejoicing in a wonderful way according to their nature, began to stretch their mouths and gaze at him. And Francis, *passing through their midst, went on his way* and returned, touched their heads and bodies with his tunic. finally he blessed them, and then, after he had made the sign of the cross over them, he gave them permission to fly away to some other place.[77]

Characteristically, out of this beautiful moment, Francis began to blame himself for negligence in not having preached to the birds before, seeing that they had listened to the word of God with such great reverence. And, Celano continues, that, from that day on, Francis solicitously admonished all birds, all animals and reptiles, "and even creatures that have no feeling," to praise and love their Creator. Another vignette:

When he came one day to a city called Alviano to preach the word of God, he went up *to a higher place* so that he could be seen by all and he began to ask for silence. But when all the people had fallen silent and were standing reverently at attention, a flock of swallows, chattering and making a loud noise, were building nests in that same place. Since the blessed Francis could not be heard by the people over the chattering of the birds, he spoke to them saying: "My sisters, swallows, it is now time for me to speak, for you have already spoken enough. Listen to the word of the Lord and be silent and quiet until the word of the Lord is finished." And those little birds, to the astonishment and wonder of the people standing by, immediately fell silent, and they did not move from that place until the sermon was finished.

When these men therefore saw this miracle, they were filled with the greatest admiration and said: "Truly this man is a saint and a friend of the Most High.' And they hastened with the greatest devotion to at least touch his clothing, *praising and blessing God.*

With the Saturn Return, it appears that Francis' reception by the public calmed down and matured significantly: miracles were easy, accepted, and persuasive;[78] humiliation was omnipresent but

---

77 Celano, I, #58–59.

78 Miracles abound in the life of Francis. *The Little Flowers of St. Francis* (I Fioretti) and other writings compiled by followers of Francis and early chroniclers in the early fourteenth century capture scores of miracles in a childlike simplicity that charms the heart. These legends and facts embody the Franciscan spirit delightfully and movingly.

compellingly refined; the public throughout Italy perceived Francis' poignant sincerity, which fit his ever-growing reputation as a saint among men, and Francis exhibited even more confidence in his ability to touch the people. Celano reports: "Francis' popularity [had now] reached a point where those who no more than touched his garment counted themselves lucky. When he entered any city, the clergy rejoiced, the bells were rung, the men were filled with happiness, the women rejoiced together, the children clapped their hands; and often, taking branches from the trees, they went to meet him singing."

Finally, things were as they were to be. And Rome helped once again.

Four hundred bishops and eight hundred abbots, representatives of the Emperor of Germany (and the Holy Roman Empire), the Latin Emperor of Constantinople, the Kings of France, England, Hungary, Jerusalem, Cyprus, Aragon, and many Lombard city-states were all called together in April by Pope Innocent III to meet on November 11, 1215 at the Lateran Basilica in Rome.[79]

The business before the Council was deeply serious: organizing the Fifth Crusade, in the light of their repeated failure; then, formulation of dogma to conceptualize more clearly the Holy Trinity.[80]

There was the doctrinal problem of transubstantiation [the Eucharistic miracle of the body and blood of Christ], the horrific Albigensian conquests [Inquisitorial attack upon the anti-papist Cathars in France and Spain], and the clean-up necessary in the present-day administration of the Church, focusing on sexual transgressions, pomp, and material luxury.[81]

And then there was Francis and his two Orders, making the Church face up to Christ's example.

---

79 Cristiani, 95. The Lateran Basilica of our Savior is also named the Basilica of St. John the Baptist, and we can not help but recall Francis' original name, in honor of this saint. The Basilica was then the Pope's Cathedral Church. St. Peter's Basilica was first constructed by Constantine beginning c. 332 (See Grant, 196), and St. Peter's Cathedral as we know it today (Michelangelo's remedial plans and dome) was not in place until 1546.

80 "The Father engenders the Son, the son becomes incarnate, and the Holy Spirit proceeds from the Father and the Son." The problem is with "Father and the Son [filioque]," and this problem still divides East and West within Christendom. See Green, 167.

81 Innocent III died in the next year, in 1216. The French bishop Jacques De Vitry, visiting Perugia when the Pope's body was lying in state there, recorded that the body was stripped of its robes and jewels by thieves who broke into the church. This dramatically portrays the larceny of the times. Stock and Cunningham, 32.

Innocent III was perceptive enough to see that Francis now had power; his Order protested not, but they presented themselves as an ideal that was embarrassingly missing at the highest levels of church consciousness. Francis would have his way: he would again receive definitive approbation by the Papal Court itself, for the Friars Minor and the Poor Clares.[82]

Figure 13 (below) brings Francis' horoscope to the time of this all-important Lateran Council. SA Ascendant squares natal Mars,

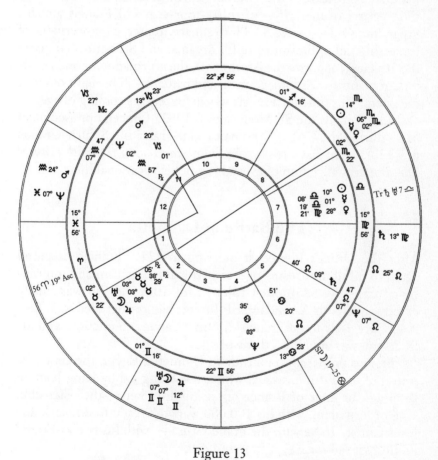

Figure 13

Inner Chart
Francis of Assisi

Outer Chart
SA Lateran Council
Nov. 11, 1215

---

82 All historians. See Cristiani, 95–96.

suggesting that administrative challenge is absorbed for the benefit of the mission's goals, probably with the help of friends (11th
House; love received, goals, reward from the profession)—and
here we recall Francis' powerful ally, Bishop Guido of Assisi and,
indeed, Pope Innocent III himself, for whom Francis literally was
a vision of the church's future.

SA Mercury-Venus were tightly opposed (full awareness of)
Francis' triple conjunction in Taurus—an affirmation of his ideals
within the structure of the Church. And most powerful of all for this
time period of maturity—of thirty-four-year old Francis and his
expanding Order—were SA Pluto square Jupiter, empowerment of
leadership, an optimism to fulfill dreams, and SA Saturn conjunct
the 7th cusp (opposite the Ascendant), the affirmation of one's position of maturity, wisdom, control, and patience, all brought out into
the open. This time for Francis was definitely his coming of age.

Additionally, the SP Moon was in 19–25 Cancer, opposed natal
Mars during the Council's convocation. Transiting Saturn-Uranus
in 7 Libra were just a few weeks from *exact conjunction with Francis'
Sun*, the crystallization of everything in his vocational life.

The Battle of Damietta

After the Order's Pentecost meeting in 1219, Francis prepared
again to fulfill his dreams of international evangelism and international Crusade. SA Jupiter, ruler of his 10th and 9th was finally
exactly square his Ascendant; SP Jupiter had retrograded to 3 Taurus 37 precisely upon Francis' Moon-Uranus conjunction; and his
SP Moon was upon his 7th cusp!

Francis prepared to journey to Damietta, Egypt, the center of
action of the Fifth Crusade, which was being led by King Jean de
Brienne—brother of Francis' first knightly hero—the ostensible
king of Jerusalem, with his 100,000 warriors ready to do battle for
Jesus Christ. To be with the grand Crusade, with his twelve Friars,
Francis set sail for Egypt in June 1219.[83]

The siege of Damietta is described as one of the most dramatic events of the thirteenth century. It was the opening of Innocent
III's new Crusade, and he had designated Egypt as the site of first

---

83 Fortini, 398–439.

attack. During the preparation years before the conquest, Innocent established a strict trade embargo throughout all of Europe against Egypt and the Levant (the broad area of Syria and upper Judea, the key ports for the Middle East). The great sultan Malik-al-Kamil had offered de Brienne quite generous terms to lift the blockade and avoid the enormous battle, but de Brienne refused those terms.

The siege upon the sultan's fearfully fortified city of Damietta with its commanding river position, double walls, twenty-two gates, 110 towers, forty-two castle-turrets, a broad navigable moat now obstructed by iron chains, and food supplies stocked for more than two years—this siege would begin tomorrow, August 29, 1219, the Day of the Decollation [beheading] of St. John the Baptist—*again* the original namesake for Francis upon his birth.

The heat was oppressive, the river and offshoot swamps were stagnating with refuse and human waste; "banners of every imaginable kind fluttered from the masts of ships: pennants, ensigns, flags of every pattern and color, flags of France, Germany, Brittany, Spain, Fisia, Holland. Companies, knights, and infantry of the Italian republics were there, equal in arms and in courage to the most powerful kingdoms ...

"White and crimson crosses shone on silk and on steel, on the castles of ships and on the mantles of knights of a multitude of orders. It [the Cross] blazed out on the habits of monks and the garments of priests. Everywhere there was the flaming emblem that was a symbol of the passionate feelings of those souls who had come here ... to liberate, defend, and hold the Holy Land from the enemies of the Holy Cross."

And Francis, after the last night of prayer, knew this battle for Christ would be lost. He spoke to the king. It was too late.

The clash of languages disordered the leadership of so great a horde. The scalding sun inflamed the Crusaders' infernal armor. The craze of thirst desiccated reason. And the god-enraged, passionate heathen backlash stained the shining Christian tunics with more blood than eyes and minds could manage. Decapitations numbered as stones upon the rocky land. The battle of Damietta was irretrievably lost.

The Holy Land — The New Rule —
The Third Order

After the overwhelming disconsolation of Damietta, Francis pressed on to the Holy Land. Little is recorded about this extended trip [a continuing Jupiter symbolism as we have seen], but the words of Monsignor Cristiani summarize this emotional visit:

> So he went to Nazareth, once the theater of Christ's "hidden life" [before Jesus's birth, the Annunciation]. There he reverenced the presence not only of his Jesus, but also of Mary His Mother, and Joseph, the humble carpenter Jesus had chosen for His foster father.
>
> We follow Francis now with greater awe to Bethlehem, the town where Christ was born. To Francis' eyes, this was indeed the world capital of "poverty." For Jesus, the Son of God, had chosen to be born there in a stable, and to receive the homage of poor shepherds and wealthy kings alike.
>
> It would be a priceless treasure to know the thoughts, feeling, and inspirations Francis experienced in this most blessed of earthly places. Was it here perhaps that he was first inspired to reproduce the Creche of Bethlehem, as he would later do at Greccio, thus making the first Christmas crib in all of Christendom?
>
> But our pilgrim must have felt even stronger emotions at the sites of Christ's sufferings than either at Nazareth or Bethlehem. We can picture him kneeling on the hill of Golgatha, praying at the Holy Sepulcher, meditating at the very places where the world was redeemed through the sufferings of the Divine Master.
>
> The vision of Christ's sufferings was to grow on Francis, and we have a proof in his stigmatization on Mount Alverna.[84]

In June–July 1219, a messenger, Brother Stefano the Simple, secretly on his own, left Italy and located Francis in Jerusalem. There was trouble: brothers in the Order had begun "to leave the way of perfection that he [Francis] had shown them and were no longer constant in love and in the practice of charity, humility, and holy poverty." Additionally, a Cardinal had imposed on the Poor Clares a departure from the Rule, which Francis and his Friars strongly opposed.[85]

---

84 Cristiani, 122–123.
85 Fortini, 436–437.

Francis returned to Italy, to Venice, on the late Summer passage. He went alone to an uninhabited lagoon island, Isola del Deserto, to fast and to pray. The experience of the Holy Land was with him deeply and lifted him quite above the bureaucratic problems pressing upon the Order ... and into his last life period.

The astrology here was subtle. Recall Figure 13 (page 131), the SA Midheaven at 27 Capricorn would come to 1 Aquarius in three and one-half years, i.e., to July 1219 by adding three and one-half degrees to the November 1215 position. This puts Francis SA MC into contact with Neptune (SA MC=Neptune) suggesting a period of "feeling lost" or, indeed, "losing it!"

Also in July 1219, transiting Saturn was Stationary-Direct (on July 10) at 9 Scorpio, square Francis' natal Saturn, always an adjustment period of how things are going in life, usually in the profession. Transiting Neptune was at 0 Taurus approaching a very important conjunction period with Francis' entire Taurus focus, another measurement of bewilderment and/or withdrawal [escape and sacrifice are very closely related throughout Francis' life].

The Secondary Progressed Moon was crossing his 7th cusp that Summer.

We see Francis getting away from his Order, from its construction, if you will. The popularity was snowballing, the numbers of friars were growing incredibly: there were now some 5,000 members in the Order.[86] The outreach was extraordinary, but it was no longer the personal mission it had been fourteen years earlier.

Francis continued on to Porziuncola. His presence was astonishingly effective, and he was able to settle things quickly within the Order. But the need to write a more precise and complete Rule was pressing. The composition of these Rules always seemed to be beyond Francis' interest and skill, so totally tied was he to the dictates of inspiration. The astrology shows us Francis returning in his life to a decidedly personal realm of experience (the Neptune focus). In reality, he could not justify the bureaucratic rules necessary for group organization with the Order's Rule for individual poverty and sacrifice. *Francis resigned from leadership of the Order.* He withdrew with the phrase, according to Celano: "From now on I am dead to you."

---

86 Yarom, 40.

Brother Elias—one of Francis first converts—had been an extremely powerful consul, lawyer/judge in Assisi, a man known for his noble birth and his extraordinary wisdom. To him—after the death of Brother Pietro di Catanio, who directed the Order for a brief time—Francis gave the title of Vicar General of the Order. Brother Elias then had the responsibility to reframe the Rule of 1221 and then write the Rule of 1223, which was finally approved by Pope Honorius III at the end of that year.[87]

In the Spring of 1221, Francis passed through Poggibonsi, a little town between Siena and Florence. He met a man named Lucchesio, who was totally caught up with earning money through cornering the grain supplies of the region and then selling at a high profit when the price rose. With the influence of Francis, Lucchesio and his wife, who had worked closely with him in the business, eventually saw the futility of their ways, sold all but their home and garden, and gave the money to the poor.

A poor man then came to Lucchesio's home, begging. Lucchesio asked his wife to get some bread for the man, but she told him that not one crumb was left. Lucchesio insisted and, when the wife went to the bread bin and opened it, she was amazed to find that it was not empty at all, but full of fresh and fragrant loaves! This miracle led Lucchieso and his wife again to Francis. They wanted to follow the way of the Order as formal disciples of Poverty, but they did not want to be separated, since "they could not get along without one another."

Francis saw "the luminous beauty of love when the union of a man and a woman is an indissoluble joining of souls. It would not be right to destroy a family, which is also a gift from God, blessed by God."[88] [We are reminded of Francis' own hallowed "marriage" to Lady Poverty, the idealized focus upon the 7th House through Mercury-Venus and the Sun.]

Francis understood in that moment that absolute renunciation should be required only for an apostle. Thus, according to tradition,

---

87 It is important to note that after Francis' death, the incipient disorganization continued, tragically in the person of Brother Elias, Francis' trusted aide. Pope Gregory IX entrusted Elias with building a basilica to honor St. Francis. In the process of doing that, Elias became a profiteering businessman; he lived in luxury, rode horseback, kept two residences, and refused to hold general meetings of the Order. He was excommunicated by the Church and was then again excommunicated by the grandly expanded Order. It is understood that, at his death, he recanted his sins. Celano xlvii-xlviii. The Rule of the Order was demanding indeed.

88 Fortini, 521.

was born the Third Order, the Secular Order, formally the "Fraternity of the Third Order of Penitence" to accommodate all who dedicated themselves to Francis' mission of humility and helping the poor but could not follow the extreme of the Rule. These members would have a different Rule: they would be prohibited from bearing arms, for example, from having hatred in their hearts, from taking any solemn oath except in those circumstances allowed by the Church. This Order now flourishes throughout the world in modern times as the "Secular Franciscan Order (S.F.O.), still lay-administered and self-governing; they are teachers, nurses, and facilitators for the poor, and counselors; "they seek souls who long for perfection in their own state."[89]

In December 1223—Fortini tells us—Francis experienced the happiest time in his life. The weather was beautiful, and Christmas was drawing near. Francis planned to recreate the birth of Jesus in a cave outside Greccio, an Umbrian *castello* near Assisi. He assembled a manger, an ox and an ass, straw, and hay. Brother Thomas of Celano was there; he tells the story:

> The day of joy drew near, the time of great rejoicing came. The brothers were called from their various places. Men and women of that neighborhood prepared with glad hearts, according to their means, candles and torches to light up that night that has lighted up all the days and years with its gleaming star.

> At length, the saint of God came [Francis], and finding all things prepared, *he saw it and was glad*. The manger was prepared, the hay had been brought, the ox and ass were led in. There simplicity was honored, poverty was exalted, humility was commended, and Greccio was made, as it were, a new Bethlehem.

> The night was lighted up like the day, and it delighted men and beasts. The people came and were filled with new joy over the new mystery. The woods rang with the voices of the crowd and the rocks made answer to their jubilation. The brothers sang, paying their debt of praise to the Lord, and the whole night resounded with their rejoicing.

> The saint of God stood before the manger, uttering sighs, overcome with love, and filled with a wonderful happiness. The solemnities of the Mass were celebrated over the manger and the priest experienced a new consolation.

---

89 Pope Pius XII, public address, July 1, 1956.

The saint of God was clothed with the vestments of the deacon, for he was a deacon, and he sang the holy Gospel in a sonorous voice. And his voice was a strong voice, a sweet voice, a clear voice, a sonorous voice, inviting all to the highest rewards. Then he preached to the people standing about, and he spoke charming words concerning the nativity of the poor King and the little town of Bethlehem. Frequently too, when he wished to call Christ *Jesus*, he would call him simply the *Child of Bethlehem*, aglow with overflowing love for him; and speaking the word *Bethlehem*, his voice was more like the bleating of a sheep. His mouth was filled more with sweet affection than with words. Besides, when he spoke the name *Child of Bethlehem* or *Jesus*, his tongue licked his lips, as it were, relishing and savoring with pleased palate the sweetness of the words.

The gifts of the Almighty were multiplied there, and a wonderful vision was seen by a certain virtuous man [the nobleman, Giovanni (Francis' first namesake, once again) who helped assemble the Creche]. For he saw a little child lying in the manger lifeless, and he saw the holy man of God [Francis] go up to it and rouse the child as from a deep sleep.

The vision was not unfitting, for the Child Jesus had been forgotten in the hearts of many; but, by the working of his grace, he was brought to life again through his servant St. Francis and stamped upon their fervent memory. At length, the solemn night celebration was brought to a close, and each one returned to his home with holy joy.[90]

The Seraph, the Stigmata, and Death

In 1213, just after creation of the Order of the Little Clares and during his frustrating first attempts to go to the Middle East, Francis met up with Count Orlando of Chiusi, a bold knight of the emperor. The count was deeply impressed by Francis and exceedingly appreciative of the Order and its example. In his name and that of his sons—"solely for reason of devotion"—Count Orlando donated to the brotherhood, without any restriction, a mountain

---

90 Celano, I, #85–86. Celano adds a note that any animals in the immediate area that were sick were freed from their ailments after eating the hay used in the Creche. Women laboring in difficult childbirth were delivered safely when some of this hay was placed upon them. Miracle cures took place among the throng attending the beautiful scene, flooded with firelight, singing, and love. An altar was built upon the spot and a church built around the altar. And the church is still there in Greccio, forty-five miles south of Assisi.

named La Verna (also *Alverna*). It was an immense, rugged cliff with a thick forest at the top, located between the Arno and Tiber rivers about sixty miles northwest of Assisi near Arezzo.

Fortini gathers together descriptions of the mountain and describes it as "tormented, wounded, and broken in some horrendous convulsion. Violent passion made grievously immobile lurks in the fearsome rock that is constantly assaulted by storms, rock that seems of another world ... a setting for a battle of titans." According to Francis, God revealed to him that the enormous fissures and the chilling precipices on this peak were made in the hour that Jesus died, when, according to the Gospel, "the rocks were split."[91]

Francis journeyed to La Verna in late August 1224. It was his sixth and final retreat to this isolated, dramatic place. The brothers had built huts of branches and mud on a rocky clearing near the top. Francis found an ultimately secluded spot, guarded by a deep fissure in the rocks for his solitary prayer vigils; no one save Brother Leo was allowed to interrupt him, and then only by calling ahead with a password warning.

This was the ultimate time of prayer and humility for Francis. In his words, as told to a Brother John by Francis in a vision after his death (one in a series of miraculous testaments of proof of the stigmata, involving visionary appearances to brothers and the touching and kissing of the wounds), here is what happened:

> I was praying in that place where [now] stands the chapel of Count Simon of Battifolle, and asked two graces of my Lord Jesus Christ; the first was, that He would grant me in this life to feel in my soul and in my body, so far as possible, all the pains that He Himself felt, during the time of His bitter Passion. The second grace which I asked of Him was like unto the first, that I might feel in my heart the excessive love which induced Him to suffer such a Passion for us sinners. And then God put it into my heart, that He would give me to feel both the one and the other, in so far as it was possible for a mere creature; which thing indeed was fulfilled in me by the impression of the Stigmata."[92]

---

91 Fortini, 551–552. Additionally, Dante described the mountain as the *crudo sasso* ("harsh crag"), "Paradiso, Canto ii, line 106. See also Matthew 27: 45, 51–52: "The earth shook, and the rocks were split; the Tombs also were opened, and many bodies of the saints who had fallen asleep were raised."

92 *The Little Flowers of St. Francis*, 242–243.

In actual life after the experience, Francis spoke sparingly about the ecstatic experience, but he gave these details on occasions, as reported by Thomas of Celano in narrative form:

> He saw *in the vision of God* a man standing above him, like a seraph with six wings, his hands extended and his feet joined together and fixed to a cross. Two of the wings were extended above his head, two were extended as if for flight, and two were wrapped around the whole body. When the blessed servant of the Most High saw these things, he was filled with the greatest wonder, but he could not understand what this vision should mean.

> Still, he was filled with happiness and he rejoiced very greatly because of the kind and gracious look with which he saw himself regarded by the seraph, whose beauty was beyond estimation; but the fact that the seraph was fixed to a cross and the sharpness of his suffering filled Francis with fear.

> And so he arose, if I may so speak [Thomas perhaps editorializing] sorrowful and joyful, and joy and grief were in him alternately. Solicitously he thought what this vision could mean, and his soul was in great anxiety to find its meaning. And while he was thus unable to come to any understanding of it and the strangeness of the vision perplexed his heart, the marks of the nails began to appear in his hands and feet, just as he had seen them a little before in the crucified man above him.

> His hands and feet seemed to be pierced through the middle by nails, with the heads of the nails appearing in the inner side of the hands and on the upper sides of the feet and their pointed ends on the opposite sides. The marks in the hands were round on the inner side, but on the outer side they were elongated; and some small pieces of flesh took on the appearance of the ends of the nails, bent and driven back and rising above the rest of the flesh. In the same way the marks of the nails were impressed upon the feet and raised in a similar way above the rest of the flesh.

> Furthermore, his right side was as though it had been pierced by a lance and had a wound in it that frequently bled so that his tunic and trousers were very often covered with his sacred blood.

> Alas, how few indeed merited to see the wound in his side while this crucified servant of the crucified Lord lived! But happy was Elias who, while the saint lived, merited to see this wound; and no less happy was Rufino who touched the wound with his own hands ...

It was Francis' custom to reveal his great secret but rarely or to no one at all, for he feared that his revealing it to anyone might have the appearance of a special affection for him, in the way in which special friends act, and that he would thereby suffer some loss in the grace that was given him.[93]

Cristiani tells the same story, as do all sources in one degree of detail or another, and then adds succinctly and dramatically:

And it seemed to Francis that his prayer was already answered. He began to burn with a consuming love and felt as though completely changed and *transformed into his Jesus.*[94]

Cristiani notes that Francis refused to tell the brothers anything about the wondrous experience, but "when the brothers washed his clothing they understood their master did indeed bear in his side, in his hands and feet, the bodily image and likeness of the wounds of our Lord Jesus Christ!" And, indeed, as we shall see, upon Francis' death, stripped naked upon the ground, the stigmata were there to be seen.

There is no doubt that the stigmata occurred within the first three weeks of September 1224 (the party left La Verna on September 30). Every source agrees. This time in Francis' life was well annotated by his followers who had become organizationally more and more sophisticated with the great increase in their numbers, and Francis had indeed become a living saint, was constantly failing in health and strength, and could die at any time. In short, records became important.

Along with St. Bonaventure (*Life of St. Francis*, Tr. Garney-Salter. London: Everyman Library, 1963), Fortini, to my knowledge, is as detailed a biographer of Francis as there is. My reading

---

93 Celano, II, #94–95. Additionally, some time afterwards as Francis showed signs that death was near, Brother Leo, Francis' sentinel upon Mount La Verna at the time of the vision, asked Francis for something personal, something written in his own hand to help Leo through any difficult time. Francis wrote the well-known benediction (Numbers 6:24–26, "The Lord Bless you and keep you ...) in Latin with a personal Blessing pointedly to Leo. Then, on the other side of the paper, Leo added specific testament in red ink (not blood) about Francis' experience with the Seraph and his reception of the stigmata. Leo also indicated the authenticity of Francis' signature—a Greek Tau, the *T-Cross*, on the outline of a mountain (Golgatha *and* La Verna?) that appeared on the paper. Exhaustive studies by historians and paleographers allow no doubt of authenticity. This paper is preserved in the sacristy of the Sacro Convento in Assisi.

94 Cristiani, 157–158.

of this climactic time in Francis' life and in our study is that Francis set up a general schedule for the brothers (corroborated as well in accounts of the stigmata in *The Little Flowers of St. Francis*): Francis was awakened each morning by a "fierce and violent falcon" tamed by Francis' presence. The Falcon nested by Francis' hut and summoned him and the brothers to prayer at every dawn.[95]

The brothers would then pray all day, with Francis off alone, watched over at a distance by Brother Leo. They would have their evening meal—or perhaps Francis would fast and continue praying through the night and into the next day(s).

Prayer would resume at "matins." This word refers to the "morning," especially in the singular, through Latin and French roots. For the Church, in the plural form, it came to mean "morning prayers," but in medieval times there was the thought that the "morning" could be *anticipated* by prayers of praise the *evening before*, i.e., matins could begin at sunset, as a first canonical hour. In fact, at that time the day was held to begin not at dawn but at sunset. It was very confusing indeed. Modern dictionaries echo this as well, giving as first definition of matins, "the night office forming with lauds the first of the canonical hours."

In the same thought with the word "matins," Fortini talks of the woodlands on the mountain top "in a light of dream, wrapped in the whiteness of the full moon."[96] This corroborates the reference to the evening prayer schedule for the brotherhood. It was during the darking of one of those nights on La Verna that Leo went to the brink of the gorge separating Francis from the rest of them to check on him, and called out the agreed-upon words that would alert Francis. But there was no answer. Three times Leo called. No answer ... finally, Francis appeared, coming forward, according to Leo, "on pierced feet, uncovers his lacerated heart, stretches out his nail-marked hands, and repeats the words of the Last Supper: 'This is my blood. Drink all of it.'"

Fortini's reference to the Full Moon was more than a romantic grace upon his historical narrative. A Full Moon *did* occur on September 1. This most specific reference probably came from records

---

95 This description explained and personalized so much for me the opening lines of a poem I have known for thirty-five years, Gerard Manley Hopkins' ecstatic *The Windhover - To Christ our Lord:* "I caught this morning morning's minion, king-/dom of daylight's dauphin, dapple-dawn-drawn Falcon, in his riding/Of the rolling level underneath him steady air, and striding/High there, how he rung upon the rein of a wimpling wing/In his ecstasy!...."

96 Fortini, 556.

of the organization of the program for the brothers' prayer vigil, drawn up upon their arrival on La Verna at the end of August, i.e., with the Full Moon of September 1.

Dating references in this medieval period within the Church were anchored to the Feast Days of Saints or of great happenings involving Saints. No one outside the Church and sometimes the courts particularly cared what date it was.[97] During the time period of Francis' fast and prayer vigil on La Verna, September 14 was the very important *Feast of the Exaltation of the Holy Cross*, certainly appropriate—and perhaps magnetic—to the dating of the stigmata.[98]

Very late on the night of this September 14, the Feast of the Holy Cross, and throughout the early hours of September 15, a *New* Moon was forming in the 29th degree of Virgo. In my opinion, it would have been too dark and exceedingly dangerous upon that heavily wooded, ominous mountain peak, alone, climbing around a precipitous gorge, for frail, preoccupied Francis to be safe. I think the brothers would have urged him that night (those nights of no moonlight) to stay closer to his hut, to pray in his hut and retire early, and to await the bright of the Moon returning in two days or so.

From most careful study of this time period early in September, I suggest that the night of Francis' stigmata was most likely seven days earlier, *on September 7*, seven days into their stay, quite possibly very near to 8 P.M. This adjustment from the 14th, the appropriate Feast Day, back to the 7th *does not affect* the Solar Arc positions or Secondary Progressed positions in Francis' horoscope at all. There is an adjustment of four degrees backward for the *Tertiary* Moon (see Figure 15 to come, page 147), with *either* position reinforcing the beautiful congruence between astrology and reality, as we shall see. The

---

97 Whitrow, 83: "The essential quality of the world was its transitoriness vis-a-vis God, not the visible change which went on unceasingly in the world. Until the fourteenth century only the church was interested in temporal measurement and division ... As late as the fifteenth century it is doubtful whether people in general knew the current year of the Christian era, since that depended on an ecclesiastical computation and was not used much in everyday life."

98 The Early Church Calendar after Francis' death designated September 17th as the *Feast Day of the Stigmata*. This was not to over-ride consensus that the stigmata occurred on the fourteenth, the Feast Day of the Exaltation of the Cross; rather, the 17th was the nearest date available for this special designation! The 14th was an extremely important Feast Day of long, long standing; the 15th was the Feast Day of our Lady of Sorrows; the 16th was the Feast Day of two other saints; so the 17th became the Day for the Stigmata. The Council of Vatican II (1962–65, ninety-three years after Vatican Council I) adjusted some Feast Days to try to bring them closer to the dates the celebrated events actually occurred, but many yet remain disparate.

position on September 7th is just ideally perfect, and not uncharacteristic of Tertiary portraits projected from correct birth times.

It remains undeniable, however, that, for either date for the stigmata, the astrology for Francis indeed shows the gift from God.

Astrology of the Stigmata

Figure 14 (page 145) is Francis' Solar Arc portrait brought forward to September 1224, the historic time of the stigmata, the fulfillment of his every prayer and deed throughout his life.

SA Neptune, the sublime focal center of Francis' being, ruler of his Ascendant as well, has finally come *to the Ascendant within 7 minutes of arc of precision*. At Francis' level, this is the mystic fulfillment of his sacrifice of being, his loss of ego, his spiritual projection of identity to the greatest possible extreme, the process begun long before in the Perugian dungeon, in the feverish bed in Spoleto, in the San Damiano chapel, and naked before his father.

SA projection of the extraordinary Moon-Uranus conjunction—the uniqueness of Francis' being, the organization of his earlier identity for materialism and the construction of his avant garde emotional individuation, also to the greatest possible extreme—has now come out of the natal square with the Neptune-Saturn *to exact square with his Pisces Ascendant axis*. This is a tremendous emphasis on the identity conversion and dual-personality fulfillment we have seen developing throughout his life.

SA Jupiter is applying to opposition with Francis' Midheaven, certainly a time for vocational and religious reward and fulfillment.

The final remarkable dimension of this Solar Arc portrait for the stigmata is *SA Saturn exactly square the Midheaven* (Saturn=MC, within 9 minutes of arc): this always signals a powerful time of life development, a major change that can often involve matters of great sacrifice for change, matters of death for change, or decision for a major change of direction, how one relates to the world. The father figure in the life is very often involved as well (here, God the Father, the paternity of the Creator).

In this month of the stigmata, it is the date of a *Progressed New Moon*. It takes place in *23 Scorpio* in Francis' *8th House*. The fulfillment of the stigmata is certainly fulfillment through death; the personality dies, loses itself, to be reborn in new light.

In this directed horoscope, we see Francis' lifetime sacrifice through SA Neptune upon the Ascendant, the dynamic intensification of his being through SA Moon-Uranus square that Ascendant, his life change through matters of death through SA Saturn square the Midheaven, and his new conceptualization of selfhood through the Progressed New Moon in Scorpio!

Figure 15 (page 147) shows the Tertiary Progressions, which are extremely time sensitive and Moon-and-angles orientated.

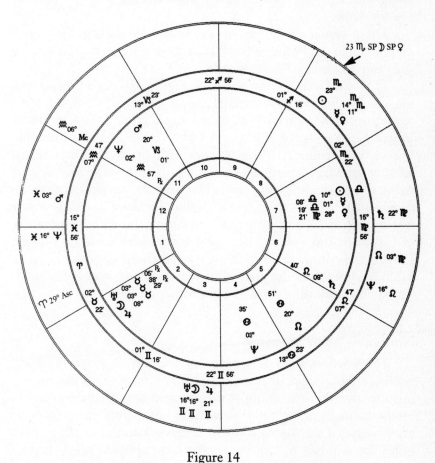

Figure 14

Inner Chart
Francis of Assisi

Outer Chart
SA Stigmata
Sept. 7, 1224

They also reinforce the portrait of stigmata fulfillment dramatically: the TP Uranus-Moon-Sun conjunction (a Tertiary New Moon,
echoing the Secondary New Moon!) is *precisely conjunct Francis'
Jupiter, ruler of his 9th and 10th*. This is certainly a signature of fulfillment, a transcendental new illumination through things Jupiterian. Jupiter is co-ruler of the Pisces Ascendant.

In turn, TP Jupiter at 16 Gemini is exactly square the Ascendant axis.

Finally, Tertiary Mars-Neptune (charismatic and, in Francis'
case, mystical uniqueness) exactly opposes natal Saturn, and,
along with the 2nd House activity, activates *the entire T-Square of
Francis' being*.

These Tertiary measurements alone are astounding. They supply a commanding echo of the magical constructs seen in the Solar
Arcs and Secondary Progressions.

The final chart for the stigmata, Figure 16 (page 148), shows
the transits for just before 8 P.M., approximately two hours after
sunset, into the matins period, arranged around Francis' natal
horoscope. Yet, again, the corroboration is formidable: the Midheaven over Mount La Verna was exactly upon Francis' mysterious
sublimated Mars (co-ruler of the Ascendant through intercepted
Aries, the militaristic swagger of his early life projection, wounds
and blood), and *the Ascendant at Mount La Verna at this time had
Neptune just about to rise at 8–9 degrees Taurus*, another accentuation
of Neptune and yet another conjunction with Francis' Jupiter.
Finally, the Moon in 23 Gemini was precisely opposed Francis'
Midheaven: another designation of matters ended, matters fulfilled,
with a new beginning promised in another realm.

Notes about the Stigmata

The word *stigmata* does not mean wounds. It properly means
marks, brands, signs, from the Latin meanings and the Greek
(also to *tattoo*). Interestingly, the connotation of shame or discredit through markings is established and cited in the word's
etymology. "The Stigmata" came to designate the marks resem-
bling the wounds of Christ crucified, manifested often during
religious ecstasy.

Francis was the first stigmatic, and there were thirty-one more
cases of stigmata up to the end of the thirteenth century, twenty-

two cases during the 14th century, and twenty-five in the fifteenth century. Out of them all, nine were declared saints by the Church.

By 1908, of the 321 cases identified by a French doctor/researcher, 229 cases had been reported from Italy (the rest France, Spain, and Portugal).[99]

Ted Harrison, a former religious affairs correspondent of the BBC, makes the very important deduction out of his research that

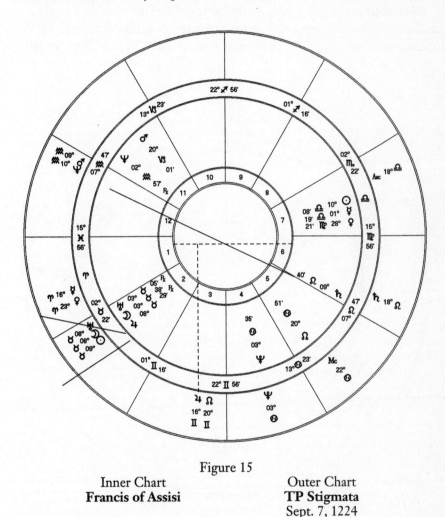

Figure 15

Inner Chart	Outer Chart
Francis of Assisi	**TP Stigmata**
	Sept. 7, 1224

---

99 Yarom, 23. Harrison, 9: "In the twentieth century [there is a] change in pattern. While Italy provides many examples, it does not dominate in quite the same way. There have been American cases, one in Australia ... and three are British (Anglicans)."

"the vast majority of cases [of the stigmata] have occurred at a time and in a place where, although remarkable, reports of stigmata could be absorbed into the culture." In other words, *it could happen*.

We can see this kind of cultural acceptance or approval, for example, in sports: when (Doctor-athlete) Roger Bannister, after extensive study, conditioning, and planning, broke the four-minute barrier in the mile race by running the mile in 3:59:04. It was an enormous accomplishment hailed throughout the world as a never-thought-possible physical breakthrough. It could be done! And after that day, May 6, 1954, the four-minute barrier was passed

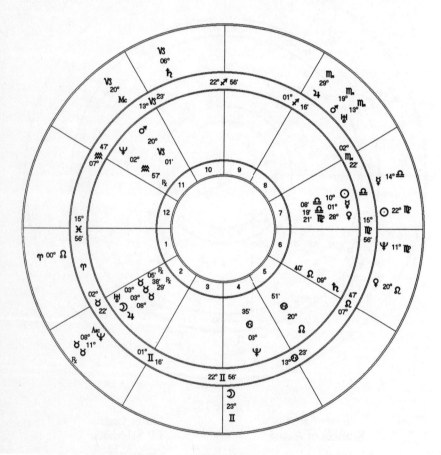

Figure 16

Inner Chart	Outer Chart
Francis of Assisi	**TR Stigmata**
	Sept. 7, 1224, 7:52 P.M. LMT

repeatedly by other runners. Races today routinely include many four-minute milers, and the record is still being lowered.

The same phenomenon of empowerment occurred after the first ascent of Mt. Everest by Edmund Hillary on May 29, 1953. So many climbers have reached the top of the world since then that there is a debris problem en route to the summit because of expeditionary camp discards.

The stigmata manifest in different ways: the wounds are in the feet and/or the hands and/or the side, and/or across the forehead and crown of the head. The wounds all or in part may bleed. Francis' wounds in his feet and hands did not bleed, but the convulsion of traumatized flesh pointedly took on the definition of nails. The wound in his side bled copiously.

In some cases, the stigmata come and go, appearing only during Holy Week or occurring only *on Good Friday,* or on every Friday, or on the Feast Day of Saint Francis. In some cases they remain: the holy Padre Pio (his church near Foggia in Italy) who joined the Capucine (a Franciscan) Order in 1902, carried the marks which originally appeared in 1918 *for fifty years,* seeping a cup of blood each day.[100]

The shape and positioning of the wounds suggest further dimension to the phenomenon: they are related to portrayals of Crucifixion scenes in Christian art. The Christian's conceptualization of nails-through-the-hands, for example, leads the stigmata to wounds in the hands. With the modern research presented in John D. Hiller's book, *Report on the Shroud of Turin* (Houghton Mifflin, 1983), explaining that the hand wounds actually were wrist wounds (otherwise the weight of the body would tear through the palms), the consciousness of the details is beginning to change, *and so has the location of the wounds.* A Maryland priest, for example, has the nailmarks in his wrists. Another contemporaneous stigmatic has wounds and visions that correspond to the illustration in her modern Bible.[101]

The mind is strongly active in this phenomenon, obviously, and this has led to off-handed, empty explanations citing psychosomaticism, which addresses how emotional pressures can bring about

---

100 Harrison, 100–113.

101 Ibid., 40. In the twelfth/thirteenth century, Christian art reflected the pained and sinful social times. The emphasis on a sweet Jesus and a beaming Virgin Mary gave way to an agonizing, wounded, ashen pale Christ figure with all the gory details of suffering depicted in glorious, brilliantly colored frescoes on the walls of churches.

organic results, but itself has no explanation. The concept of *psychogenic purpura* has been coined to label spontaneous lesions for which there is no physical explanation. The medical research talks responsibly about the masochistic dimension of the stigmata, about the ability to endure pain for long periods of time, to the point of actual enjoyment of hardship.[102]

The profile assembled by researchers—medical, psychiatric, religious, and journalistic—of the stigmatic, is a person usually female (outnumbering men seven to one);[103] able to do with minimal food or astounding lapses of eating (to the incapability of eating); a strange body odor; instances of levitation; piercing, telepathic insight; chronic ill health; difficult childhood; and a link with, even immunity to fire and/or feverish states. All stigmatics report and evidence a conspicuously altered state of consciousness, the preparedness for visionary experience and multiple personality manifestation. The profile can be detailed more exactly and, indeed, expanded, but this is the general overview as gathered by Harrison and Yarom.

The dimension of ill health in Francis' case can not be denied. Astrologically, it is perfectly clear: natal Saturn, within the extreme opposition with Neptune, is in the 6th (sickness) and is co-ruler of the 12th (chronic illness); the Sun, ruler of the 6th, is squared by Pluto; Uranus, ruler of the 12th is exactly conjunct Francis' Moon; and Neptune, ruling the Ascendant, receives the opposition from Saturn.

The dimension of fever and fire is pronounced throughout Francis' life. He endured debilitating, long-lasting sieges of fever as a prisoner in the Perugian dungeon, during the next step toward his conversion when he was in Spoleto (aborting his expedition to become a knight), and many other times in his life, and almost perpetually in the later years. The fevers were always well documented because they emphasized his suffering, his personal neglect, his selflessness.[104]

---

102 Harrison, 15.

103 Due in great part to the Catholic clergy's exclusion of women, to most of culture throughout history excluding expression, position, and fulfilling relevance to women; in short, a heightened suffering and alienation for women, and therefore, through intensified piety, increased projection through that suffering for significance in Christ's suffering.

104 In a Vatican-authorized medical inquiry into stigmatic Padre Pio's case, it is recorded that, on one occasion, the temperature of his body broke the mercury tube in the thermometer. Harrison, 107.

Fortini tells us explicitly that Francis had always been fascinated by fire. "Staring at it had always been a great joy ... At times he had not hesitated to feed it with his own habit."[105]

When Francis was in Damietta, in Egypt, a prostitute offered herself to him. Francis told how her bed was ready and that the woman was very beautiful. He took her instead to a great fire (proving Mars sublimated) that was burning in the grand kitchen, in a large roasting brazier. He then threw himself upon the fire and invited the woman to join him.[106]

Shortly after Damietta, Francis offered several times in his sermons to throw himself into fire to prove his faith.

When Francis was near death, after the stigmata, his discomfort complicated by severe eye problems (Sun; Moon), a doctor tried to treat him, with a cauterizing operation:

> When the doctor appeared, armed with the cautery that he would heat in the fire till it glowed, Francis began to tremble with terror. He knew perfectly well what they were planning to make him endure so as to get rid of his ophthalmia—they hoped. The incandescent iron was to burn both temples from the top of the ear to the arches of the eyebrows. Unable to bear this spectacle, his faithful companions, Leo, Rufino, Angelo, and Masseo walked off.
>
> Only Elias remained; he heard Francis address the fire with a prayer of childlike faith: "My Brother Fire, the Most High has given you a splendor that all creatures envy. Show yourself now to be kind and courteous to me ... I pray the Magnificent Lord to temper this fiery heat so that I may have the strength to bear his burning caress.[107]
>
> Elias held Francis' hand and reported that it trembled no more. Although the smell of burning flesh nauseated other brothers, Francis had no pain.

Francis fasted continuously; he barely ate. Stigmatics in history have shown extreme independence from food. There is the

---

105 Fortini, 563–64. And then is added: "Next to fire, he loved water ..." This is a most appropriate description of Francis' musing in terms of his sublimated Mars, ruler of Aries intercepted within his Ascendant, and the dominant pervasiveness of the Piscean Ascendant itself.

106 Fortini, 422, "undeniable historical fact." Additionally: great numbers of prostitutes followed the Crusader armies. There were the women who accompanied their "men of lineage," riding with them, fully armored, into battle, and also involved in "amorous intrigues that provoked all sorts of passions, violent jealousies, and bloody feuds."

107 Green, 261.

well-known case of St. Catherine of Siena (born 1347; one of a number of stigmatics who died at thirty-three years of age, at which age it is believed Christ died) who went, it is said, for eight years without taking any food or liquid, other than the Blessed Sacrament. Some modern stigmatics have had to be hospitalized not necessarily because they are malnourished but because the medical establishment insisted that they must be fed.

Why was Francis the first stigmatic? Did God suddenly decide to open this direct channel to identification with Christ's suffering and love, to break the barrier that allowed the phenomenon to be repeated often from then on throughout the world? The answer probably is that the time was right for this specific mystical religious experience to manifest through the mind, into the body, in terms espoused by the current religious teachings and depiction. The Church philosophy of Francis' time was extremely tied to *Corpus Christi*, the Body of Christ, instead of to the Virgin Birth or the Resurrection, or intellectual interpretations of the Holy Ghost, as have dominated in other times. The times made the stigmata possible. Francis' person made the stigmata happen.

At the outset of her psychoanalytic study of Francis, Israeli psychotherapist Nitza Yarom presents William James' caution of identifying as a state of illness certain physiological and psychological phenomena that occur during a religious or mystical experience. The "religious genius" will exhibit the kinds of behaviors that are considered abnormal or pathological, but it is these very energies that give such people "religious authority" and impact.

What is fighting to be said throughout all the medical studies of the stigmata and Francis in particular is that we do not understand the phenomenon of religious intensity (the mystical experience). We are frightened by it since—unlike most other intense behavioral syndromes—religious intensity carries with it some kind of other-worldliness that implies divine approval. So, although we feel left out of something as special as the religious experience seems to be, and we do not understand it at all, we too must approve of it.

Astrologically, our analysis has led us through a conversion between two personalities, bridging a split or division. That is not only objectively clear historically, but it is also subjectively rewarding in appreciating the life of Francis. Yarom does not mention this premise but dissects the fragile state of Francis' core being in terms of Francis' Oedipal conflicts and his bi-sexual web of anxiety. Does this help us to understand his conversion and ecstasy more; his inspiration of history, and, indeed, his uniqueness in all of Creation?

What is "wrong" with being close to God? It is reasonable that being close to God does alter the human being and that that alteration may indeed appear aberrant. The mystical realm belongs to those who get there. Perhaps the ideated electrodes and cerebral scalpels of today's psychology *are not valid in early thirteenth-century life*. For any analysis to be meaningful, it must be couched in terms and at the level of the object of that analysis, framed in terms of the subject's cultural values, but acceptance seems to me to be more enriching.

Using insight that is pertinent to those times of old, Yarom points out that Francis certainly felt disillusionment as a knight: he lost in battle, he was sick and in prison; he failed again in his trip to de Brienne, when he had to turn back at Spoleto. He had to feel shame, and then he converted that shame, that disillusionment to religion. Why not? The astrologer can say that Francis was perfectly prepared for that switch. *It was supposed to be that way.*

As we have seen through Francis' identity change, religion—in terms appropriate to his times *and* to his personality, i.e., sacrifice, living the way Christ lived, which would guarantee spiritual success—did provide for him the alternate path. Again, the astrologer sees this as the way things are supposed to develop.

It is engaging to consider medical comments on the symptoms of Francis' chronic illness, that they relate, for one example, to a form of malaria. Yarom quotes the details supplied by St. Bonaventure about the hideous personal living conditions Francis endured, serving the Lord in "cold and nakedness," the suffering from "diverse ailments so grievously that scarce one of his limbs was free from pain and sore suffering." The symptomology—the shivering, the skin color, the fevers, the weight loss, the eye problems to the edge of blindness—becomes more meaningful if we can label it.

For an astrologer, within the reliance upon vast spectra of living symbolisms, the poetical must not be forgotten. For example, that Francis began his "career" by disrobing completely before his father, the bishop, and the assembled public, and ended his life asking to be laid naked upon the ground is symbolic, beautifully so. It completes a circle of intent and avowal in Francis' life, and, very important to understand, it was a means of making a statement *that was typical of Francis' time*. He lived at a time when the well-turned, epigrammatic phrase was in high style (his dialogue with Pope Innocent III, for example); there were Latin puns hidden in practically everyone's Italian sentences. Naked before one's father to be reborn is poetic and inspired. It is also emphatic, convincing, and memorable.

Yarom rests much of her analysis on Francis' not being able to "allow himself masculine phallic existence. He could not actualize himself as a knight, a merchant, or a family man. His more pronounced characteristics were feminine. He was, above all, the promoter of love ... the feminine role that he cannot fulfill as a young adult in normal life (leading to homosexuality) can be well fulfilled in a religious vocation, especially at a time when romantic love and religious passion have become important to the contemporary man ... And by turning sexuality into preoccupation with the body, by the use of the defense mechanism of conversion, St. Francis finds an outlet."[108]

Astrologically, we were able to appreciate much of these insights through the Jung-labeled archetype (timeless symbol) of the *anima* (see page 123). Indeed, Francis may have been surrounded by the facts and rumors of rampant homosexuality among the clergy in his time, but did not Francis give all that potential up too when he took off his clothes? He desperately wanted to be free from the world as he was living it, as he was hurt by it, as he saw it being worsened by others. Francis was not a reaction, he was a *new* example.

Francis was saintly, perhaps *the* most celebrated and pan-religion saint in history. In that sense, Francis was free. He was freer than we who do not quite understand. Along with him, perhaps the best we can do to get closer to him is to believe in miracles also.

The Death of Francis

Francis was now hallowed among men for his historical, transcendental reception of the stigmata. His dreadfully ill state was the talk of every city. The people of Assisi wanted Francis to die *in Assisi*—soon, before fate, accident, or even abduction might establish another of the feuding cities of Umbria (or Tuscany) as the terminal city of Francis' holy life. Celano says that when Francis himself asked that he be brought once again to the Porziuncola chapel, the center of the brotherhood, on the outskirts of Assisi (and when Elias actually had him moved yet again inside the walls of Assisi for burial immediately after Francis' death, to ensure the

---

108 Yarom, 58–60.

body's safety from militarized relic-hunters), "The whole city rejoiced at the coming of the Holy Father."

Francis died on Saturday evening, just after sunset, October 3, 1226, probably about 5:38 P.M. (my timing; see death chart, Figure 17, page 157). Then, on Sunday morning, as soon as it was light, a funeral procession was formed: the brothers bore tree branches and torches raised high, and band musicians played with joy. The body was taken first to the San Damiano church and the quarters there of the Poor Clares so that Clare and the other Poor Ladies could see their beloved Francis' body and kiss its hands. The procession continued then to the small church of Saint George, where Francis had first preached, and he was buried.[109]

After Francis' funeral, Elias wrote a detailed encyclical letter to all the ministers of the Franciscans describing the final days in great detail. He categorically stated that "not one part of his [Francis'] body was free from excessive suffering, and because of the tightening of his sinews all his limbs were stiff, exactly like those of a dead man." Interestingly, this rigorous bodily condition disappeared immediately upon Francis' death: Elias and others picked up Francis' body, washed it and wrapped him in beggar's sack cloth, and they noted how limp and flexible the body was ... and they all saw the stigmata.

Several days before he actually died, Francis had himself stretched out naked on the ground (or floor; differing references are made). Celano tells us that he covered his side wound with his hand, that he called for bread for the final Eucharist.

There are many reports of contemporaneous visions of Francis before Bishops and Ministers of the Order, as he was dying. Francis is to have announced that he was "leaving the world." There are many stories like theses—quite beautiful indeed—that create for history the perfect medieval living-fresco of inspired, Christ-like death.

A particularly lovely occurrence repeated in every narrative, speaks of a multitude of larks—birds that are seen and heard to sing exclusively in daylight hours, in the light of the midday sun— assembling in the dark of evening on the roof of Francis' cell, singing their honor and farewell to their dead brother.

The stories tell us of the brothers singing also, of Francis singing with his final strength. He had just dictated his final verses, *The Canticle to the Sun*, and his voice was yet inspired with strength and light.

---

109 Smith, 194, quoting Celano in the main.

Arnaldo Fortini, whose biography of Francis combines memorably humble devotion with professorial scholarship—in truly remarkable translation by Helen Moak—takes us to the end:

> Francis died just after darkness had settled. Evening was coming on. In the wood the trees were still glowing in a soft and rosy light, though Porziuncola itself, where everyone knelt around Francis, lay in darkness.
>
> After a long pause of shadow and silence, Francis' lips opened on his last invocation—David's prayer in a cave, the prayer of souls sore-oppressed: "With a loud voice I cry out to the Lord; with a loud voice I beseech the Lord."
>
> The brothers made the response in subdued voices: "My complaint I pour out before him; before him I lay bare my distress."
>
> From the edge of paradise, as if on a threshold that opened to light, Francis' voice rose again. He spoke for all troubled and abused souls in the last message of his exhausted heart.
>
> "I look to the right to see, but there is no one who pays me heed. I have lost all means of escape. There is no one who cares for my life."
>
> He cried out in pain. His cry shook the dark walls and flowed out through the door, wide open to gather in the last light of the evening. The tops of the trees were no longer visible, but in the west the skies still burned in fire and blood.
>
> And then there was silence. Francis was dead.[110]

And we know that the Larks came with their song.

Figure 17 (page 157) is Francis' Solar Arc portrait to the date of his death. It is a miracle of confirmation of the birth date and time we defined at the beginning of this study.

The Arc accumulation measures exactly 45 degrees 13 minutes. This is the accumulated *semisquare*, always a time of conspicuous development in anyone's life, a time when all behavioral resources, psychological needs, and personality expression make a special statement in relation to the world.[111]

---

110 Fortini, 614.

111 The arc distance between the natal Sun and the SA-SP Sun, the basis of the Solar Arc direction technique total 45 degrees. Bill Clinton was elected President of the United States in November 1994 in the month of his SA semisquare; O. J. Simpson's estranged wife and her friend were killed in the month of Simpson's SA semi-square.

Remembering our initial analytical grasp of Neptune, it is a wonderment of astrology to have seen this symbol of mysticism, sanctity, and sacrifice, of dissolution and dualism reach Francis' Ascendant precisely for the experience of the stigmata (see Figure 14, page 145). This had to have been the beginning of his death. It was an experience apart from this world (historically, even with Francis in some accounts and artistic depictions, actual corporal levitation is indicated within the stigmatic's experience).

Now, at actual mundane death, Neptune is semisquare its natal position, still within orb of the Ascendant, and semisquare Uranus-Moon. The grand synthesis of birth potential is powerfully reiterated.

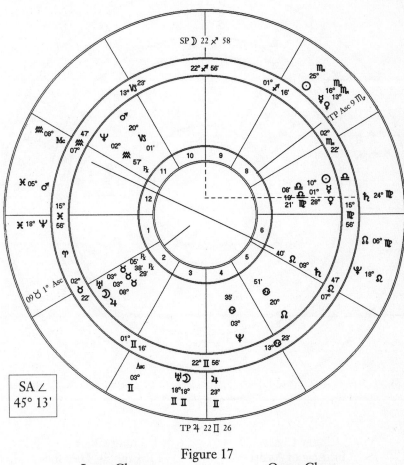

Figure 17

<table>
<tr><td>Inner Chart</td><td>Outer Chart</td></tr>
<tr><td>**Francis of Assisi**</td><td>**SA Death**
Oct. 3, 1226</td></tr>
</table>

SA Jupiter is opposed Francis' Midheaven: his mission is fulfilled and rewarded.

At the stigmata (see Figure 14, page 145), SA Saturn was precisely square to Francis' Midheaven. Now, at his death, the SA MC is opposed natal Saturn: the time of fulfillment, major development, change. Undeniably for Francis, death is fulfillment and freedom. His whole life was dedicated to this moment.

The Secondary Progressed Moon on the day of Francis' death was precisely conjunct his Midheaven! Again and again, angular contacts of epic import; again the fulfillment of every need of life.

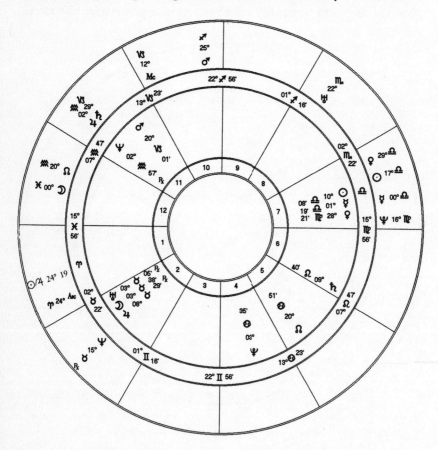

Figure 18

Inner Chart	Outer Chart
Francis of Assisi	**TR Francis' Death**

Oct. 3, 1226, 5:38 p.m. LMT
Porziuncola, Italy.
12E37 43N04

Figure 17 (page 157) also shows the highly sensitive Tertiary positions for Francis' death: coincidentally TP Jupiter is *precisely* conjunct the fourth cusp opposed the Midheaven! The TP Ascendant at 9 Scorpio is opposed natal Jupiter!

Figure 18 (page 158) shows the transits at the chapel of Porziuncola (just outside the walls of Assisi) in the outside ring, for the time close to when Francis died, just after sunset. Note the Ascendant at 24 Aries, the Descendant at 24 Libra, with the Sun at 17 Libra just having crossed below the horizon into the 6th House of the transit chart.

This death Ascendant at Porziuncola made the Midpoint picture: Tr. Asc=natal Sun/Jupiter: fulfillment, success, and happiness.

Pluto at 16 Virgo was very close to or exactly conjunct Francis' natal horizon.

Transiting Jupiter, ruler of Francis' Midheaven and 9th House, out of the grand T-Square construct that was the design of Francis' entire life, had come to exact conjunct with his transcendental Neptune.

Epilogue

So many of the books about Francis have personal statements by the authors as epilogues. This suggests that there has been more than an academic involvement with the subject. Indeed, that is the case for me as well. As I came near to the end of this study, I hoped that it would not get too long because I wanted some space at the end in which to make such a personal statement, although I did not know what I wanted to say.

I have just finished the page above. It is 4:12 in the afternoon, Sunday, December 4, 1994. I forewent the football game of the day and continued working because of my involvement with the end of Francis' life. After all the reading, my companionship with Francis has become very close throughout eight consecutive fourteen-hour writing days. It has been more than an academic involvement.

I hesitated to introduce some last charts of significance, extending the story further. But I must, in the light of a personal, final chart that then follows.

Figure 19 (page 160) shows Francis' horoscope arced to May 25, 1230, three and one-half years after his death, after he was canonized (July 16, 1228). This May date is when Francis' remains were taken from the little church of San Giorgio to the new Basilica di San

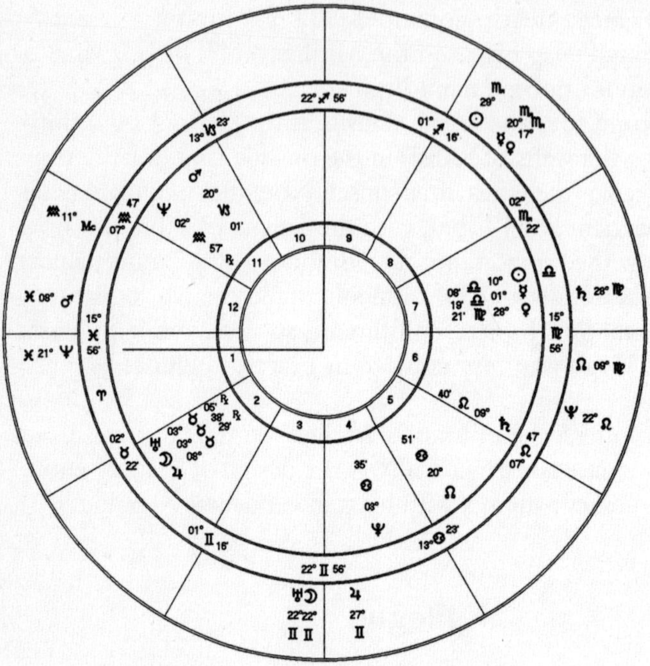

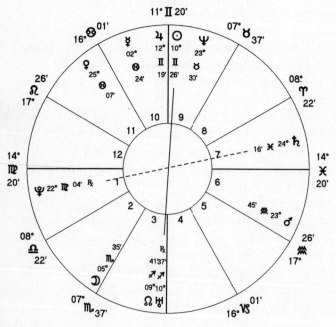

Figure 19
SA Reburial
May 25, 1230

Figure 20
Reburial
May 25, 1230
12:00 P.M. LMT
Assisi, Italy
12E37   43N04
Placidus Houses

Francesco that had been built in record time, thanks to Brother Elias' direction and his wheeling and dealing (see page 141).

This horoscope lives along with Francis' spirit. On his date, SA Neptune was *within 5 minutes of precise square to Francis' natal Midheaven!* SA Uranus-Moon, Francis' all-powerful identity focus, had come to precise opposition with the Midheaven as well!

In Figure 20 (page 160), the transits of that day are shown, for the moment around noon, when the festivities of extombing, processing, and planning a midday mass to honor the retombing of Francis' remains surely would have been at their peak. Note that the Sun is exactly opposed by Uranus, in valid placement at the

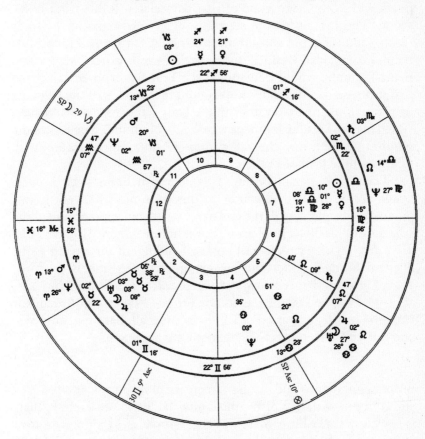

Figure 21

Inner Chart
Francis of Assisi

Outer Chart
SA Writing
Dec. 4, 1994

Placidus Houses

Midheaven, with Jupiter, that glorious morning. Note as well that transiting Saturn and Pluto were in opposition, *both square to Francis' natal Midheaven!*

This is extraordinary energy, power, and even danger—for a dead person.

"As the elaborate procession was nearing its destination [the new Basilica], armed men of the commune, acting in collaboration with Brother Elias, seized the coffin, carried it into the church, barred the doors, and buried it in an excavation [that had been made] in solid rock."[112]

This strange occurrence is captured in Francis' horoscope after death and in the horoscope of that day related to his natal horoscope. The reason for the startling seizure (Uranus) of the body (Pluto) and the rapid entombment (Uranus, Saturn), accomplished behind barricaded Basilica doors, is that the brothers were afraid that the public would demand to see Francis' exposed body and that, because of natural decomposition, the wounds of the stigmata would no longer be visible. With the body safely hidden from view, "the danger of disillusionment vanished" (Neptune). Such were the mindset of the times, the veneration of saints, the obsession with relics, and the love of Francis.

Then, on a personal note, I wondered if Francis' birth chart would speak through direction to this time now, 813 years, two months, and eight days to the end of my writing in appreciation of the astrology of his life. The chart is shown here as Figure 21 (page 161).

I may be very tired—and now self-indulgent for having sacrificed my football game—but I was stunned to see Francis' SA Midheaven after all that time *conjunct the Ascendant I had rectified for him, the 16th degree of Pisces.* I was stunned to see Francis' SP Ascendant from the rectified position of 16 Pisces, after all that time, now precisely at 10 Cancer, precisely opposed my natal Sun.

From beginning to end, we have seen astrology in remarkable synchronization with one of the most unusual lives ever lived. Francis is so relevant for humankind, as an example of sacrifice and love unparalleled. It is reasonable indeed, then, to feel that God would want signs in the heavens to show, as eloquently as in history, the extraordinary being of Francis.

September 26, 1181 at 4:41 P.M. *Ecco il Santo!*

---

112 Fortini, 620, note h.

Bibliography

Armstrong, Karen. *A History of God*. New York: Ballantine Books, 1993.

Brown, Raphael. *The Little Flowers of St. Francis*. New York: Hanover House, 1958.

Campbell, Joseph. Editor. *The Portable Jung*. New York: Viking Penguin, 1971.

Catholic Encyclopedia. Nashville TN: Thomas Nelson Publications, 1986.

Celano, Thomas of. [Tr. Placid Hermann, O.F.M.] *Saint Francis of Assisi*. Chicago: Franciscan Herald Press, 1963.

Cristiani, Msgr. Leon. [Tr. Bouchard, M. Angeline] *Saint Francis of Assisi*. Boston: Daughters of St. Paul, 1983.

Cunningham, Lawrence. Editor. *Brother Francis*. New York: Harper & Row, 1972.

Eerdman. *Eerdman's Handbook of the History of Christianity*. Grand Rapids MI: Eerdman's Publishing Company, 1977.

Fortini, Arnaldo. [Tr. Helen Moak] *Francis of Assisi*. New York: Crossroad, 1992.

Goodrich, Norma Lorre. *The Holy Grail*. New York: HarperCollins, 1992.

Grant, Michael. *Constantine The Great*. New York: Scribners, 1994.

Green, Julien. *God's Fool: the Life and Times of Francis of Assisi*. San Francisco: Harper & Row, 1983.

Hall, Angus. *Strange Cults*. New York: Doubleday, 1976.

Harrison, Ted. *Stigmata: A Medieval Phenomenon in a Modern Age*. New York: St. Martin's Press, 1994.

Jung, Carl G. *Psychology & Religion*. New Haven: Yale University Press, 1938/66.

The Little Flowers of St. Francis of Assisi. Paterson, NJ: St. Anthony Guild Press, 1958.

McManners, John. Editor. *Oxford Illustrated History of Christianity*. London: Oxford University Press, 1990.

Munkasey, Michael. *The Astrological Thesaurus, House Keywords*. St. Paul, MN: Llewellyn Publications, 1992.

Pardoe, Rosemary and Darroll. *The Female Pope*. London: Crucible Thorsens, 1988.

Smith, John Holland. *Francis of Assisi*. New York: Scribner's Sons, 1972.

Sogyal, Rinpoche. *The Tibetan Book of Living and Dying*. HarperSanFrancisco, 1993.

Stock, Dennis and Cunningham, Lawrence. *Saint Francis of Assisi*. San Francisco: Harper & Row, 1981.

Tyl, Noel. *Holistic Astrology*. St. Paul, MN: Llewellyn Publications, 1980.

_____. *Synthesis & Counseling in Astrology*. St. Paul, MN: Llewellyn Publications, 1994.

_____. Editor. *Exploring Consciousness in the Horoscope*. St. Paul, MN: Llewellyn Publications, 1993.

Whitrow, G. J. *Time in History*. London: Oxford University Press, 1988.

Yarom, Nitza. *Body, Blood and Sexuality*. New York: Peter Lange Publishing, 1992.

Personal conversations and discussion with Alan J. Ouimet, S.F.O. (Secular Franciscan Order).

Index

Dracula
The Life of Legend

Following the path of the sun, civilization moves inexorably from the East to the West. Conquest leads the way and, throughout history, every country—some still known and many long forgotten except in name—has had its time to rule the known world. Giants came and went and returned again, and Turkey (the early Anatolia) had dominance and domain longer than most. In the middle of the fifteenth century, with a crescent of occupation already accosting

An astrological rectification of the birth date and time of Prince Vlad Dracula of Wallachia

✦

Europe from across the Adriatic, Turkey moved to secure its religious, trade, and political anchor back in Constantinople, at the entrance to the Black Sea and the wealth of the East.

This arc of influence above Greece from the Adriatic, from Bosnia to Constantinople (now Istanbul)—lands collectively known as the Balkans—has always been a nerve nexus for the world, its dendrites extending further East along the border of the Mediterranean and then south down through the Levant, and down the Rift Valley that is Israel. This is where all politics, faiths, and trade routes have always come together between East and West—to confuse, challenge, and conquer the efforts men made to survive and prosper.

In the middle of the fifteenth century the battles raged incessantly. Countries still fought about which god would prevail for what profit, which force commanded how much respect. The Turks were then the invading hordes. They were the center of all European defensive attention and they had to be defeated. It was into this combative, dangerous world and into this time of the Turks that Dracula was born. It was the world that would extol his loyalty to the Christian faith and cringe at his demonic cruelty.

In Florence, during the last weeks of June and the first week of July 1439, there was an attempt to end the religious schism between the Roman and Eastern Orthodox arms of Christianity, between West and East. The Eastern Emperor, John VIII Paleologus, had put out a call for help to save ancient Byzantium (then Constantinople) from the Ottoman Turks. The threat had been there for many, many years and now an ultimate confrontation was imminent.[1]

The call was heard. The Emperor and Pope Eugenius IV decided to meet in Ferrara, Italy, about 100 miles southwest of Venice. During the initial deliberations, an outbreak of the plague occurred in Ferrara, and the Pope and the Patriarch—and more than 700 scholars, theologians, interpreters, and officials comprising the convention—were persuaded to reconvene in glorious, healthy Florence, 100 miles further south.[2]

It is recorded that this extraordinary ecumenical convocation marched and processed into Florence during a torrential wind and rainstorm; all the delegates and their servants, and the horses, the pompous banners and vestments, were totally drenched. In the wake of the plague in Ferrara, the wet parade into Florence was another poor omen indeed.

In spite of a grand gap between West and East in terms of doctrine and observance, theological issues were somehow stabilized and adjusted to a political flexibility, to a secure defensive position against the Turks. On July 5, there was a grand ceremony in the Duomo,[3] and it was announced to the world, "Let the

---

1 *Ottoman* is the designation for Turkey's vast empire. The term was derived through English mispronunciation of the name of the great Sultan Osman I who entered Asia Minor in the late thirteenth Century. The Turks then entered the Balkans in 1345, securing Constantinople in 1453. At its Zenith under Sultan Suleiman I in the mid-sixteenth century—having annexed lands extending to the Persian Gulf, embracing the entire southern coastline of the Mediterranean as well, including Alexandria—Suleiman began to advance into Austria. He failed to capture Vienna, and the Ottoman Empire began its decline. The Turkish fleet was annihilated in the Eastern Mediterranean in 1571.

2 Hibbert, 92.

3 The "Cathedral, the Dome;" the great Cathedral of Florence—Santa Maria del Fiore—had just been enlarged with Brunelleschi's first-ever grand dome on March 25, 1436, just three years before the ecumenical conference.

heavens rejoice and the earth exult: the wall which divided the Western and Eastern Churches has fallen. Peace and concord have returned."[4]

Figure 1 (page 171) is drawn for the approximate time of this grand announcement to the world. The Sun and Pluto in conjunction at the Midheaven opposed by Jupiter in Capricorn certainly shows the establishment of grand, new perspective in terms of religious and philosophical dogma, but Jupiter which rules the 3rd, the House of treaty signings, is *retrograde*. This is another poor omen indeed: the extraordinary potential and resourcefulness (Jupiter-Pluto) of the treaty are tentative, vulnerable, undecided; and the anchor to the vision is undefended in the chart's northern hemisphere. [This opposition axis keyed by retrograde Jupiter is also square the Ascendant.]

The dramatic idealism of it all seen in the Mercury-Venus conjunction in Leo *is challenged by the square from Mars*. This is the final omen: the ruler of the West (the 7th), Mars, is still at odds with the ruler of the East, Venus (the Ascendant). [Or perhaps this can be reversed since the Council took place in the West, i.e., the Ascendant signifies the Western power and the Descendant the Eastern.] And this Mars is also conjunct the Moon, dispositor of the Sun-Pluto conjunction and *ruler of the 10th*.

Deep within the entire problem is the assumed God-sanction of rightness propelling the Roman Catholic cause: the West demands respect and adherence to its dogma, which is especially focused within the singular issue of the rift, the conceptual assimilation of the Holy Trinity (Neptune in the 11th, recognition expected, squared by Uranus).[5]

The treaty was soon abandoned. It was a symptom of the times: princely allegiances were easily washed away in the wake of opportunism. Dracula swam these currents and was eventually drowned by them, as we shall see.

---

4 Hibbert, 93.

5 Father and Son and Holy Ghost: "The Father engenders the Son, the son becomes incarnate, and the Holy Spirit proceeds from the Father and the Son." Western faith was confronted by Greek (Eastern) logic. The problem is with "Father and Son *[filioque]*," and this problem still divides East and West within Christendom. See Green, 167; Grant, 168.

The Fall of Constantinople

By the time of Constantine (c. 280–337), Rome, the eternal city, had ceased to be the political center of the empire. Rome was simply too far removed from overland trade routes West to East, too distanced from defensive positions for its northern cities to control its outreach to the expanding world. Additionally, powerful conquerors like Constantine did not want to be headquartered in Rome so close to the Senate and its edicts.

Constantine decided on a new site for a new capital. He rebuilt the ancient city of Byzantium. The site was near where he had enjoyed a great military victory (the defeat of the "pagan rival" Licinius, giving Constantine "possession of the East"), and its magnificent harbor allowed defense by sea as well as land. He inaugurated and dedicated his new Constantinople in 326. It was the key city-symbol for the two halves of the known world.[6]

The fall of Constantinople to the Turks, when Dracula was twenty-one years old—besides being a milestone of world history—establishes the arena and political climate for Dracula's life: the deadly intrigues, the battles of vengeance with the Turks after his imprisonment as a child, the hideous tortures he employed, his bitter determination to kill the king of Poland, the duplistic treaties with the Turks and Hungarians, his second long imprisonment and third rise to the throne, and his mysterious assassination, with his head displayed on a spike *in Constantinople*.

Figure 2 (page 173) is the signal conjunction of Saturn and Neptune in 1450. This conjunction occurs every thirty-five or thirty-six years as a generational statement. In this Figure from the perspective of Constantinople (thirty-two months before the city's fall), the Sun is depressed by the massive conjunction. The Sun rules the 10th, the "party in power," the Christians. It is put down strongly by doctrinaire coercion (Saturn in Virgo), compounded by subterfuge, revolutionary turnover, and upset (Neptune).

---

6   Grant, 116–122. Grant observes, "It was possible to see where the future lay, and the new foundation [Constantinople] marked a definitive transfer of the epicenter of the [Roman] empire to the east, which was richer than Italy and the western provinces, and would house imperial rulers long after the west had gone."

    Groh, 268–269 recounts the long debate about Constantine's faith, his Christianity. Recent authentication of a sermon Constantine preached sometime between 317 and 324 shows that the mighty ruler declared publicly that the (Roman) Christian God was indeed his sponsor and driving power. Constantine was baptized on his deathbed (337) and buried in the Church of the Holy Apostles in Constantinople, where he had had erected six coffins, symbolizing the apostles, on either side of his resting place.

Pluto is opposed by Mars, both rulers of the Ascendant, and this axis is squared by the Ascendant axis as well, dramatically describing the battle-force that can be brought upon the people.

Venus, ruler of the 7th—the other forces, the Turks—forms an arm of the T-Square, square the Mars-Pluto axis. Venus is in the 12th (hidden enemies) and supportively trined by the Moon in the 4th, the "party out of power," the infidels, the Turks. The Moon's rulership of the 9th and the Mercury-Jupiter square (each planet in

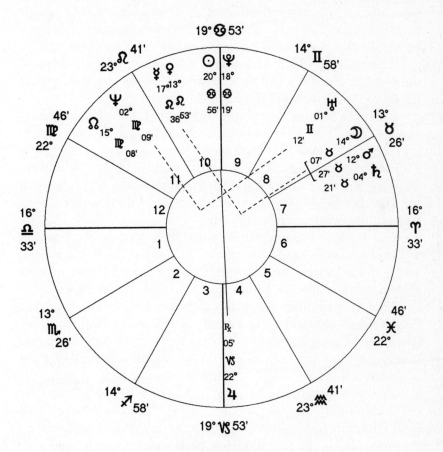

Figure 1
Ecumenical Council
July 5, 1439, 12:00 P.M. LMT
Florence, Italy
11E15 43N46
Placidus Houses

its own sign) show the tension of dogma in the background of the epochal anxiety.

Figure 3 (page 173) shows the Solar Eclipse that occurred thirty days before the grand battles. The invading Turks and the defensive Christians saw the Eclipse of the Sun form in the early afternoon in the western sky above the Turks' encampment.

After the Eclipse there were other omens, and a heavy atmosphere of gloom and doom pervaded Constantinople: the dome of the great Saint Sophia cathedral glowed red. The Christians saw the light as a threatening reflection of the Turkish campfires outside their walls; the Turks saw the light as a confirming sign from heaven that Islam would finally prevail to enlighten the ancient city.

The Eclipse, which darkened the Moon, threatened to fulfill the prophecy held dear by the Christians that the city would never fall while the Moon was bright in the heavens!

During a solemn procession within the city to bring a heavy statue of the Blessed Virgin to the cathedral to invoke God's blessing, the statue came loose and fell to the ground; a violent storm with thunder and lightning then broke out; there was widespread flooding; and then a thick fog settled over the city—highly unusual for May. It was said that God had brought in the fog in order to conceal His departure from the city.

Finally, there was the prophecy that the *last* emperor of the city of Constantinople would have the same name as the first emperor, and that was indeed the case with Constantine XI Dragases, now awaiting with his people complete annihilation by the Turks.[7]

The Eclipse chart has brought Neptune forward from the Grand Conjunction chart to a Midheaven position over Constantinople, opposing Jupiter. This opposition with Jupiter augurs poorly for the Christians since Jupiter rules the Ascendant here at Constantinople.

Mercury, ruler of the 7th, the Turks (the attackers), is "caught up" within the Eclipse, is part of it, and is related by *trine* to Neptune. Mercury and Jupiter-Neptune rule the Virgo-Pisces axis on the 9th–3rd axis, the axis of dogma, philosophy, religious teaching.

Saturn in the 10th, the Christian power, is retrograde and opposed Venus, the Midheaven ruler and dispositor of the Eclipse, the Christians in power, the gloom and doom.

---

7 Reported by the Greek historian Chalcondyles and retrieved by Florescu and McNally, *Dracula: Prince of Many Faces*, 70–73.

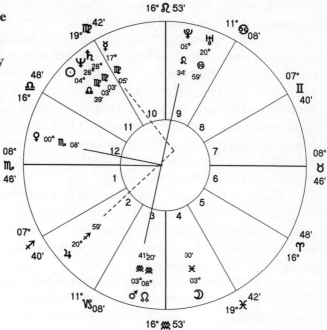

Figure 2
Saturn-Neptune
Sept. 19, 1450
8:51 A.M. LMT
Istanbul, Turkey
28E58 41N01
Placidus Houses

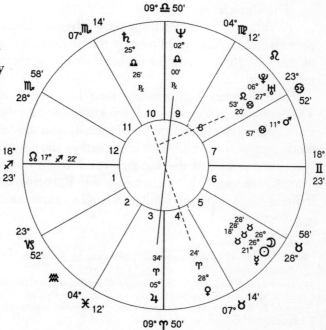

Figure 3
Solar Eclipse
May 8, 1453
8:55 P.M. LMT
Istanbul, Turkey
28E58 41N01
Placidus Houses

This Saturn-Venus axis is squared by Uranus. Saturn and Uranus both rule the 2nd House, Constantinople's resources, which were severely depleted by this time before the battle. The build-up of Turkish annexation had been protracted over several years, and thousands of Constantinople's citizenry had left the city for safety elsewhere. The city had shrunk from some one-million inhabitants to about 60,000 now facing the Turks, with many of the remaining population being non-military clergy. The Christians simply could not defend their nine miles of border facing the sea and the five miles on land. Reinforcements would not come. Politics—and omens—had got in the way.[8]

Finally, Mars in Cancer is peregrine (yet exactly semisquare the Eclipse) and can run away with the horoscope.[9] Mars rules the 4th (and the 12th), the opposing political power, and Mars rules force. The Turkish army numbered 100,000 men, and the Sultan himself, Mehmed II, was on the scene.

Mars also rules gunpowder, which had just been incorporated into Middle Eastern warfare. The Turks had had a monstrous cannon built, nicknamed the "Basilica": it was twenty-seven feet long, had a forty-eight-inch bore, and was capable of firing projectiles weighing 600 pounds, propelled by 150 pounds of gunpowder.[10]

The scene was set.

A Turkish astrologer must have advised Sultan Mehmed who personally gave the signal to start the battle at 1:30 in the morning on May 29; Jupiter would have been visible on the horizon, having just risen in Aries.

The "Basilica" had smashed open the city walls the days before. The Sultan's European mercenaries now stormed those walls. They were followed by the Sultan's bodyguards who were ready to kill any mercenary who turned back or lagged in the advance. Then came the elite troops and the military band drumming a rapid march-beat. Constantinople fell, and so did Emperor Constantine XI, fighting like a common soldier in hand to hand combat.

---

8 Ibid., 72.

9 See Tyl, 155–190. *Peregrination:* not making any Ptolemaic aspect, nor in a sign of rulership or exaltation.

10 Florescu and McNally, 73. The weight of Basilica was such that it required 700 men and fifteen pair of oxen to pull it into position. The shot left a crater six feet deep. It could be fired only seven times in twenty-four hours because of the danger of overheating and explosion.

Some 4,000 Christians were killed and 50,000 men, women, and children were enslaved. Sultan Mehmed waited the traditional three days to allow his army the rewards of looting and then entered the city, going directly to the cathedral to pray to Allah. Florescu and McNally report that it was believed then that the Prophet Mohammed had said, "Blessed be he who conquers Constantinople." And so it was: Mehmed was named Conqueror, and a turning point in history was established.

The Ottoman Empire was now geographically part of Europe. The Pope, who had provided no support for defense, wrote: "The light of Christianity has suddenly gone out. We shall not see it again in our lifetime."[11]

Along with cyclical occurrences of the Black Death (bubonic plague), tuberculosis, syphilis, leprosy, and small pox; natural disasters like floods and earthquakes; constant intrusions westward, north, and south by the warring Turks; and intricate and compelling webs of superstitions that fatalized behaviors, this siege of Constantinople represented a culmination of all things fearsome. It affected all states and nations, especially Wallachia (now southern Romania) to the northwest of Constantinople; Transylvania and Moldavia further to the north; and Hungary just further west. Times were very, very difficult and dangerous.

Dracula's Father and the Order of the Dragon

As his son will be, Vlad the father was born in Wallachia, a state about the size of the State of New York, with a population of about 500,000.[12] Two classes—Boyars (wealthy land-owners with political power) and peasants—made up the population. The army amounted to about ten percent of the citizenry. All were ruled by a prince.

Growing up, Vlad spent much time in Hungary and in Germany, especially Nuremberg, the center of operations for the Holy Roman Empire, where he enjoyed the many alliance treaties with Wallachia. It is suggested that Vlad had been converted to Roman Catholicism from the Eastern Orthodox. Upon his father's death, Vlad the son would be determined to secure the Wallachian throne for himself.[13]

---

11 Ibid., 75.
12 Ibid., 30.
13 The right of progenitor succession was not established in Wallachia. The Boyars determined succession. Politics, international alliances, and subterfuge were key determining factors.

Vlad the father needed powerful support to commandeer the Wallachian boyars to his side. He sought support from the Polish king. This threatened to disrupt extant alliances, and the potential crumpled. Next, the twenty-eight-year old aspirant went to mighty Constantinople, willing even to marry a Byzantine princess if that would help his cause. Vlad was overwhelmed by the city's courtly glamour and the spiritual power centered in the holy shrine of St. Sophia. But no major support could be rallied and no marriage opportunity came about.

The fifth Crusade against the Turks was being organized by the Roman Emperor in Nuremberg in early 1430. Vlad went to this center of excitement and his life was changed.[14]

Vlad the father was inducted into the Order of the Dragon, a very private, knight-like fraternity among young European elitists, sworn to protect the Christian cause (Roman and Eastern Orthodox) at all times, with special mention being given to the Franciscan Brothers Minor. The Order of the Dragon was ratified by the Roman Emperor, and a golden necklace was given to Vlad bearing the seal of the Order. It was to be with him to the death and then with his son until death and further, the mysterious threads within his casket (discussed later). Vlad the father was now indisputably in fine company, in an alliance, a brotherhood that extended throughout eastern Europe.

Vlad was not to become Prince for several years (his half-brother ruled). When he returned to Wallachia, he was given the post of military governor of Transylvania, another state in the region, contiguous to and north of Wallachia ... and he was given a new name.

The boyars knew of Vlad's induction into the Order of the Dragon. They now called him "Dracul." Florescu and McNally point out that the word *drac* means "dragon" or, indeed, "devil" (the dragon symbolized the devil); *-ul* was simply the definite article "the." The peasants gravitated to the demonic meaning more than the loftier symbolic one, and this would condition strongly the historical view of Dracul and, especially, of his son.

---

14 These Crusades were an echo of the papal Crusades to rescue Jerusalem from the Moslems. These "Holy Land" Crusades began in 1095 and ended in 1291. Then, attention shifted away from the Moslems and onto the Turks, away from Jerusalem and onto Constantinople, and the *Eastern* Crusades began.

Dracul married,[15] and three sons were born: Prince Mircea (1428), Vlad Dracula *[vlahd drah'-koo-lah]* (i.e., "son of Dracul") in 1431, and Radu "The Handsome" (1435).

Florescu writes that Vlad Dracula was "born in Sighisoara, under the sign of Sagittarius, in November or, more likely, December 1431."[16] In personal discussion with Professor Florescu, he has explained to me that this birth month/sign datum for Dracula came from an historian colleague in Bucharest who also researched Dracula and who was knowledgeable in astrology. I only hoped that it was not a superficial astrological assignment to fit Dracula's infamy as "Vlad the Impaler," impaling many tens of thousands of victims on stakes (Sagittarius) and planting them in groves and along roads (for miles) as displays of his authority and might. My astrological study—which we shall now analyze together—agrees with Sagittarius for several reasons. Additionally, in the process of rectification and in the light of new data presented—with astrology filling in some gaps in the historical record—the date and time were brought together conclusively, as will be reported later.

The Astrology

Theoretical justification of Sagittarius is not difficult: the key is to appreciate the sign's *energy for self-assertion,* for what is right, its drive to affect thought, to impose opinion.[17] The Sagittarian life-energy fights for acknowledgment and respect. Undeniably, Dracula needed to be respected, to be feared to the extreme. He had to have reasons, and those reasons were surely framed in his early life conditioning.

When Dracula was very young, his father took him and his younger brother (Radu) to do business with the great Sultan Murad (the father of Mehmed II, conqueror-to-be of Constantinople). The negotiations with the Sultan ended with Dracul leaving young Vlad

---

15 The role of women in the life of Dracul or his son is barely noticeable. Such was the way of the times: it reflected the "harem philosophy" of the Ottomans that spilled over into the eastern European states and the style of keeping genealogical history. Women were lost to the bidding of the men. There was little distinction between servant, concubine, or wife.

16 Florescu and McNally, 45.

17 Tyl, *Synthesis and Counseling,* 76, 94–95.

and Radu in the Sultan's household *as hostages*; in this way the Sultan would hold Vlad to his word. We shall see how this long imprisonment in Dracula's youth builds within him an extreme drive for vengeance, compounded by his father's murder by the king of Poland and his older brother being buried alive by his own people (the boyars) in Tirgoviste.

Additionally, Dracula became totally caught up with internationalism, treaties and alliances, and many different languages. His political philosophy was to create maximum strength in his own realm in order to be powerful elsewhere. In other words, his strength would have to be known far and wide and converted into fear in order for respect and compliance to be inspired.

Savage acts became the rule of his reign. Dracula's murder record within the major time of his rule—just six years—is numbered from 40,000 to 100,000 people (conservatively, that is about thirty killings per day for six years), a calculation made by various historians and by the papal nuncio, the bishop of Erlau, near the end of Dracula's career in 1475.[18] Impalement was his favored method of execution according to all the histories (German, Russian, Hungarian, Turkish, Romanian). Stakes stood permanently prepared in his palace courtyard, as a deterrent, as an advertisement. To this day, to the Romanians, Prince Vlad is not known as "Dracula" but as "Vlad Tepes (*tsep-pesh*)," *Vlad the Impaler.*

Dracula combined physical torture with "moral torture."[19] He liked to obtain confessions prior to punishment, as the researchers say, "to put a man in the wrong before he was executed." This was a forced justification for the murder to follow.

Dracula placed inordinate emphasis on words, on artful polemics (along with his great language skill, a 3rd House emphasis): an adversary could talk himself out of death if his words were clever and included flattery of Dracula, self-debasement, and a daring statement welcoming whatever "justice" Dracula would deem appropriate.

We must assume the Sagittarius position for the Sun and build out from that center through the rest of the planets to establish Dracula's life portrait.

Figure 4 (page 179) shows the ephemeris pages for November–December 1431. Inspecting the planetary positions Jupiter through Pluto, we see that there is one major aspect in formation

---

18 Florescu and McNally, 104.
19 Ibid., 106.

between two of the "heavy" planets: Saturn and Uranus make a square in cardinal signs during the whole Sagittarian period. This aspect highlights an ego-dramatic intensification of extraordinary ambition. If it is tied into the other planetary pictures, Dracula's administrative power would be well delineated.

Another dimension of this Saturn-Uranus relationship that is very important in Dracula's life is *the intensification of conservatism, of dogma, of rigid ways of doing things.* Normally, Saturn-Uranus contacts suggest a struggle between the conservative and the avant-

+ 0:00 UT				Geocentric Tropical Longitudes for NOV 1431								
Date	Sid.Time	Sun	Moon	Node	Mercury	Venus	Mars	Jupiter	Saturn	Uranus	Neptune	Pluto
13	4:00:31	29♏03 02	01✕17	12≈57	17♐47	16♑15	26♐01	12Ⅱ11R	21♑26	25♈51R	18♌32R	09♋30R
14	4:04:28	00♐04 04	15 20	12 54	19 10	17 18	26 47	12 03	21 31	25 50	18 32	09 29
15	4:08:25	01 04 55	29 40	12 50	20 31	18 20	27 33	11 55	21 37	25 48	18 32	09 28
16	4:12:21	02 05 47	14♈13	12 47	21 50	19 22	28 19	11 47	21 42	25 46	18 32	09 28
17	4:16:18	03 06 40	28 57	12 44	23 08	20 23	29 05	11 39	21 48	25 44	18 32	09 27
18	4:20:14	04 07 34	13♉43	12 41	24 24	21 24	29 51	11 31	21 53	25 42	18 31	09 26
19	4:24:11	05 08 30	28 24	12 38	25 37	22 25	00≈37	11 23	21 59	25 41	18 31	09 25
20	4:28:07	06 09 26	12Ⅱ52	12 35	26 48	23 25	01 23	11 15	22 04	25 39	18 31	09 24
21	4:32:04	07 10 23	27 00	12 31	27 56	24 24	02 09	11 07	22 10	25 37	18 31	09 23
22	4:36:01	08 11 21	10♋44	12 28	29 00	25 24	02 56	10 59	22 16	25 36	18 30	09 21
23	4:39:57	09 12 20	24 02	12 25	00♑00	26 22	03 42	10 51	22 21	25 34	18 30	09 20
24	4:43:54	10 13 20	06♌54	12 22	00 55	27 21	04 28	10 42	22 27	25 32	18 30	09 19
25	4:47:50	11 14 22	19 24	12 19	01 45	28 19	05 14	10 34	22 33	25 31	18 29	09 18
26	4:51:47	12 15 24	01♍37	12 15	02 29	29 16	06 00	10 26	22 39	25 29	18 29	09 17
27	4:55:43	13 16 28	13 36	12 12	03 06	00≈13	06 47	10 18	22 45	25 28	18 28	09 16
28	4:59:40	14 17 32	25 28	12 09	03 35	01 09	07 33	10 10	22 51	25 27	18 28	09 15
29	5:03:36	15 18 37	07♎18	12 06	03 56	02 05	08 19	10 02	22 57	25 25	18 27	09 14
30	5:07:33	16 19 44	19 10	12 03	04 07	03 00	09 06	09 54	23 04	25 24	18 27	09 13

+ 0:00 UT				Geocentric Tropical Longitudes for DEC 1431								
Date	Sid.Time	Sun	Moon	Node	Mercury	Venus	Mars	Jupiter	Saturn	Uranus	Neptune	Pluto
1	5:11:30	17♐20 51	01♏09	12≈00	04♑07R	03≈54	09≈52	09Ⅱ46R	23♑10	25♈23R	18♌26R	09♋12R
2	5:15:26	18 21 59	13 18	11 56	03 57	04 48	10 38	09 38	23 16	25 21	18 25	09 10
3	5:19:23	19 23 07	25 40	11 53	03 34	05 41	11 25	09 30	23 22	25 20	18 25	09 09
4	5:23:19	20 24 17	08♐16	11 50	03 01	06 34	12 11	09 22	23 29	25 19	18 24	09 08
5	5:27:16	21 25 27	21 06	11 47	02 15	07 25	12 57	09 14	23 35	25 18	18 23	09 07
6	5:31:12	22 26 37	04♑09	11 44	01 19	08 16	13 44	09 06	23 41	25 17	18 23	09 06
7	5:35:09	23 27 48	17 24	11 40	00 14	09 06	14 30	08 58	23 48	25 16	18 22	09 04
8	5:39:06	24 28 59	00≈51	11 37	29♐00	09 56	15 16	08 51	23 54	25 15	18 21	09 03
9	5:43:02	25 30 10	14 27	11 34	27 41	10 44	16 03	08 43	24 01	25 14	18 20	09 02
10	5:46:59	26 31 21	28 13	11 31	26 19	11 32	16 49	08 36	24 08	25 13	18 19	09 01
11	5:50:55	27 32 32	12✕07	11 28	24 57	12 19	17 36	08 28	24 14	25 13	18 18	09 00
12	5:54:52	28 33 43	26 09	11 25	23 38	13 05	18 22	08 21	24 21	25 12	18 17	08 58
13	5:58:48	29 34 53	10♈18	11 21	22 23	13 49	19 08	08 14	24 28	25 11	18 16	08 57
14	6:02:45	00♑36 04	24 33	11 18	21 16	14 33	19 55	08 07	24 34	25 10	18 15	08 56
15	6:06:41	01 37 14	08♉50	11 15	20 17	15 16	20 41	08 00	24 41	25 10	18 14	08 55

Copyright (C) 1987 Matrix Software, Big Rapids MI 49307

Figure 4
Ephemeris for November–December 1431

garde, the potential for radical change from the old way to the new way of doing things. For Dracula, this is mutated into his arch-conservative enforcement of his will through avant-garde methods, his ways of meting out his personal sense of justice.

Indeed, everything Dracula did served his ambition and needs for power, even his conversion to Roman Catholicism late in life to please King Matthias of Hungary, to get out of prison, to have his sins forgiven, was a strategy to regain the throne. This *is* a fight between Saturn and Uranus, with Saturn in Capricorn dominating for most of Dracula's life.

We can see a conjunction of Venus and Mars in Aquarius for the second half of the Sagittarian period. This could be quite important to capture the sexual emphasis—the "morbid sexual deviation," especially toward women—that is revealed through Dracula's tortures: the symbolism of the constant impaling, his excision of women's and men's genitalia. One story related in all the histories (from a Slavic narrative) is that a concubine told Dracula she was pregnant with his child; after having her examined, Dracula knew it was impossible; and literally had her ripped open to reveal that fact.[20]

This Venus-Mars conjunction in Aquarius—normally a social-ly-aware relationship thrust for anything but evil; rather, for innovative good—could be distorted within the whole astrological portrait *by the opposition this conjunction can make with Neptune* in the second week of December.

In December, the Moon positions range from Scorpio to early Aries. The lure of the Scorpio Moon is extremely strong through the association of complex sexuality and brutality with the sign of Scorpio, which is easily overstated in astrological studies. But looking very carefully at the ephemeris page, we see that Pluto—except for a possible relationship with the Moon—will be peregrine, very powerful in its lack of Ptolemaic contact with the Sun or the other planets. This Pluto itself could take up the Scorpio banner.

Throughout the study of Dracula's history, there is an extreme awareness of defensiveness, a pervasiveness of self-protection: from his obsession with building walls (the walls of Bucharest especially, raising that city to the rank of princely residence; founded in the

---

20 "Realizing he had been made an object of ridicule, [Dracula] had her womb cut open from her sexual organs to her breasts. As the unfortunate woman lay dying, writhing in excruciating pain, Dracula cynically remarked: 'Let the world see where I have been.'" Ibid., 107.

mid-thirteenth century but matured in strength by Dracula during his reign), fortifying monasteries, building mountain fortresses and his notorious Castle Dracula;[21] to his need for spiritual atonement, his building of many churches and monasteries, of being often in the company of prelates of the Church. Dracula liked to think of himself as a protector of the whole Orthodox world, not merely the Romanian church.[22]

All this is a very clear mixture of Sagittarius and Scorpio, of Scorpio and Sagittarius. There is the energy for power and personal conviction, the dastardly action upon it, and then the defensiveness about it all, rationalizing it through religion.[23]

Dracula gathered beggars and the infirm and ill street people together in a banquet hall and fed them richly. He then burned down the barricaded building, including all the people, to improve the health of his State. He was cleansing his realm.

Defensiveness, walls, atonement; inspiration and rationalization; again, Scorpio and Sagittarius. With the Sagittarius Sun, Scorpio must be emphasized in Dracula's horoscope. But is it through the Moon?

Figure 5 (page 183) is the noon chart for the Scorpio Moon possibility, December 1 or 2 (into 3). Figure 6 (page 183) is the noon chart for the Capricorn Moon possibility, since, on December 7, this Moon is conjunct Saturn in Capricorn, therefore involved with the Uranus square. Would this deep press upon the Moon tell us something? Is that the coldness and lethal administrative power we are talking about, then rationalized by the Sagittarian energy? Could the Scorpio component then be fitted *to the Ascendant*?

In Figure 5, there is a curious separation in the whole-form of the portrait: the Moon-square-Neptune unit is clearly separate from the Saturn-square-Uranus unit. The Venus-Mars subgroup is trined Jupiter, and alone; the Sun is trine Neptune, and all these units are

---

21 Ibid., 88.

22 Ibid., 97–98.

23 To show Dracula's love of the bon mot in the light of his torture/atonement syndrome: "Two monks came to visit the palace at Tirgoviste. [They] climbed to the top of the Chindia Tower and were shown by Dracula the customary scene of horror in the court-yard below, which was strewn with impaled cadavers. Dracula was evidently expecting some form of protest. Instead of reproof, one of the two monks reacted quite meekly, 'You are appointed by God to punish the evildoers.' The prince hardly expected this enunciation of the doctrine of divine right, and consequently spared and rewarded the monk." The second monk spoke his mind and was impaled on the spot. From a German narrative, Florescu and McNally, 98.

separated centrally by the Mercury-Pluto opposition. The display seems fragmented, disunited. Indeed, a case could be made for a division (a schism) in Dracula's psyche, but that does not really hold up in the reality of his life: Dracula was well-integrated in actions, he was thoroughly committed to how he was; he was not one way one moment and another way at another time; duplistic in allegiances but singularly focused in performance.

Figure 6 (page 183) brings a surprise into view: a Fire Grand Trine among the Sun, Uranus, and Neptune. This construct is an arch defense mechanism, a closed circuit of motivational self-sufficiency. Dracula does as he pleases. He is driven, potentially obsessed, with proving himself in dramatic fashion, commanding respect. He is a law unto himself.[24]

The way into or out of a Grand Trine is through any planet in opposition or square to one of the corners. Here, the outlet would be through Mars, which opposes Neptune within the Grand Trine, and through Saturn, which squares Uranus within the construct. Mars and Saturn, life and death at the ultimate level; killing at the despotic level. And are not "walls" part of the significance of the defensive Grand Trine complex?

Figure 6 suddenly overpowers Figure 5. The Moon now in a Cardinal sign captures Dracula's getting-things-done persona. After all, when Vlad the father lay dying,[25] he sent on to his son the gold necklace of the Order of the Dragon, transferring the sworn duty to protect the Christian faith. Dracula was privileged and highly motivated by this act.

In his life of mayhem, Dracula was not only working out some deep personal psycho-tragic knots, he was pursuing a duty passed on by his father, he was administering his realm to accomplish something. What rationalization! The Capricorn austerity and organizational power—and, indeed, the sign's religiously rationalized inquisitorial nature—definitely gain answer from reality.

---

24 Tyl, *Synthesis & Counseling*, 284–302. The Grand Trine construct is found disproportionately often in the horoscopes of criminals: one takes one's own road. Actions are sustained by deeply personal justifications, but while the defense is strong *the freedom is curtailed*. In other words, after a while, the tail wags the dog.

25 The heroic Hungarian prince, John Hunyadi decided to eliminate Dracul who, in spite of his duplistic dealings with the Turks and the Eastern Christians, had blamed Hunyadi for a particular Christian defeat. Hunyadi collusively and artfully discredited Dracul and then motivated the prince who would become Vladislav II, King of Poland, to pursue and kill Dracul.

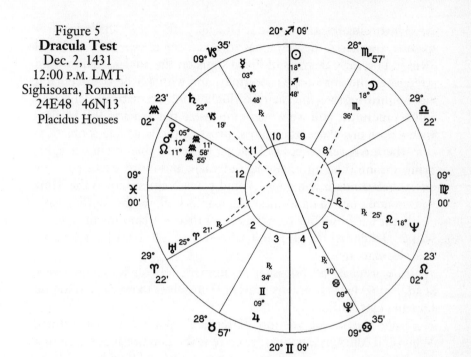

Figure 5
Dracula Test
Dec. 2, 1431
12:00 P.M. LMT
Sighisoara, Romania
24E48   46N13
Placidus Houses

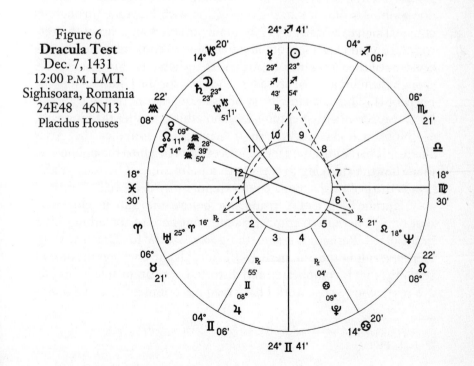

Figure 6
Dracula Test
Dec. 7, 1431
12:00 P.M. LMT
Sighisoara, Romania
24E48   46N13
Placidus Houses

The timing tests throughout Dracula's life—as we shall see—frequently emphasize degree areas in Fixed signs, especially 0–3 and 10–13. The early degrees of Fixed signs on the angles, then, would strengthen the horoscope powerfully, and with a Scorpio Ascendant we would preserve the Scorpio dimensions dramatically, through Pluto peregrine, and we would emphasize the 3rd and 9th Houses with Capricorn there, the mental process, the language sophistication, the many references to Dracula's considerable intelligence, his brilliant mind, the international outreach, and more. Picture it: this Scorpio Ascendant alinement would place Neptune upon the Midheaven and Mars in opposition, angular as well, on the fourth cusp!

Figure 7 shows our rectification of Prince Vlad Dracula's horoscope: December 7, 1431 at 3:18 A.M. in Sighisoara [*ziggy-shwa'-rah*], Romania.

The unity of this horoscope is immediately obvious, and several additional measurements present themselves to reveal and define Dracula extraordinarily well.

Note the retrogradation pattern: all planets except Saturn, Venus and Mars are retrograde. Here is the definite suggestion of a psycho-contrapuntal level to everything about Dracula, to all he does. Venus is drawn into the opposition with Neptune through its conjunction with Mars: this Neptunian touch is an echo of the retrogradation, and it is most telling here since Venus rules the 7th, the presentation Vlad Dracula makes to others, to his public. He thought himself a social crusader—not just for the Church—but for his people. This is a clear twist of the Aquarian potential signified here; the aspect with Neptune, i.e., something is other than it seems.

Note that Mercury is in 0 Capricorn, conjunct the Aries Point.[26] This brings the mental process forward into the public eye, identifies the thinking process with a public line. The retrogradation is the personal agenda counterpoint at work as well.

Neptune is oriental, rising last before the Sun in clockwise motion.[27] There is an emphatic statement here of something ideal or idealized. Perhaps it is something *unattainable* for Dracula. With Neptune ruling the 5th, perhaps the ideal is the core significance of sexuality, that is complicated and distorted or unattainable in his life. No researcher whose work I have read has not mentioned Dracula's

---

26 Tyl, *Synthesis & Counseling*, 303–311. The Aries Point suggests public focus.
27 Ibid., 497.

obsessive psychosexual difficulty—often stated as an inclination to impotence—that he was ineffective sexually and overcompensated for this deep undercutting of his masculine power.

The deeper and deeper we get into understanding Dracula, the more and more Neptune and its concomitant pathologies manifest themselves. The broad conjunction with the Midheaven tells us that every transit, arc, or progression to the Midheaven will work *through the Neptune veil* and, in turn, engage the sense of a powerful, angular Mars, conjunct Venus. With the nodal axis involved as

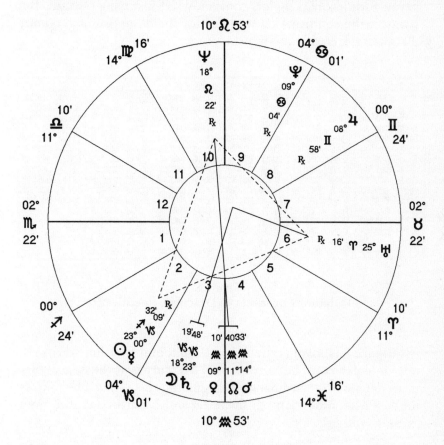

Figure 7
Dracula
Dec. 7, 1431, 3:18 P.M. LMT
Sighisoara, Romania
24E48 46N13
Placidus Houses

well, *the public thrust for all personal difficulties is strongly suggested.* With Venus' rulership of the 12th as well, the mix gains even more relevance within the swirl of psychological impedimenta.

With the retrogradation pattern, with the powerful and dominating Neptune, with the depression below the horizon and the accentuation of the mental axis (Saturn ruling the 3rd, holding the Moon-Saturn conjunction; the Moon ruling the 9th holding Pluto peregrine), with the walled-in defensive behavior of the Grand Trine and the lethal outlets through Mars and Uranus-Saturn, we have a formidably complex, constantly self-justifying portrait. But where is the confirmation we need for the despotism and cruelty that twist the credibility of history?

Midpoint Sort: 90° Dial											
☿	000°09'	♄/♇	016°26'	♇/☊	025°22'	♀/Mc	040°01'	☉/♅	054°24'	♂/♅	079°55'
☉/♇	001°18'	☉/Mc	017°12'	♂/♇	026°49'	♀/☊	040°25'	☿/♅	057°42'	♀/Asc	080°46'
♃/♄	001°23'	☉/☊	017°35'	♆/♇	028°43'	Mc	040°53'	☉/Asc	057°57'	Mc/Asc	081°37'
☿/♇	004°37'	☽	018°19'	☽/♀	028°45'	☊/Mc	041°17'	☿/Asc	061°15'	♅/♆	081°49'
☽/☉	005°56'	☉/♂	019°03'	♅/Asc	028°49'	☊	041°40'	♅/♇	062°10'	☊/Asc	082°01'
☉/♄	008°40'	☿/♀	019°39'	☽/Mc	029°36'	♀/♂	041°52'	♇/Asc	065°43'	♂/Asc	083°28'
♇	009°04'	☿/Mc	020°31'	☽/☊	030°00'	♂/Mc	042°43'	☽/♅	066°48'	☉	083°32'
♀/♃	009°04'	☿/☊	020°54'	☽/♂	031°26'	♂/☊	043°07'	♃	068°58'	♃/♇	084°01'
☽/☿	009°14'	☉/♆	020°57'	♀/♄	031°29'	♀/♆	043°46'	♄/♅	069°32'	♆/Asc	085°22'
♃/Mc	009°55'	☽/♄	021°04'	♄/Mc	032°21'	♂	044°33'	☽/Asc	070°21'	☉/☿	086°50'
♃/☊	010°19'	☿/♂	022°21'	Asc	032°22'	♆/Mc	044°37'	♄/Asc	073°05'	☽/♃	088°39'
♂/♃	011°46'	♄	023°48'	♄/☊	032°44'	♆/☊	045°01'	☉/♃	076°15'		
☿/♄	011°59'	♀/♇	024°07'	☽/♆	033°20'	♂/♆	046°27'	♀/♅	077°13'		
♃/♆	013°40'	☿/♆	024°15'	♂/♄	034°11'	♃/♅	047°07'	♅/Mc	078°04'		
☽/♇	013°42'	♇/Mc	024°59'	♄/♆	036°05'	♆	048°22'	♅/☊	078°28'		
☉/♀	016°21'	♅	025°16'	♀	039°10'	♃/Asc	050°40'	☿/♃	079°33'		

Figure 8
Midpoint Locations — Dracula's Rectification

Figure 8 (above) is the Table of midpoint locations throughout Dracula's rectified horoscope.[28] Mercury is at the Aries Point (zero degree of a Cardinal sign) beginning the Table. The following key Midpoint Pictures shape Dracula's horoscope into even greater synthesis:

28 In the Table, 0 degree = the beginning of Cardinal sign positions; 30+=0 of Fixed signs and further; 60=0 Mutable and further. The "equals" sign in Midpoint Pictures connotes the relation of any planet or point *by the extended family of the fourth harmonic* (conjunction, semisquare, square, sesqui-quadrate or opposition) to the midpoint of the planetary pair.

✦ Mercury=Sun/Pluto: Extraordinary mental projection; "lording it over" someone; great salesmanship.[29]

✦ Pluto=Sun/Saturn: The pressure to change (enforce) personal values.

✦ Pluto=Venus/Jupiter: Popularity; the world view. [Dracula was highly praised and widely known for his deep understanding of the Turks (through his imprisonment, learning their language and ways), his dedication to Eastern Orthodoxy, and his willingness to be part of all Crusade activity against the Turks.]

✦ Pluto=Jupiter/MC: Great recognition and publicity.

✦ Asc=Saturn/MC: Cold, calculating ambitious drive.

✦ Asc=Moon/Neptune: Losing ego definition [Perhaps the psychosexual part of his complex personality; Neptune rules the 5th.]

✦ Asc=Mars/Saturn: The center of the personality deals with matters of life and death, or deals with matters in a life-or-death way. This is an extreme manifestation of what Ebertin called the "death axis."[30]

✦ Mars=Venus/Neptune: Sexual drive has difficulty being fulfilled; easy self-delusion.

✦ Mars=Neptune/MC: Personal flair, sensual image [many descriptions of Dracula's single extant life-portrait use the word "sensual"].

✦ Sun=MC/Asc: The quest to be one's own person. Individualism.

✦ Sun=Uranus/Neptune: Extremely high self-regard [echoing Venus' trine with Jupiter, ruler of the self-worth 2nd].

---

29 These Midpoint Picture capsule-images are taken practically verbatim from Tyl, *Synthesis & Counseling*, the Appendix or Tyl, *Prediction in Astrology*, the Appendix.

30 Reinhold Ebertin, the founder of the Cosmobiological School of Astrology, and a masterful pioneer with Midpoint Pictures, named the Mars/Saturn midpoint the "death axis." This is an extreme statement indeed, and indeed Dracula's horoscope does call for the extreme. Hardin and Harvey (see bibliography) suggest that Mars/Saturn "can also denote an authoritarian manner, a 'killer instinct' or a need to center [oneself] through hard or ascetic work ... making the snap 'life or death' decisions ..."

I add that normally there is a drying up, a struggle to end things, a coldness, dealing with death matters in many different senses of the words. For example, Jackie Kennedy-Onassis had natal Sun=Mars/Saturn; see Tyl, *Synthesis & Counseling*, 43, 314, 526.

- ✦ Sun=Mars/Asc: Adjusting things by force.

- ✦ Sun=Jupiter/Pluto: Successful use of strong personality power; keeping things in one's own grip.

- ✦ Sun=Neptune/Asc: Discomfort, frustration [surely from things sexual, with Neptune ruling the 5th].

Dracula was at his best in diplomacy, running double-deals with the Turks and the Orthodox Christian and Roman Catholic countries: the 3rd and 9th Houses are very strong in his horoscope, the Neptune all-pervasive.

Finally, within our initial orientation, we can look at the horoscope in barest form, just as a fifteenth-century astrologer would have looked at it, without Neptune, Pluto, and Uranus, not knowing for sure where Venus or Mars was, having a reasonably good idea that the Moon was in the middle of Capricorn conjunct Saturn. The Sagittarian internationalism, judicial ethic, and self-presentation power would be clear. The austere administrative thrust through Moon-Saturn would be acknowledged, with a concomitant fear factor, and all would be blessed or at least made easy by Jupiter, the only planet visible (above the horizon), in opposition (by sign) with the Sun: *recognition by God*. Dracula was special indeed.

Early Imprisonment, Freedom, Vengeance

Dracul the father was a crafty politician. He saw the Turks gaining an enormous hold on territories surrounding his little princedom. The Turks had destroyed the Serbs and the Bulgars and were now planning a siege upon the Greeks. Dracul signed an alliance with the Turks *against his own patron*, the Holy Roman Emperor Sigismund, and certainly against his holy commission in the Order of the Dragon!

Even the Turks got so they did not easily trust Dracul. Sultan Murad II lured Dracul into a meeting in the spring of 1442. Dracul took young Dracula and younger Radu with him to the meeting. The Wallachian party did not receive a good reception: the children were spirited away and the father was immediately put into chains and confronted by the Sultan. Dracul had to reconfirm his oath of loyalty to Murad; to do this and claim his own freedom, he offered his own sons as hostages. The children's imprisonment would last for six years. Dracul and his sons would never see each other again.

In March–May 1442, Dracula was almost ten and one-half years old. Solar Arc Pluto (see page 183; add 10 degrees to Pluto at 9 Cancer) was opposing his Moon and going on to the midpoint of Moon/Saturn and Saturn itself, rulers of the 3rd–9th axis, over the six-year period of incarceration, in a foreign country, as it were. At the same time, transiting Pluto at 21 Cancer emphasized the same mental axis, the same core-significant, sensitive planetary picture.

Here is the confinement, the pain, the disorientation, the emotional hurt, the isolation, and repression that formed the needs for vengeance and vindication in Dracula's adult life. This is a secure beginning to ground our rectification, but we must look ahead to clear-cut developmental contacts with the angles of the horoscope.

McNally and Florescu point to this time as a clue to Dracula's "shifty nature and perverse personality. From that time onward, Dracula held human nature in low esteem. Life was cheap—after all, his own life was in danger should his father prove disloyal to the Sultan—and morality was not essential in matters of state."[31]

> Dracula's Turkish captors related that the boy exhibited trickery, cunning, insubordination, and brutality, and "inspired fright in his own guards." Dracula had gotten a taste for revenge and showed it.[32]
>
> However, at the same time, Dracula received a splendid education in the finest Byzantine tradition. The Sultan had an eye to the future, of course, and was grooming Dracula (and his brother) to be important allies in the conquests ahead. Dracula was taught philosophy under the crack of a whip. He learned Turkish perfectly and observed constantly the insidious ways of politics and the brutal ways of war.

Back at home, Dracul the father allowed his oldest son Mircea to cooperate with the Christian forces at the battle of Varna and thereby broke his vow to the Sultan. Dracul thought that his children would be "butchered" for his act, which he rationalized as

---

31 McNally & Florescu, *In Search of Dracula*, 21.

32 Ibid., 22. Additionally, Dracula developed an intense hatred for his younger brother "Radu the Handsome" whose good looks and compliant nature installed him as minion of the Turkish courtiers.

piety and loyalty to Rome, as a move to ensure Christian peace. Dracula learned of his father's treachery and felt abandoned and alienated to the core. The Sultan spared the sons any punishment for their father's treason.

Dracul then turned against the heroic Hungarian leader John Hunyadi, who then chose to eliminate Dracul for his duplicities. Hunyadi accomplished this indirectly by seeding fear and suspicion of Dracul in the mind of the Polish prince Vladislav, a Hungarian ally, who then organized the final attack on Dracul.

Dracul's oldest son was the first to die for treason, buried alive by his own people. Dracul tried to escape the closing net of intrigue and assassination. Knowing the end was near, he sent on to Dracula his gold medal from the Order of the Dragon. Dracul was caught and beheaded in November–December 1447.[33]

Figure 9 (page 191) shows the Lunar Eclipse of September 24, 1447, just two months before the death of Dracul, for Tirgoviste, Romania, the seat of the Wallachian throne. Note that the Eclipse axis in 9 Aries-Libra is precisely square to Dracula's natal, peregrine Pluto in 9 Cancer and that the Pluto in this Eclipse chart, at 1 Leo, is square to Dracula's natal Ascendant, as we have rectified it (page 183). This synastry promises a tremendous change in life perspective for Dracula, not quite sixteen years old.

Upon his father's murder, Dracula was freed by the Sultan and was made an officer in the Turkish army. Learning of the eradication of his family, Dracula formulated far-reaching plans for vengeance. We can easily presume a traditional-respect and personal-hatred relationship with the memory of his father. Dracula was a young, brilliant, intrepid warrior with much psychological baggage, with grudges to settle with the world. With that energy, motivation, and sense of rightness, he was able to build upon his freedom quickly.

Figure 10 (page 192) shows the Solar Arc picture for Dracula's freedom and his attack to regain his father's throne. SA Saturn has come to opposition with the Midheaven, promising a "major change in the family or in the profession; possible death concerns within the extended family circle; the father figure; an extremely important time of life development."[34] This is a key angular confirmation of the rectified time we have established.

---

33 *East European Monographs*, 14, through Romanian Embassy, see Bibliography.

34 Tyl, *Prediction*, Appendix, 317; *Synthesis*, Appendix, 845.

SA-SP Sun has come to opposition with natal Pluto illuminating Dracula's need for power and confirming new life perspectives. The SA Ascendant was squaring his all-important Neptune, promising that his specialness would gain recognition (the Turks were backing his effort to regain his father's throne, i.e., to continue the alliance with the Turks).

Yet, two other measurements threaten to undermine the entire picture: Solar Arc Uranus was promising sudden upset of the political/professional position through its square with the Midheaven

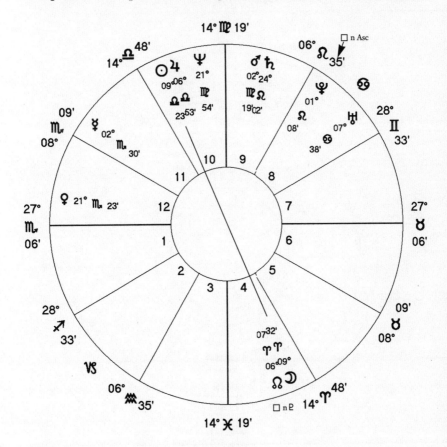

Figure 9
Lunar Eclipse
Sept. 24, 1447, 10:17 A.M. LMT
Tirgoviste, Romania
25E27 44N56
Placidus Houses

and, transiting Neptune was squaring the Sun, promising further duplicity in political dealings (the Sun rules the 10th) and possible overturn of the status quo.

Supported by the Turkish cavalry and other troops, Dracula led a bold and *successful coup of the Wallachian throne*, but his tenure was short-lived, only two months! The Polish prince who had killed his father, Vladislav II, overthrew Dracula with Hungarian forces, and Dracula had to flee for his life. Although he was free of the Turks, the young prince was imperiled from all other sides.

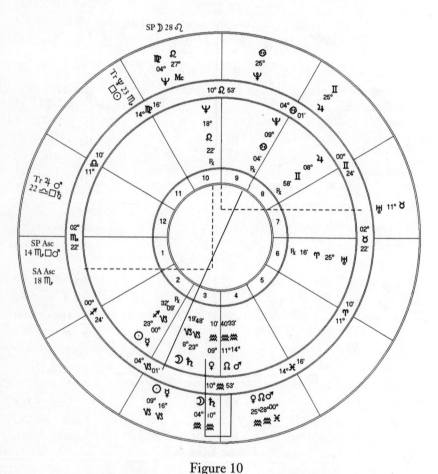

Figure 10

Inner Chart
Dracula

Outer Chart
SA Freedom
Dec. 15, 1447

Dracula hid away in Moldavia and then Transylvania, which was under the rule of the Hungarian hero Hunyadi, who had set up Dracula's father for murder by the Polish prince. Politically in the most chicanerous of times, Hunyadi and Vladislav, who was in control of Wallachia, Dracula's family base, began to drift apart, and Hunyadi saw it beneficial to make peace with Dracula! A very tricky meeting took place in January 1453—Dracula was just twenty-one: the Secondary Progressed Moon was at 29 Libra conjoining Dracula's Ascendant for a new start within sixty days, and transiting Jupiter was square its natal position.

A deal was made: Dracula took a prominent military appointment in Hunyadi's army, at that time highly reputed and successful; Dracula would counsel Hunyadi about Turkish ways, tactics, and plans.

As the siege upon Constantinople was begun, the only real hope of the Byzantines was placed upon the armies of John Hunyadi, with Vlad Dracula at his side. The invading Sultan Mehmed II had been in the same court learning with young Dracula during his imprisonment with Mehmed's father. Mehmed had gotten close to Radu, Dracula's handsome younger brother. Now all of them could meet on the battlefield at Constantinople, such were the fractured alliances and collusion of the times ... but it was not yet to be. Hunyadi's army did not go to the aid of Constantinople but saw to protecting its own borders in Transylvania (now commanded by Dracula) and the great fortress at Belgrade, guarding the approach to Hungary.[35]

Details about the fall of Constantinople struck fear into the heart of eastern Europe. Wallachia, Transylvania, and Hungary were in grave, immediate danger. The brutality of the Turks was one of their great weapons: tales were told of their use of impalement to kill captives. The impaled bodies displayed around conquered cities were silent, efficient sentinels. We shall see these tables turned by Dracula later.

Vladislav II began to shift allegiances to the Turkish side. That is all Hunyadi needed: as defenses against the Turks' push onward to Belgrade and Hungary were mounted, Dracula was given leave to mount an offensive against Vladislav II.

---

35 Florescu and McNally, *Dracula*, 70–71.

Dracula's allegiances at this time were to Hunyadi and Hungary and to the Christian cause, the pledge implicit in the Order of the Dragon. His rupture with his former Turkish protectors was out in the open, and his attack on Vladislav II was fully in order. In July 1456—while the Turks and Hunyadi fought at Belgrade, Dracula met Vladislav II near Tirgoviste. Dracula had the satisfaction of killing—in hand-to-hand combat—the man who had killed his father. Vengeance was his—and so once again was the throne: by August 22, Dracula was prince of Wallachia, Prince Vlad, son of Vlad the Great, sovereign and ruler of Ungro-Wallachia and of the duchies of Amlas and Fagaras.[36]

Figure 11 (page 195) shows the Solar Arc positions as they had developed to this time of victory for Dracula. In the eight and one-half years since his freedom, Dracula's SA Saturn had proceeded past the opposition with the Midheaven and now opposed his key natal Neptune. This measurement normally corresponds to a bewilderment, a frustration, a giving up under difficult circumstances, but the awesome transiting conjunction of Uranus and Pluto was *conjunct* natal Neptune and the SA Moon in 13 Aquarius was applying to conjunction with natal Mars. The picture is one of extreme force through collusion, through deception or chicanery, precisely what occurred within the Vladislav-Hunyadi-Dracula triumvirate. This is reinforced by transiting Neptune at 9 Libra exactly square Dracula's peregrine Pluto. (The Secondary Progressed Moon was opposed Jupiter.)

Figure 12 (page 196) shows the Tertiary progression for Dracula's second ascent to the throne after the murder of Vladislav II. The TP MC is applying to conjunction with Pluto, the TP Sun is square the key Neptune, and the TP Moon opposes that Neptune. TP Saturn is square to the rectified Ascendant, and TP Uranus is opposing that Ascendant. These two charts show a powerful portrait throughout astrology's spectrum of predictive measurement; a determined, nefarious ascent to power.

Just two months before this vital time, in June 1456, when Dracula began his pursuit of Vladislav II, a comet was sighted in

---

36 Ibid., 76–81. Fighting against the 90,000-strong Turkish army, Hunyadi's forces in the battle of Belgrade were reinforced from an unlikely source. A seventy-year-old, gaunt, mystical Franciscan monk, now canonized as Saint John of Capistrano, brought a band of some 8,000 inexperienced peasants and clergymen to help Hunyadi. The determination and fanaticism of these crusaders were extraordinary and played an important role in the Hungarian victory. Shortly after the repelling the Turks, both leaders died of the plague.

the night sky and was visible for seven weeks and four days over central and eastern Europe. As with the Eclipse over Constantinople, here again was a powerful omen. The Turks under Mehmed II saw it as the significator of their defeat by Hunyadi, but promising a second opportunity to fight again since Hunyadi died immediately after his victory. Dracula's people saw the comet as a positive omen, with Dracula returning to the ancestral throne. In fact, the only Dracula coin yet discovered depicts on one side the profile of the Wallachian eagle with a cross in its beak, and on the other side a crescent mounted *on a star trailing six undulating rays in its wake.*

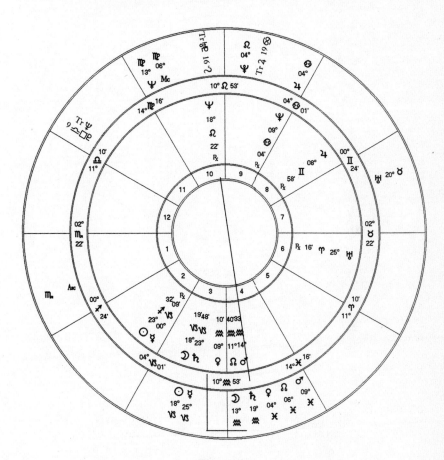

Figure 11

Inner Chart	Outer Chart
Dracula	**SA Regains Throne**
	Aug. 22, 1456

This was Halley's comet, 221 years before its formal identification and study![37]

And as we look ahead into Dracula's future, we must note from Figure 11 (page 195) that transiting Uranus-Pluto will be making a brutally forceful opposition with his natal Mars for another year and Solar Arc Pluto is inexorably approaching conjunction with the

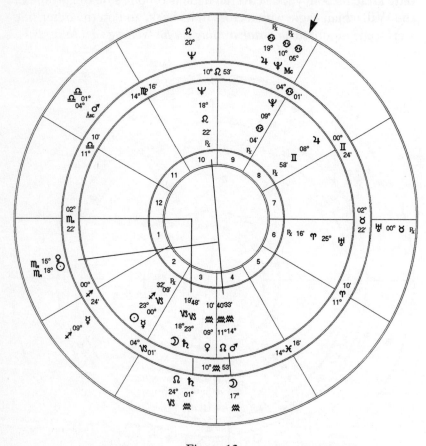

Figure 12

Inner Chart
Dracula

Outer Chart
TP Regains Throne
Aug. 22, 1456

---

37 Florescu and McNally, 82–83. English astronomer Edmund Halley (1636–1742) identified this first periodic comet in 1677. The very bright comet has a period of about sev-
enty-six years, and records of its appearances go back to 240 B.C. (studied earliest by the
Chinese). Its last appearance within earth vision was in 1986; the next will be in 2061.

Midheaven, due in 1462 (6 degrees/years further into the future). We must see also that transiting Neptune from 9 Libra (in Figure 11, page 195) will proceed on to Dracula's Ascendant in about ten years.

Dracula's Brutal Rule

We have a detailed physical description of Dracula in words from a papal representative to the region, and we have a life-sized portrait painting (at the Amras Museum near Innsbruck, Austria), from which a miniature was copied and is displayed at the Kunsthistorisches Museum in Vienna. The verbal and painted portraits agree. Dracula had an unusual, even bizarre appearance, singularly arresting and strange. [This image is portrayed on the cover of this volume.]

Three traits dominate: a tremendously thick growth of hair, worn in curled ringlets close to the sides of his face, down, over, and below his shoulders; a heavy frankfurter-shaped mustache that reached out wider than his gaunt face and rested lumpily above a vanished upper lip and a protruding lower lip. One gets the impression of a jutting jaw and a slender nose, the tip of which is too close to the bottom lip. And the third arresting feature was his eyes, overly large, perhaps bulging, establishing a kind of gaze beyond or through things, an almond-shaped openness that is alarming and mysterious. He was clean shaven, although the painting reveals a heavy beard beginning its return.[38]

Here is the verbal description from Niccolo Modrussa, the papal legate to Buda, who knew Prince Dracula later in his life:

> He was not very tall, but very stocky and strong, with a cold and terrible appearance, a strong and aquiline nose, swollen nostrils, a thin and reddish face in which the very long eyelashes frame large wide-open green eyes; the bushy black eyebrows made them appear threatening. His face and chin were shaven, but for a

---

38 It is interesting to note that, for the ancient Egyptians, for example, hair was a liability in battle; soldiers were clean shaven and bald. The word "barbarian," meaning bearded one, comes from Roman times when the wealthy and aristocrats were clean shaven and the slaves and lower classes were not. In Turkey, it was quite the opposite: flowing beards conferred status and it was slaves who were forced to shave. In Dracula's time and region, long drooping mustaches were the rule among princes. His was stiff and differently, meticulously groomed, and, though clean shaven, he appears to have had a shadow of a beard at all times.

moustache. The swollen temples increased the bulk of his head. A bull's neck connected [with] his head from which black curly locks hung on his wide-shouldered person.[39]

Florescu and McNally see the portrait as "overpowering, haughty, authoritarian." The astrologer sees the Scorpio Ascendant powerfully presented through Dracula's obvious hirsute nature and stocky build. The Mars rulership of Scorpio and its prominence in the horoscope, in Aquarius, suggest the ruddiness, the redness in the verbal description; and, in the painted portrait, Dracula is wearing rich red silk robes and a pink topaz and pearl headpiece.

— ✦ —

The ruins of Dracula's palace at Tirgoviste can still be distinguished from more massive remains of later additions. In the main, what is left is the Chindia Tower and the ruins of a cellar where Florescu and McNally found clear outlines of cells. It is recorded in histories that it was from the Chindia Tower that Dracula presided over the tortures that were administered in the courtyard below.

Dracula's political philosophy was simply to build and keep power. The mere flicker of possible confrontation triggered an overwhelming, annihilating response. Immediately upon seizing the throne, for example, Dracula conducted a massive purge of the hostile noble families, allying the small but powerful boyar class to his way of doing things. Florescu records the oldest Romanian historical chronicle of a typical event:

The Spring of 1457, during the Easter celebrations that the boyars were attending at the palace: Dracula had found out that the boyars of Tirgoviste had buried one of his brothers alive. In order to know the truth he searched for his brother in the grave and found him lying face downward. So when Easter Day came, while all the citizens were feasting and the young ones were dancing he surrounded them ... led them together with their wives and children, just as they were dressed up for Easter, to Poenari [a reference to Castle Dracula], where they were put to work [for months] until their clothes were torn and they were left naked.

---

39 Florescu and McNally, 85, and other sources.

The record is repeated by the Greek historian Chalcondyles, citing some 200 boyars and their wives, as well as leading citizens of Tirgoviste: "They were seized by Dracula's men as they were finishing their meal in the main banqueting hall of the palace, following the elaborate Easter ritual at the Paraclete Chapel. In Dracula's ingenious mind, one aspect of the punishment had a utilitarian purpose: the reconstruction of the famous castle high up on the Arges ... the old boyars and their wives were selected out from the main body and immediately impaled ... the others formed work gangs to build the castle over several months."[40]

The walls of the castle—and walls were Dracula's obsession—were double conventional fortress-width to withstand the heaviest Turkish cannon fire.

In his purge of the nobles and most boyars (land-holding, politically strong citizenry), Dracula impaled, according to German accounts, some 20,000 people, including entire families. In their place, he built up a different kind of nobility, the *armasi*, who carried out Dracula's style of justice. Many of the *armasi* were foreigners, adventurers and mercenaries, who "were well paid and devoid of principles." They were Dracula's "impalers par excellence."

Dracula saw himself as a judge, an administer of justice—a very pronounced confirmation of Sagittarian characteristics, especially with his Moon ruling his 9th, holding Pluto peregrine. This self-regard was a part of the extraordinary attention he paid to atonement for his heinous acts. He frequented monasteries, he built monasteries and churches, and he punished evil-doers with a savagery almost unimaginable. He did all sorts of "good works" to redeem himself before God. Florescu points out perfectly what we see astrologically: "In [Dracula's] tortured mind, cruelty and religiosity were deeply intertwined, and he would occasionally use religious grounds to justify a crime." And we must remember that always in the background was his Dragon oath, inherited from his father, which established him as a leading Christian crusader.

Here is how Dracula kept the law against adultery: "If any wife had an affair outside of marriage, Dracula ordered her sexual organs cut. She was then skinned alive and exposed in her skinless flesh in a public square, her skin hanging separately from a pole or

---

40 Ibid., 91–92.

placed on a table in the middle of the marketplace. The same punishment was applied to maidens who did not keep their virginity, and also to unchaste widows. For lesser offenses, Dracula was known to have the nipple of a woman's breast cut off. He also once had a red-hot iron stake shoved into a woman's vagina, making the instrument penetrate her entrails and emerge from her mouth. He then had the woman tied to a pole naked and left her exposed there until the flesh fell from the body, and the bones detached themselves from their sockets."[41]

"Vlad the Impaler"—as Dracula is known to Rumanians today—perfected the Turkish torture:

Stakes stood permanently prepared in the courtyard of the palace of Tirgoviste, in various strategic places, in public squares, and in the vicinity of the capital. Dracula was often present at the time of punishment. Usually, it is said, the stakes were carefully rounded at the end and bathed in oil so that the entrails of the victims should not be pierced by a wound too quickly fatal when the victim's legs were stretched wide apart and two horses (one attached to each leg) were sent [to pull] in different directions, while attendants held the stake and body firmly in place. Not all of Dracula's impalement victims were, however, pierced from the buttocks up. Judging from several prints, men, women, and children were also impaled through the heart, the navel, the stomach, and the chest.

Dracula decapitated, cut off noses, ears, sexual organs, and limbs. He blinded, strangled, hanged, burned, boiled, skinned, roasted, hacked ("like cabbage," specifies a German narrative), nailed, buried alive, and had his victims stabbed ... If he did not practice cannibalism, German [folklore] mentions that he compelled others to eat human flesh ... he stuck stakes in both breasts of mothers and thrust their babies onto them ... innumerable people were hanging from each tree branch.[42]

Every source speculates the reason behind such savagery, and all sources suggest sexual pathology, specifying the symbolism of Dracula's ritualized obsession with impalement, and the cutting off of sexual organs. The impalement could have substituted from his own inadequacy. Additionally, Russian narratives in particular confirm Dracula's anger toward women.

---

41 Ibid., 104.
42 Ibid., 104–106.

In his own lifetime, Dracula became famous for his crusade for Christendom, his helping the poor of his principality, and his horrific ways of justice (Mercury=Aries Point, notoriety). He actually became the subject of contemporary horror literature: refugees from Dracula's reign reported the horrific tales to monks who copied down the details and kept them in monastery libraries.

The astrologer can recognize the wanton, reckless, overriding power force of peregrine Pluto, ruler of the Ascendant; the depression and pain in the mental axis, the Moon-Saturn conjunction squared by Uranus; the Ascendant square the midpoint of Mars/Saturn; the mutual reception between Mars and Uranus; Venus drawn into the conjunction with Mars and the opposition with Neptune, ruler of the sexuality 5th. We see the harshness of focus within the parental axis, the drive for vengeance, the elaborate defense mechanism (Fire Grand Trine) establishing for Dracula the law unto himself.

The Great Battle

Pope Pius II saw the Turkish threat growing yet again in eastern Europe. At the council of Mantua in 1459, the pope inaugurated yet another crusade against the Turkish Sultan Mehmed, asking Christendom to raise 100,000 gold ducats.

With John Hunyadi dead, his younger son Matthias rose to the throne of Hungary. His hold on the position was initially insecure so he could not answer the pope's call. Many potentates sent verbal support but, caught up in nationalistic squabbles, did not commit troops or money.

Dracula was the only sovereign to respond immediately. He was admired for his courage and his eagerness to fight for Christianity. It would be Dracula who would meet the Turkish onslaught, Mehmed II with whom he had grown up in the Turkish court during his early imprisonment.

An added complication was that Dracula's younger brother, Radu the Handsome, who resided in Turkish Constantinople, was now *positioned and poised to seize the Wallachian throne from Dracula.* The grand battle, the show-down for East and West was set for the spring of 1462.

Dracula's army numbered only about 31,000, including boys and women. Along with swords and bows and arrows, the army's weapons included scythes, hammers, and scimitars. Dracula was planning on help from Matthias in Hungary, help which would never come.

Sultan Mehmed knew of the poor response to the pope's plea, and decided to strike at Wallachia as soon as he could. His forces outnumbered Dracula's *ten to one*.

During the winter early in 1462, Dracula had some preliminary skirmishes with Turkish forces along the Danube. He attacked quickly and stealthily and was able to defeat several Turkish strongholds, burning them as he made hasty retreat with his outnumbered and exhausted forces. Dracula was proud to send on to the pope a detailed statistical list of all Turks killed in the different places. He was a blood-drenched hero, controling the entire length of the Danube.[43]

The time came for Mehmed to launch a full-scale invasion of Wallachia; he would be compelled to invade the country by land from Bulgaria.

Dracula knew what was to come. He implored Matthias of Hungary to enter the effort. He even expressed his readiness to conclude a marriage with a member of the royal family, meaning he would abandon his Eastern Orthodox Christianity and become a Roman Catholic. Matthias would not cooperate—and Mehmed approached from Constantinople with his forces numbering almost 300,000 men and 120 cannons![44]

Yet, historians report that morale among the Wallachians was extremely high: "Dracula had a talent for inspiring enthusiasm in his men; he exhorted them to glorious and sometimes sacrificial action."[45]

But the Turks were able finally to cross the Danube on June 4, 1462 and the high point of the mighty battle—from Dracula's perspective—occurred during the night of June 17, 1462.

Figure 13 (page 203) shows us that Solar Arc Pluto has arrived at Dracula's Midheaven, a major test of our rectification. This measurement is life-significant: dramatic changes of perspective are practically assured. There can be transformations of many

43 Ibid., 134; *In Search of Dracula*, 49.
44 Florescu and McNally, *Prince of Many Faces*, 138–139.
45 Ibid., 141.

kinds. Professional adjustments are major. In short, it is a life-milestone time that is so large in impact that change is invariably decidedly disruptive.

At the same time, SA Moon opposes Dracula's keystone Neptune, a time of insecurity and doubt. SA-SP Sun is conjunct Saturn suggesting the enormous awareness of responsibility Dracula manifested in answering the papal plea for leadership of the crusade.

And finally, transiting Saturn that summer was transiting 10–12 Aquarius, exactly opposed the Midheaven we have set for the

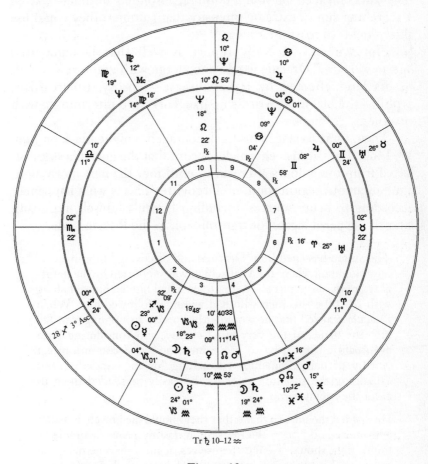

Figure 13

Inner Chart
Dracula

Outer Chart
SA War/Capture
June 17, 1462

bloodied prince. This time—this mighty battle—would be the change of a lifetime for Dracula, just thirty years old.

As the Turks made it across the Danube, Dracula had to adopt creative "retreat tactics." He would draw the Turks deep into his land, surround them, and isolate sections of the Sultan's army. Dracula would wear down the invading hordes, destroy the resources of his own land, depopulating villages, burning towns, destroying crops and cattle, diverting streams, poisoning wells, turning flatlands into mire and swamps, pitting the land with traps. The Turks invaded but found nothing, absolutely nothing—except a scorching sun of extreme intensity that summer; they could use their shields to roast their meat.[46]

Florescu and McNally report as well that Dracula used "germ warfare." Dracula would encourage with grand rewards all in his land affected by lethal disease—leprosy, tuberculosis, syphilis, the plague—to dress up like Turks and intermingle with the enemy soldiers.

Then, Dracula staged his final, courageous night attack on June 17, 1462. The Turkish chronicles record that the guerrilla skirmish lasted from three hours after sunset until four the next morning in a mountainous region south of Tirgoviste. This is what happened, according to many sources, including Dracula himself, reporting later to the papal legate for transmission to the Roman curia:

> The sultan besieged him [Dracula] and discovered him in a certain mountain where the Wallachian was supported by the natural strength of the place. There Dracula had hidden himself along with 24,000 of his men who had willingly followed him. When Dracula realized that he would either perish from hunger or fall into the hands of the very cruel enemy, and considering both eventualities unworthy of brave men, he dared commit an act worthy of being remembered: calling his men together and explaining the situation to them, he easily persuaded them to enter the enemy camp.
>
> He divided the men so that either they should die bravely in battle with glory and honor or else, should destiny prove favorable to them, they should avenge themselves against the enemy in an exceptional manner. So, making use of some Turkish prisoners, who had been caught at twilight when they were wandering about

---

46 Ibid., 144.

imprudently, at nightfall Dracula penetrated into the Turkish camp with part of his troops, all the way up the fortifications. And during the entire night he sped like lightning in every direction and caused great slaughter, so much that, had the other commander to whom he had entrusted his remaining forces been equally brave, or had the Turks not fully obeyed the repeated orders from the sultan not to abandon their garrisons, the Wallachian undoubtedly would have gained the greatest and most brilliant victory.

Dracula carried out an incredible massacre without losing many men in such a major encounter, though many were wounded. He abandoned the enemy camp before daybreak and returned to the same mountain from which he had come. No one dared pursue him, since he had caused such terror and turmoil.[47]

The account offered by the Greek historian Chalcondyles is more detailed and seems more realistic: Dracula rushed the camp with some 7,000 to 10,000 troops. With torches and flares, they tried to locate the Sultan's tent but couldn't. The Ottoman cavalry and jannisary guards got into action and warded off much of Dracula's attack. Some 2,000 Wallachian prisoners were taken; Dracula lost 5,000 men and the Turks 15,000 in the night of slaughter.

A few days later, the Turks attacked Tirgoviste. There the Sultan Mehmed and his men came upon Dracula's most infamous scene of horror, the "forest of the impaled." Strung out for over a mile, many thousands of stakes of various heights held the carcasses of some 20,000 Turkish captives. This was Dracula's tactic to destroy the Turkish spirit.

Mehmed was disgusted: Dracula's land was not worth this price of victory. He retreated eastward! And then the plague erupted.

The Turks saw all of this as a curse linked to Dracula. The military forces were overwhelmed with illness. Radu the Handsome, with a lifetime of Turkish support behind him, was sent into Wallachia to win over the people and usurp his brother's throne. He succeeded. [Note Saturn's rulership of the brother-3rd House, with SA-SP Sun illuminating natal Saturn and transiting Saturn opposing Dracula's Midheaven.]

Dracula's army on-the-run melted away. There was no help coming from anywhere. At a secret mountain retreat, surrounded by overwhelming Turkish forces, Dracula used a subterranean

---

47 Ibid., 146.

passageway to try to escape. He purloined some horses who were reshod backwards to leave a confusing trail. He went to a Hungarian fortress at Koenigstein to hope against hope for the arrival of King Matthias from Hungary.

Matthias had indeed finally started off to help Dracula and the two met up in as much secrecy as could be arranged. But two very strange things happened: Matthias knew that Dracula's brother, Radu, was now installed as the new Prince of Wallachia, and Matthias had given official recognition to the new Prince; and a series of letters (the so-called "Rothel" letters) supposedly from Dracula to Sultan Mehmed begging forgiveness and reconciliation were intercepted by Matthias' spies. The king and his men—in full frontal deception of Dracula—carefully plotted his end. Dracula was in the dark.[48]

After weeks of discussion and planning, Dracula took a force of Matthias' soldiers and set off ostensibly to attack Radu. En route over the rugged mountainous region, the army and its horses and cannons were being lowered off a cliff into a valley by pulley-supported platforms. In this moment, on December 6–7, 1462, under secret orders from the Hungarian king, the head Hungarian officer took Dracula prisoner.[49]

On this night, there was a Lunar Eclipse at 24 Gemini-Sagittarius conjunct Dracula's Sun. It was his birthday. Figure 14 (page 207) shows that Eclipse: note that the Sun-Moon axis is squared by Uranus; that transiting Neptune is rising [the duplicities] and exactly square to Dracula's natal Uranus; and, of course, transiting Saturn is still precisely opposed Dracula's Midheaven.

Dracula, under palace arrest by Matthias, king of Hungary, now became a living legend in the Hungarian court ... for almost thirteen years.

---

48 These letters were revealed only recently to be forgeries by Romanian historian Radu Constantinescu. The letters had been written in clumsy Latin syntax, which was most uncharacteristic of Dracula's style. Everything about the letters went against logic, e.g. offering the Turks help in abducting the Hungarian king while Dracula was planning with the king against the Turks, especially in the wake of the enormous battle period that had lasted almost eight months! The letters have now been ascribed to one Johann Reudell, a Catholic chaplain who had earlier suffered losses under Dracula's plundering actions. The ploy was to discredit Dracula even further than his reputation as psychopath and killer in the eyes of the Church, which was nevertheless compelled to praise Dracula's pro-Christian activities.

49 Ibid., 159.

Marriage — Conversion — Freedom — Death

Dracula was imprisoned in Hungary in its best times, the "Hungarian Renaissance," wherein Matthias played the role likened historically to that to be played by Lorenzo de Medici in Florence twenty years later. Learning and the arts flourished. Material affluence was everywhere. Royal treasures were displayed to all visitors. Hungary was the paragon of western cultural splendor.

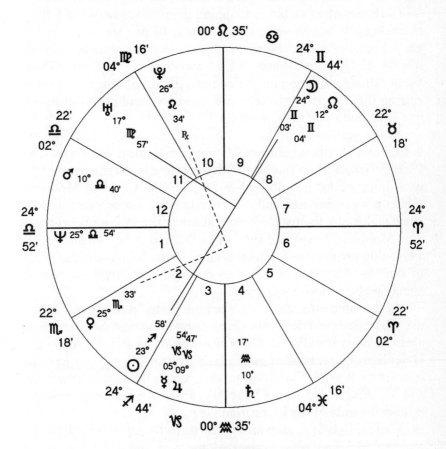

Figure 14
Lunar Eclipse
Dec. 7, 1462, 2:34 A.M. LMT
Tirgoviste, Romania
25E27   44N56
Placidus Houses

Matthias would put Dracula on display to visiting delegations. Florescu says, "the king knew the psychological impact that this confrontation would entail—the awesome 'Impaler Prince,' even as a captive, had the power of sending shivers down the spines of the Turkish delegates. It was a way of signaling to the king's foes that Matthias would keep Dracula in reserve, just in case the Sultan violated the provisions of [the] treaty."

There are accounts of Dracula's bizarre behavior in jail: catching mice and having birds brought to him for impalement; cutting off the heads of some birds, stripping them of feathers and letting them loose. While these descriptions may be projections of frightened, ghoulish minds, there *is* confirmation from supposedly credible sources like the Bishop of Erlau, writing to Pope Sixtus IV in 1476: "Unable to forget his wickedness, [Dracula] caught mice and, cutting them up into pieces, stuck them on small pieces of wood, just as he had stuck men on stakes."[50]

In the grandness of Hungarian life at this time, it was awkward indeed that Matthias continued his inaction against the Turks. The Church remarked on this often. Matthias finally got the opportunity to improve his position when Stephen the Great of Moldavia (Dracula's cousin) attacked a Hungarian outpost of great importance on his way to oust Radu and take over the Wallachian throne. The Moldavians captured the city of Bucharest on November 24, 1473, along with all of Radu's treasures. Radu, beaten and lost, died of syphilis. Matthias now had to contend with Stephen. A new enemy was too close for comfort.

At the same time, there was the impulse to "rehabilitate" Dracula. Dracula could lead Matthias' crusade against Stephen and, again, against the Turks. There was one provision, however: for Dracula to be reinstalled as Wallachian prince he would have to convert to Roman Catholicism, abandoning Eastern Orthodoxy, and Matthias would accept Dracula's earlier offer to marry into the extended family of the Hungarian king.

Further details are not known, historically, except that Dracula accepted Matthias' offer, converted, married, and had two sons, all before his military reappearance in July 1475. Deductive reasoning begins to place the marriage and birth of the children into the mid-1460s. New research shared by McNally and Florescu in *In Search of Dracula* points in this direction.

---

50 Ibid., 163.

In personal discussion with Professor Florescu, I was able to contribute strongly a tenable time and life-development scenario. Figure 15 (below) shows Dracula's horoscope for June 1466, the mid-time between March 1466 and September 1466.

Most important to note is that transiting Neptune finally arrives at Dracula's Ascendant, a time of change, when identity is altered, when ego changes. Within that same time period, transiting Saturn squares the Sun, ruler of the 10th; tr Jupiter conjoins Uranus; tr Uranus squares his Mercury. All these measurements suggest rethinking one's position. They show change.

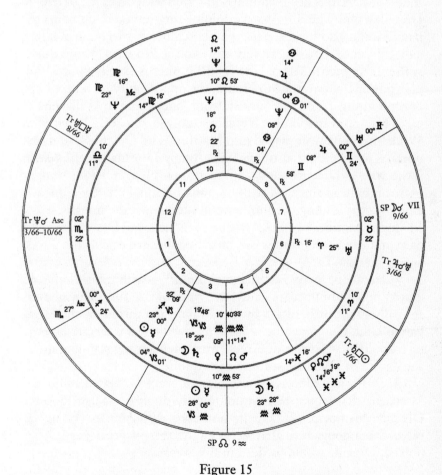

Figure 15

Inner Chart	Outer Chart
Dracula	**SA Marriage/Conversion**
	June 1, 1466

Marriage is clearly suggested by the Secondary Progressed Moon's position on the 7th cusp in September 1466; and the SP Nodal axis conjunct Venus (children as well).

In the background, SA Pluto moves to the midpoint of Neptune/Midheaven (at 14 Leo 37), suggesting strange circumstances altering life perspective, one's professional position.

Figure 16 (page 211) shows the Tertiary Progression positions at a time of possible (probable) marriage; the chart once again clearly supports Dracula's birth time and our suggestion of the mid-1466 date for his new strategy. Note that TP MC is square to Neptune—always, this key Neptune is involved with every major turn in Dracula's life. The TP Moon conjoins the Sun (and, conjoins the natal Moon, also for marriage, on September 5, two months later), and TP Venus-Uranus are very close to the 7th cusp (Venus exactly there one month later). Finally, TP Jupiter is exactly upon Dracula's power Pluto in the 9th House, the opportunity for a new start, beyond Hungary, on the Turkish front, once again in Wallachia.

This "conversion" by Dracula absolved him of all past sins. While this maneuver played into Matthias' and Dracula's hands for political strategies, it also touched strongly Dracula's deepest *needs for atonement*. Dracula was again "even" in his ledger before God, or even a bit ahead since he, with the rank of captain in the Hungarian army, was leading yet another crusade against the infidels!

In the summer of 1475, Matthias, Stephen, and Dracula signed a pact, and a renewed front was formally established against the Turks.

In January 1476—*precisely the exact date of Dracula's semi-square Solar Arc*, at age forty-four and one month[51]—with transiting Pluto exactly squared Dracula's natal Sun, ruler of the 10th, Dracula was formally given recognition for the Wallachian throne by the Hungarian Diet. On November 26, 1476 Dracula was reinvested by the metropolitan at Curtea de Arges, with a few boyars standing by, as the Prince of Wallachia—for the third time.

McNally and Florescu point out that everyone feared and hated Dracula: what would this pathologically duplistic sadist do next? Dracula did not bring his wife and sons with him to Wallachia; researchers conjecture that he knew he was in great peril. And, indeed, Dracula would be dead in five weeks.

---

51 The Sun's passage for a winter birth in the northern hemisphere is slightly faster than the average, so the Solar Arc of 45 degrees accumulates faster, earlier in life. See Tyl, *Synthesis*, 204–216.

Dracula was killed during another violent clash with Turkish forces. Again, his own 2,000 soldiers were outnumbered two to one. Researchers (especially the Austrian chronicler Jacob Unrest) confirm the fact that Dracula was killed by a hired assassin from the Turkish camp. The killer had enlisted (been captured) into Dracula's circle as a slave. The Turk was instructed to attack Dracula from the back, to cut off his head, and bring it to the Sultan.

That is what happened "in the last days of December." Then, Dracula's head was taken to Constantinople and exposed high on a stake to confirm that the Great Impaler was finally dead.[52]

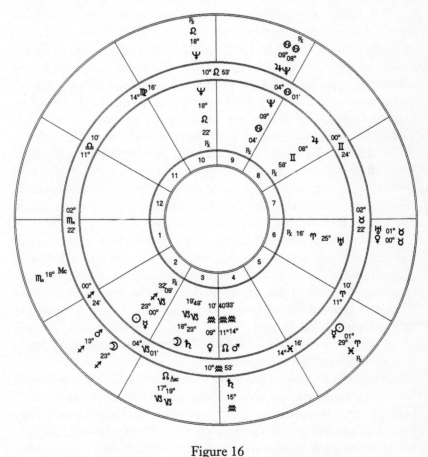

Figure 16

Inner Chart
Dracula

Outer Chart
TP Marriage/Conversion
July 11, 1466

---

52 McNally and Florescu, *Dracula*, 174-175; Florescu and McNally, *In Search of Dracula*, 102–103.

Chronicles and folklore place Dracula's burial in the fortified monastery of Snagov (*place of death*) on an island in one of Europe's deepest lakes. Dating back to the thirteenth century, the fort-monastery was extremely safe from siege, protected always by the harshest terrain, the waters, and, in winter, the thick ice—that could be shattered by a cannon shot, drowning enemies advancing over it. The protection walls were built right up to lakeside. The installation was a tiny town unto itself, in the gloomiest of sur-roundings. For over 100 years from the mid-thirteenth century, Wallachian princes built onto and improved the fortress. The last improvements were made by Dracula.

The abbey was used for imprisonment and torture; excavations reveal decapitated skeletons with their heads placed neatly beside body bones. In the nineteenth century, the abbey was a formal prison, haunted by violence; a bridge from the mainland to the island collapsed under the weight of chained prisoners who were all pulled under the reedy-clogged waters to their death. Earthquakes, violent storms—all reminders of the curse connected with the Abbey through the person of Vlad Dracula fill the history of Snagov.

Tradition had it that Dracula's body was buried in front of the main altar of the church on Snagov, there to be trampled and defiled by the priests during every mass. Excavation there revealed a neat grave pit empty except for anachronistic animal bones placed there by earlier searchers as decoys. It is a mystery.

But the extraordinary Dracula researchers, whose superb works have guided our study—Professors Florescu and McNally—dug elsewhere, chiefly at the *entrance* to the church. There they found a headless skeleton in threads of proper raiment for a prince. Tiny treasure clues—including reference to the Order of the Dragon and to his father, Vlad Dracul—were found with the bones, as well. Most creative deduction by teams of researchers suggests strongly that this stormy spot is indeed the dismal grave of Dracula.[53]

Figure 17 (opposite) shows in the outer ring of Dracula's natal horoscope the Lunar Eclipse just preceding Dracula's re-investiture and his death. The portents are dire indeed: the Eclipse axis is con-joined by transiting Pluto and all are square Dracula's Sun; there is a massive Mars-Uranus square to Saturn that connects tightly with

---

53 Ibid., Chapter 8.

Dracula's own Mars in the 4th House, suggesting strongly the sudden deathly danger from the home encampment. Transiting Saturn in December 1476 (three months later) had retrograded back to 20 Cancer opposed Dracula's Moon, and transiting Mars on December 27—surely the night of the death blow—was exactly conjunct Dracula's 4th cusp, opposed his Midheaven. Time and time again, at the turning points of Dracula's life, we have seen his birth day and birth time convincingly reinforced.

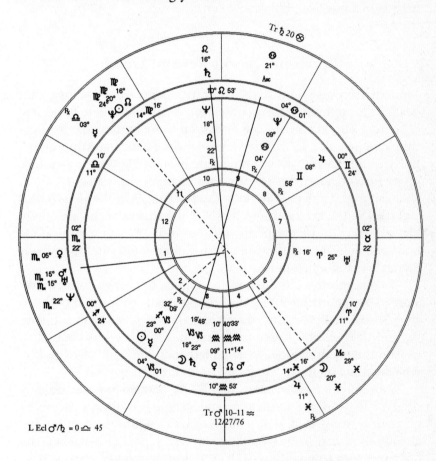

Figure 17

Inner Chart
Dracula

Outer Chart
Lunar Eclipse 1476
Sept. 4, 1476, 3:30 A.M. LMT
Tirgoviste, Romania
25E27   44N56

Interestingly, the Mars/Saturn midpoint—Ebertin's "death axis (see pages 183 and 187)—of the Eclipse chart is at 00 Libra 45, conjunct the Aries Point, i.e., Dracula's Mercury as well. Mercury in Dracula's horoscope always represented his notoriety, as we have seen, and we see as well that Mercury rules his 8th. In death, a tortured personality left the world. His body is decayed, his head is gone, but this life lives on, linked to folklore older than history, to the concept of vampirism, in macabre alteration through the imagination of a novelist, 420 years later.

Epilogue: Blood Beyond Death

Modern preconceptions to the contrary, bodies are active long after death. Throughout history, observing dead bodies left unburied, exhuming buried corpses, we have seen those bodies change position, change color, move, bleed, grow hair. There are extraordinarily dynamic considerations in the state of a dead body: the moisture of its surrounding, the temperature changes, insect activity, soil chemistry; gravity's pull on body fluids, changes in the veins (color and size) as the skin starts to be shed; distension of the abdomen, bloated erection of the penis, blisters formed at pressure points upon the body, blood flowing afresh from the mouth, the eyeballs liquefying, and much more.[54]

To our ancestors, if the body continued to change color, move, alter its shape, to have blood trickling fresh from the mouth, to show sexual readiness, etc., then the body continued to live. Living beyond death was a fearsome thing, and folklore was created to explain the phenomenon, to assimilate it and make it manageable. The dead *had* to die, or the living were threatened.

Subsequent deaths, then, could be blamed on the already dead.[55] To stop the epidemic (and vampirism always seems to occur in concentrated waves, much as UFO sightings seem to), the already dead had to be (re)killed *properly*. Upon exhumation, the body was seen to be different than in death—most often, just days or weeks after burial—reinforcing the suspicion that the corpse had indeed taken on the identity of a vampire. This would justify the ritual termination of the spirit through elaborate means, most

---

54 Barber, 83–119.
55 Ibid., 3.

popularly by impaling the vampire through the heart (or navel) with a wooden stake, during daylight hours, preferably using a stake fashioned from the wood of an Ash tree.[56]

Blood is the medium of life; it is vitality. The vampire needs blood to live on, of course. And, as well, the vampire needs company in the loneliness of the night world. By ingesting blood from a living neck or breast, vampires form community with the living, stay alive themselves, and the killing threat multiplies.

The belief in vampires is universal and timeless. It has been documented in every extant culture. The body of vampire folklore is very close to the practice of animal and human sacrifice: blood supplies energy, satisfies gods, keeps influence alive. Blood is dangerous and important.

Since some bats suck blood for sustenance and were named "vampire bats" (probably first by Cortes in his conquest of Mexico) the quality of flight became part of the vampire archetype. Our fear of vampires ascribed ugliness to them; ideas of Satan, then—the devil we fear—took winged, ugly form, threatening to drain life away from the path to God.

The earliest derivations of the word *vampire* have a common root from most of the Mediterranean languages: from *vam* meaning blood and *pyr* meaning monster. Slovakian forms are *vampir, vapir, vepir, veryr, vopyr, upier.* The Romanians have many names for a variety of vampires, most commonly *strigoi,* an evil creature who sleeps during daylight hours, flies at night, can take animal form and sucks the blood from sleeping children. Other languages transliterate words for "red-faced with drink, drinking and growling, restless in death."[57]

These fears, myths, and myriad embellishments have endured and multiplied throughout time. Evil—the taking of life—fascinates eternally. Evil generates sin, which is exciting in its threat. We are aroused by and attracted to the dangerous, the deviant, the demonic. Ian Fleming has suggested that *without* the seven deadly sins, our lives

---

56 Wood from the ash-tree is fundamental to many primal folk beliefs, beginning perhaps with reference to Ashtoreth (or Asherah), a mother figure, fertility symbol, a goddess of sexual intercourse, the consort of Baal, the Canaanite god (though at Ugarit she was El's wife, mother of seventy sons). Her name means "upright." She was a tree goddess as well, represented either by a tree or by a sacred wooden pole or pillar. See Grant, *Ancient Israel,* 24.

Additionally, in Teutonic legend, Wotan's staff, carrying the magic Runes of fate, was fashioned from ash.

57 Mascetti, 198–199.

would go flat ... "How drab and empty life would be without them ... it [would be] as if Leonardo, Titian, Rembrandt, and Van Gogh had been required to paint without using the primary colors."[58]

Is it that we humans darkly identify with evil characters, with vampires, with someone like Dracula? Is it that our deepest urges, prohibited from seeing the light of life, are discharged through an alter ego monster-form. Is it that this identification is licensed, that it is allowed by the fact that we know well that good *will win* in the end and evil *will be* conquered? Is it that security needs fear to define itself? Is it that religion requires the rivalry represented by evil?

As blood and living are vital, so is the perpetration of bloody evil vital; it is a vivid, active, filled-with-life-accentuated occurrence: the adrenaline, the fear, the danger, the inscrutable motives, the incomprehensible repercussions. We recognize and, to varying degrees, identify with such extremes. We feel more alive and, indeed, at the same time, more protected by not being evil ourselves; we are protected by our mores, laws, and religion.

For example, a celebrity's murder trial fascinates hundreds of millions of people. It is not for its gory details as much as for the vital excitation of the startling, gruesome event and the vitally important question of its just outcome. We are involved. It is the public celebrity's fame that gives us permission to take part in the drama: he or she belongs to us and we belong in the picture. We identify with the process of evaluation and punishment and, in that sense, each of us knows good *and* evil.

But Dracula was not a vampire and was not known as one. He was revered by his people for his public works, his excessively stringent but highly effective laws and punishments, his bravery, and his loyalties to the Church. Peasants in Romania, in the region around Castle Dracula do/did *not* connect Vlad Tepes (the Impaler) and the vampire(s) in their folklore.[59] Vlad the Impaler's only overlap is simply that he impaled people, but they were alive and well. Folk tales do cite one instance of his dining in his courtyard of torture and dipping his bread into the blood of a nearby victim, but blood was not his elixir of life.[60]

How did Dracula the life merge with the vampire legend? The answer is not difficult, but for it to be sound, we must approach it

---

58 Quoted in Plantinga, 91–92.
59 McNally and Florescu, *In Search of Dracula*, 123.
60 Florescu and McNally, *Dracula: Prince of Many Faces*, 120; and other sources.

through the outline of Bram Stoker's life, the man whose sensuous gothic novel, *Dracula*, created the merger in 1897 and ignited a popularity for the vampire theme that commands four-star cultural attention still a century later.

Bram Stoker and Dracula

What little is known about Abraham Stoker, an Irish theater critic, manager of theatrical events, and novelist, is consistently strange. From birth he was so ill and feeble with a never-diagnosed disease that he was not expected to live and was confined to his bed for the first eight years of his life; he never experienced standing up and walking before he was nine! McNally and Florescu suggest that Stoker could look back on this experience and know "what it would be like for a vampire to be bound to his coffin and native soil."[61]

Bram took his father's abbreviated name, from Abraham. Bram's "strong-willed mother" was most indulgent of him and influenced his early childhood strongly with Irish fairy tales and (entertaining) horror stories, her remembrance of a cholera epidemic in 1832, etc. The diversion of all this fell upon a most sensitive mind and facile imagination.[62]

Through private tutelage, Bram was able to enter Trinity College, Dublin in 1864. He had mysteriously overcome his childhood illness and developed into a star athlete! He was popular with his fellow students and was elected president of the very important Philosophical Society. He was an avid theater buff and graduated with honors in science.

Stoker was born on November 8, 1847 in Dublin. I have found that cursory rectification tests suggest a revealing starting point when the birth time is set at 1:58 P.M., LMT (Figure 18, page 219). The New Moon birth in Scorpio in the 8th House emphasizes occult interests (which abounded in his life) and also personal privacy (echoed by the heavy rectification pattern in the Ascendant, including the co-rulers of the Ascendant, Uranus and Saturn).

---

61 McNally and Florescu, 137; all Chapter 11.

62 When Bram was twelve, a great deal of public attention focused on the union of the two Romanian states, Moldavia and Wallachia, and researchers point to this time as Bram's initial introduction to that mysterious part of Europe.

The weakness at birth is often ascribable to New Moon birth, i.e., the Moon has not light of its own), especially when closer to exact; and here as well, we see the potential debilitation of Neptune retrograde conjunct the Ascendant. Mars retrograde corroborates a lowered vitality also. This horoscope birth-time hypothesis certainly shows a repressed, weakened system, with enormous energy roiling beneath the surface. Clearly, the threat of debilitation is present. We can note the Solar Arc of Ascendant to Saturn, i.e., out of Neptune's way, to occur at nine, when Bram was free of bed and illness, when his "spine" was established, with transiting Jupiter-Pluto conjunct his Mars and tr Uranus squared the suggested Ascendant (Spring 1857).

Stoker's horoscope shows a highly emphasized Jupiter, with its square to the Uranus-Pluto conjunction (Jupiter=Uranus-Pluto) promising a drive to success; the severe retrogradation pattern in the northern hemisphere (and the Sun-Moon in Scorpio in the 8th) suggests at the same time great obstacles en route to that success. Jupiter here rules the Midheaven and trines the Sun-Moon conjunction. This drive can certainly corroborate young Stoker's athletic success and popularity (Moon rules the athletics 5th with Jupiter there; Sun rules the 7th; Uranus-Pluto in Aries, applied power, trine the Midheaven).

Venus, the final dispositor of the horoscope, in its own sign Libra in the 7th, suggests popularity as well, and conjunct the Nodal Axis testifies unequivocally to the great maternal influence in Bram's life, specifically in terms of the 3rd House, ideas, thinking, writing.[63]

Through Pluto's rulership of the 9th holding Mercury in Sagittarius (disposed by Jupiter), we begin to see *writing in terms of publication;* we see *internationalism* (and Stoker made professional trips to many countries including several visits to the United States). In other words, the power focus of Uranus-Pluto squared by Jupiter and trine the Midheaven has very much to do with Stoker's profession and his/its international thrust, and, early on, the revival of his vitality into athletic strength.

A rare photograph of Stoker at about age fifty-five shows a strong, barrel-chested man, with a textual reference made to red-

---

63 I have researched the Lunar Nodal axis as lunar symbolism in relation to the Sun. In that axis, I have learned to see the process of the feminine meeting the masculine, taking in the Sun's light and transmitting it further, ingesting the seed and putting forth the fruit. I see maternal influence. I see the potential for a knot of complication through the mother, or, indeed, an amalgamation of strengths through maternal influence, in terms of the planet or angle configurated by conjunction or square with the Nodal axis. See Tyl, *Synthesis & Counseling*, 49–65.

dish hair and bushy eyebrows. Without any doubt the photograph portrays fixed-sign dominance and certainly supports reference to Aquarius and Uranus.

Midpoint pictures reveal a great deal in our test horoscope for Stoker: the Aries Point=Mercury/Jupiter (29 Virgo 30), a clear reference to writing for the public. The Aries Point is also focused at the midpoint of Saturn-Pluto suggesting the image of *a struggle in public or pathology exposed.* This joins the extraordinary retrogradation pattern and Sun-Moon position to suggest *a contrapuntal world*

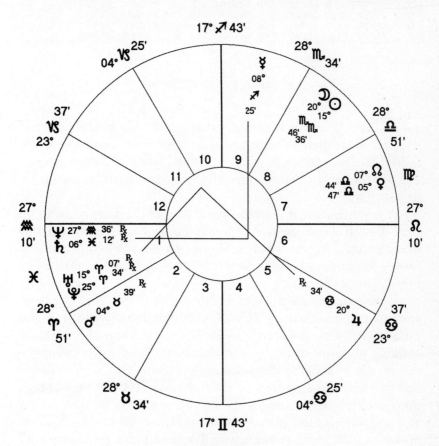

Figure 18
Bram Stoker (Rectification)
Nov. 8, 1847, 1:58 A.M. LMT
Dublin, Ireland
06E15   53N20
Placidus Houses

BRAM STOKER NOV 08, 1847

Midpoint Sort: 90° Dial

♄/♇	000°53'	♅	015°07'	♄/Mc	026°57'	☽/♂	042°43'	♃/☊	059°09'	Mc	077°43'
♂/Asc	000°55'	♀/♇	015°41'	☽/♀	028°17'	☊/Mc	042°44'	☽/☿	059°36'	☉/♃	078°05'
♂/♆	001°07'	♇/☊	016°39'	☽/☊	029°15'	♃/♄	043°23'	☉/Mc	061°39'	☽/♃	080°40'
♃/Mc	004°09'	☿/Asc	017°48'	♂/♇	030°06'	☉	045°36'	♄/Asc	061°41'	♀/♄	081°00'
♂/♄	005°26'	☿/♆	018°00'	☉/♅	030°21'	♅/Mc	046°25'	♄/♆	061°54'	♅/Asc	081°09'
♀	005°47'	♀/♂	020°13'	☽/♅	032°57'	☿/♇	046°59'	♃/♅	062°51'	♅/♆	081°21'
☉/Asc	006°23'	♅/♇	020°20'	♂	034°39'	☽/☉	048°11'	☽/Mc	064°15'	♄/☊	081°58'
☉/♆	006°36'	♃	020°34'	☉/♇	035°35'	☽	050°46'	♄	066°12'	♄/♅	085°40'
♀/☊	006°46'	♂/☊	021°12'	☿/♀	037°06'	☿/♂	051°32'	♃/♇	068°04'	♇/Asc	086°22'
☊	007°44'	☿/♄	022°18'	☿/☊	038°05'	♇/Mc	051°38'	☿	068°25'	♆/♇	086°35'
☽/Asc	008°58'	Mc/Asc	022°27'	☽/♇	038°10'	♂/Mc	056°11'	♂/♃	072°37'	☿/♃	089°30'
☽/♆	009°11'	♆/Mc	022°39'	♃/Asc	038°52'	☉/☿	057°00'	☿/Mc	073°04'		
♀/♅	010°27'	♂/♅	024°53'	♃/♆	039°05'	Asc	057°10'	♀/Asc	076°29'		
☉/♄	010°54'	♇	025°34'	☉/♂	040°07'	♆/Asc	057°23'	♀/♆	076°41'		
♅/☊	011°26'	☉/♀	025°41'	♀/Mc	041°45'	♆	057°36'	☊/Asc	077°27'		
☽/♄	013°29'	☉/☊	026°40'	☿/♅	041°46'	♀/♃	058°11'	♆/☊	077°40'		

Figure 19
Bram Stoker — Midpoint

within Stoker, a deep private realm that somehow is brought out and discharged publicly. This is the inspiration of the creative artist, indeed, but we can see that this repressed world is very, very difficult for Stoker. In one manifestation, it threatened his life in his earliest days.

A key measurement here—regardless of the time of birth on that day—is *Venus opposed the midpoint of Mars-Saturn (Venus= Mars/Saturn)*. Again, this is reference to the other realm within Stoker, kept beneath the surface that is polished by Venus in Libra in the 7th.

As the measurements accumulate, synthesis suggests the presence of real problems, problems with emotional expression and relationship. Everywhere we look, we see a stratum of frustration working itself out through the imagination, the dogged self-application, and a very smooth public presentation. This Venus= Mars/ Saturn picture is a passionate effort to make something work; in this case, life itself to begin with, then his emotional tie with others, and undoubtedly the management of difficult sexual issues. That Stoker's professional pursuits would be a cathartic pipeline for all this is clear, corroborated by the redeeming and importantly synthesizing picture Midheaven=Sun/Jupiter and Venus being *exactly quintile (72 degrees, creativity) the Midheaven.*

In the "winter" of 1876, probably February, Stoker, aged twenty-eight—with published drama reviews and horror stories already to his credit—met the celebrated Shakespearean actor Sir Henry Irving. Stoker's notes state that, at a reading by Irving, he [Stoker] broke into "uncontrollable hysterics." McNally and Florescu add: "In a way he [Stoker] fell in love with Henry Irving and began working immediately in a part-time capacity [personal manager] that was to continue for the rest of Irving's life."

At this time, transiting Saturn was conjunct the Ascendant-Neptune position we have for Stoker, and SA Moon was conjunct his Midheaven, a tremendous vocational excitation as well as an emotional vulnerability or emotional assertion. Stoker became Irving's private secretary and confidant and theatrical manager *for twenty-seven years*. Stoker called their friendship, "as profound, as close, as lasting as can be between two men."[64]

McNally and Florescu add to this: "But there was more to the relationship than [even] that. Irving held such a fascination for Stoker that he achieved an extraordinary dominance over him. Indeed, in life Irving was lord and master to Stoker as in fiction [in Stoker's *Dracula*] 'Dracula' is to Renfield."

There is no doubt here that the underpinning of Stoker's personality was vulnerable to dominance, was open to exploitation, was masochistic, and deeply repressed. There is little doubt that homosexuality was an enormous problem for Bram Stoker in Victorian England, in his life, and in his bizarre relationship with Henry Irving.

During the early years, Stoker had married and moved to London in the Spring of 1878: SA Sun, ruler of the marriage-partner 7th, was at 16 Sagittarius 30 applying to the Midheaven; transiting Uranus was at 27 Leo conjunct the seventh cusp; and the Secondary Progressed Ascendant was at 16 Taurus opposed Stoker's Sun. This is a powerful group of measurements corroborating the rectification of Stoker's horoscope.

Astrologer David Monks (see Bibliography) has accomplished a very sensitive and clever deduction of the horoscope of the *fictional* Dracula from Stoker's extraordinary novel.[65] His observa-

---

64 The researchers quote Stoker's Personal Reminiscences of Henry Irving; see *In Search of Dracula*, 141.

65 Monk's speculative horoscope for Dracula, based on the chronology and location of his first appearance ("birth") in the novel is May 4, 1893 at 9:25 P.M., LMT in the Borgo Pass, 47 North 17, 25 East 08. The year is deduced by Monk most craftily through Van Helsing's comments on the death of Charcot, the French pioneer of hypnotism and hypnotherapy. Charcot died on August 16, 1893. Van Helsing is speaking on September 26th in the novel, a month later. Mina Harker's diary makes references to a Thursday, etc. The year has to be 1893; the year of Charcot's death, the time reference of the remark, and the time setting of the novel.

tions and those of the commentaries he quotes point to "the great submerged force of the Victorian libido breaking out to punish the repressive society which had imprisoned it." Monks suggests that Stoker's novel's phenomenal success was that it spoke on a subtle level to the Unconscious. He calls attention to the novel's seduction of a coyly hesitant man by the vampire women, an extreme reversal of everything thought normal or not allowed to be thought about at all.[66]

With regard to Stoker's horoscope, which Monks used with a noon mark, he notes the Venus in Libra and points out Stoker's marriage and the friendship with Irving. He adds factually: "Both these relationships were flawed. After the birth of his son, Noel, the marriage ran out of sexual steam, while the Stoker/Irving arrangement saw Bram very much as second fiddle, a role he was only too happy to accept. His admiration for the actor [Irving] seems to have been a naive adulation which belittled his own standing."

There is simply no doubt in astrological analysis that Neptune is the planet that leads synthesis to the signification of masochism. Barbara Watters pointed up courageously twenty-five years ago at the beginning of the psychological maturation of astrological analysis that Neptune rules the unconscious with a compulsive power, that it represents the illusion of reality, that it signifies martyrdom, the need to "suffer in public."[67]

There is no doubt that masochism and surely homosexuality played a powerful role in Stoker's relationship with Irving, in the release of Stoker's inner world through the horror stories depicting passive men, extensive oral fixations (sucking blood, i.e., always "kissing"), and indeed, the ultimate end, impalement with a stake.[68]

66　It is interesting indeed to note that Monks' fictional "Dracula" horoscope has a 4 Libra 32 Midheaven conjunct the Venus in Stoker's horoscope, i.e., therefore "Dracula's" MC=Stoker's Mars/Saturn; and our real-life Vlad Dracula has Ascendant=Mars/Saturn, with these horoscopes conceived independently.

67　Watters, Chapter VIII. As well, we must note that in 1912 Alan Leo wrote "Neptune allows the soul to leave the body," (*Art of Synthesis*, page 115) when Neptune was the last known planet, when theosophy had influenced spiritual understanding strongly at the turn of the last century. The Leo view and the Watters (and others since) view are not disparate; the questions are simply why does the soul leave the body, what is the unconscious going to do with the potentials presented to it? Freud did not create psychoanalytic morphology, nor did Jung create archetypes, nor did the Greeks invent their glorious fables: they exposed them in terms appropriate for understanding the times, for use within the extant ethos.

68　Stoker was fascinated with masks and masquerades (Neptune). In one of his last books, entitled *Famous Imposters* (1910), he probed into histories of women who took on the outward appearance of men and vice versa. See McNally and Florescu, *In Search of Dracula*, 154.

Stoker was well aware of vampire legends, especially through the Irish writer Joseph Sheridan LeFanu whose lesbian (symbolical presentation, of course) vampire novel *Carmilla* was one of the greatest, most inflaming vampire stories ever written; *The Vampyre*, written by John Polidori, Lord Byron's personal physician and lover (1819; published first under Byron's name); and particularly Emily de Laszkowska Gerard's *Land Beyond the Forest* (1888), in which

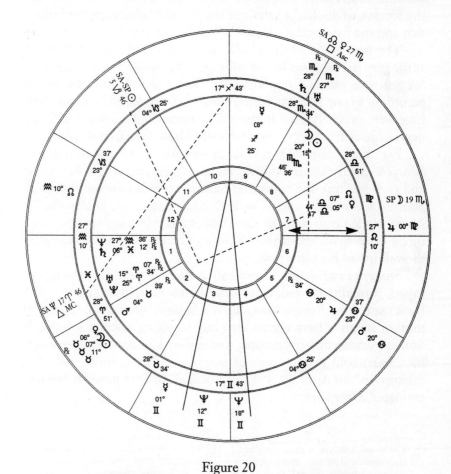

Figure 20

Inner Chart	Outer Chart
Bram Stoker	**Dracula Publication Transits**
Nov. 8, 1847, 1:58 A.M. LMT	May 1, 1897, 12:00 P.M. Z00
Dublin, Ireland	Dublin, Ireland
06W15 53N20	06W15 53N20

Placidus Houses

Romanian superstitions (Transylvanian; literally, "beyond the for-est") were presented to beguile readers.

Stoker prodded his reader's minds beyond what was known; eastern Europe was the lure; real names from the region provided exotic and powerful details. Surely, Stoker knew of Prince Dracula and his reputation as the Impaler. It was an easy mixture then to place the powerful sounding and exotic name of "Dracula" into extant vampire tales wrapped in travelogue mists of lands beyond the forests, to discharge safely an imagination afire with the forbid-den and the frustrating. "Dracula" set Stoker free.[69]

The novel—called the *Un-Dead* until it was changed to *Dracula* at the very last moment before printing—was published in May 1897. SA Sun was within 1 minute of arc exactly square Stoker's Venus, according to our 1:58 P.M. birth time. Solar Arc Ascendant and Nep-tune were precisely trine to the Midheaven, and SA Pluto was 1-1/2 degrees away from opposition with the Midheaven (not shown).

Figure 20 (page 223) reveals as well SA Node–Venus in 27–26 Scorpio exactly square the Ascendant (tremendous public thrust and recognition); the transiting Saturn-Uranus conjunction in 27 Scorpio was exactly square Stoker's Ascendant; and, finally, the SP Moon at 19 Virgo squared the Midheaven. Here is dramatic testi-mony once again about the viability of Stoker's horoscope angles, the validity of his birth time.

Stoker's imagination focused all vampire legends into the black-caped, formally dressed, handsome aristocrat named "Dracula," a far scream from Prince Vlad, the life behind the legend. Over 250 motion pictures have reeled into our teetering unconscious since Stoker's extraordinary creation, and millions of copies of the novel have been sold in hundreds of languages. Bram Stoker died "of exhaustion" on April 20, 1912 in London, in near poverty. He was cremated ... for sure.

---

69 The name "Dracula" *is* powerful: there are the most open vowel [ah] and the most closed [u, pronounced *oo*] contrasting each other—ah-oo-ah; the strongly stroked, rolled "r" led explosively by the "d"; and, above all, the pivotal, hard, menacing sound of "k". An extra-ordinary number of power words and epic historical names carry their strength through the "k" sound, ending or beginning in "k" (or hard "c") for effect: Kaaba (the most sacred shrine of Islam in the courtyard of the Great Mos*que* (also the "k" sound); Kabbalah, Franz Kafka, Kamikaze, Immanuel Kant, Herbert von Karajan, Kennedy, J. Arthur Rank, Kissinger, Elektra, Socrates, The Koran, Krishna, Moby Dick, Christ, square, kleptoma-nia, wreck, peak, crazy, cool, captivate, kill, and many slang-sexual words. *Drrra'-Koo-Laaah* has clear kinetic impact.

Bibliography

Bao-Lin Liu and Fiala, Alan D. *Canon of Lunar Eclipses 1500 B.C.–A.D. 3000.* Richmond, VA: Willmann-Bell, Inc., 1992.

Barber, Paul. *Vampires, Burial, and Death: Folklore and Reality.* New Haven: Yale University Press, 1988.

Florescu, Radu R. and McNally, Raymond T. *Dracula: Prince of Many Faces.* New York: Little, Brown and Company, 1989.

Grant, Michael. *Constantine the Great.* New York: Charles Scribner's Sons, 1993.

_____. *The History of Ancient Israel.* New York: Charles Scribner's Sons, 1984.

Green, Julien. *God's Fool: the Life and Times of Francis of Assisi.* San Francisco: Harper & Row, 1983.

Groh, Dennis E. "The Religion of the Empire: Christianity from Constantine to the Arab Conquest." *Christianity and Rabbinic Judaism,* Herschel Shanks, Editor. Washington, DC: Biblical Archaeological Society, 1992.

Hale, John. *The Civilization of Europe in the Renaissance.* New York: Atheneum, 1994.

Hardin, Michael and Harvey, Charles. *Working with Astrology: The Psychology of Harmonics, Midpoints and Astro*Carto*Graphy.* London: Arkana, Penguin Books, 1990.

Hibbert, Christopher. *Florence: The Biography of a City.* New York: W. W. Norton, 1993.

Mascetti, Manuela Dunn. *Vampire.* New York: Penguin, 1992.

McNally, Raymond T. & Florescu, Radu. *In Search of Dracula.* Boston: Houghton Mifflin, 1994.

Michelsen, Neil F. *The Tables of Planetary Phenomena.* San Diego: ACS Publications, 1990.

Monks, David. "Astrology, Vampires and Sex," article in the *Bulletin of the Irish Astrological Association.* Dublin, 1994.

Plantinga, Cornelius. *Not the Way It's Supposed to Be—A Breviary of Sin.* Grand Rapids, MI: Wm B. Eerdmans, 1995.

Stoker, Bram. *Dracula.*

Tyl, Noel. *Prediction in Astrology.* St. Paul, MN: Llewellyn Publications, 1991.

—————. *Synthesis & Counseling in Astrology*. St. Paul, MN: Llewellyn Publications, 1993.

—————. Editor. *Sexuality in the Horoscope*. St. Paul MN: Llewellyn Publications, 1994.

Watters, Barbara H. *Sex and the Outer Planets*. Washington D.C.: Valhalla Paperback; 1971.

Discussion with Boston College Professor of History, Radu R. Florescu, the world's leading Dracula researcher, with Professor Raymond T. McNally.

Discussion with Romanian Embassy Cultural Counselor, Ioana Ieronim, Washington D.C.; reference: *East European Monographs*, "Dracula— Essays on the Life and Times of Vlad Tepes," edited by Kurt W. Treptow, distributed through the Embassy, by Columbia University Press, New York; 1991.

Index

Leonardo da Vinci
The Mind as Master

An astrological rectification of the birth date and time of Leonardo da Vinci

✦

Giorgio Vasari (1511–1574) was a masterful painter, with many portraits shown in Florence and the Vatican, including the definitive portrait of Lorenzo de' Medici. He was also a superb architect—one of his designs was the Uffizi Gallery in Florence and another was the tomb of Michelangelo, with whom he had studied. But perhaps above all, as a rhapsodic writer, Vasari was the inventor of art history.

In 1550—with revisions made in a second edition in 1568—Vasari's *Vite de' più eccellenti architettori, pittori e scultori italiani* (The lives of the most excellent Italian architects, painters and sculptors) reflected the light of Italy's classical revival as a rebirth of fine art. He set forth for the first time the concept of "renaissance."[1]

While Vasari's work was filled with editorialization, Florentine nationalism, and a definite awareness of the sensual captivation intrinsic to legend, it was the singularly authoritative record of

---

1 Vasari's great work contained 120 biographies, all recounted in adventurous style, filled with love of the subject, awe of the personages depicted, and the sense of their collective world significance. The stories are based on eye-witness accounts experienced by Vasari or secondarily gleaned through interviews with people who knew the masters. At the time of publication, Vasari was superintendent of fine arts for the Grand Duke Cosimo de' Medici. See Penguin Classics, *Lives of the Artists*, Ed. George Bull.

    The term "Renaissance" was first formally applied to the era by Swiss historian Jakob Burckhardt in 1860, but the idea, the spirit, and recognition of the movement was born first with Vasari.

the artistic times. It is he who monumentalized this bloom of fifteenth-sixteenth century Italy, the 200 years of intellectual and aesthetic glory that ended the darkness of the Middle Ages and illuminated for all time to follow the nobility of man's creativity. It is Vasari who introduced "Il Divino" to history: "Celestial influences may shower extraordinary gifts on certain human beings, which is an effect of nature; but there is something supernatural in the accumulation in one individual of so much beauty, grace, and might." The divine one was Leonardo da Vinci.

Leonardo embodied everything excellent about man, about the Renaissance. He possessed every noble quality: prodigious physical skill and strength, generosity, kindness, eloquence, love of the wild, and a "terrible strength in argument, sustained by intelligence and memory." There was the subtlety of his mind, "which never ceased to devise inventions"; his aptitude for mathematics, science, music, poetry. And even more, Leonardo was a man of "physical beauty beyond compare."[2]

Other writers followed suit, adding their reminiscences and histories of the period to Vasari's. Great attention was given to the early splendor of Giotto, the perspective refinements of Masaccio, and the age of perfection culminating in the works of Michelangelo and Raphael. There were Ghiberti, Brunelleschi, Donatello, Alberti, Verrocchio, Botticelli, and many others, but there was always the special, incomparably beautiful presence of Leonardo whose tall silhouette was famous in the streets of both Florence and Milan, whose knee-length, rose-colored capes went against long-draping fashion, whose beard, hair, and thick eyebrows (in his later years) fulfilled the philosopher image. In his painting, *The School of Athens*, Raphael captured Leonardo in the image of Plato, paying homage to Leonardo by choosing him to represent the man then esteemed as the greatest thinker of all time. Leonardo was declared "the true model of the dignity of knowledge, like Hermes Trismegistus and Prometheus in antiquity."[3]

This regard of Leonardo as a *philosopher* above any other description is most telling. The Renaissance symbolized a return, literally a rebirth, of ancient philosophers (some even say a reincarnation cluster from ancient Greece). The entire style of study and

---

2   All sources. Bramly, 5.
3   A description by Giovanni Paolo Lomazzo (c. 1590), quoted by Bramly, 6.

expression of thought changed, in Italy and then throughout Europe. Important personages identifying with ultimate ideals were seen as restless seekers experimenting in many directions with all kinds of subjects, looking for arcane truths, for eternal principles— and their beauty. Philosophers were magicians (Magi), and Leonardo was honored until his death as the paradigm.[4]

Leonardo was a meticulous note taker. After about the age of thirty, he wrote *everything* down, all his observations of the world about him from the complex aerodynamics of a bird's wing in flight—and how man could fly—to the detailed working concept to divert from its course the Arno, Tuscany's river of life, to bypass and finally defeat enemy Pisa 120 miles downstream; from grocery lists and domestic memos to the amount of wax needed to make the proper number of candles for his own funeral; from anagram witticisms written in musical *solfeggio* notation to detailed rules for living a healthy life. There were solutions to all conceivable problems like putting the thread onto a screw, mass producing needles, remaining underwater safely; there were copious scientific considerations of optics, aerodynamics, anatomy, watchmaking, acoustics, mechanics; creating the better olive press, automatic door closure devices, intensified lamps, folding furniture, better toilets, cranes, and on and on and on. But there was *never* any personal revelation, never any emotional insight. There was only the applied work of the mind.

The notebooks—estimated by scholars to total about 7,000 pages retrieved from probably 20,000,[5] the rest being yet undiscovered or lost—only came to light and systematic study in the 1870s. These stupendous observations and studies, almost all of them extremely beyond Leonardo's own time, revealed an inventive genius, a mind of concentrated analytical skill beyond description or measure. Here was painter, sculptor, philosopher, systematically reinventing the world. The qualities of his mind and spirit recovered from the notebooks portray Leonardo as the singular individual in all of history to attain such consistent universal brilliance.[6]

Vasari and later sources—and Leonardo's notebooks—focus on Leonardo's presence, his mind, his reputation as a man of learning. Benvenuto Cellini quotes Francis I, King of France, under whose protectorate Leonardo died, as saying that "never had there been a

---

4   Garin, 123 (Chapter Five).
5   Turner, 5. Other sources.
6   For most thorough study of the inventive realm of Leonardo, see Hart.

man who knew as many things as Leonardo, not only about sculpture, painting, and architecture, but also about philosophy, for he was a very great philosopher."[7]

Vasari gushes about artistic details of Leonardo's work told to him by expert eyewitnesses (Vasari was eight years old when Leonardo died). Leonardo was the ultimate master of *chiaroscuro* (molding form through manipulation of extremes of light and shade) and *contraposto* (showing movement through turns of the body about its axis). He changed art forever by showing *attitude* in paintings; he pursued, discovered, and revealed the nerves, musculature, and blood-flow process that lifted and colored the mystery of a smile; he captured the personality of hair; he captured *thought* in his brush strokes; and above all perhaps, he applied a neo-classic (indeed, Euclidian) geometry to the organization of his paintings that set an ideal for all art to follow. The power in this geometry was its suggestion of the inherent order of creation.[8]

But Leonardo left no central monument for his art. We point to the Sistine Chapel for Michelangelo, the Grand Rooms at the Vatican for Raphael, the dome of the Duomo in Florence for Brunelleschi, St. Peter's in Rome for Bramante. We have little to cite for Leonardo—the genius *who rarely finished a work of art.*

Time and time and time again in his life, Leonardo accepted commissions and then walked away from the work unfinished, or he made mistakes with innovative binding agents, for example, and a fresco two years in the preparation would drip off the wall. Of the thirteen works that do survive and are confirmed to be largely by Leonardo's own hand, even four, perhaps five of these are unfinished, including the *Mona Lisa* (after some eight years of work!). The extraordinary, epoch-changing masterpiece, *The Last Supper,* even in Vasari's time, just forty to fifty years after completion, was said to have deteriorated to no more than "a dazzling stain."[9]

---

7 All sources. Bramly, 8.

8 See Turner, Chapter 11, "The Body as Nature and Culture," and Chapter 12, "A Blessed Rage for Order."

9 Bramly, 296. By 1624, there was hardly anything left of *The Last Supper* to see. Restorations good and bad have kept some image alive.

   In light of Leonardo's habitual incompleteness and frequent project failure, Vasari tried to explain the romantic grandness of Leonardo's life and work by introducing the concept of perfectionism: "He began many things and never finished any of them, since it seemed to him that the hand was not able to attain to the perfection of art in exactly the things which he conceived: seeing that he imagined difficulties so subtle and marvellous, that they could never be expressed by the hand, no matter how skillful." All sources; see Gould, 13.

Vasari's veneration of Leonardo through the memories and conviction of the genius' contemporaries became the base of legend.
The *Mona Lisa* was there with her enigmatic, mystic smile; the
unfinished *Adoration of the Magi*, with its extraordinary geometry; the
unfinished *Saint Jerome* with its depiction of poignant suffering; the
unfinished *Virgin and Child with Saint Anne and a Lamb*, a happy swirl
of exquisitely controlled movement and spirit, and a few other paintings; Rubens' sketch of part of Leonardo's plan for the grand fresco
The Battle of Anghiari and the master's own instructions about battle
portrayal in his notes for a *Treatise on Painting* show the extraordinary power of Leonardo's mastery of composition and anatomy. For
just over 300 years, Leonardo was like a celestial Nova, but the glow
was not yet clarified; its existence was known, but its light had not
fully reached our eyes.

Then, when the thousands of pages of his notes were discovered
just before the turn of this century, to the meagre but marvelous
legacy of his art were added *the revelations of Leonardo's mind*. The
explosion of this man's presence took on infinitely more detail, far,
far beyond painting. The Renaissance man was born, and the longer
the list of Leonardo's "discoveries" became, the more Leonardo
appeared to move beyond all human measure. Here was someone
exploring human flight, exploring the ocean bed, obsessed with
omniscience, who could also paint the perfect smile, who knew the
workings of humankind in anatomical detail, who could make musical instruments and sing songs of his own creation, who was eloquent beyond telling, who could create dramatic pageants that would
rival twentieth-century stagecraft. But again, there was mystery:
Leonardo wrote these thousands and thousands of pages of notes
backward from left to right, with inverted characters! His manu-
scripts that described so incredibly many inventions *had to be read
with a mirror,* and not one machine or battlement apparatus put forth
on these pages *had been built to endure or survive!* The Nova became
even brighter, but it was still unclear.[10]

As more and more information accumulated, Leonardo took on
more and more mystery. Was he supernatural? Was he hiding messages in his work too advanced for the rest of humanity? His obses-
sions with knowing, with detail; his illegitimate birth and thus

---

10 Leonardo was left-handed, and this style of writing is not uncommon to left-handers. All
   sources. Bramly, 13.

disqualification from university studies, from a traditional career, from certain trades like medicine, law, or banking; his extreme and continual fear of slander and degradation; his sensitivity which threatened to go beyond practical management; his disinclination to complete his works; his misanthropic inaccessibility—all added to the legend and defined him distinctly apart from other mortals.[11]

The brighter the light became, the more the mystery developed, and the greater became our need somehow to explain the magnificent Leonardo.

Then there was Sigmund Freud. In 1916, after some twenty-five years of his formulation of what became known as psychoanalysis, as Leonardo's newly discovered notes were challenging the academic world, Freud published *Leonardo da Vinci: A Psychosexual Study of an Infantile Reminiscence* (original title). Freud took a rare subjective thought from Leonardo's notes (the only piece of information about his childhood in the notes)—a dream of a vulture that flew down to Leonardo's cradle and struck its tail against his lips—and created a homoerotic full-scale analysis of Leonardo's neuroses.[12]

There was an error in Freud's German translation of Leonardo's notes. For example, "vulture" should have been "kite" (a kind of hawk), which in retrospect does much to mitigate the amplification of Freud's theorization, involving the Egyptian archetype of the vulture with the appropriate goddess, etc. But Freud's hypothesis remained: Leonardo's story revealed an unconscious wish to commit the act of fellatio. The early experience of sucking at the breast and his having been taken away from his mother shortly after birth had been transformed into the discomforting report about a bird and its tail smacking at Leonardo's lips.

Freud took the sketchy facts known about Leonardo at the time (illegitimate birth, mother and father marrying others during Leonardo's first year) and hypothesized that his father left him to be brought up by his mother Caterina in her home. Caterina was over-tender with Leonardo and over-eroticized her relations with him—

---

11 Vallentin, 114; Bramly, 36.

12 Leonardo's words: "I seem to have been destined to write in such a detailed manner on the subject of the kite, for in one of my earliest childhood memories, it seems to me that when I was in my cradle, a kite flew down and opened my mouth with its tail and struck me many times with the tail on the inside of my lips." Bramly, 49. Also Merejcovski, probably the source Freud read, the German translation from the Italian through the author's Russian(!), 387 ... in some versions, the phrase is added, "as though to signify that all life long I would speak of wings."

as the kite memory supposedly showed. Somewhere between the age of three and five, according to Freud (and to inaccurate biographical details), Leonardo's tie with his mother was broken. He was returned to his father's household and to the care of a [his father's new] young and childless wife. At about this same stage, Leonardo had to repress his sexual interest in and curiosity about his mother Caterina. He achieved this repression by identifying himself *with her* and thereby forcing himself to choose love objects like himself. In Leonardo's case, the repression of sex interest was severe. He sublimated much of his sexual energy and interests into curiosity and a craving for knowledge. Freud stated that "What an artist creates provides at the same time an outlet for his sexual desire."[13]

Freud takes this theory full-blown into a dramatic analysis of Leonardo's whole life. For example, likening Leonardo's use of dark caves in his paintings and drawings to portrayal of the vulva; to his clumsy portrayal of the vulva in his otherwise spectacularly refined anatomical drawings; to the explanation of the Virgin and St. Anne (her mother) appearing together as equal in age to symbolize parallel or competitive mothers, etc.[14]

Freud saw Leonardo's cold and bitter notes about humanity as emphasizing extremely conservative behavior, the manifestation of a severe and puritanical conscience. He hung much upon Leonardo's observation that "Intellectual passion drives out sensuality."

In reality, there is little doubt that Leonardo was indeed a homosexual.[15] Homosexuality was rampant in Florence; in Germany, the word "Florenzer" became synonymous with homosexual. The legal penalty (burning at the stake!) was not enforced; the government considered public brothels as an alternative. The authorities turned an almost blind eye to the situation, and this saved Leonardo, as we shall see, when he was brought before the authorities on a charge of sodomy in his early years. We shall learn of his very long relationship with Salai, his young ward, and more.

---

13 Freud/Farrell introduction. It is explained that, when Leonardo refers to the kite's tail striking him many times against the lips, he is referring not only to the experience of sucking, but also to the experience or memory in which his mother pressed innumerable passionate kisses on his mouth. Hence, Freud explains the passive character of the fantasy equating with Leonardo's adult wish to play the passive partner in a homosexual act of sucking a penis.

14 Freud did not recognize that it was traditional in the Renaissance to portray the Virgin Mary and St. Anne as young women together as the idealization of perfection.

15 All major sources, except Vallentin. See Gould, 22.

When Freud's exercise was added to the lore of Leonardo, the legend became inflamed with prurient speculations: the psychosexual explanations only created more mystery. Other commentaries followed. Intriguing questions about his maternal complex came to the fore and are still there: who is/was the Mona Lisa? Is this actually Caterina as Leonardo remembered her, as she should have been? Is that why Leonardo spent eight years with this portrait, never really finishing it, keeping it with him to his death?

What emerges from any study of Leonardo is *not* an extensive statement about art—there is so little to go on. It is *not* a marvellous catalogue of inventions that steals thunder from eighteenth and nineteenth century scientists—there are thousands of pages of drawings and detailed notes, but no thing ever completed or preserved. It is *not* a library of treatises—there were so many begun, on optics, flight, anatomy, water, and more, but none ever published. Rather, it is the monumentality of the man's mind, his observations of the world around him, and his crystalization of the creative process.

Leonardo's Birth

In the very small village of Vinci, a long day's ride from Florence, a peasant girl named Caterina gave birth to the "love child" conceived with Ser Piero da Vinci, an up-and-coming Notary. The date was Saturday, April 15, 1452, and the time was "at the third hour of the night."[16]

Ser Piero's father (*Ser* is a title given to a Notary), Antonio—Leonardo's grandfather—was attending the birth and recorded it in a book very important to the family. His entry was complete with the name of the priest who baptized Leonardo and the names of the witnesses to the ceremony. We do not know when Antonio's entry was made and we do not know when the baptism took place, but we can assume a good level of accuracy with this record since Antonio was himself a Notary, in a long family line of middle-level legal officials, and the book in which he wrote the expanded entry was a "notarial" book.

---

16 Bramly, 37–38, the only reference to have the time and its source: a photocopy of grandfather Antonio's entry on the last page of a notarial book that had belonged to Leonardo's great-great-grandfather. The entry reads: "1452: There was born to me a grandson, son of Ser Piero my son, on 15 April, a Saturday, at the third hour of the night. He bears the name Leonardo." As was usual in the case of an illegitimate child, the mother's name was not recorded.

In Italy in the Renaissance, the night began at sunset. Sunset on that day in April in Vinci occurred at 6:50 P.M. (with a 4 Scorpio Ascendant). But "night" was surely confirmed by a darkened sky, which would have occurred closer to 7:15 or 8:00 P.M. Three hours later ("at the third hour of the night") would mean approximately 10:15–11:00 P.M., giving an Ascendant of 14 Sagittarius and a Midheaven of 7 Libra at 10:15 P.M. (see Figure 1 below).

The very beginning of study of Leonardo's life brings quickly forward from all sources the facts of his tall figure, his extraordinary

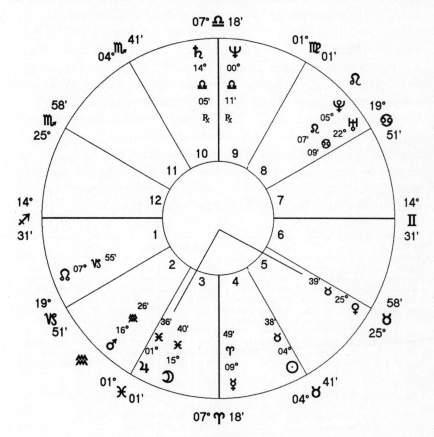

Figure 1
Leonard da Vinci (Test)
April 15, 1452, 10:15 P.M. LMT
Vinci, Italy
10E55 43N47
Placidus Houses

beauty of presence, his extreme love of the outdoors (he was the first to depict landscapes as pictures in themselves and not just as background to portraits), his great pleasure with animals (buying birds from vendors just to free them and observe close at hand their anatomy in flight); his passion for horses, of which he did extremely detailed anatomical studies; his thoroughly reinforced reputation as a philosopher. All of this suggests a Sagittarian Ascendant, which indeed was the sign on the eastern horizon when he was born, and, on that night and day, Jupiter, the Ascendant ruler, was squared (across the sign line) by Venus in Taurus, a strong suggestion indeed of the importance of aesthetics and personal beauty.

As well, the general chronology of Leonardo's life points strongly to the time "in late 1482 or early 1483," at age thirty when Leonardo left Florence in Tuscany to seek his fame in in Lombardy, delivering a silver lyre he had created as a gift to Lodovico Sforza, the powerful ruler of Milan, from the great Lorenzo de' Medici in Florence.[17] General perusal of the ephemeris for late 1482 and early 1483 (see Figure 2 below) shows transiting Uranus at 17 Sagittarius in December 1482 (just beyond the 10:15 P.M. Ascendant of 14 Sagittarius), the transit that so reliably signals major geographic displacement, individual change of a life-significant nature. (Leonardo would remain in Milan for most of his adult life.)

+ 0:00 UT		Geocentric Tropical Longitudes for 1482								
Date	Sid. Time	Sun/Earth	Mercury	Venus	Mars	Jupitor	Saturn	Uranus	Neptune	Pluto
JUN 1	17:12:32	18♊39 08	06♉01R	16♊58	18♒03	01♍42	18♎52R	13♐23R	06♐03R	06♎07R
JUL 1	19:10:48	17♋14 49	03♋02D	23♋50	24 33	06 12	19 00D	12 17	05 22	06 16D
JUL 31	21:09:04	15♌57 24	02♍09	00♍48	20 37R	11 55	20 33	11 39	05 01	06 53
AUG 30	23:07:21	14♍59 37	11♎21	07♎45	14 46	18 16	23 13	11 43D	05 08D	07 52
SEP 29	1:05:38	14♎30 06	00 11R	14♏34	19 04D	24 43	26 34	12 33	05 42	09 02
OCT 29	3:03:54	14♏30 41	07♏31D	21♐08	01♓44	00♎40	00♏09	13 58	06 39	10 09
NOV 28	5:02:11	14♐55 01	24♐51	27♑08	18 30	05 28	03 27	15 44	07 46	11 00
DEC 28	7:00:28	15♑29 42	00♒15R	01♒39	07♈05	08 19	05 58	17 30	08 49	11 25
JAN 27	8:58:44	15♒58 03	19♑55D	02♈12	26 20	08 33R	07 14	18 57	09 36	11 17R
FEB 26	10:57:01	16♓05 25	00♓58	21 28	15♉45	06 08	06 58R	19 48	09 56	10 42
MAR 28	12:55:18	15♈43 30	29♈10	13 17R	05♊04	02 23	05 23	19 53R	09 47R	09 54
APR 27	14:53:34	14♉52 10	23♉17R	08 02D	24 13	29♍30	03 11	19 15	09 13	09 08
MAY 27	16:51:51	13♊38 36	20 39D	28 13	13♋14	29 00D	01 20	18 08	08 26	08 41
JUN 26	18:50:08	12♋14 56	09♋40	27♉52	02♌10	01♎04	00 38D	16 58	07 42	08 42D

Figure 2
Leonardo da Vinci, age 30

---

17 All sources. See Vallentin, 69.

Recalculating the test chart for an Ascendant of 17 Sagittarius gives 10:30 P.M., with a Midheaven of 11 Libra 23, and also gives us an early surprise: the ephemeris record (see Figure 2, page 238) shows that, in December 1482, along with transiting Uranus in 17 Sagittarius, *transiting Pluto would be in 11 Libra 25!* As well, transiting Saturn would have just opposed Leonardo's Sun. These are mighty measurements—two of them angular—working together to support this major move in Leonardo's life.

In other words, the birth time of 10:30 P.M.—surely within the reference made by Antonio, "at the third hour of the night"—would indicate for Leonardo powerful, life-changing, simultaneous angular transits. Testing in this way throughout Leonardo's life repeatedly reinforced this time of 10:30 P.M. conclusively, as we shall see.[18]

At first glance, Leonardo's horoscope, Figure 3 (page 240), drawn for 10:30 P.M., presents four initial considerations.

The Dominating Saturn

Saturn is almost exactly overhead. It is easy to imagine the symbolic influence Renaissance astrologers would have given to this Saturn: exalted in Libra, overseeing the entire horoscope, the only planet above the horizon, born on Saturn's day (Saturday)![19]

This Saturn is ennobled by sign placement in Libra: ambition directed through social awareness; and by elevation: austerity, nobility, a rigorous behavioral code, alone in a crowd—these are the impressions we learn of Leonardo in every source of information about him.

All of Leonardo's inventions were somehow directed to make things better for people, to please authorities, to fulfill civic programs: from the plans to build a bridge for the Turks from Istanbul to Pera;[20] to retrieve land from the marshes near Rome; to making

---

18 The earlier horoscope for 10:15 P.M. is very tempting indeed with the clear signature MC=Saturn/Neptune, as our analysis will suggest, i.e., the interplay between a Neptune complex and a Saturn complex of measurements; perhaps the disinclination to finish his works. But such a midpoint picture, its severe debilitation, is left behind by Leonardo's extraordinary eventual success. The 10:30 P.M. time responds throughout Leonardo's life much more appropriately.

19 Of course, Uranus, Neptune, and Pluto were not yet known.

20 This bridge was conceived to be the link between Asia and Europe. Leonardo's design was "amazingly modern," with a colossal span of 240 meters (almost the length of three football fields). In his proposal, Leonardo also itemized many of his other inventions: his ability to build windmills, an automatic bilge pump for ships, and more. Bramly, 326. So often, it seems, Leonardo presented so much to others so as to defy credibility. No response came from the Turks.

rope, minting coins, building mirrors, creating bizarre theatrical costumes. A. Richard Turner captures this Libra dimension—and, as well, Leonardo's *Mars in Aquarius*, beautifully trine Saturn—in his phrase, "Leonardo's manifold practical projects [were] to rearrange God's creation in a way useful to humans."[21]

This Saturn is retrograde, clearly suggesting his estrangement from his father, and, as well, his illegitimacy, his feelings of

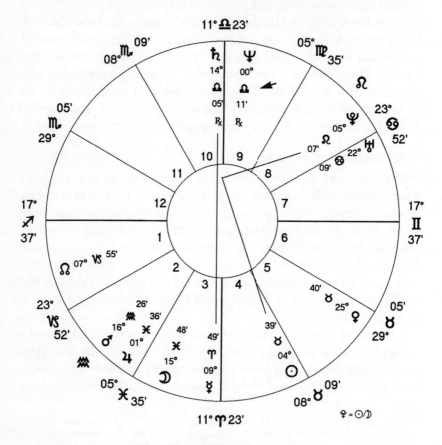

Figure 3
Leonard da Vinci
April 15, 1452, 10:30 P.M. LMT
Vinci, Italy
10E55 43N47
Placidus Houses

---

21 Turner, 213.

inferiority (we hear often his embarrassment that he can not speak Latin with the intelligentsia of Florence, how hard he worked to learn, how he never achieved that facility; how sensitive he was that he was not formally educated).[22]

Saturn rules the 2nd House: Leonardo's undermined sense of self-worth was at one and the same time overcompensatorily self-aware in excellence and intrinsically self-demeaning that he was not working hard enough.[23] The question is begged always, "Whom was Leonardo trying to please?" The search for his father's closeness and his mother's love, for family togetherness are emphasized always in every turn of narrative about Leonardo's life.

This Saturn is opposed to Mercury—a key aspect which will be covered in detail later—and Mercury is the ruler of Leonardo's 7th House: we can see these deep dark feelings projected onto society as a defense against the pain Leonardo felt personally. For example, biographer Bramly suggests "Virtue persecuted" as a perfect epitaph for Leonardo.[24] Bramly sees Leonardo's identification with Jesus in *The Last Supper* (on the eve of betrayal) as one expression of Leonardo's constant fear of being socially maligned and persecuted. An angry and pained view of man grew within Leonardo throughout his life: he wrote, speaking of bone structure, muscles, and organs, "I do not think that rough men, of bad habits and little intelligence, deserve such a fine instrument and such a variety of mechanisms." In short, Leonardo did not think that others appreciated the marvel of human life; thus they felt no obligation to respect it: "How many people there are who could be described as mere channels for food, producers of excrement, fillers of latrines, for they have no other purpose in this world; they practice no virtue whatsoever; all that remains after them is a full latrine."[25]

---

22 For full study of the Saturn retrograde phenomenon, please see Tyl, *Synthesis & Counseling*, 38–47.

23 Even on his deathbed, Leonardo is supposed to have recognized (to the King of France) "how much he had offended God by not working on his art as much as he should have." All sources.

24 Bramly, 279.

25 Bramly, 280.

Neptune at the Aries Point[26]

This position of Neptune—lushly trine to Venus in its own sign of Taurus (the final dispositor of the horoscope)—is a dramatic statement of Leonardo's extraordinary thrust of imagination, vision, aesthetics, sensitivity and, in counterpoint, his anxious turn of mind about his social acceptance. This Neptune is also "at" (i.e., squaring) the Midpoint of Moon/Saturn suggesting feelings of inferiority, melancholy, frustration, unfulfillment, and even the disinclination to finish what one starts.[27] Much more will be discovered about this Neptune position later.

The Sun-Moon blend, Taurus and Pisces, suggests tremendous energy to work with the intangible and to give it form, an extremely high potential for creativity, a great need for understanding and sympathy from others. The need for a goal so that all of the feeling is somehow worthwhile introduces the Saturn concept (ambition) in Libra, its opposition to Mercury ruler of the 7th, the thrust of the Sagittarian Ascendant (we can note that Neptune is quincunx Jupiter, both planets dispositing the Moon in Pisces).[28]

The Sun is square with Pluto, a statement of personal power held back, dampened, even stifled, as in the image of a blanket covering a grenade. This square almost invariably suggests something haunting, repressing, or constricting a powerful personal thrust; some contrapuntal developmental concept that impinges upon the normal flow of progress.[29]

In managing the Sun-Pluto square, Leonardo will have to work through difficulty. The difficulty is deep and psychological: Pluto in

---

26 Key to zodiacal conceptualization is the point of zero-Aries, of course. But this awareness relates as well to 0 Libra by opposition (the same axis) and to 0 Cancer and 0 Capricorn by square. In short, "0-Cardinals" is our orientation to the world around us. Any natal planet or point at 0 degree of any Cardinal sign is by definition configurated with "the Aries Point;" the planet's or point's symbolism will be given a decided push out into the world, a public boost, exposure. See, Tyl, *Synthesis & Counseling*, 312–321.

27 See "Solar Arc Analysis Directory," practical for analysis of natal Midpoint pictures as well, Tyl, *Synthesis & Counseling*, Appendix; or Tyl, *Prediction in Astrology*, Llewellyn, 1991, Appendix. Additionally, Leonardo loved conjuring, creating tricks with a natural science orientation for his friends. "He conscientiously prepared his surprises with almost pedantic seriousness." Vallentin, 32.

28 See Tyl, *Synthesis & Counseling*, Sun-Moon blend Section beginning page 76.

29 A modern example: Charles, the Prince of Wales (November 14, 1948 at 9:14 P.M., GMT in London) has the Sun square Pluto. The Sun rules his Ascendant. The would-be king has a stifling influence in his life, clearly symbolized by his Moon-Node conjunction in the 10th, opposed his Mercury. This influence working against his personal power is clearly his mother, Queen Elizabeth. See Tyl, *Synthesis & Counseling*, 50–52.

the 8th so very often suggests that psychological or spiritual assistance will be sought sometime to work out difficult concerns in life, usually those connected to early development, family upset, and the problems with interpersonal values that follow. Learning about the pressures and understanding their role in development help free the personal potential, help to remove the blanket. Empowerment follows struggle; freedom is achieved through assimilation of difficult considerations and refinement of one's approach to life. The best ending to the development scenario of Sun square Pluto shows the personality strength—in this case, Leonardo's creativity and its orientation to his world—matured, reinforced, and confirmed by the very tensions that threatened to debilitate it early on.

We can begin to agree with historians and biographers that Leonardo's illegitimacy and his "neuroses" born out of the early family disorganization are of deep concern within his development. We note also the suppression into the northern hemisphere of all planets within Saturn's orbit, suggesting much unfinished business in the early development; we see the awesome Saturn-Mercury opposition hard on the parental axis, and the Sun receiving the Pluto square within the parental 4th.

In our first overview of this horoscope, led by the dominating Saturn in Libra upon the Midheaven, we have gained corroboration of Leonardo's austere characterological presence, the severity of his mind. This is complemented by the Sagittarian Ascendant with Jupiter square Venus which fits Leonardo's tall figure and extraordinary personal beauty, described by all biographers, his occasional jocularity, his enthusiasms, etc.

We can feel extreme sensitivity and the need to give it all form and value (the Sun Moon blend) and we can strongly suspect a smothering or fuming frustration within all of this drive (the Sun-Pluto square), behind which we can suspect with good reason a deeply entrenched dissatisfaction that is linked to the break-up of the early home.

Through Mercury's relationship with Saturn and Mercury's rulership of the 7th, we see projection of personal anxiety, upset, and depression upon society in general, relationships in particular.[30] His homosexuality is an outgrowth of these concerns (and others) and further individualizes Leonardo's growth.

---

30 See Tyl "Defense Mechanisms, projection," *Synthesis & Counseling*, 655.

Going Deeper

Leonardo's mind is the dominant theme in all presentations of his life: the philosopher, the intellect, the thinker, the imaginer, the analyst, the inventor, the social critic ... image after image out of his life behavior bring focus to the role of his mind, to the symbolism of his Mercury in Aries. It is "on fire," if you will, and ignites his entire being. Through its trine with Pluto, Mercury is an easy conduit for the Sun-Pluto syndrome into Leonardo's psyche; through its tight semisquare with Venus in Taurus, Mercury is idealistically tied to his all-encompassing sense of aesthetics; and through the Cardinal opposition with Saturn on the Midheaven axis, Mercury is made dominatingly serious. We can recall Vasari's description of Leonardo's "terrible strength in argument, sustained by intelligence and memory," an obvious emphasis of 3rd House dimensions (ruled by Neptune).[31]

Additionally, Mercury is only 24 minutes of arc away from the precise midpoint position between Sun and Moon (see Figure 4, page 245). It is undeniable that any planet conjunct, square, or opposed to the Sun-Moon midpoint will work to dominate the life.[32]

And so Leonardo's Mercury is life-dominant. More than anything painterly, architectural, or even inventive, the mind and its workings are Leonardo's life signature. Leonardo's mind designed his every action, perceived every nuance of life that it could, noted in arch objectivity every detail accessible to the eye, and drove every glimmer of awareness this man had about the world into the consciousness of all time. His "rule" for his life was a commandment from this Mercury: *nota ogni cosa*, take note of every thing[33]; and his working premise, *pittura e cosa mentale*, painting is something mental.[34]

And further, Mercury is *square the Lunar Nodal axis*, an undeniable indication of extreme maternal influence. The subject of his relationship with his mother—even before any awareness of Freud's hypothesis—must be a dominant theme in Leonardo's

---

31 All sources. But, as well, Vasari wrote of Leonardo's generosity and kindness, perhaps overstated in his deification of Leonardo. Largesse does not come through in the more careful biographies; Leonardo was too poor and too unrecognized for too long in his life to be the bubbling courtier.

32 This observation through my experience is corroborated in the literature, especially in the Cosmobiological School in Europe. It is very well presented in Harding and Harvey, Chapter 4, by Harvey. Also, see Tyl, *Synthesis & Counseling*, Section 2, C.

33 Vallentin, 270.

34 Garin, 193.

Midpoint Sort: 90° Dial											
♆	000°11'	♀/♃	013°38'	☿/♀	032°45'	♃/♇	048°21'	♄/♅	063°07'	☉/♇	079°53'
♀/♇	000°24'	♄	014°05'	♀/Mc	033°32'	☽/♅	048°59'	☉/☊	066°17'	☿/♃	080°43'
☉/♃	003°07'	♅/☊	015°02'	♂/♅	034°18'	♆/☊	049°03'	♀/Asc	066°39'	♃/Mc	081°30'
♅/Asc	004°53'	♂/Asc	017°02'	☉	034°39'	☿/☊	053°52'	☿/♇	067°28'	♃/♄	082°50'
☿/♆	005°00'	☉/♆	017°25'	♃/☊	034°45'	♂/♃	054°01'	♇/Mc	068°15'	☽/♆	083°00'
♆/Mc	005°47'	☽/♀	020°44'	♀/♄	034°53'	☊/Mc	054°39'	♂/♆	068°19'	♀/♅	083°55'
♀/♂	006°03'	♇/☊	021°31'	♇	035°07'	☽/♇	055°28'	☽/♃	068°42'	☉/♂	085°32'
♄/♆	007°08'	♅	022°09'	♆/Asc	038°54'	♀	055°40'	♄/♇	069°36'	☊/Asc	087°46'
☊	007°55'	☉/☿	022°14'	♂/♇	040°47'	♄/☊	056°00'	☿/♂	073°08'	☽/☿	087°49'
☿	009°49'	☉/Mc	023°01'	☽/☊	041°51'	☉/Asc	056°08'	☉/♅	073°24'	☽/Mc	088°36'
☽/☉	010°13'	☉/♄	024°22'	♃/♅	041°53'	♅/♆	056°10'	♂/Mc	073°55'	☽/♄	089°57'
☿/Mc	010°36'	♃/Asc	024°37'	☿/Asc	043°43'	☿/♅	060°59'	♂/♄	075°16'		
♇/Asc	011°22'	♂/☊	027°11'	Mc/Asc	044°30'	☽/♂	061°07'	☽	075°48'		
Mc	011°23'	♀/♆	027°56'	☉/♀	045°09	♃	061°36'	♃/♆	075°53'		
☿/♄	011°57'	♅/♇	028°38'	♄/Asc	045°51'	♅/Mc	061°46'	♀/☊	076°47'		
♄/Mc	012°44'	☽/Asc	031°43'	♂	046°26'	♆/♇	062°39'	Asc	077°37'		

Figure 4
Leonardo da Vinci, April 15, 1452

life. That relationship, its discomfort, is the blanket upon his power, warming it to life and continuously conditioning its full claim to living.[35]

This Mercury in Aries is the first way Leonardo's sensorium perceives the world; the fiery sparks of Mercury bombard the ultra-sensitive Moon-screen in Pisces. There is a lightning-fast consideration process that is embraced by awareness of the intangible. Together, the brazen sense of proud knowing and the sensually fragile sense of receptivity and understanding nourish creative form and expression.

Saturn represents fear, recognition of the potentials for control and repression. Within this opposition, Mercury gains all-too-keen awareness of Fire fears, the fears of being ignored, not being recognized, not being listened to. This is compounded by the fact of Leonardo's illegitimacy and the way his society regarded that condition. The Saturn-Mercury contact defines gnawing insecurity and

---

35 Indeed, Freud's dramatic hypothesis—right or wrong—colors one's view of Leonardo because of its potential validity. It stimulated much counter-analysis in the literature. Biographer Vallentin, for example, writing in 1938, does not even mention Freud. Yet, she offers this perspective: "But the child was carefully kept away from his own mother [*capturing the break that had to have been there*]. Leonardo's development was permanently influenced by the fact that he grew up [*after weaning*] as a motherless child, bereft of the primitive, irreplaceable tenderness and natural warmth of mother love ... This incomplete acceptance, this sense of admittance only with reservations, coloured Leonardo's whole personal development and outlook on life. From early childhood the boy was thrown back upon himself; he had lost the happiness and the tyranny[!] of mother love, and gained unfettered liberty to reap impressions from the world around him." Vallentin, 7.

paranoia. Leonardo suspected and feared others; others did not easily understand or appreciate Leonardo.

Bramly observes: "Above all other things, Leonardo feared jealousy and the malicious gossip it gave rise to, the bad reputation that scandal could create. He complains of it in near-paranoid fashion. He believes he has never done any wrong; yet he is pursued, attacked, persecuted. Falsehood, scandal, ingratitude, lies, hatred, insults, ill repute—all these words recur insistently in his writings."[36] In Leonardo's horoscope, jealousy is keyed to Mercury as ruler of the 7th; malicious gossip is a 9th House concern (the third House, communication, of the 7th), here also keyed by Mercury, ruler of the 9th. The 9th House holds Neptune conjunct the Aries Point and adds layers of intensity to Leonardo's paranoia.

Leonardo's conservative reactions were his tight defenses against his fears. Time and time again in the books written about Leonardo we read descriptions like, "He would give full vent to his high spirits in the company of young men of his own age, but in his own conduct he showed a sobriety and prudence beyond his years, as though a sure instinct held him back from any sort of over-indulgence or excess."[37]

This Mercury connection with Saturn—its severity and residual conservatism, i.e., inspiration tightly controlled—was self-protection, withdrawal from his fears of rumor, debasement, and rejection, and was also key to his management of libido, as we shall see, turning his opinion of sex to disgust and revulsion, except when true emotions were involved beyond bestial behavior.[38]

Neptune Complex

One of Germany's premiere astrologers in this century was Thomas Ring (1892–1983). His approach was classical and philosophical. He appears to have been fascinated by the astrology of famous people, by the archetypal significance shown in the horoscope symbols of people developed in life beyond measure. He published a short analysis of Leonardo. Knowing that Leonardo

---

36 Bramly, 128.

37 Vallentin, 34.

38 Venus in Taurus and ruling the 5th House emphasizes the need for refinement and perfection in matters sexual. Any ugliness is abhorrent.

was born "at the third hour of the night," he set his horoscope rectification at 9:49 P.M., exactly three hours after sunset. This horoscope gave an Ascendant of 9 Sagittarius and a Midheaven of 00 Libra. Ring was undoubtedly confirmed in his presentation by the exact conjunction of Neptune with the Midheaven.[39]

Ring observes that Leonardo was a secret man, that he dealt privately with the finite and the infinite, within the clash of the practical and the universal. Ring spotted one key dimension leading from the elevated position of Neptune deep into Leonardo's sensorium: the exact aspect of *165 degrees* between Neptune and the Moon. [Fifteen degrees beyond a quincunx; 15 degrees short of an opposition.]

This aspect was barely recognized, understood, or taught when Ring was doing his work. We know it now as formed within the 24th harmonic; it is called a *Quindecile*.[40] Ring called it the "Abtrennungsaspekt," the separation aspect, in the sense of divorce, disruption, upheaval. I should like to add, "compulsion," *the response* to such upset in life, the obsessive nature in response to trauma.

Michael Munkasey, an expert with harmonics, amplifies this observation of separation significance and compulsion: he suggests that the aspect defines something that overrides common sense, that puts life out of balance, that drives the entire life in order to play out the energies symbolized. Michael puts it quickly and memorably as, "You can not escape the planets involved."

In astrology, Neptune symbolizes the soul or, as Alan Leo put it, "Neptune allows the soul to leave the body."[41] And I might add, Neptune allows things soulful *to enter* as well, to identify inspiration, vision, the unknown. For Ring, Leonardo's soul symbol in such demanding contact with the Moon introduced deep within Leonardo the soul of the mother beautiful, and it was mystified throughout Leonardo's whole life.

---

39 Ring, *Astrologische Menschen Kunde*, Vol. 1, 297; analysis in *Genius und Daemon*, 45–47.

40 This harmonic is based upon 360 divided by 24, or 15 degrees. The family of aspects includes 15 degrees, 75 degrees, 105 degrees, and 165 (all multiples of 15) as chief aspects in the harmonic since they stand alone from other aspects. We may note that President Bill Clinton (August 19, 1946 at 8:51 A.M., CST in Hope, AR) has the 105 degree aspect between his Mars and Uranus (suggesting a sexual compulsion and a drive to be before the public) and 75 degrees between Mercury and Jupiter (suggesting an academic, learning compulsion). Arnold Schwarzenegger (July 30, 1947 at 4:10 A.M., CED in Graz, Austria) has the 165 degree quindecile between Moon and Mars (enormous drive for action).

41 Leo, Alan, *The Art of Synthesis*, London: Fowler. 1968; 115.

This beautifully apt description suggests a whole realm of psycho-ethereal sensation to balance in Leonardo's existence the arch-detailed perceptive data of the Mercury-Saturn construct. In the process, it is reasonable that Leonardo's personal feelings and emotions become lost; they could find no manageable point of reference. Thus the austere, dry, private, lone position of the master.[42]

Without family connections, Leonardo created glorious and dramatic mother images (Madonnas), and Ring echoed Freud's symbolisms of the caves/wombs appearing threatening and foreboding in Leonard's work. In this scenario, Ring saw the male as someone allowed [asking permission] to enter the cave only as *Anstossbefruchter*, as "driving seed-planter."[43]

We are now ready to work with this extraordinary horoscope of genius, corroborated substantially in all studies of Leonardo's character, throughout his life time, testing the birthtime we have selected through the sensitivity of the astrological angles to Arcs Progressions, and Transits. All the while, we will be clarifying the brilliant light of this extraordinary individual, this Nova in the history of man.

The Family Shifts

To trace the foundation of Leonardo's development and complexes, we must work carefully with the earliest years, specifically the family shift very soon after birth and then, as a teenager, away from home into his apprenticeship in an art studio in Florence. In the process, we will be fine-tuning the horoscope and learning as much as we can about Leonardo's mother. Although historians are not sure, astrology does offer confirmation that she eventually returns in Leonardo's life much later, as we shall see.

From Leonardo's natal horoscope (see Figure 3, page 240) we can see the suggestion of a powerful time of family change in the very early years: note that the Solar Arc projection of the Midheaven will

---

42 Gould, 23: "All we know of Leonardo is consonant with the image of the tough intellectual homosexual in all ages—the combination of physical strength, great beauty and spectacular ability offset by a certain isolation arising, in this case, from his illegitimacy and continuing as a marked aloofness throughout his life."

43 Ring did not mention Pluto and its square with the Sun. With Pluto having been discovered only some twelve–fifteen years before his writing about Leonardo, computations of Pluto's position even at that time were unreliable, let alone for 500 years earlier.

bring it to Saturn in 2 degrees 42 minutes (14 Libra 5 minus 11 Libra 23), which is approximately two years and eight months (5 minutes of arc per month abbreviation of SA movement).[44]

At the same time, we can project (anticipate) Leonardo's Secondary Progressed Moon to place it at that future time as well. The SP Moon will be crossing the fourth cusp in approximately twenty-six months (abbreviating SP Moon passage as one degree per month; 26 degrees/months from 15 Pisces to 11 Aries), which is approximately two years and two months!

In two years and two to eight months, June–December 1454, the ephemeris indicates that transiting Pluto will enter exact sextile with the Midheaven from 11 Leo and that transiting Uranus will be at 4 Leo, *exactly square Leonardo's Sun!*

Look at the Moon at 15 Pisces: in 2 years+ (2 degrees+), the Solar Arc advance of the Moon would be to 17 Pisces square the Ascendant, and SA Mercury would be exactly conjunct the 4th cusp!

These measurements suggest a major family shift shortly after Leonardo's second birthday.

When we include the Tertiary Progressions for June 26, 1454, at two years and two months of age, we find the TP Moon at precisely *11 Aries*, conjunct the 4th cusp also![45]

The traditional chronology of Leonardo's earliest years is based on several tax declarations by the da Vinci family. In a 1457 tax document, when Leonardo was five, the earliest evidence researchers have, it is noted that Leonardo is claimed by Antonio, his paternal grandfather. There were tax reductions to be gained for illegitimate children; Antonio applied, but was not granted such consideration. Researchers also know that Caterina, Leonardo's mother, married a man nicknamed Accattabriga soon after Leonardo's birth and that Ser Piero, Leonardo's father, married a young woman named Albiera very soon after the birth and went to live in Florence.

The astrology says that Leonardo remained with Caterina until shortly after his second birthday and was shifted over to his grandfather's home when Caterina married and moved to a smaller place called Campo Zeppo, about thirty minutes' walk from Vinci. *Or,*

---

44 See Tyl, *Synthesis & Counseling*, 204–216 and Tyl, *Prediction in Astrology*.

45 Tertiary Progression takes each day after birth as symbolism for one Lunar Month of life. Tertiaries are Lunar orientated and extremely sensitive; the Moon progresses approximately 3 degrees per week of life, the Sun, 1 degree per month. Tertiary contact with the natal angles is of paramount importance, therefore Tertiaries are a most sensitive test for rectification.

the astrology shows the shift in Leonardo's life caused by Caterina's marriage, and then, perhaps three or four months later (as the Secondary Progressed Moon went on to oppose Saturn) the separation from his mother. Perhaps Caterina tried to make a go of it with Leonardo and her new husband; it didn't work; it was better for all to put/to leave the boy with the grandparents.[46]

But, Leonardo had to be breast-fed. Hiring a wet-nurse was out of the question socially and financially. In all probability, Caterina stayed with Leonardo, living with the grandparents, and then, after Leonardo was weaned, Caterina left Leonardo with Antonio and went with her husband to their own home. Perhaps the weaning and the separation coincided harshly—and perhaps a kite did indeed come to his cradle. Leonardo's precocious perception recorded the effect, processed and stored it forever. Or did such a dream grow to rescue trauma?

Bramly writes, "Leonardo, who later spent much time studying the mechanisms of childbirth and the development of the fetus, wrote and repeated that 'a single soul governs the two bodies' (of mother and unborn child). He considered—in an astonishingly modern insight—that 'desires, fears, and suffering are common to this creature as to all the other animate parts of the body, so that something desired by the mother will be imprinted on the members of the child within her when she experiences the desire, and a sudden terror may kill both mother and child.'"[47]

When Leonardo was a teenager, he was continuously prying into things, exploring the hillsides, studying strange flowers, watching the darting movements of animals, ruminating about things hidden in caves, wondering why sea shells were on hilltops. He sketched what he saw, his imagination took form, he discovered the joy of portrayal.

From an early age, Leonardo permitted none of the household to enter his room. He hoarded his collection of things gathered during his journeys into the hills; Vallentin even suggests "the high odour of animals he had caught and the stench of dried and decaying fish and larvae mingled with the heavy scent of fading flowers." In his aloneness and throughout his lifetime, Leonardo defined himself through his discoveries.

---

46 Bramly, 39–45.
47 Bramly, 46.

Vasari tells us that Ser Piero maintained some contact with his son and actually sold some of Leonardo's early drawings in Florence; that Piero really took notice of the boy's talent when Leonardo fashioned a monster-theme creation on a board (or shield) presented to him for decoration. It was startling: a fire-belching monster leaping from the surface. Piero sold it in Florence for a handsome profit.

Ser Piero's commercial success with his son's work induced Piero to send Leonardo as an apprentice to an established painter in Florence. Piero approached the master painter and teacher Andrea del Verrocchio. Verrocchio (1435–1488) was most impressed with Leonardo's early work and accepted him.

When did this key shift occur in Leonardo's life? Normally, apprenticeships of this sort began when the young student was twelve or thirteen years old. Not of privileged family, Leonardo probably remained in the hills longer, to 1465 or 1466 (Bramly) or 1467 (Turner) or 1468 (Vallentin). The decision to send him to Florence might in fact have been prompted by the death of Antonio, the grandfather. As well at that time, Ser Piero began his *second* marriage.

The astrologer sees several family events coinciding in time: the father's remarriage, the grandfather's (father surrogate) death, leaving Vinci, and entering a great artist's school as apprentice in Florence, the Tuscan capital, flourishing at that time as one of the greatest cities of Europe. We can anticipate major Transit and Progression activity affecting the angles of Leonardo's horoscope. We are led by the ephemeris notation (not shown): transiting Saturn was in 7–11 Aries in Leonardo's fifteenth birthday month, April 1467. This transit of Saturn across the 4th cusp is a highly reliable indicator of Leonardo's new start, as well as his father's new start. Calculation of the Secondary Progressed Moon's position for that month places it at 12 Libra, exactly conjunct Leonardo's Midheaven—extremely important corroboration of the Saturn transit—definitely stating the turning point onto Leonardo's career path.

Figure 5 (page 252) shows Leonardo's natal horoscope surrounded in the outer ring by the full transits for 6:00 A.M. April 18, 1467, a feasible departure time for the full day's trip to Florence, just three days after his fifteenth birthday.[48]

---

48 We can imagine that much could have been made of this coincidence with Leonardo's birthday: what a new start, the becoming a man, leaving the past behind, entering the fabulous city of Florence on completely new footing!

Note that the SP Ascendant is squaring Neptune (new, public art/sensory influence), that the Tertiary Mars is exactly conjunct the fourth cusp and TP Moon is exactly conjunct Uranus. Transiting Neptune is opposing the Sun. These measurements define the strong bloom of individuation, an artist's individuation.

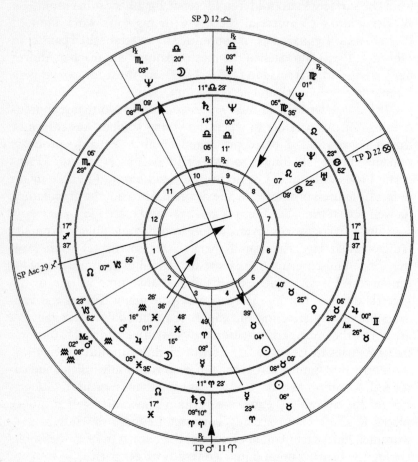

Figure 5

Inner Chart	Outer Chart
Leonard da Vinci	**Transits: Florence**
Apr. 15, 1452, 10:30 P.M. LMT	Apr. 18, 1467, 6:00 A.M. LMT
Vinci, Italy	Vinci, Italy
10E55 43N47	10E55 43N47

Placidus Houses

There is little doubt that this focused time in Leonardo's life was extremely important. Transiting Mars had been squaring Leonardo's Sun just before his birthday; the Ascendant that morning of probable departure was conjunct the powerful Venus. This is a compelling portrait of Leonardo's entrance into a new world. What a time of opportunity, with transiting Pluto exactly opposed Jupiter, ruler of Leonardo's Ascendant![49]

Scandal in Florence

Florence began as Florentia, "the flourishing town": for the Etruscans and then the Romans, emerging from histories of battles and sieges, occupations and upheavals to become the blooming flower of intelligence, creativity, and business in the Renaissance. The name of Lorenzo de' Medici, The Magnificent One, and his extended family dominated the era through their patronage of the arts and the thrusts of exploration and discovery that revived Europe in the mode of classical achievement. Lorenzo was not personally a man of universal mind, but he promoted spiritual interests, was extremely diversified in his pursuits, and sought to make these dimensions vanguard to his rule.[50]

The city itself was a gleaming, busy work of art: the streets alined at right angles, fifty public squares adorned with sculpture and bedecked with blazingly colorful family, guild, and government banners; forty-four gold and silversmiths and jewelers displaying their luxurious creations in open shops; 180 churches, with the central cathedral crowned by Brunelleschi's wondrous dome. Some 70,000 people were supported by 270 woolen-goods shops, eighty-three shops belonging to members of the silk guild, sixty-six apothecaries' shops, eighty-three shops kept by woodworkers, fifty-four by sculptors and stonecutters, seventy butcher shops, thirty-three banks whose cashiers dealt with their customers

---

49 Additionally, SA Mars (not shown) was 40' from exact conjunction with Jupiter. Also, we can look backward into time from this chart and note the transit of Uranus over Neptune for the preceding eighteen months as the time when Ser Piero recognized the intense development of Leonardo's talent. We can look forward two months to see the SP Moon conjoining Saturn, giving a span of time of approximately four to six months of planning for change, affecting change, and anchoring change.

50 Burckhardt, Chapter Six, "The Furtherers of Humanism."

while sitting outside their premises behind counters on which their quills and inkwells, ledgers, and abacuses were laid upon expensive carpets.[51]

And this was the city where the greatest artists since Hellenic times had developed and produced their masterpieces of creativity, scholarship, and wisdom.

Leonardo learned well from Master Verrocchio. He modeled in clay, wax, and gypsum; he painted in tempera (using an albuminous medium—egg whites—as paint carrier); he began working with the new oils; there was carving, filing, and soldering. He was part of the team that assisted the teacher with major works of art in many mediums. Eventually, Leonardo was working on entire figures in large works done by Verrocchio. In his private time, Leonardo began drawing from nature.

The earliest extant sketch made by Leonardo as a young man is a pen-drawing of a landscape, the first we know of when nature was portrayed for its own sake, i.e., the first true landscape in Western art. Leonardo dated the drawing—which was "an extremely rare phenomenon at the time"—he dated it emphatically and decoratively, *5 August 1473*. He was twenty-one years old.[52]

On the reverse side of this detailed yet expansive, perhaps theatrical landscape there is a hasty sketch of a hill and a stone arch among trees. A male nude appears in the sky, and above a smiling face there is the sentence (written in normal style): "I, stopping (or staying) at Antonio's, am content (*io morando dant. sono chontento*).[53]

Bramly can not explain this except to note that the landscape shows a rugged yet serene scene in vivid detail, "as if to etch it forever in memory, as if it represented in the artist's secret heart the setting for some moment of great emotion." That is the end of this intriguing glimpse into the beautiful, young Leonardo.

Figure 6 (page 255) is the horoscope of that date, of that landscape's position in Leonardo's life: here is SA SP Sun exactly conjunct Venus, *simultaneously* with SA Pluto square Venus; with SA Venus conjunct the 7th cusp of relationships!

---

51 Hibbert, 100–102, after the detailed report of a Medici agent, Benedetto Dei.
52 All sources. See Bramly, 85, for photo presentation of the landscape.
53 Bramly, 84.

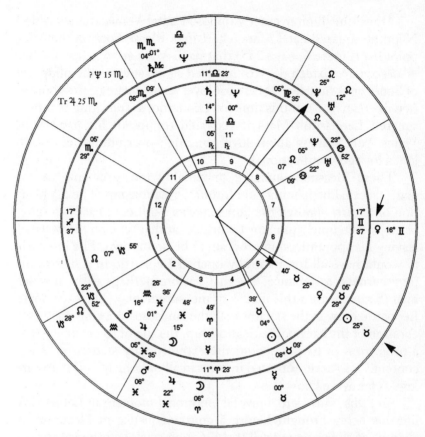

Solar Arc Midpoint Pictures for June 10, 1473 to Oct. 10, 1473

Jun 1473	Mc ⊡ ♀/♌ ☿ ⊡ ♂/♄	Being known for one's art or appreciation of things cultural; significant romantic fulfillment. Thoughts don't know where to go; any alternative seems inappropriate; indecision; separating from issues.
Jul 1473	♇ ⊡ ☿/Mc ♌ ⊡ ☉/♅	A major turning point is possible; the power picture is clear; persuasion dominates. Meeting unusual or intense people; quick new associations.
Aug 1473	♇ □ ♀ ♆ ☍ ☽/♅ ♄ ☍ ☉ ♅ ⊡ ♌/Asc	Intensification of love desires; affairs; compulsiveness; wasting emotions. Dreaminess; fantasies about love, the erotis; possible misdirection of love; being duped. The sense of difficulty, overwork, depletion, confinement, discipline; the fear of loss; "aloneness"; possibly grief. All for the avant–garde; unusual associations; upbeat ways of doing things with other people.
Sep 1473	♅ ⊡ ☽/♀ ♄ □ ♃/♌	Sudden, innovative thoughts and plans; irritability about progress; getting on with things hastily. Working with others by the rules; getting things perfectly clear; holding back in strategic reserve; slowing things down for safety; maybe "missing the boat" through caution.

© Tyl/Matrix

Figure 6

Inner Chart	Outer Chart
Leonard da Vinci	**SA Landscape**
Apr. 15, 1452, 10:30 P.M. LMT	Aug. 5, 1473

Transiting Jupiter exactly opposed natal Venus and transiting Neptune squared natal Mars (charisma). Please note on the Mid-point list (Figure 6, page 255) that natal Mars at 16 Aquarius (See *46 degrees 26*; sixteen degrees in Fixed signs) squares the midpoint of Sun/Venus (natally, "Desire for love; sexual feelings; the application of creativity"); at this time for Leonardo, as transiting Neptune squared Leonardo's Mars it activated (opposed) his natal Sun/Venus, "dreaminess about love potential; overindulgences of all kinds for ego gratification").[54]

These measurements are undeniably measurements of romance, sexual happening, and intimate relationship. The SA position of Saturn opposed the Sun suggests a difficult, hard-working, perhaps even lonely time for Leonardo, at that time on the verge of leaving his apprenticeship program to be on his own. The insecurity would have all too naturally opened Leonardo to a significant togetherness, a romance, a sexual liaison, perhaps with an older man (Saturn within this matrix of measurements). The nude male Leonardo drew in the sky was real; the landscape drawing was a celebration of the liaison, the relationship, the site of its occurrence or a projection of its perfection; the extraordinary statement "I am content," was never repeated in print in all of Leonardo's later writings as far as we know.[55]

And this leads us to a pivotal emotional moment in Leonardo's life: his being brought before a court of justice in Florence on charges of sodomy on April 9, 1476, one week before his twenty-fourth birthday, three years after the landscape drawing.

In Florence at that time, there were special letter boxes known as *tamburi* ("drums," because of their shape). These depositories for anonymous citizen complaints were also called *Buchi della Verita* (Mouths of Truth). One could denounce one's neighbor all too easily—and frequently. In the case of homosexuality, the charge would be serious indeed. Someone wrote an accusation of Leonardo.

Several people were charged along with Leonardo, one of them from a celebrated family, for engaging in sodomy with a certain

---

54 See Tyl, *Synthesis & Counseling* or *Prediction in Astrology*, Appendix. Additional observation: at the same time as Tr Neptune=Mars=Sun/Venus; Tr. Neptune=Saturn/Ascendant ("depressing and introverted life situations"), i.e., natally Leonardo's Mars also= Saturn/Asc ("struggling with inhibitions and control").

55 Bramly opines that this moment of tranquility, "of pure happiness," corresponded to the landscape drawn on a visit home, when Leonardo perhaps saw his mother. The astrology says different.

Jacopo Saltarelli, aged seventeen. The charge was reviewed by the court, and on June 7 it was dismissed.

Leonardo was deeply jarred by this. We read that the questioning by the Board of Inquiry was incessant and grossly detailed, that Leonardo's sensibilities were pummeled by crass, heavy-mouthed officials. Astrologically (just three years after the landscape chart, Figure 6, see page 255), we can see SA MC coming to square with Pluto and opposing the Sun. This strong measurement also suggests that a major reorientation of Leonardo's career was in the offing, a push into new directions. Indeed, Leonardo was leaving Verrocchio to go it alone.

The scandal before the court imploded powerfully upon Leonardo's sense of aesthetics and fairness; the blanket was smothering the grenade (the natal Sun-Pluto square). All the vulnerabilities to distrusting (fearing) relationships were exacerbated (natal Mercury's key position opposed Saturn and ruling the 7th). Biographers relate this shocking time to Leonardo's lifelong withdrawal thereafter from relationships, to his pronounced disgust for sexual copulation. He wrote later, "The act of coupling and the members [sex organs] engaged in it are so ugly that if it were not for the faces and adornments of the actors [the people going through the ritual], and the impulses sustained, the human race would die out ... He who does not restrain his lustful appetites places himself on the same level as the beasts."[56]

The acquittal certainly did not do very much to erase the smear Leonardo felt, even in rampantly homosexual Florence. He was surely embarrassed for Verrocchio, for his father and, dare we feel, for his mother. The fact that he was open to such attack, such potential defamation shocked him deeply, and throughout his life his mistrust of others, his misogyny, was always traceable back to this incident by some thought construct or direct reference in his notes. This incident took its position very clearly within the counterpoint-retrogradation symbolism of Saturn in Libra.

Leonardo gradually left Verrocchio's care and tutelage and through lonely times worked and waited for significant commissions.

In 1478, the day after Leonardo's birthday, the powerful Pazzi banking family attempted a public coup against the Medici. The clash occurred in the grand cathedral just as Mass ended. Flashing

---

56 All sources. See Bramly, 123.

daggers and loud shouts rang out as the Pazzi people assaulted Lorenzo de' Medici and his family. A bloody scene, a hysterical riot, and a frantic chase through corridors and up and down towers were recorded by witnesses frozen in their tracks by the surprise and horror. The Pazzi lost and, in those hours of terror, eighty victims lost their lives.

Florence was plunged into a mass of troubles. The Pope was enraged, and King Ferdinand of Naples saw the opportunity to reach northward to punish the Florentines "for their arrogance." After two years of battles, Lorenzo finally settled a shaky truce.

Out of these unsettled times, in 1480, Leonardo finally received his first important commission: an altarpiece in the grand style, for which he would paint what was to become one of the most important works of all art history, *The Adoration of the Magi.*[57]

Leonardo worked with plan after plan after plan, with unheard of mathematical precision in the geometric organization of the figures. Time went by. The groundwork of the painting was completed, and the composition was clear, but after September 28, 1481, when the monks recorded their last contact with the artist (bringing Leonardo a cask of wine, perhaps to urge him on), work stopped, and the painting, already a masterpiece in its preparation, remained unfinished.

Transiting Saturn was at 15 Libra, signalling Leonardo's Saturn return, a return of his entire psychological make-up to another point of change.[58]

Vasari explained Leonardo's failure to complete *The Adoration* with an allusion to Leonardo's perfectionism, i.e., that the hand would never achieve what the mind knew to be. Leonardo's supreme achievement here was, as the German philosopher Oswald Spengler put it, "the clarity of intent."

No one can adequately explain this moment of Leonardo's turn of mind. Perhaps the monks who commissioned *The Adoration* reneged on their contract (it was complicated and unusual,

---

57 For its geometry (triangulation) principles, the contraposto technique of bodies turning upon their own axis, and the humanism of reactions. Legendary art historian Bernard Berenson (1865–1959), a specialist in Renaissance painting, acclaimed *The Adoration*, "Truly a great masterpiece and perhaps the quattrocento produced nothing greater." This is high praise from the sole prestigious critic who normally cast harsh judgment on Leonardo's work. All sources, see Bramly, 164.

58 Additionally, transiting Pluto at 6 Virgo was at the midpoint of Neptune/Midheaven: "strange happenings on the job." See Tyl, *Synthesis & Counseling* or *Prediction*, Appendix.

arranged by Ser Piero for his son), and Leonardo felt once again taken advantage of and assailed by unfeeling mortals, and this in turn resurrected bitterness and disgust with regard to the scandal past. Yet, we astrologers know all too well that the die was cast for Leonardo to alter the course of his life dramatically at his Saturn return. In his continued pain of having been scandalized, Leonardo had to leave Florence and begin again.

In Milan

Leonardo felt that he had been passed over by Lorenzo de' Medici; he had not been invited to place one of his works into the de' Medici collection. Leonardo watched as his artist colleagues left for sparkling commissions available in Rome and elsewhere. He felt shunned by the literati of Florence, since he spoke hardly any Latin and was not University educated (Mercury ruler of the 9th House opposed Saturn).

Leonardo was a skilled musician. His playing of the lyre and his singing were regarded as "without equal." And finally, it was Leonardo's musical achievement that caught the ear of Lorenzo. Il Magnifico saw that Leonardo had made a splendid silver lyre, fashioning the frame of the small harp in the bizarre form of a horse's skull. The lyre possessed a wondrous tone, and he thought it would do much for political good will if this lyre were given as a gift to the Count of Milan, the powerful Lodovico Sforza ("force" in Italian).

Leonardo saw his opportunity: he declared his willingness to part with the lyre and *deliver the gift to Sforza himself.* Armed with Lorenzo's letter of recommendation, Leonardo set out for Milan, for his new life.[59]

Scholars do not know exactly when Leonardo left Florence; we are told that it was at the end of 1482 or early 1483 (Vallentin), the end of 1481 or early 1482 (Hart), in 1482 (Bramly) or in 1481 (Turner). But the astrology is exceptionally clear: in December 1482, the ephemeris shows transiting Uranus at 17 Sagittarius and Pluto at 11 Libra, *each planet exactly on an angle in Leonardo's horoscope!*

Figure 7 (page 260) shows Leonardo's Solar Arc positions for December 15, 1482: note SA Moon opposed Saturn just about to

---

59 All sources. See Vallentin, 65–67.

free itself from a year or more of heavy work, depression, and ultra-sensitivity. Note how this insight is painfully corroborated by the simultaneous transit of Saturn opposed his Sun from 4–5 Scorpio.

The mighty transits over the Midheaven and Ascendant answer to the SA Mars position exactly upon Leonardo's natal Moon: "the strong drive to fulfill needs, to let it fly; disruption, hyperactivity."[60]

Figure 8 (page 261) shows the Tertiary Progressions for this key date in the outer ring around Leonardo's natal horoscope: the Sun

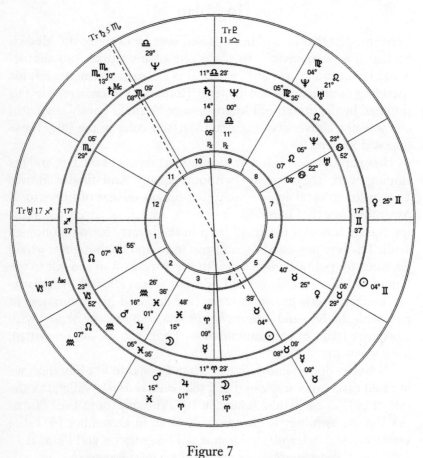

Figure 7

Inner Chart
Leonard da Vinci

Outer Chart
SA to Milan
Dec. 15, 1482

---

60 Tyl, *Synthesis & Counseling* or *Prediction in Astrology*, Appendix.

is precisely conjunct the 7th cusp, lifting itself above the horizon to new visibility; TP Venus has returned precisely, affirmatively to its natal position; TP Jupiter is precisely upon the young master's all-powerful Mercury; and TP Node is conjunct the Ascendant, promising new relationships and associations.

These measurements show conclusively that change was essential in the development of Leonardo's life, and they confirm, once again, the accuracy of the 10:30 P.M. birth time.

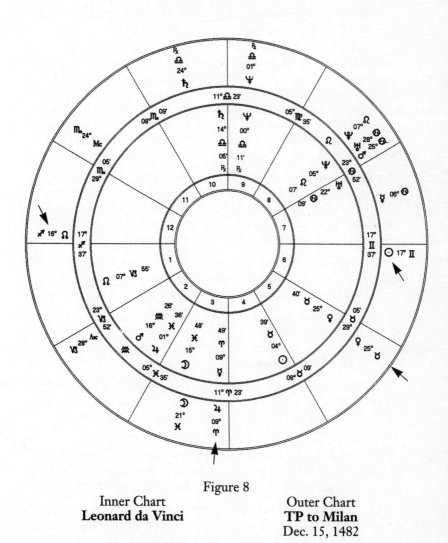

Figure 8

Inner Chart
Leonard da Vinci

Outer Chart
TP to Milan
Dec. 15, 1482

Milan was three times larger than Florence, yet it did not compare with Florence in terms of the arts and humanities. Lodovico Sforza ruled with an iron hand. Because of his swarthy complexion and gruff ways, he was nicknamed Il Moro (the Moor).

The thirty-year old Leonardo presented himself to the court of Milan, with Lorenzo's letter, the lyre, and a very carefully composed letter of his own. Leonardo's letter is simply astonishing; the easy self-intensification of Uranus natally trine his Moon, the emboldened professional thrust of Pluto natally square his Sun, the excessive display of his ambition, his Saturn-need to be useful and of service—all of this explodes:

> Most Illustrious Lord, having by now sufficiently considered the experience of those men who claim to be skilled inventors of machines of war, and having realized that the said machines in no way differ from those commonly employed, I shall endeavor, without prejudice to anyone else, to reveal my secrets to Your Excellency, for whom I offer to execute, at your convenience, all the items briefly noted below.
>
> 1. I have a model of very strong but light bridges, extremely easy to carry, by means of which you will be able to pursue or if necessary flee any enemy; I have others, which are sturdy and will resist fire as well as attack, and are easy to lay down and take up. I also know ways to burn and destroy those of the enemy.
>
> 2. During a siege, I know how to dry up the water of the moats and how to construct an infinite number of bridges, covered ways, scaling ladders, and other machines for this type of enterprise.
>
> 3. If because of the height of the embankment, and the strength of the place or its site, it should be impossible to reduce it by bombardment, I know methods of destroying any citadel or fortress, even if it is built on rock.
>
> 4. I also have models of mortars that are very practical and easy to transport, with which I can project stones so that they seem to be raining down; and their smoke will plunge the enemy into terror, to his great hurt and confusion.
>
> 9. [Sic] And if battle is to be joined at sea, I have many very efficient machines for both attack and defense; and vessels that will resist even the heaviest cannon fire, fumes, and gunpowder.
>
> 5. I know how to use paths and secret underground tunnels, dug without noise and following tortuous routes, to reach a given place, even if it means passing below a moat or a river.

6. I will make covered vehicles, safe and unassailable, which will penetrate enemy ranks with their artillery and destroy the most powerful troops; the infantry may follow them without meeting obstacles or suffering damage.

7. In case of need, I will make large bombards, mortars, and fire-throwing engines, of beautiful and practical design, which will be different from those presently in use.

8. Where bombardment would fail, I can make catapults, man-gonels, *trabocchi*, or other unusual machines of marvelous efficiency, not in common use. In short, whatever the situation, I can invent an infinite variety or machines for both attack and defense.

10. In peacetime, I think I can give perfect satisfaction and be the equal of any man in architecture, in the design of buildings public and private, or to conduct water from one place to another.

Item: I can carry out sculpture in marble, bronze, and clay; and in painting can do any kind of work as well as any man, whoever he is.

Moreover, the bronze horse could be made that will be to the immortal glory and eternal honor of the lord your father of blessed memory and of the illustrious house of Sforza.

And if any of the items mentioned above appears to anyone impossible or impractical, I am ready to give a demonstration in your park or in any other place that should please Your Excellency—to whom I recommend myself in all humility.[61]

Vasari wrote that Il Moro was incredibly moved by Leonardo's presentation of talent and implored him to begin work on an altarpiece representing the Nativity, which he would send to the emperor. But that is *not* what happened. Leonardo had to languish—probably due to the Duke's doubting of such an arrogant and self-possessed young man. No practical leader could trust such a dreamer. Leonardo would have to wait for some nine years to prove himself.

Leonardo stuck it out, studying, studying, studying to fill the gaps in his formal education, following his inborn compulsion to perceive and to know. He began his notebooks. He compiled endless lists of synonyms (some 7,000–8,000 words). Vallentin reports that he was able later to declare with pride that "I possess so many words in my mother tongue that I am more likely to have trouble with the right understanding of things than from the lack of words

with which to express my mind's conception of them." The dominance, reliance, and strength of Mercury are obvious.

Leonardo adds, "As iron rusts when it is not used and water
gets foul from standing or turns to ice when exposed to cold, so the
intellect degenerates without exercise."[62]

Leonardo suffered for acceptance and busyness, for recogni-
tion. He formed a loose partnership with another artist family (de
Predis brothers) and, with transiting Jupiter precisely upon his
Neptune, gained a commission to paint *The Virgin of the Rocks.*

He dreamed of far-away places and drew ideas and inventions
for their societies. He became remote to others, tight unto himself.
He developed an antipathy against society. His notes revealed the
lowest opinion of mankind.

The plague came to Milan in 1484, for two years.

At this time, Leonardo worked hard: he designed a city plan to
bring fresh air into houses, to organize shops and living quarters creatively, to improve urban waste disposal, to build spiral staircases,
updraft chimneys for smoke removal, bay windows for maximum light,
clean stables, etc.; in short, dream cities for the rich and the poor. He
was dedicated to the removal of the horror of dirt and poverty.

He staged elaborate pageants utilizing gears and cog-wheels as
no one had dreamed possible, capturing in one of them, the
"Masque of the Planets" the motions of all the planets in the solar
system.[63] When he found himself meditating upon new ideas too
long in the early morning, he created an alarm clock to rouse him
to his workbench. Mechanical invention dominated his mind.
Roasting spits. Olive presses. Steam power. Gear differentials. Tri-
cycles. Bicycles.

Leonardo's work with the pageants pleased Sforza. He now
believed what Leonardo could do (and Leonardo was more credible, eight years older). In the Spring of 1490, they began seriously
to consider the immense monument to Il Moro's father. *Transiting
Jupiter was conjunct Leonardo's Sun.*

---

62 Vallentin, 109. Leonardo "gave memory higher rank than will and reason"; memory was
man's only defense against time the destroyer, and it was man's most precious possession, of which only death could rob him. Again, Mercury opposed Saturn.

63 This "Masque of the Planets" was held on January 13, 1490 in the Castello Sforzesco.
The theme was chosen by Lodovico on the advice of his astrologer Ambrogio da Varese
in gratitude for having saved Il Moro's life during a serious illness. Leonardo had some
respect for astrology, but had scant regard for astrologers who, he said, got fat on the
credulity of the foolish. Bramly, 221.

At the same time, Leonardo began his deepest study to date, in the field of optics, which led to many inventions, including the camera obscura (a device to accept and project light images trough a pinhole into a darkened enclosure), addressing the problems of the time of light transmission, refraction, image inversion, binocular vision, perspective, three-dimensionality, etc.

On July 22, 1490, Leonardo noted cryptically, "Giacomo arrived." Leonardo took in a ten-year-old apprentice, naming him "Salai," a Tuscan word meaning a "demon." Salai was troublesome and hyperactive all his life, according to all sources, but he was beautiful, and it becomes clear that Leonardo's and Salai's master/apprentice relationship developed into a sexual one. Salai remained with Leonardo throughout the master's life.

The Caterina Enigma

Three years later, we read in Leonardo's notebook, on two separate lines: "16 July / Caterina came, 16 July 1493." This is noted emphatically [the repetition of the date].

Does the emphasis betray hidden emotion? On the facing page is a list of names from Leonardo's childhood. Bramly notes that meetings (this with Caterina) characteristically summon up memories. Is this list tied to Caterina?

The name again appears some six months later in Leonardo's notes about costs and budget. Then there is nothing further until the day of Caterina's funeral (not dated) approximately a year or two later: Leonardo notes the expenses, which were excessive for a housekeeper or servant, but not generous for a beloved mother.[64]

Bramly points out with great sensitivity that at this time in his life Leonardo was possessed with a sense of keen fulfillment, what Pasteur called "the inner god, which leads to everything." Nothing seemed impossible for him; he could attempt anything—and he could *understand* anything. He composed treatise after treatise; with supreme self-confidence, he sought to penetrate the secrets of art, water, air, mankind, the world (he was now interested in geology, in fossils, and in mountain formation); he investigated the origins of milk, colic, tears, drunkenness, madness, and dreams; as if it came under the senses, he talked of "writing what the soul is"; he dreamed of flying like an

---

64 Bramly, 243–244.

eagle or a kite and began to draw plans of "flying machines." And there was the giant horse being planned for Il Moro.[65]

Leonardo's sense of accomplishment, personal power, and inspiration suggests a freedom ... the blanket sliding away from the grenade, a more direct acknowledgment of personal power, *with difficulties moved out of the way or with problems being solved*. Astrologically, we should expect to find Plutonic emphasis and *an activation of the maternal complex*, the quindecile aspect (Neptune-Moon).

Figure 9 (page 267) shows Leonardo's horoscope brought forward to the date of the "Caterina" entry, July 16, 1493. Most dramatically, we see transiting Pluto at 4 Scorpio exactly opposed the Sun (the awareness of full life perspective and personal power, or the push into that direction); we see Solar Arc Pluto at 14 Virgo 45 opposing *the Moon* ("extreme emotional intensity, upheavals, exaggerated new plans," and also the mother figure).

The SP Moon at 29 Virgo is almost precisely conjunct Leonardo's Neptune, part of the quindecile mother-separation/compulsion aspect; SA Uranus is exactly opposed his Jupiter, ruler of his Ascendant ("the big break, boundless optimism").

We see *extreme* personal empowerment and the awakening of the maternal complex as we studied initially. These large measurements are reinforced by transiting Neptune's exact square with natal Neptune, the SA Sun exactly trine to Saturn. And—as is shown in Figure 10 (page 268), the Tertiary Progressions for this date—the TP Sun along with TP Saturn are exactly opposed natal Sun, creating a T-Square with natal Pluto, which is, in turn, exactly emphasized by TP Uranus!

Additionally, the most sensitive TP Moon is conjunct Venus, ruler of Leonardo's Midheaven and the TP Midheaven itself is precisely conjunct the 4th cusp.[66]

There is absolutely no doubt that Leonardo sent for his mother, in her early sixties, probably widowed, to live with him in Milan. Her coming was a release, a closure of emotions, a part of his flush of extraordinary success, and a clear period of maturation in Leonardo's life. The astrology of this all-important time of Leonardo's life is unqualifiedly astounding.

---

65 Bramly, 245.

66 Additionally, the TP Node is square to the Moon/Jupiter midpoint signifying "successful contacts," professionally here and also in terms of the Moon and the quindecile complex. All interpretations quoted for Arcs and midpoint pictures are from Tyl, *Synthesis & Counseling* and *Prediction in Astrology*, the Appendix.

The Sforza Horse Monument

The model for the Sforza horse monument—Lodovico's father astride a battle steed with front hooves raised in excitement over the body of a trampled enemy—was so colossal "that it took men's breath away." To solve the center of gravity problems would be a formidable achievement for Leonardo; solving the casting problems would revolutionize sculpture and the foundry industry. Leonardo's plans for the monument for Maximilian Sforza became a monument to his own design capabilities. In the process, with

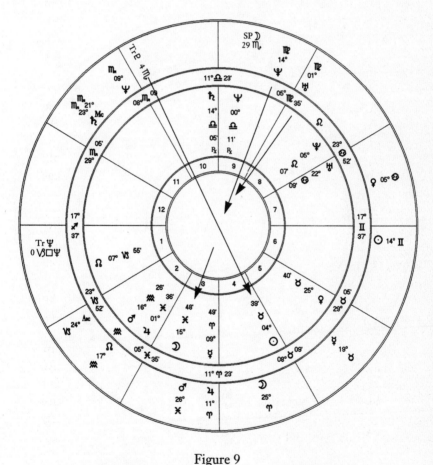

Figure 9

Inner Chart
Leonard da Vinci

Outer Chart
SA Caterina
July 16, 1493

clear Plutonic impact upon the art world, Leonardo became extremely famous.

But in all the might of his ascendancy, Leonardo could not hold off politics and war, namely Charles VIII, king of France, at the head of the largest army in Europe, who had crossed the Alps and now marched into Italy. City after city opened its doors in capitulation to this army; all of Italy—from Milan to Naples—was conquered, and not one cannon was fired.

It was late in 1494, and in a program to reinforce defenses for the future, the metal allocated for the colossal equestrian statue was

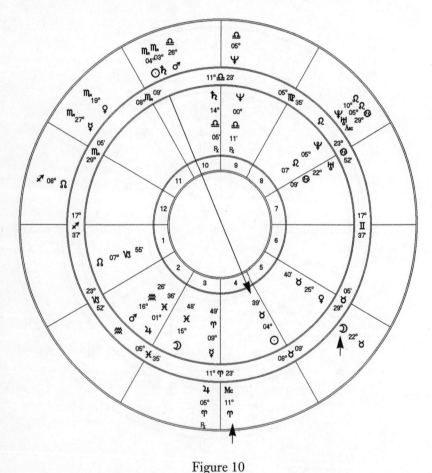

Figure 10

Inner Chart
Leonard da Vinci (Test)

Outer Chart
TP Caterina
July 16, 1493

necessarily diverted, in November 1495, to building canon and other weapons. While the drawings and construction studies remain, the monument was never finished.

The Last Supper

Through covert means, *Lodovico Sforza had himself invited Charles' siege upon Italy.* With great cleverness he had planned and succeeded in subjugating the House of Aragon (the remains of Spanish rule of Italy), humiliated the Pope, confirmed himself with the powerful Este family, benefitted from the fall of the Medici in Florence, and established an alliance with the king of France. Sforza was the mightiest prince in Italy, and Milan was (for the moment) returned to stability.

Lodovico commissioned Leonardo to paint *The Last Supper* on the dining room wall of a monastery building alongside the church he was refurbishing—Santa Maria delle Grazie. The Dominican monastery was to be the burial place for Lodovico and his wife Beatrice.

We do not know an exact date for the beginning of Leonardo's work on *The Last Supper*, but all authorities agree that the commission was given by Sforza in 1495 and that the work was completed in 1498. (There are many references in the histories to Leonardo standing before the wall for hours, leaving without touching the work or making just two or three ministrations with his brush and then retiring to study his plans, his mind's vision. He would search the streets and piazze to find people with extraordinary faces; he would follow them through the streets and sketch their visages and movements for one or the other of the thirteen personages planned for the mural. Astrologically we can take mid-year 1496 as a mid-point for the creation of this extraordinary fresco. Figure 11 (page 270) shows the Solar Arc positions and key transits for that time.

Again, we see extraordinary corroboration in the horoscope: SA Sun was exactly on the horizon ("Recognition; being seen for who one is"); SA Jupiter opposed Saturn ("ambition given the go-ahead signal; patience pays off; feeling more right than right"); and above all, *SA Pluto had moved to precise square with the Ascendant-Descendant axis*, signaling an "extremely important time of life, taking command of things, identity transformation, a life milestone."

Additionally transiting Saturn was in 9–10 Aries just crossing the fourth cusp, an extraordinary new start, and transiting Jupiter was at 3 Scorpio opposing Leonardo's Sun.

The Last Supper and the *Mona Lisa* (see page 279) were to become Leonardo's most known and celebrated works of art. *The Last Supper's* organization and spiritual impact changed the face of art forever. Leonardo's functional space was articulated on the end wall of the room to elongate the real space of the room length, to fool the eye; his management of perspective was theatrical to the

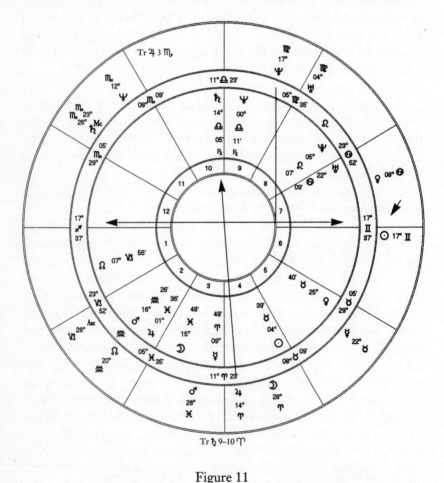

Figure 11

Inner Chart	Outer Chart
Leonard da Vinci	**SA Last Supper**
	June 8, 1496

extreme, accommodating thirteen individually expressive bodies in one plane, creating points of focus that reinforced the divine position of Jesus in the central space of the painting, along the longitudinal center of the room; the geometry within the painting was a full study of Euclidian discoveries; each apostle was modeled to speak a life development of individualistic qualities; Judas was so anti-conventionally *near* Jesus, before the fact of betrayal, yet so obvious to all after the fact; and each person was endowed with an individualistic response, captured in a split second of animated time, to Jesus's statement, "Verily I say unto you that one of you shall betray me."

Leonardo used an experimental medium to hold his color upon the wall, and it proved to be disastrously flawed. The mural began to disintegrate during Leonardo's lifetime; his major success was threatened with disappearance.[67]

The German genius poet/dramatist, Wolfgang Goethe first saw *The Last Supper* in 1788, and with his own vision stimulated by the remains of Leonardo's work (reinforced by clumsy touch-ups) wrote, "*The Last Supper* is the true key to the vault of artistic concepts. In its genre it is a unique work to which nothing can be compared."[68]

At this same time, Leonardo was studying and inventing: machines to produce needles, machines to make rope, an ingenious industrial spinning wheel, the principles of which would not be realized again for 200 years; the principles of flight, aerodynamics, pressures and currents, principles of gliding, the propeller, the parachute, all to be adapted for man; and above all the machinery of war, every conceivable device to improve and economize the production of weaponry, including gunpowder, attack and defense machines; and designs for concepts absolutely incredible to late fifteenth-century minds: a helicopter, an armored battle vehicle, a submarine, all conceived in detailed design particulars.

New sieges came upon Italy from the French, this time by Louis XII, and Milan capitulated on September 14, 1499, again without a shot being fired. The Comte de Ligny, commander of the

---

67 All sources. See Turner, 36; 276–297.

68 Letter to Goethe's patron Karl August in Weimar, quoted in Turner, 94. Goethe later (in 1815–16) wrote an extensive, beautifully constructed essay about *The Last Supper*, which has been widely circulated in art literature. His grand and insightful attention to *The Last Supper* imbedded the masterpiece in the art consciousness of the western world. Along with other great witnesses and writers, Goethe depicted *The Last Supper* as image given to literature, as immediacy given to history, as life given to the record of Jesus.

French armies, is thought to have invited Leonardo to work with the French against Tuscany as a battle engineer. While this appears traitorous to us now, "those scruples," according to Bramly, were not known at the time. Leonardo made notes about this liaison with de Ligny and added the code of anagrams to his mirror-written script: for example, "Go and find *ingil* [Ligny] and tell him you [Leonardo] will wait for him at *amor* [Roma] and that you will go with him to *ilopan* [Napoli]."[69]

Astrologically, we should expect to find something covert, even duplistic in Leonardo's horoscope development at this time; and we do: transiting Neptune was at 12 Capricorn *exactly square to his Midheaven* and the accumulated *Solar Arc semisquare* had peaked! Again, Leonardo was restless, his services ready for the asking, courting change.

At the same time, August–September 1499, Leonardo's SP Moon was conjunct his Ascendant. He traveled to Mantua, Venice, and returned to Florence.

During this trip which only took two or three months, Leonardo spilled out his inventions and ideas on municipal authorities in an effort to be hired for the realization of his extraordinary plans. Chief among them were sub-marine plans for the Venetians against the Turks, the reclaiming of land from the sea, and the enormous bridge to Asia from Istanbul (for the Turks!). But no commissions were offered.

Cesare Borgia

There is simply no despot in Renaissance history as criminal, evil, and fearsome as Cesare Borgia. To historians—as it did to the people of his time—his name suggests "cruelty, deception, impiety, lust, and incest." Borgia was the illegitimate son of Pope Alexander VI and a Roman courtesan. Borgia himself became a cardinal at age sixteen and was defrocked at twenty-two. His liaison with his sister Lucrezia was legend in his time and his arrangements of her marriages for political gain were legion; he would summarily dispatch the suitors and spouses involved. He is said to have had his own brother stabbed to death; to have arranged orgies for his father the

69 Bramly, 306.

pope's entertainment. He was even described as "more execrable than the Turk!" He habitually dressed in black.[70]

Cesare's mission was to conquer central Italy. He was determined to fulfill the glory of his namesake, Julius Caesar. Figure 12 (page 274) is the horoscope of Cesare Borgia, carefully and thoroughly rectified by astrologer Basil Fearrington.

Borgia's Mars-Saturn conjunction in Leo at the Ascendant, through monarchical imposition, demands the getting away with murder and, dare we say, the doing of murder to fulfill ambition. The dramatic ruler.

It is very interesting to note that Borgia's Midheaven is quindecile (recall Leonardo's compulsion aspect of Neptune-Moon, see page 247) to his Sun, which is conjoined by Pluto. This is a compulsion, a powerfully driving thrust of ego-assertion, didactic and unemotional (Virgo), stimulated by some early development problems. Additionally, note Uranus square Mars-Saturn and Neptune square Moon, tyrannical enforcement and duplicity within the despotic profile of (at the quality level established for) Borgia's life.

Two midpoint pictures round out the dreadful burden within this horoscope: Pluto=Mars/Uranus ("Force, shock") and Moon= Pluto/ Ascendant ("dramatic personal projection"). Pluto oriental, i.e., rising last before the Sun (clockwise motion) suggests strongly the collection of power through affiliation with or annexation of others.[71]

To fulfill his dream as a military engineer, Leonardo had met his man in Cesare Borgia. Note that Borgia had Pluto conjunct the Sun and Leonardo, Pluto square the Sun, that Borgia's Midheaven received Leonardo's Saturn through opposition, and his Jupiter on the Descendant was square Leonardo's Sun. The men met in terms of power, Borgia using it, Leonardo building it. To top if all off, both Leonardo and Cesare Borgia were illegitimately born. Note that Borgia's horoscope in the main is suppressed below the horizon ("unfinished business" in the early development), echoed by the 8th House Moon placement and the retrogradation of Jupiter at the horizon. Each of these men was possessed in his achievements with a scorn of convention and a quindecile compulsion.

---

70 All sources. See Bramly, 321–322. And especially, Chamberlin, 191–205.
71 See Tyl, "the Oriental Planet," Section 3A, *Synthesis & Counseling*.

Leonardo began his new post in "March–June" 1502. Figure 13 (page 275) again captures this move in Leonardo's life clearly and emphatically: SA Ascendant came to exact opposition with the all-important Pluto power center, again freeing it within the square with the Sun! SA Moon and transiting Jupiter were conjoining the Sun *and both were squaring Pluto!* Transiting Pluto at 0 Sagittarius was square Leonardo's Jupiter, ruler of his Ascendant!

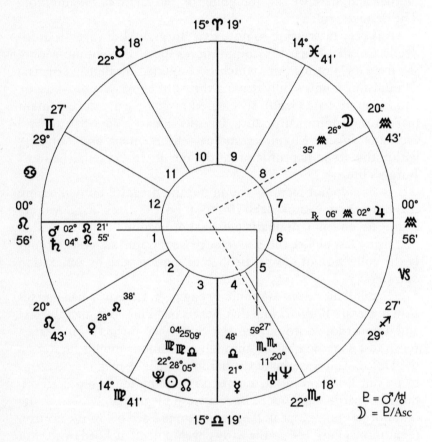

Figure 12
Cesare Borgia
Sept. 13, 1475, 00:55 A.M. LMT
Rome, Italy
12E29 41N54
(Rectification by Basil Fearrington)
Placidus Houses

At this time, Leonardo met Niccoló Machiavelli who had been sent by the Signoria of Florence to observe Cesare Borgia, what he was doing and how he was going about it. Borgia's exploits and tactics were to become the centerpiece of Machiavelli's *The Prince*, which Napoleon regarded as "the only book worth reading."[72]

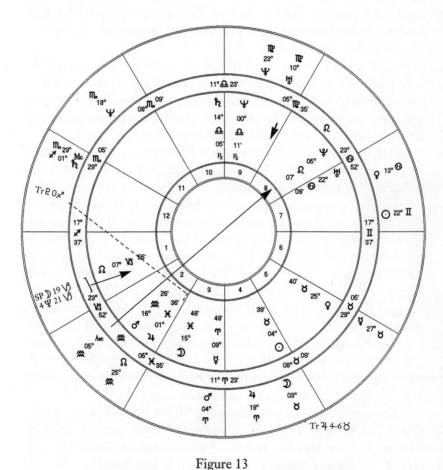

Figure 13

Inner Chart
Leonard da Vinci

Outer Chart
SA Borgia Work
Mar. 15, 1502

---

72 Please see Fearrington's life study and rectification of Machiavelli's horoscope in Tyl-ed., *Astrology Looks at History*, "The Princely Warlord," Llewellyn Publications, 1995.

Leonardo worked separately from his patron, probably never witnessing any of the horrors. Historians do not know why Leonardo—without any notation in his notebooks—then left Borgia and was back in Florence by March 1503. Since he was withdrawing long-held savings from the bank in Florence, it can be conjectured that he perhaps had not been paid by Borgia (so often the case between patron and protege, i.e., the affiliation was deemed recompense enough). Perhaps Leonardo saw Borgia's end coming, which occurred in August 1503 when his father, Pope Alexander VI died. Borgia lost his power at the top, if you will, and was exiled, first to Naples and then to Spain.

Astrologically, we can see in Figure 13 (page 275), during the year with Borgia, that Leonardo's SA Moon would strengthen its conjunction with the Sun. Perhaps Leonardo had second thoughts about military bombast for another's glory. Perhaps he wanted to return to being his own artist on his own terms.

Back in Florence, Leonardo at age fifty-one—still extraordinarily celebrated throughout all of Italy—began two very important commissions, neither one of which would be completed.

The first was the grand plan—backed strongly by Machiavelli—to defeat Pisa once and for all by diverting the flow of the Arno, the river coursing thorough both cities. This would be a tremendous task of earth removal and water management. An enormous effort was mounted, with workers paid the highest wages, but the war was won by other means, and all work was stopped. Then Leonardo adapted the work to peaceful purposes—his automatic cranes, his gigantic treadmills to dredge up earth—proposing a canal from Florence to Pisa (a distance of 120 miles). Horrible weather hampered progress; there were deaths on the job; friction developed when wages were lowered; and the project became "the ridiculous dream of an eccentric." It was abandoned in October 1504.[73]

The second commission from the Signoria of Florence was to depict *The Battle of Anghiari*—a celebrated battle between the Florentines and the Milanese in 1440—on the expansive end wall of its Grand Council Chamber. This commission became crucially important to Leonardo and to onlookers throughout Florence because the young, sensational, brooding, ruthlessly powerful of body and talent, perpetually stone-dust dirty, brutally acerbic sculp-

---

73 All sources. See Vallentin, 346.

tor/painter Michelangelo Buonarroti, aged twenty-eight, wanting to challenge the aging master, had wrangled the commission for the wall at the other end of the Chamber![74]

Michelangelo had been a star in Lorenzo de' Medici's household and a student of the master Ghirlandaio. He had sculpted the gigantic masterpiece *David* just the year before. Interestingly, Michelangelo was born with Pluto opposite his Mars-Sun conjunction in Pisces; this moody power structure was the apex of an enormously self-defensive Water Grand Trine.[75] There is an annotated, caustic chance meeting in a public square between the great master and the younger genius: Leonardo suggested some questions he was being asked by the public be cast Michelangelo's way, who was just passing by. Michelangelo thought he was being patronized. He barked back to Leonardo accusations about the latter being unable to finish any artwork, ending with, "And the stupid people of Milan had faith in you?" The stab hurt Leonardo to the quick.[76]

Shortly after Leonardo began planning *The Battle*, Ser Piero died (SP Moon was exactly on Leonardo's Mars, ruler of his 4th). The only evidence of emotion is shown through a strange entry of the date in Leonardo's notebook: "At 7 A.M. on Wednesday, July 9, 1504, Ser Piero da Vinci, my father, notary to the Podesta, died, at seven in the morning. He was eighty years old, and left ten sons and two daughters." Leonardo had accounted Ser Piero's age incorrectly (at most he was sevnty-seven) and he was wrong about the date: it was not a Wednesday but a Tuesday. Scholars do not know what to make of the coldness of this important data and its clumsiness of entry.[77] Was it Leonardo's resentment of Piero's early-life abandonment of him, certainly part of his mother-complex anchored to the same condition?

Leonardo was to give up on *The Battle* (and Michelangelo never got started either—nude soldiers bathing was his theme—because he was called to Rome by Pope Julius II to design his tomb and articulate the Sistine chapel) when his binding agent within

---

74 Reliably timed birth data for Michelangelo from several sources, including his own notes and those of his father: March 06, 1475 at 1:45 A.M., LMT, in Caprese Michel, Italy.

75 Michelangelo wrote that he "delighted in melancholy" (Sonnet LXXXI). "He laboured at all times under a sense of persecution, interpreting entirely innocent phrases as uttered in malice, with intent to humiliate him (Sun-Moon in Pisces; Saturn retrograde in the 7th square the Nodal axis). See Vallentin, 349.

76 Bramly, 343–345.

77 Vallentin, 343.

the colors failed; Leonardo watched helplessly as the colossal drawing on the wall dripped off completely, forever gone. It was Spring 1505, just six months after the colossal failure of the Pisa canal; *transiting Uranus was exactly square to Leonardo's Ascendant:* change beginning again, and perhaps with it the slide from the pinnacle of fame.

Leonardo had become totally fascinated yet again with natural history. This diversion could very well have undermined his attentiveness to the Pisa project and to the *Battle* fresco, frustrating in turn everyone's efforts on his behalf.

Leonardo was intrigued with fossilized crustaceans found on mountain tops. Had they been caught up in Noah's deluge? Crustaceans can't swim! Where did the water go if the earth had been completely inundated? He made grand deductions (correct) about changes in the earth's land and water areas over geological time. Leonardo conjectured and formulated the concept of sea level. He hypothesized principles of erosion. He applied his mind to explaining the destruction of Sodom and Gomorrah by natural forces. He thought he had discovered the soul of the world! He began to manage a heretofore unknown force: steam.[78]

It is breathtaking to see these grand concepts being worked night and day by this man's shining mind, and, as vividly, to see him in his suffering so isolated from others, driven somehow to make up—now with Caterina's death—the separation traumas of his earliest childhood, working through his bitter contempt for family relationships. The extraordinary quindecile aspect (see page 247) between Neptune and the Piscean Moon inexorably drove Leonardo to private martyrdom, sublimated so much anxiety, supported inspiration, and birthed visionary accomplishment.

---

78 Vallentin, 336–339

Mona Lisa

Vasari tells us that Leonardo undertook a commission from a certain Francesco del Giocondo: to portray his wife, Monna Lisa. And Vasari notes that after four years of effort, Leonardo still had not finished the painting.

Francesco del Giocondo was a wealthy man, married for the third time in 1495, to a woman named Lisa di Gherardini. In 1505, Monna (an Italian title for "Mistress, Dame, Lady") Lisa was about twenty-six or twenty-seven years old.[79]

Vasari had never seen the *Monna Lisa*, but gives a detailed description of the portrait's quality and detail from expert witnesses and from copies made by other masters and students. We must note in particular that Vasari was the only person to provide the Monna Lisa story. Consequently, many other stories were presented: that the woman Leonardo depicted so intriguingly sensitively was a favorite mistress of Giuliano de' Medici, was a mistress of Charles d'Amboise, or was even the celebrated grand dame Isabella d'Este (who so eagerly wanted Leonardo to do her portrait only to be curiously and perpetually avoided by Leonardo), or this duchess or that. There is serious conjecture that Leonardo was painting the ideal woman, finally discharging his deep maternal complex. Why else was it never finished? If it were a commission, wouldn't the commissioner have insisted on having the painting after years and years of waiting? Would he not have sued Leonardo? Perhaps the commissioner's wife died in the meantime and he wanted nothing more of it? But wouldn't he want the portrait even more? Had Leonardo fallen in love with the painting himself?

With Leonardo's artistic example, painting had become focused on capturing life precisely, realistically, and in psychological depth; portraits were to reveal not just features but temperament. There was heightened interest in capturing a transient thought or mood on the faces depicted. Vasari put it, "At that time accomplished artists were setting themselves to the intelligent investigation and zealous imitation of the true properties of the natural world." Leonardo himself had acclaimed that "the painter can even induce men to fall in love with a picture that does not portray any living

---

79 Bramly, 362. The portrait to which Leonardo himself never gave a title is known as *La Gioconda* ("Mrs. Gioconda"; also, the smiling woman) in Italy, La Jaconde in France, and Mona Lisa in English and German-speaking countries.

woman. It once happened to me that I made a picture representing a sacred subject which was bought by one who loved it—and [who] then wished to remove the symbols of divinity in order that he might kiss it without misgivings."[80]

Some historians claim that the *Mona Lisa* is a portrait of the artist, of Leonardo himself, in the guise of the idealized woman, the woman of his life, Caterina, Leonardo's mother "La Caterina." These researchers have explored computer analysis of the painting, X-rays, etc. to support their hypothesis.

Not one word about the painting or the man who supposedly commissioned it is found even obliquely in what we have of Leonardo's notebooks. The concept about the painting is like the conceptualization in the painting itself, *sfumato*, smoky, as seen through a veil, a mist, a soft focus. Perhaps elsewhere in Leonardo's notes, yet to be discovered, the answer will be revealed.

The famous smile was supposedly achieved (Vasari) by Leonardo composing music and having it played by instrumentalists in his studio during the model's sittings. After Vasari, historians gushed with romantic reaction to the portrait: the subject's Christlike peace defying time; she who has experienced all pleasure and all pain, full of compassion and understanding.

The portrait has suffered over the centuries: strips of about seven centimeters (almost three inches) have been cut from each side; two pillars that originally framed the background landscape have disappeared; her superbly rendered eyebrows (according to Vasari) have disappeared; sensitive tones of color that allowed the onlooker "to see the pulsing of the veins in the hollow of the throat" are no longer visible.

Astrology can not help with this dilemma. The chronology of Leonardo's life and suggestions through Vasari begin to establish 1505, perhaps toward the end of the year, as the time that Mona Lisa was begun. At that time, SA Uranus was at almost 14 Virgo, moving into *opposition with Leonardo's Moon within the Neptune-Moon* quindecile complex. This transit matrix could well have been the catalytic witness to Leonardo's portrayal of the ideal woman, la Caterina, a memorial of perfection.

---

80 Hale, 215, 434–435. Additionally, Bramly reports that one of the attendants in the Louvre fell in love with the *Mona Lisa*, which it was his duty to guard. He talked to her and was jealous of tourists who came too close, claiming that she sometimes smiled back at them. He was encouraged to take early retirement. Page 396.

The *Mona Lisa* never left Leonardo until his death in 1519; King Francis I, caring for Leonardo in France, kept the painting. It later entered the Louvre Museum in Paris.

And it was stolen! On August 22, 1911, this most famous painting in the world was stolen one night from the Louvre, where it had hung for over a century. The painting was not recovered until December 13, 1913, when it was found in Florence in the possession of a painter named Vincenzo Perugia.

This theft and the global resurrection of *Mona Lisa* awareness can help us confirm Leonardo's birth time still more. The horo-

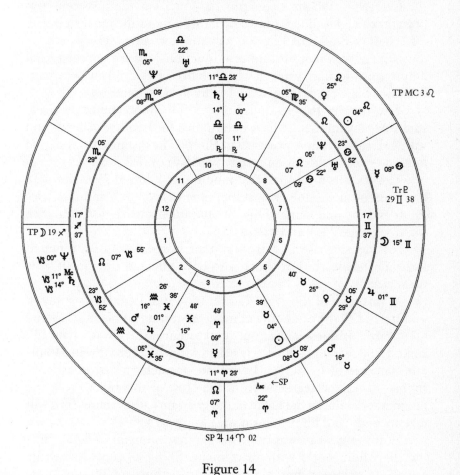

Figure 14

Inner Chart	Outer Chart
Leonard da Vinci)	**SA Mona Lisa Theft**
	Aug. 22, 1911

scope on page 281 (Figure 14) shows the Solar Arcs for Leonardo brought forward to that August 22nd in 1911 when his *quindeccential* masterwork was stolen. It is astounding what we see: 143,290 days after Leonardo's death; 459 years, four months, and six days after his birth, the day chosen by a thief to steal the Mona Lisa was WITHIN 2 MINUTES OF ARC THE EXACT 5TH OCCURRENCE OF LEONARDO'S 90-DEGREE SQUARE SOLAR ARC! Every planet and every point in the horoscope was, for the fifth time in Leonardo's extended life, precisely square its natal position as we have timed his birth—within 2 minutes of arc!

Everything about Leonardo da Vinci was emphasized, was brought to highest focus once again, throughout the modern world. The theft of the Mona Lisa was a major news story everywhere.

Note as well that SP Jupiter was within 3' of arc opposed natal Saturn (justification, proving what's right); SP Ascendant was exactly square his Uranus (heightened individual recognition).

The Tertiary Progressions brought TP Moon almost precisely to the Ascendant that we have determined for Leonardo's birth, and the Midheaven almost precisely to Pluto. The distance from partile here in terms of the Moon is only two days of real time!

The transits are equally astounding: tr Pluto at 29 Gemini 38 was square Leonardo's critical Neptune (within 32') and the Aries Point and the midpoints of his Moon/Saturn and Venus/Pluto (See Figure 4, page 245); and more!

It is no surprise in astrology that horoscopes of the famed live on after death. For those who have affected time itself, it is no accident.

At this time of the *Mona Lisa*, 1505–1506, Leonardo's study of gliding and flight came to a climax: his testing of his model, "the great bird." In Fiesole, just outside Florence, there was a bare hill some 1,300 feet high, popularly called Monte Cecero (Swan Mountain, because of its shape). Leonardo was determined to attempt flight—in utmost secrecy—from the crest of this hill: "From the mountain that bears the name of the great bird, the famous bird will take its flight and fill the world with his great fame."[81]

To his mind, this was to be his greatest moment of fame, "filling the whole world with amazement, filling all records with its fame, and bringing eternal glory to its birthplace." But we know

---

81 Most sources. See Vallentin, 367–368.

not of the results; and knowing not in this frame of expectation is failure. The test took place at the time of the *Battle's* failure to hold to the wall of the Grand Council Chamber. No witness to the flight attempt ever came forward.

Also at this time, Leonardo immersed himself in the study of anatomy. His dissection of corpses—some thirty in all, an unheard of number at that time: men, women, fetuses, the extremely aged—and his work with slaughtered animals were explained within a characteristic grandness of plan: "I am revealing to men the origin of the prime and perhaps the secondary cause of their being ... I want to work miracles (*voglio far miracoli*)." Leonardo eventually was able to make diagnoses in many cases as modern as today's; for example, the first report in the history of medicine of a death from arteriosclerosis, another from pulmonary tuberculosis. He was able to describe in detail—in pictured detail—the development of the fetus within the mother's womb, the accurate curvature of the spine, the automatic neuromuscular system, the lachrymal canal through which "the tears rise into the eyes from the heart."[82]

Researchers have noted that Leonardo, in his studies of the reproductive organs, gave short shrift to the female: his drawings were incomplete (without clitoris or labia minora) and the vaginal orifice was grotesquely out of proportion. Leonardo thought [surely in a bias against women, perhaps for the early hurt in relation to La Caterina] that the private parts of a woman were disproportionate to those of her partner. He writes, "In general, woman's desire is the opposite of man's. She wishes the size of the man's member to be as large as possible, while the man desires the opposite of the woman's genital parts, so that neither ever attains what is desired."[83] This depiction was eventually corrected, and extraordinary deductions were made about fertilization and the gestation process. For the penis, Leonardo believed it to have a life of its own(!): "This animal often has a soul and an intelligence which are

---

82 All sources. See Vallentin, 392. His working conditions were so difficult, even macabre: fighting the hot Italian climate and its effects on decomposition, eschewing embalming fluids because of their tainting the natural state of the body, working at nights so as not to draw attention to his labor, the restraint of nausea, etc. And there was the stigma attached to tampering with the dead: a papal bull issued in 1300 by Boniface VIII established excommunication as the penalty for those who eviscerated the bodies of the dead. This bull was aimed at horrible practices in the Crusades but was generalized as well to the study of anatomy. Ibid, 389.

83 Bramly, 119–121.

independent of the man." He declared the testicles to be the seat of emotional energy.[84]

Leonardo's studies in anatomy became one of the major monuments of his mind; his practical goal was to show the incompetency of physicians and his idealized goal was to "write down what the soul is." These studies continued to absorb him completely between 1508 and 1511, the period of his most exact drawings and studies, with SA Pluto conjunct Neptune (concerns of death matters, unusual experiences, etc.).[85]

To Rome

Commissions came to Leonardo from Milan as well at this time. He shuttled between the two cities. His notebooks filled up with studies on mechanics, geometry, geology, painting, and, of course, anatomy. He began work on a bypass of the River Adda at Tre Corni, but he soon had to return to Florence to assist the sculptor Rustici with a bronze group for the Baptistry. Then he was back in Milan, concentrating on muscles and the dynamics of fluids, and a second equestrian monument, which never got beyond the sketch stage. And there was the masterpiece of the *Madonna and Child and Saint Anne*.[86]

Again in this time period, politics and war interrupted the course of life. Louis XII was engaged in expansionist policies and invaded Italy, beginning with Milan. But forces formed in Venice with allies brought in from Germany and Spain rallied around Pope Julius II, and Louis was eventually driven out. In the process, the Pope had stirred up the Swiss—the formidable mercenaries of Europe at the time—and they attacked where the French had failed, beginning with an invasion of Milan and its territory. Then the French came back at the Swiss, back and forth until September 1513, when the French were finally routed and the Swiss were in control, and the Milanese knew not to whom allegiance was due.

---

84 Vallentin, 403–404. There are several decidedly homosexual doodles in the notebooks attributed to Salai (bearing his name), Leonardo's life-long ward and companion.

85 Leonardo was intent on publishing treatises on every subject imaginable. He came close to this fulfillment in anatomy through his meeting and planned collaboration with the young anatomist Marcantonio della Torre, but della Torre died prematurely shortly after meeting with the master.

86 Turner, 49.

By this time, Leonardo desperately needed a patron. Commissions had all but vanished during the wartimes. He decided to forsake the city of his choice and to journey to Rome. He needed a new patron—the Sforza family was gone, Borgia was gone, the Florentine government was a shambles. It was the beginning of the unhappiest time of his life.

Figure 15 (below) clearly shows this time of change—September 24, 1513, when Leonardo left Milan—again reinforcing the reliability of the birth time through the sensitivity of the angles.

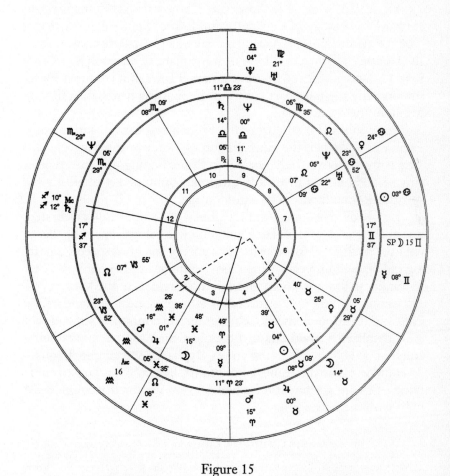

Figure 15

Inner Chart	Outer Chart
Leonard da Vinci	**SA To Rome**
	Sept. 24, 1513

Note that the SP Moon was exactly upon the 7th cusp (2 degrees orb, i.e., two months, certainly within the planning period for such a major change).

SA Moon was square to Mars ("Strong drive to fulfill needs, to 'let it fly;' disruption,") and SA Ascendant was conjunct Mars ("The fighting spirit, robustness"). SA MC was square to Leonardo's extraordinary Mercury: Leonardo needed his points of view recognized once gain by a powerful patron/partner. Overall, we can say that Leonardo, at sixty-one, was looking to start over again, elsewhere, at a new level.

Figure 16 (page 287) shows the Tertiary Progressions brought forward to the day of departure for Rome, September 24, 1513. The TP Moon and TP Ascendant were at 15–16 Aries *exactly opposite Leonardo's Saturn;* TP Uranus was square Leonardo's Sun. Note that TP Saturn was at 6 Scorpio square TP Uranus conjunct Pluto, symbolizing the fall-apart nature of Leonardo's battle-torn time in Milan in the recent past.[87]

Pope Julius II died during the French evacuation, and the new Pope was a Medici, the younger son of Lorenzo the Magnificent! Artists from all over Italy flocked to Rome hoping that the art-sensitive Leo X would distribute glorious commissions to all for the spirit of Rome. It was to be a golden age.

Leo X did encourage the arts, but Leonardo, while celebrated, was no longer in fashion. His reputation was being eclipsed by that of younger rivals who worked with high energy and great speed. Appearing old beyond his years, with a long white beard, Leonardo was left to wander in solitary gloom through the corridors of the Vatican.

Leonardo was being sustained at a very meagre standard by Giuliano de' Medici, the Pope's brother, on a monthly stipend that was "insulting": hundreds of times less than the payments being commanded by the glittering young Raphael, for example. Leonardo could not play the games of the court, he could not bow to curry favor of the powerful, and he had no stamina for the competitive fight with the new *maestrini*.

---

87 Also, it is important to note that transiting Pluto came to Leonardo's Ascendant between October 1509 and October 1510. This was his peak study time for anatomy, dealing with dissections of the dead, as we have discussed. Normally, this powerful transit would have signaled an enormous shift of life perspective, but Leonardo's environment did not cooperate; he could not shift out of the circumstances he was in until three years later in September 1513. This transit was confined to another level, his search for the soul within the bodies of the dead.

The art world of Rome—of all Christendom—was focused around the new Cathedral of St. Peter. Donato Bramante, the great architect who had collaborated with Leonardo long before at the court of Milan, had earlier persuaded Pope Julius to pull down the thousand-year-old basilica of St. Peter and adopt plans for the grandest cathedral the world would ever see. Work had begun on the new St. Peter's in 1506 and would last until 1667(!), utilizing the genius of Bramante, Raphael, Sangallo, Michelangelo, Maderno, and Bernini. Armies of workmen were involved, and all artists

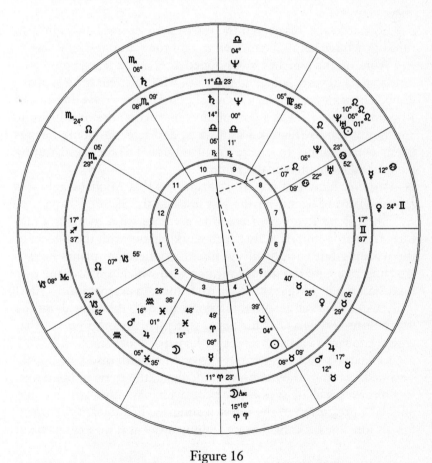

Figure 16

Inner Chart
Leonard da Vinci (Test)

Outer Chart
TP To Rome
Sept. 24, 1513

coveted the inspiration and work being realized there; all wanted to be a part of the conception.[88]

Leonardo threw himself into the study of motion, percussion, weight, air, botany and, in anatomy, very specifically the lungs and the larynx. He produced plans for machines to make rope and mint coins.

Finally, the Pope got around to commissioning Leonardo to drain the marshes, a vast area on either side of the Appian Way in Rome, that were "a breeding ground for fever." Leonardo's experience with canals came to the fore again, as did his innovative mapping abilities, creating the first aerial-view maps, i.e., looking directly down upon a site instead of from an oblique three-quarter angle viewpoint.

Leonardo also pioneered the use of solar energy, the light captured by a huge parabolic mirror, to boil the water in dyers' vats.

Work on the marshes was stopped after a few years, completed only some 370 years later, and the work with solar energy was abandoned to await *our* modern times. Leonardo was traveling out of Rome to other cities as a consultant on art commissions, his time and attentiveness fractured as always, and later in Rome he was given commissions to create involved and technically daunting pageant amusements for the Pope.[89]

Another blow to Leonardo's pride was that Michelangelo was now the hero of Rome, having just finished the Sistine Chapel.

Then Pope Leo gave Leonardo a commission to paint a picture. Leonardo immediately began working, not with the subject of the painting but with distilling juices from certain plants he was studying to create the proper varnish with which to finish the picture. Vasari tells us that the Pope exclaimed, in exasperation, "Alas! This man will never get anything done, for he is thinking about the end before he begins." This papal statement was the phrase that ended Leonardo's artistic career at the papal court.[90]

Leonardo's sketches became heavy, filled with disasters; people stranded, victimized by nature: the Deluge, the ruins of buildings. In short, in his chalk studies, he portrayed massacres, which could only be a projection of the bitter feelings he had toward the world for his loneliness. As his life was falling away, it is no exaggeration

---

88 Bramante seems to have forgotten his old friendship with Leonardo. Raphael had become Bramante's protege.

89 Bramly, 379–398 for Leonardo's Rome experience.

90 All sources. See Vallentin, 456.

to say that this awesome man who could move the world with his chalk was dreaming of the annihilation of mankind.

Leonardo's patron, Giuliano de' Medici died in March 1516. Leonardo was again abandoned: *transiting Saturn was precisely upon his rectified Ascendant*, and transiting Pluto was still square his Neptune, as it was for so long during the Rome years.

But an astrologer would have seen hope. Figure 17 (page 290) shows Leonardo's portrait for this pivotal time: again, as we have seen so often in key moments of individuality, Leonardo's Uranus is highlighted, this time by the Secondary Progressed Moon exactly in conjunction.

Note the positive, supportive measurements: SA Jupiter is applying to conjunction with the Sun; SA Ascendant is square Venus, ruler of his Midheaven; the SA SP Sun is applying to the Nodal Axis, suggesting a new relationship, a new patron; transiting Jupiter at 11 Cancer is square the Midheaven. Transiting Uranus was at 0 Taurus approaching Leonardo's most responsive Sun. Some new association must come out of this lonely time.[91]

Leonardo decided to abandon Rome and go to France, where his reputation was still very grand, thanks to the appreciation earlier of King Louis XII. Leonardo and his household, which included Salai, another apprentice of some years standing (and heir-to-be) Francesco Melzi, and a new servant, left Rome in the Spring of 1517, surely in April, *with transiting Uranus conjunct his Sun.*

The group took three months for the journey, going through Florence, Milan, and into France through Grenoble and Lyon to meet the young, robust King of France, Francis I. The king received Leonardo with excitement and honor and settled him and his companions in comfort in a manor house of their own, in Amboise, connected with the royal house by an underground tunnel which the King used daily to go see Leonardo and have long, long discussions with the master. Francis gave his "favorite painter, engineer, and architect" a handsome income.

Leonardo helped Francis with plans for a castle and devised court entertainments, his grand, intricate pageants that some thirty years before had finally secured the trust of Lodovico Sforza.

---

91   Looking ahead: we can see SA Pluto 3+ degrees away from opposition with Leonardo's dominating Mercury and SA Saturn 2+ degrees away from conjunction with Leonardo's Ascendant. The period from mid-1518 to mid-1519 will be critical for the old master.

On April 23, eight days after his sixty-seventh birthday, Leonardo recorded his last will and testament. Vasari tells us that Leonardo had been ill for many months and had "desired scrupulously to be informed of Catholic practice and of the good and holy Christian religion. Then, after many tears, he repented and confessed. Since he could no longer stand upright, he had himself supported by his friends and servants in order to receive the holy sacrament in piety outside his bed."[92]

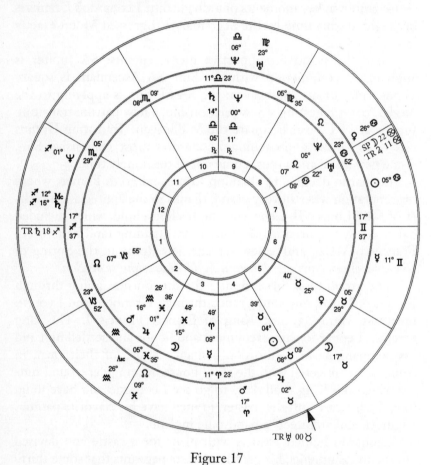

Figure 17

Inner Chart	Outer Chart
Leonard da Vinci	**SA Medici Death**
	Mar. 15, 1516

92 Bramly, 406.

Leonardo's will seems to confirm this last-minute turn to religion, which he had assiduously avoided throughout his notebook records of his life. His specifications for his funeral were precise and painstaking, but absolutely nothing is specified for his burial, for his tombstone or epitaph. He portioned out his estate, with the bulk going to young Melzi [who later shared many details with Vasari personally], including the notebooks.

Leonardo died quietly in the manor house on May 2, 1519.

Figure 18 (below) is Leonardo's death horoscope, our final proof for Leonardo's rectified birth time.

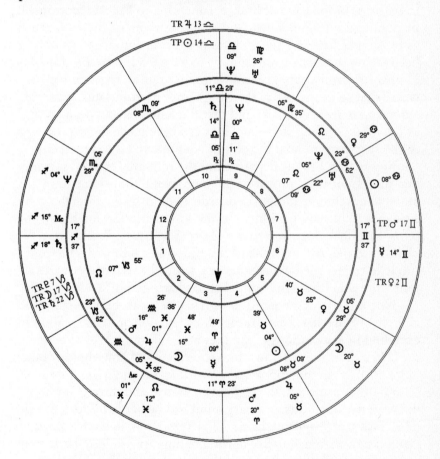

Figure 18

Inner Chart	Outer Chart
Leonard da Vinci (Test)	**SA da Vinci's Death**
	May 2, 1519

SA Pluto had come to exact opposition with Leonardo's domi-
nating Mercury. SA Saturn had just crossed Leonardo's Ascendant.
Note that the SP Ascendant was conjunct Jupiter, suggesting a
peaceful passing. TP Mars was precisely opposing, attacking,
Leonardo's Ascendant; the TP Moon opposed his Uranus, and the
TP Sun was exactly conjunct his Saturn.

The transits are similarly clear: transiting Jupiter is conjunct
Leonardo's Saturn, Pluto upon his Nodal Axis, Saturn opposed his
Uranus, and, in peace, transiting Venus square his Jupiter.

There is a nice story told in the life studies that Leonardo died
in the arms of the King of France, lamenting to Francis "how much
he [Leonardo] had offended God by not working on his art as much
as he should have."[93] Yet, Francis is historically logged as having
been seeing to business too far away to have made it back in time for
Leonardo's swift passing. However, most recent research has suggested that someone else in the King's place had officiated at the ceremony away from Amboise and that the King, having been advised
of Leonardo's failing state, could indeed have made the trip back to
Amboise in time to hold the philosopher safe in his last moments.

Biographer Bramly departs from the romantic ending, suggesting that Leonardo probably did *not* spend time lamenting his
underachievement; rather, Leonardo (would have) used the time
available to explain his illness to the king and describe his symptoms! In a final, deep bow to the Master's Mercury, Bramly says, "If
he had had pen and ink at hand and the strength to write, he would
surely have recorded in his notebook with what reluctance and suffering the soul leaves the body that has harbored it."[94]

Not a trace of Leonardo's burial place can be detected, the
churchyard having been ravaged by Napoleon and randomly
exploited by generations of families and pillaged by stone masons,
the lead coffins melted down for war efforts and household goods.

Through the notebooks, *The Last Supper*, the *Mona Lisa*, and
several other paintings, throughout the world and throughout time,
the presence of an extraordinary mind had been established, a veritable Nova of explosive light. That mind was inventive beyond
imagination and imaginative beyond telling. And indeed, perhaps it
is the ultimate contentment with this excellence that mystically sus-
tains the haunting, privately proud smile of La Caterina.

---

93 All sources. See Bramly, 407.
94 Ibid., 408.

Bibliography

Bramly, Serge. *Leonardo: Discovering the Life of Leonardo Da Vinci*. Tr. Sian Reynolds. New York: HarperCollins. 1991.

Burckhardt, Jacob. *The Civilization of the Renaissance in Italy*. New York: Harper & Row. 1958.

Chamberlin, E. R. *The Bad Popes*. New York: Dorset. 1969.

Freud, Sigmund. *Leonardo da Vinci and a Memory of His Childhood*. Tr. Alan Tyson. Harmondsworth, Eng.: Pelican Books. 1963. Introduction Copyright, Brian A. Farrell, "On Freud's Study of Leonardo," 1963.

Garin, Eugenio. Editor. *Renaissance Characters*. Chicago: University of Chicago. 1991.

Gould, Cecil. *Leonardo: The Artist and the Non-Artist*. Boston: New York Graphic Society. 1975.

Hale, John. *The Civilization of Europe in the Renaissance*. New York: Athenum. 1994.

Harding, Michael and Harvey, Charles. *Working with Astrology: the Psychology of Harmonics, Midpoints and Astro*Carto*Graphy*. London: Arkana. 1990.

Hart, Ivor B. *The World of Leonardo da Vinci*. New York: Viking Press. 1961.

Hibbert, Christopher. *Florence—The Biography of a City*. New York: Norton & Company. 1993.

Mannering, Douglas. *The Art of Leonardo Da Vinci*. New York: Excalibur. 1981.

MacCurdy, Edward. Editor. *The Notebooks of Leonardo Da Vinci*, Vol I. New York: George Braziller, 1939.

McLanathan, Richard. *Images of the Universe: Leonardo Da Vinci, the Artist as Scientist*. Garden City, NY: Doubleday. 1966.

Merejcovski, Dmitri. *The Romance of Leonardo Da Vinci*. Tr. Bernard Guilbert Guerney. New York: Heritage Reprints. 1938.

Munkasey, Michael. *The Astrological Thesaurus, Book 1: House Keywords*. St. Paul, MN: Llewellyn. 1992.

Ring, Thomas. *Astrologische Menschenkunde*. Freiburg: Bauer Verlag. 1956.

_____. *Genius und Daemon*. Publication data not available.

Sypher, Wylie, "Leonardo's Mystery," in *Book Week* publication, September 25, 1966.

Turner, A. Richard. *Inventing Leonardo*. New York: Knopf. 1993.

Tyl, Noel. *Prediction in Astrology*. St. Paul, MN: Llewellyn Publications, 1991.

_____. *Synthesis & Counseling in Astrology*. St. Paul, MN: Llewellyn Publications, 1994.

Vallentin, Antonin. *Leonardo Da Vinci*. Tr. E. W. Dickes. New York: Viking Press. 1938.

Williams, Trevor I. *The History of Invention*. London: Macdonald & Co. 1987.

Zubov, V. P. *Leonardo Da Vinci*. Tr. David M. Krause. Cambridge: Harvard University Press. 1968.

Index

Beethoven
Da Da Da
Da

T he key. Tonality.
In music, the key is the sound grounding of any piece, the central tone (tonality) around which the music is composed. A tonal color is established, and, not surprisingly, tests have shown that non-musicians and musicians alike react similarly to keys, to tonalities, so strong is the archetypal manifestation of a color, a mood, an energy level through the sound.

An astrological rectification of the birth date and time of Ludwig van Beethoven

For example, play on the piano (or have played for you) in the middle register, with the right hand, the notes E and then A, in that order, going down from the E to the A. Do you hear the sound of an "ending," the sound of bringing the music to a final stopping point? That progression (musicians call it the dominant-tonic progression) is the same in every key, in various colors; the fifth degree of the scale always leads to, calls out for, the first degree.

Play the notes again, this time adding a C# after the E: E-C#-A. This C# is called the "third" of the chord; the three notes together establish the grounding sound of the key of A-Major. Now play them in reverse: A-C#-E and hold each note down as you play the others. To most of us, A-Major is the color red—play the chord strongly—hear the sounding of bright finality.

Now, try playing the A and then the *D* below it: this is the same progression, the same sound of coming to rest, but the A has become the dominant of a different key, the key of D, a scale of entirely different coloration (play the notes A, F#, and D downward; D-F#-A upward, for the grounding in D-Major).

Astrologically, we can translate this to the Sun being the base (tonic) of a key (a particular life-coloring sign) and the Moon being the dominant (fifth degree), and the Ascendant being the third degree, a very important variable within the scale. They all go together; they must. Each relies on the other to establish the whole.

A second example, please: play the D-F#-A triad (the group of three notes that work together as the tonic or root chord of D-Major). Listen to it intently. Next, *move the F# down one-half step*, i.e., to the white key just below it, abutting it, F-natural. Now, play the notes D-F-A together. Just listen to the change accomplished by altering the third degree of the scale (the Ascendant)!

That change of key is a change from D-Major to D-*Minor*, perhaps Sagittarius to Scorpio; all the difference in the world when the composer wants to adjust mood coloration.

Beethoven played tricks with these tonal regimens, these well-tempered concepts of acoustics. He planned his earth-shaking Ninth Symphony with a grounding in D-minor (D-F-A), but instead of establishing that key clearly at the outset of the work, as a composer should and must traditionally, he introduced the deep grounding of an A (played by the big double-basses) and repeated over it fleetingly (with the violins), many times, the notes A to E. There is no "D" in sight!

Surprisingly and daringly, this A beginning the Ninth Symphony emerges (along with the E) as part of the *dominant chord* of the D-Minor scale (the chord built upon the fifth degree of D-minor, A-C-E); Beethoven then leads us dramatically and innovatively back to the base tonality instead of establishing it clearly at the outset for our maximum listening comfort. Beethoven creates tension and drama in unique ways.

The title of this chapter on the life of Beethoven captures the most famous of all his musical phrases, the rhythmic statement (G, G, G to E-flat; a descending major third), from the very beginning of his Fifth Symphony. Beethoven played a trick here as well (sixteen years before the Ninth): using the dominant of G (and tipped off by the E-flat), he leads the listener into the key of C-minor (perhaps Beethoven's most favored key, C-E-flat-G), the grounding of this symphony, but then he ends it in the key of *C-Major* (C-E-G), the transition from night to daylight! Beethoven did the same in his final Symphony, beginning in D-minor and ending in D-Major, again darkness to light. This individualistic creative way captures symbolically the essence of Beethoven's shadowed realm of neurosis giving birth to genius illumination.

In his defiance of established structure and practice, Beethoven created grand new forms for his inspiration. In the "Da-Da-Da Da Fifth," the rhythmic motif dominates the work, even to the point of displacing any particular melody to lead the ear to fulfillment. In so many, many ways—technically and inspirationally—Beethoven transformed music from the Classical Era to the Romantic Era.[1]

Such avant-garde practice dominated Beethoven's personal life as well. For almost fifty years, Beethoven *denied the year in which he was born;* he avoided this grounding tonality as best he could. Even more, there is no valid statement anywhere in the biographical sources with regard to the date on which he was born; we only have the December *date* of his Christening.

Beethoven even ignored his parentage.

There are reasons for all this, to be sure: psychological games being played out at the core of Beethoven's identity, which have been extremely well-annotated throughout a century of study and will be revealed in our rectification process.

Our objective here, then, is to determine the *astrological* tonality of Beethoven's birth: to establish the key, the major and minor colorations, the principle themes, and, most helpfully, the rhythms in time that lead us to knowing measurement and appreciation of Beethoven's rebellious life and inspired genius. That is the challenge to astrology, with its own music of Sun, Moon, Ascendant, aspects, and development sounds.

---

1 Indeed, the so-called modern music of any era usually makes a departure from established practice in terms of tonalities and progressions. The twelve-tone scale conceived by Austrian born Arnold Shoenberg (1874–1951), for example, dictates that each note of the entire chromatic scale be sounded in composition before any note can be repeated! This *atonal* (against the establishment of a central key) movement influenced twentieth-century music dramatically.

Birth Date and Lineage

Bonn, Germany in 1770 was a neat, clean, elegant city at a picturesque bend in the Rhine river in the southwest of the country. Its population numbered about 12,000 persons. The archbishop and the Elector (a very important prince-like figure) were established there. Bonn was bustling with courtiers, politicos, servants, and small businessmen. While Bonn's artistic and cultural life was well-developed and influential, the music capital of the Holy Roman Empire was clearly Vienna, and serious artists had to go there to make their mark in the world.

Beethoven's paternal grandfather, Ludwig van Beethoven (1712–73), was a bass singer with a secure position in the chapel at the court in Bonn. He had come from Belgium—and the Flemish "van" in his name becomes very important in his namesake grandson's life, in contradistinction to the powerful, nobility-signifying "von" in German.

Kapellmeister Ludwig's son was Johann (1740–92), also a career musician, as violinist, singer, and harpsichordist. He continued the family's musical tradition by teaching his own son, our Ludwig (1770–1827) music in brutal, intense, tyrannical fashion. Johann suffered a lifelong shadow from the celebrity and grandness of his father (who also disapproved of Johann's marriage) and from the precociousness of his son, our Ludwig. Johann got lost in the young boy's excellence, and in his eclipsed state, turned to drink and became unstable.

Beethoven's mother, Maria Magdalena Keverich, held things together. She was "born on" (a rare mention of birth date, since the Christening date was *the* date of importance in those times) December 19, 1746, three days after what would be the birth date of her genius son, as we shall see. Frau Beethoven had a Sun-Jupiter conjunction in Sagittarius, with the Moon probably in Pisces, with a Water Grand Trine, all suggesting a philosophical way of managing life, with keen private reliance on some inner, sustaining spiritual sense. She is portrayed as pious, kind, grave, and resigned; pained, suffering, and righteous.

Three things are important here in reference to the mother. Maria Magdalena was herself born into a family that was racked with pain: a father who died when she was twelve and a mother who was a cook in the court, had six children, four of whom died, a nervous breakdown, a problem with drink, and a precipitous death in abject poverty. Second, Maria Magdalena saw all of this as a "chain of sorrows," which she identified with the married state.

In a discussion with young Caecilia Fischer [a key source of biography since the Beethovens had rented a flat in the home of Caecilia and her brother's parents], Maria Magdalena remarked: "If you want to take my good advice, remain single, and then you will have the most tranquil, most beautiful, most pleasurable life. For what is marriage? A little joy, but then a chain of sorrows."[2] Caecilia reported carefully that the young Ludwig, probably aged five, was in the room at the time and overheard this conversation distinctly.

Third, Maria Magdalena herself had seven children with Johann, four of whom died. A key consideration here is that her *first* Beethoven child, who was christened on April 2, 1769, was named Ludwig Maria, after grandfather Kapellmeister Ludwig and the mother, but this Ludwig lived for only six days. Our Ludwig, the master to be, was born twenty months later in mid-December 1770.

From these background details, we can anticipate dimensions of parental tension, family anxiety, to be prevalent in Beethoven's life and, of course, in his horoscope. He would be born into a very, very difficult life space: a stoic, suffering mother, a lowly, "ne'er-do-well" father with a tyrannical, driving temperament, the pervasive specter of a luminous grandfather, and an earlier namesake born first, ahead of him, and dead. From the heights to which we know Beethoven ascended creatively and conceptually, we can hypothesize that his formative family concerns were commensurately deeply imbedded in his emotional makeup, in the patterning of his relationships with the world. We can anticipate that many explanations of much behavior will be reasonably and clearly rooted in these family tensions. That is how humankind develops; through echo, alteration, or denial of inherited circumstances.

Ludwig van Beethoven was *baptized* in the Saint Remigius Parish Church in Bonn on December 17, 1770. There is simply no doubt about this. The christening certificate in the Registry at Bonn exists today, and it is clear as a bell: "... *de decima septima Decembris Baptizatus est Ludovicus.*" Every detail is presented in legible Latin: the sponsors were Beethoven's grandfather, the

---

2 Solomon, 9.

Kapellmeister, and the wife of the next-door neighbor, Johann Baum, clerk of the electoral cellar, etc.[3]

It is reported in almost all sources that it was the custom at the time in the Catholic Rhine country not to postpone the baptism beyond twenty-four hours after the birth of a child. Thayer (see Bibliography), the most voluminous and respectedly definitive biographer of Beethoven, says that "it is in the highest degree probable that Beethoven was born on December 16, 1770."[4]

Here and there in other sources, there is a confusion between "being born" and "being christened (or baptized)." Schindler (see Bibliography) says flatly that Beethoven "was *born* in Bonn on 17 December 1770," but there is an editor's footnote that corrects this statement to the date of Beethoven's baptism, suggesting that birth on the 16th is probable.

Kendall (see Bibliography) says "the date of his birth has usually been taken to have occurred two days previously, on the 15th of December, and certainly he [Beethoven] seems to have regarded that date as his birthday, though there is a tradition [of other researchers, saying the 16th] so that 16 December would seem more probable."[5] It seems as if Kendall didn't really care to check this out; and where Beethoven's alleged own reference to the 15th comes from I have been unable to uncover. It is Beethoven's *nephew's* reference to the 15th (in a letter to the master) that is jarring in the scheme of things, and probably influenced Kendall.[6] [This nephew, Karl, will figure prominently in Beethoven's life and our rectification, for other reasons.]

Even (Dr.) Franz Wegeler (see Bibliography), a close friend of Beethoven for many, many years, states, "Our Ludwig was born on 17 December 1770," but there is an accompanying editorial comment that this mistake is "incomprehensible." I think that Wegeler, five years older than Ludwig, confused baptism with birth under the protracted duress of helping Beethoven in his extraordinary custody battle for his nephew: the baptismal certificate which Wegeler procured for Beethoven at his behest assumed great importance in finally establishing his birth year and negating Beethoven's tacit approval of the story *that he was of noble birth.*

---

3   Thayer, Volume 1, 53; and other sources.
4   Ibid., 53.
5   Kendall, 10.
6   Wegeler and Ries, note 171.

In summary, then, the swirl of conjecture about the birth date is complicated by several considerations:

First — Noble Birth

Beethoven appeared to *deny* his family beginning.[7] Instead of his reality, he held on to a "Family Romance," a very powerful life-pervasive psychodynamic defense structure. The Family Romance is a fantasy structure conceived by Sigmund Freud and Otto Rank whereby the child replaces one or both of his parents with elevated surrogates—heroes, celebrities, kings, or nobles. Biographer Solomon integrates this concept into Beethoven's life adroitly, meaningfully. It becomes an important astrological point of analysis as well.

Beethoven felt deeply special. He lived with his genius while being completely aware of it. It is undeniable that he thought there must have been more about his origins to support, justify, and lead to his noble excellence.

Additionally, in a time of frequent misspellings and typographical errors, Beethoven was not uncomfortable with the occasional change in his name from "van" to the German nobility's "von" [of the lineage of]. Faced with his greatness and his regular appearances in the highest social circles, people assumed that he did have the noble birth that was provocatively suggested by the prefix to his surname.[8]

Rumor had it that Beethoven was the (illegitimate) son of King Friedrich Wilhelm II of Prussia (and the cook's char-daughter). Beethoven let that rumor live quietly, in between the lines of his thoughts and in between the thoughts of all those around him, until the month before he died![9]

---

7 Schindler wrote: "Beethoven himself as a rule did not speak of his early youth, and when he did he seemed uncertain and confused," 46.

8 For example, the announcements and a review of a concert on March 29, 1795 refer to "Herr Ludwig von Beethoven," as does an announcement for a concert in 1797. Even Goethe wrote of "von" Beethoven; the police filed a secret report on "Herr von Beethoven." Solomon, 87–88.

9 In a long, intimate letter to Wegeler—answering a Wegeler letter one year late(!) Beethoven wrote, "You say that I have been mentioned elsewhere as being the natural son of the late King of Prussia. Well, the same thing was said to me a long time ago. But I have adopted the principle of neither writing anything about myself nor replying to anything that has been written about me. Hence, I gladly leave it to you to make known to the world the integrity of my parents and especially of my mother." Beethoven delayed mailing this extremely late letter two months more, just a few weeks before his death. Solomon, 286.

It is fascinating to note that Beethoven sought and received permission to dedicate his last symphony, the Chorale Ninth, to Friedrich Wilhelm III, the scion of Beethoven's imagined father. In a dedicatory passage in the score, Beethoven wrote, "Your Majesty is not only the supreme father of your subjects but also the patron of arts and sciences ... I too, since I am a native of Bonn, am fortunate enough to regard myself as one of your subjects."[10] I can not help reading here Beethoven's private paternity claim presented to the unknowing son of Friedrich Wilhelm II, in fantasy, *his half brother!* I can not help acknowledging that the dominant theme of the Ninth Symphony (using much of Schiller's *Ode to Joy* as text) is *brotherhood.*

Beethoven was advised that he would receive a commendation, a decoration from the King for his grand accomplishment and dedication of the Ninth. Beethoven told Wegeler that he hoped and expected that a Royal Order would be forthcoming as a token of appreciation. Finally, he would become a noble!

But Beethoven received *no* decoration. Instead, along with a small note of appreciation, he was to be sent a diamond ring *(Brillantring)*. The ring arrived; not a diamond, but a cheap "reddish-looking stone," which was appraised at low value. Proudly above it all and embarrassed to anger—and undoubtedly deeply hurt—Beethoven insisted that the ring be sold.

According to his friend, Karl Holz (whom Beethoven authorized to write his biography), who urged Beethoven to keep the ring, Beethoven rose up before him and "with indescribable dignity and self-consciousness proclaimed: 'I too am a King!'"

Second — The Earlier Ludwig

The master loved his namesake, the Kapellmeister, and he could well have felt put out that his mother's first-born had been given the grandfather's name first (undoubtedly to put father Johann back into the Kapellmeister's good graces). But Beethoven could just as easily have seen his *own* soul waiting for the *better* time, the stronger body into which to be born. We don't know, but Beethoven often said that *his* Christening date was *that of the dead*

---

10 Ibid., 288.

first Ludwig, and that he himself had been born two years later than in reality, in 1772! Bizarre denial.

There is no logic in this, no rational deduction possible. Some theorists suggest that Johann changed Beethoven's birth date (in publicity) to make him two years younger and appear even more precocious than he was, perhaps to compete with the memories of the astounding Mozart child some fifteen years earlier. But there is absolutely no shred of evidence to support this. Johann did *not* falsify the birth information; *Ludwig* did.

Third — The Pain of the Father

Johann "inflicted" teaching upon Beethoven. Beginning at age four or so, Johann used his tutelage of young Ludwig as a means to reassert his importance in the family circle. His father, the much-loved Kapellmeister, had just died (and young Ludwig kept a portrait of the grandfather with him all his life), and Johann clearly saw Ludwig's extraordinary potential. All sources say that Johann conducted his teaching of the supremely gifted child (initially clavier and violin) in a brutal manner. There were witnesses that Ludwig was forced to *stand* on a little footstool at the clavier, weeping, to play his lessons; that the father was implacably severe, not merely strict, but cruel. Young Ludwig would at times be punished and locked up in the cellar.[11]

Biographers report uniformly what Solomon words so aptly: "We have, then, a matrix of family circumstances, actions, and attitudes which might well have led to permanent disillusionment and despair. It is testimony to Beethoven's strength and resiliency of character that he was able to withstand these stresses.... Apparently abandoning any hope of establishing warm and loving relationships, Beethoven largely withdrew from the society of his fellows and playmates, and from his parents as well."[12]

Beethoven was unable to learn anything at school much beyond simple addition in arithmetic. He amazed those around him by how gifted he was in music and how ungifted he was in everything else. It seems that young Ludwig retreated into the fantasy of his music, a "protective cloak of his daydreams." And here

---

11 Ibid., 16.
12 Ibid., 19.

Solomon appends Freud's well-known theory that "unsatisfied wishes are the driving power behind fantasies; every separate fantasy contains the fulfillment of a wish, and improves on unsatisfactory reality." We will return to this Neptunian signification of psychological defense later.

The Family Romance of noble birth was a fantasy component used to discharge the anxiety of namesake complications with his grandfather whom Beethoven adored as a father surrogate and model, even though the old man died when Beethoven was three; his earlier-born dead brother, the original namesake for Ludwig; and the tyranny of his father Johann's teaching and discipline, all within a sorrow-full existence. How possibly could he, *the* Beethoven, come from such mean surroundings? He *had* to have been born of privilege and fanfare, somehow a noble!

For rectification, we are strongly alerted then to a focus of developmental tension that *must* involve the parental axis somehow, within the 4th–10th House axis and/or involving the significators of these two Houses. There will surely be a tie-in as well with the 7th House of relationships, a lifelong frustration for Beethoven.

Clearly, these bold, initial deductions about Beethoven's personality development call attention to the *angles of the horoscope:* they will be highly accentuated, we can be sure. But what are the *planetary values* we are working with? In our general orientation, we must be astrologically sure of December 16, 1770 as the date of birth. To make that judgment, we must cast an eye to the 15th as well, the reference made by nephew Karl.

Here in Figure 1 (page 307), we see the planets at noon on December 16, 1770. Let's get a general feel for the planetary energies and the aspect groups. With this orientation, we will then be able to zero in on the Moon position, test the timing of development with Solar Arcs and Transits, and then determine an Ascendant. We will be building the root chord of Beethoven's life tonality.

Beethoven's planetary positions for the 16th show the Sun and Mercury and almost surely the Moon in Sagittarius: here is an extraordinary thrust of opinionation. This is a brilliant Sun-Moon combination indeed, focusing strongly on nervous cerebral energy, ideas, spirited devotion to everything one believes in, a tenacity to one's personal point of view. With Mercury involved as well, very close to the Sun, we have a fired up train of thought for sure, a series of locomotives!

Also, we can expect a very strong affinity with the out-of-doors, with Nature, with exuberance, with the sheer exercise of selfhood.

Mars opposes Mercury exactly at the core of the triple conjunction in Sagittarius. Mars in Gemini suggests an intense need to apply energies in communication, to champion diversity and anything cerebral, and to do it always powerfully and drivingly in the life. This Mars opposition axis with the Sun-Mercury and probably the Moon in Sagittarius is perhaps the most dramatically impelling

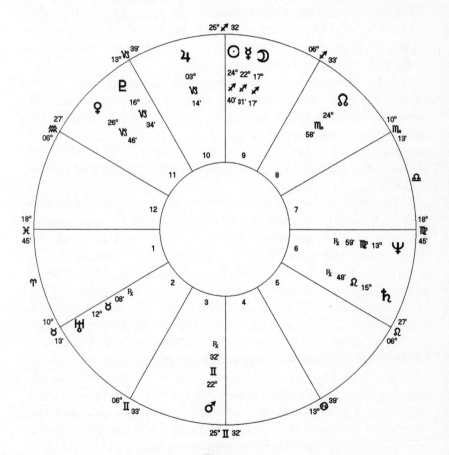

Figure 1
Beethoven/Planetary Orientation
Dec. 16, 1770, 12:00 P.M. LMT
Bonn, Germany
07E05   50N44
Placidus Houses

drive, thrust, imposition-of-thought picture possible in the astro-logical lexicon. This is enormous tension expressed in cerebral and creative pursuits, in arch-opinionation, and self-assertion.[13]

Mars is retrograde: there is an important psychodynamic counterpoint here, which usually corresponds to some rationaliza-tion, some superiorly conceived justification for one's energy. The energy goes in before it goes out, for censorship, adjustment, or camouflage. There can be a smoldering, a brooding, a delayed reac-tion. We have already seen the great scope of problems in Beethoven's home life and his concerns about lineage. These could fill out the retrogradation premise of this Mars, especially if this high-tension axis with the Sun-Mercury and probably the Moon *is tied in with the parental axis.*

On Beethoven's birth date, Saturn was also retrograde: we can expect "difficult (even inferiority) feelings taken on in the early home life through relationship with the father figure, usually the father, who somehow was taken out of the picture early; or was there but absent or passive; or was so tyrannical ... one or any com-bination of these ... so as not to have given the guidance of author-itative love."[14]

Here we have part of Beethoven's father-family syndrome (the grandfather's shadow, the father's brutality) which we must capture astrologically. Additionally, Saturn in Leo almost always suggests that ambition will be fulfilled through dramatic means, that the ego center will be put forward strongly, *in showy fashion.* We can sense an overcompensatory development here, out of the coercion of the home and the father's program and into the freedom of dramatic self-expression far away from it all. We can feel especially sure about this deduction because Beethoven's Saturn in Leo is trining his Mercury and Sun. Will it also be trining his Moon?

Saturn is squared by Uranus in Taurus: any relationship between these two planets is always a suggestion of there being new ways of doing things or the breaking away from tradition and embracing the avant garde; the modern, the new, and the different all beckon. This is a forceful identification with a generation gap,

---

13 Martin Luther King (January 15, 1929 at 11:21 A.M., CST in Atlanta, Jim Lewis rectifi-cation) had a most pronounced Mars in Gemini, retrograde and opposed Saturn in Sagit-tarius. It figures dramatically in King's philosophy of non-violent rebellion. See Tyl, *Synthesis & Counseling.*

14 Ibid., 40.

with any new way of looking at things. This is often a backdrop significator of rebelliousness, the promise for change.

Uranus-Neptune-and-Pluto comprise a Grand Trine, a classic defense-mechanism of practical self-sufficiency (in Earth).[15] An epithet to describe this construct would be "I don't need your help" or "I can and will do it my way." It defines individuation and it encourages over-doing things to prove one's point. It can easily develop within home life pressures *to establish and protect a private sense of self-worth*, to ward off anxiety about esteem issues. It is very important to note that with any Grand Trine construct *relationships are denied to a great degree.* In other words, self-protecting measures work naturally against relationship and the exchange of resources with others. So often we can easily get the feeling through a Grand Trine of someone being a law unto one's self.

The way for the defensive energies to get out of a Grand Trine and into the flow of life development offensively is through a square or opposition formed with one of the points of the Grand Trine. We have just discussed that Uranus squares Saturn and that Uranus is within the Grand Trine. This is a key, then, Uranus: the planet of electrifying individuality, rebellion, and genius. Beethoven was indeed a law for himself only to follow.

Here we must make special note of something remarkable: the planet Uranus was discovered by Sir William Herschel in the night sky over London on March 13, 1781, probably around 11:00 P.M., LMT.[16] At the moment of discovery, Uranus was positioned at 24 Gemini 27, opposed by Mars at 23 Sagittarius, a fitting image of the symbolism established for all time for Uranus. Now, as we prepare this rectification of Beethoven's horoscope, please note that *the planet Uranus upon its discovery for all of time to come was exactly opposed, in full awareness of, Beethoven's Sun!*

The fact that the Earth Grand Trine exists without the Sun or Moon's involvement (statistically more infrequent) suggests that Beethoven's defensive construct of practical self-sufficiency existed *separately* from the major thrust of his personality. In short, his extreme independence, while self-protecting on the one hand, will probably operate as an isolating *complex* on the other.

---

15 Ibid., section beginning 282.

16 Jawer, Jeff. "The Discovery of the Outer Planets," Tyl, *How to Personalize the Outer Planets.* Llewellyn, 1992.

Schindler reports that Beethoven had three ancient Egyptian inscriptions "framed and mounted under glass, on his work table."[17] They read as follows:

I am that which is.

I am Everything that is, that was, and that will be.
No Mortal Man has lifted my Veil.

He is of Himself Alone, and it is to this Aloneness that All
Things owe their Being.

Solomon states that these inscriptions, so close to Beethoven's feelings, are "poignant reminders of the master's withdrawal to an impregnable self-sufficiency, a self-sufficiency which ultimately prevailed against his longings for love." The formidable Grand Trine.

Yes, we must ask here, "isolating from what?" Will it be relationships, from which Beethoven showed early withdrawal? Will the withdrawal be just because of his deafness? Will the withdrawal be from *a particular kind* of relationship? We can see that *none of the planetary bodies in the test horoscope is in a Water sign.* If this holds up, emotional identification will be difficult for Beethoven; characteristically with this astrology, he will want to relate *to some exalted extreme* in order to gain emotional orientation. Is it that he will be isolated then from *normal* emotional relationships? Is there an emotional relationship complex here born out of the early home life difficulties, defended by the self-isolation and superiority feelings (Saturn retrograde in Leo), and discharged in creative genius?

Venus in this noon-test chart, Figure 1 (page 307), is in Capricorn and is peregrine, i.e., not in Ptolemaic aspect (or essential dignity) to any other body.[18] Usually the peregrine planet trumpets its symbolic significance throughout all that the personality does, through what it represents to society. It becomes a most significant singleton. In effect, it dominates, it permeates, it colors the life behaviorally, strongly, in terms of the planetary archetype. It can run wild. Here, Venus is in *Capricorn*, which usually corresponds to a delayed socio-emotional maturation. This could be another indi-

---

17 Schindler-MacArdle, 365; Thayer-Forbes, 481–482.
18 Tyl, *Synthesis & Counseling in Astrology*, section beginning 155.

cation of relationship difficulties for Beethoven, running amuck with the personality's development, the tension finally discharging itself into extraordinary creativity, i.e., relationship fulfillment through *ideals* expressed at another level.

Jupiter, the planetary symbol of enthusiasm, of one's hope (need) for a particular kind of reward, is also powerful in this horoscope: it is also peregrine, also in Capricorn. Jupiter in Capricorn commands opportunities to prove the Self's authority and importance. Jupiter is also the dispositor of the Sun, Mercury, and probably the Moon, and possibly the Midheaven.

For the Romans and the Italian ancients before them, Jupiter (*Diespiter* in early Latin) was the god of the sky, the supreme deity. Jupiter was also Jove, the Greek Zeus, Yahweh, Jehovah. Jupiter could influence the course of history and clarify the future. On the hundredth anniversary of Beethoven's death in 1927, the musicologist Hans Joachim Moser, describing a classicistic commemorative statue to the master, said: "Beethoven is deified; as a 'superman,' a 'Prometheus,' indeed a 'Jupiter,' the naked Olympian is enthroned above the neo-baroque bombast of highly-colored marble and golden bronze, above Alpine peak, eagle and thundercloud, with the clenched fists of the C-minor Symphony [the Fifth] and the bitter, tight-pressed lips of the first movement of the Ninth." Beethoven was Diespiter, the Jupiterian archetype.[19]

Astrologically, then, we have clear indications so far of the drive and drama, the developmental tension and the compensatory behaviors, the potential break away to freedoms, the isolationist protectionism, the possible psychological complexes about family and relationships.

But *where is the music?* Shouldn't we see something about inspiration, about imagination, fantasy, beauty, idealizations, even the self-deception and charade that, as we shall see, issued from Beethoven's complexes? What about Neptune?

In the noon-test horoscope, Neptune is also within the Earth Grand Trine. Pluto is placed within it too. Obviously, in our rectification reach for Beethoven's genius, we want to see if and how the awesome Grand Trine structure (not involving the Sun or Moon) is fed into the arena of the personal planets. Uranus squares Saturn, as we have seen, and this Saturn clearly reaches to relate by

---

19 Notes, Beethoven/Bernstein, 66, *Deutsche Grammophon*, 1980.

trine to the Sagittarius group. When we "move" the Moon within Sagittarius, we can at best get a semisextile relationship with Pluto from somewhere near the noon mark, and with a small adjustment we can clarify *the square with Neptune*. In *this* way, the three outer planets, the grand defensive structure of practical self-sufficiency, the management of structure (Earth), *would definitely have an escape outlet into the dynamically charged Sagittarian-Gemini axis*. This would integrate the entire horoscope, save for the two peregrine planets, Venus and Jupiter!

Neptune square the Moon suggests a lack of realism, a daydreaming, a romantic reverie, an imagination, a distancing through idealization. Without Water emphasis in the horoscope, with Venus peregrine, with Neptune possibly squaring the Moon and— through the Moon—Mercury and the Sun as well, we easily see the master alone, inspired, reaching for the unattainable. A key to our detailed study later will be the formative problems in Beethoven's life relationships reflected in the dramatic pathos of his music, the themes of longing that abound, suggested pointedly, for example, by his song cycle *An Die Ferne Geliebte*, "To the Distant Beloved." We shall see that we are guided to some surprising astrology about Neptune by all of this.

Specifics about the Moon

The Moon entered Sagittarius very early in the morning of December 15, 1770, two and one-half days before the christening ceremony at St. Remigius Church (see Figure 2, page 313). We must remember that Catholic tradition in that area of Germany was for baptism to take place within twenty-four hours of the birth (see page 302).

For Beethoven's Moon *not* to have been in Sagittarius, the birth would have had to occur at this very early time or earlier, so long before the baptism.

If Beethoven's birth had taken place during the very early hours of the 15th, we would have known about it, I think: this birth time would have disrupted the household, even late at night the day before, and the neighbors would have remembered, especially the Fischers from whom the Beethovens rented and whose children compiled myriad details about the Beethoven early family life as reliable source data for biographers. That early morning birth did not happen.

Additionally, Beethoven absolutely could not have had a Libran Ascendant. It does not fit the "chord." Summarily, Beethoven was labeled a "misanthrope" by many, many people all his life, i.e., as someone who hates mankind. Even at age ten, Beethoven was described this way, by a local cellist (Bernhard Maeurer) gathering details of the budding genius for posterity: "Outside of music he [Beethoven] understood nothing of social life; consequently he was ill-humored with other people, did not

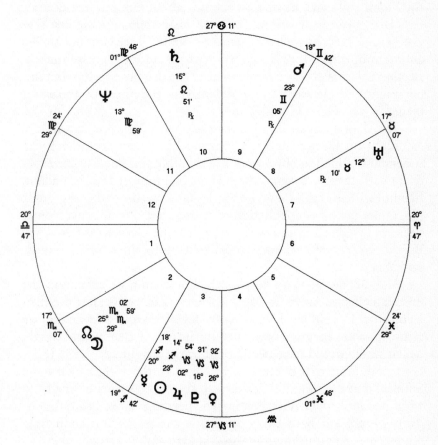

Figure 2
Beethoven/Time Orientation
Dec. 15, 1770, 2:22 A.M. LMT
Bonn, Germany
07E05   50N44
Placidus Houses

know how to converse with them, and withdrew into himself, so that he was looked upon as a misanthrope."[20]

Beethoven was clenched-fist tenacious to a fault—even to his last gesture on his deathbed—a world to himself. All the sketches, paintings, and busts of Beethoven portray a stocky, chunky, ruddy-faced rebel. The Ascendant *must* be in a fixed sign, and we will investigate this thoroughly in a moment.

Everything points to the fact that Beethoven was born *later*, i.e., with the Moon in Sagittarius. How much later? Within Sagittarius, the Moon will make its first aspect only about one and one-quarter days later, near dawn on the 16th, *the square with Neptune*, see Figure 3 (page 315). As we have seen above and will see later in detailed annotation, the Moon's square with Neptune is essential in Beethoven's makeup as complement to the driving Sagittarian temperament and the earthbound defensiveness defined by the outer planets in the Earth Grand Trine.

The Moon began its square in orb with Neptune just before Midnight on December 15. Very quickly, we can note the Virgo Ascendant, which is absolutely not possible for Beethoven, especially with the increasingly important Neptune at the Ascendant. Beethoven was no aesthete; he was a titanic hero—and every single biography uses this appellation over and over again, conveniently keyed to his Third Symphony, the Eroica (the heroic), written when Beethoven was thirty-four years old, changing the course of musical history.[21]

And, of course, as we develop the hours later, we encounter the unsuitable Libra Ascendant again (twenty-four hours after the conjecture on December 15). To consider a Scorpio Ascendant, we again en-counter the early morning image of Beethoven's birth, which surely would have been noted by the neighbors.

It is definite that Beethoven was born on the 16th, which was a Sunday; that the time did not disturb the night; that the time fit in with the family day. With Beethoven "needing" a fixed sign Ascendant, we are left with two options: Aquarius or Taurus, in time sequence, each affording the Moon square with Neptune.

---

20 Solomon, 20.

21 Autexier's book (see Bibliography) is entitled *Beethoven: The Composer as Hero*; Solomon names Beethoven's early years in Vienna, "The Heroic Period"; the concept of "hero" is everywhere, the rapport references to Napoleon, etc.

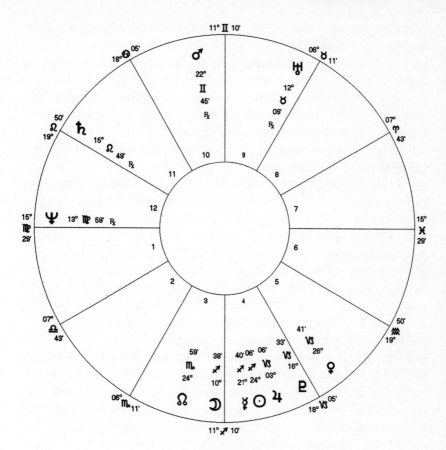

Figure 3
Beethoven/Moon-Neptune Orientation
Dec. 15, 1770, 11:00 P.M. LMT
Bonn, Germany
07E05 50N44
Placidus Houses

The Ascendant Variable

Figure 4 (page 317) is the speculative chart for Beethoven that appears most in the international archives of astrological data. There are other speculative times, and what ties most of them together is the fascination with a Taurus Ascendant and the sense of *structuring music*, the fact that Uranus would be rising, Pluto would be at the Midheaven, and the Sun-Mercury-Moon conjunction would be locked away in the 8th House, squared by Neptune, and

Neptune itself would be transiting the Midheaven upon Beethoven's death (March 26, 1827). All of these points of surmise are valid starts to rectification, as we are doing in another direction in this chapter.

Yes, here is the suggestion of ascendant genius, mega-public exposure and hidden, frustrated personal needs, the anxiety about finance (which plagued Beethoven lifelong, out of the insecurity of his early home situation, even when he was very well off in later years) through Mercury's rulership of the 2nd.

Certain things bother me about this speculation: peregrine Jupiter rules and is positioned in the 9th House, suggesting a tremendous level of formal study, for travel, even religion to pervade the life. But Beethoven could not exist in a school setting, despised teaching others, was himself totally self-taught (except in the very most elementary school lessons), was not religious, and Beethoven never went anywhere except to Vienna! He never returned to Bonn; he was invited to England but never went. He concertized in Prague, about 200 miles away, and he journeyed to the countryside every summer, but so did everybody else, after a fashion. In short, Beethoven was not a learned man, and he stayed put, while all other great virtuoso musicians and composers traveled far and wide throughout Europe. Beethoven lived a very solitary, routined life. He had no social graces; and, except for his music, no social ammunition, i.e., no resources with which to be attractive.

When Beethoven arrived in Vienna in November 1792, aged twenty-two, he began a fitful year of study with the old Master Haydn, a close friend of Mozart who had died just eleven months before. It is said that Haydn, once very angry with Beethoven, called him an atheist.[22] That was the prevailing view of Beethoven's religiousness, according to Solomon. Beethoven composed only two major works of religious nature, the *Mass in C* and the epic *Missa Solemnis*, which has never been at home in Church or the Concert Hall. Beethoven suggested that the *Missa Solemnis* could be performed as a "grand oratorio," a *secular* form, which is exactly how it was premiered.

Clearly, Beethoven had a non-sectarian view about the *Missa Solemnis*. While he understood the communication of religious feelings and fervor, it is clear throughout his life that religion was not

---

22 Thayer-Forbes, 141.

front and center as a 9th House peregrine Jupiter would suggest. I feel that Beethoven composed the *Missa Solemnis* at the end of his life to show off his ability to master the form of liturgical music, so neglected was that form in his career output. Music historians, for the most part, agree.

As well, I am uncomfortable with the Pluto rulership of the 7th placed in the Midheaven, at the Midheaven. This suggests gigantic public exposure and, indeed, *relationships* auguring well for the career, supporting Beethoven's place in the sun. It is perfect, we think. But it

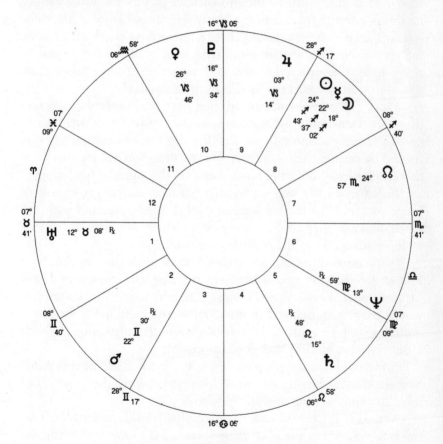

Figure 4
Beethoven/Common Speculative
Dec. 16, 1770, 1:29 P.M. LMT
Bonn, Germany
07E05   50N44
Placidus Houses

is so easy to romanticize the lives of geniuses in retrospect, to endow them with extraordinary attributes and place them into special settings. The view of the world smitten at Beethoven's feet, of definite exhibitionism—this Pluto ruling the 7th hugging the Midheaven—is *not* Beethoven, who was called a misanthrope even at age ten; who, when asked to play the piano at social gatherings, even those of his patrons, would fly into a rage, stomp out of the room and go home, whose music was often performed in cold, dimly lit, sparsely attended concert halls, whose symphonies were initially found shocking, who did not always attract the audience we picture for him. In short, he did not traffic the world opulently. He would enter a Bierstube (tavern), take a seat in a distant corner, do nothing but think all alone for several hours, and then *un*thinkingly offer to pay for a meal he never had! If he ordered a meal and the waiter made a mistake, he would disgustedly hurl the food back at the waiter!

Pluto is magnificently positioned here and superbly aspected; there is no tension in sight! *Pluto is the only referent to relationships, to the 7th House.* As we shall see, Beethoven's life was completely distressed by relationship problems. Our rectification will have to show this emphatically and offer an explanation through the symbology.

Beethoven's life was outwardly "so uneventful, yet so full of inner pathos." All of this became "inextricably blended with the particular qualities of his music to produce a composite image which fascinated the age of Romanticism."[23]

I am uncomfortable with this Venus peregrine in the 10th House: Beethoven's Venus-concerns running wild *through or within the profession?* These Venus issues, concerns (needs) in Capricorn would have been delayed in maturation and fulfillment, be unrequited somehow (chronically, as we know from his life). Twelfth House maybe, but not the 10th! Impossible.

And could Saturn retrograde really be the ruler of this Midheaven, this leadership of music history, comprised of sounds of rebellion and heroism and an "Ode to Joy"?

And, very important now in our study of development, *this Taurus-rising chart does not allow major Solar Arcs to angles* to transpire significantly during Beethoven's lifetime of gigantic achievement and jagged change.[24] For example, Uranus can never arc to an

---

23 The New Grove, 149–150.

24 Please see Tyl, *Prediction in Astrology*; Tyl, *Synthesis & Counseling*, sections beginning 204, 327, 392.

opposition with the Midheaven; Pluto can never square the Sun nor reach the Ascendant; Neptune reaches the 7th only in Beethoven's last years of life when relationships were no longer important in his make-up.

The Midheaven does significantly seem to arc to an opposition with Saturn, a square to Uranus, and opposition with Neptune. But this is Pluto more than it is the MC (since the conjunction arcs together)!

Additionally, major transits to these angles in this chart *do not correspond* to major events in Beethoven's life with drama and clarity, yet Beethoven's life is completely angular and sharply delineated with powerful turns of destiny. It is a life of distinct eras, clearly etched in his personal history of activity. This chart appears divined with only minimal reference to the *development* of Beethoven's life potentials within life time.

What about these major developments: the almost twenty-three-year-old pianist deciding to make his get-away to Vienna [the composer's Mecca] early in November 1792, as his father lay dying, never to return? Wouldn't a transit of Uranus conjunct the 7th cusp fit in here? It does, as we shall see with another birth time. How about Beethoven's tortured confrontation with his incipient deafness in the epic *Heiligenstadt Letter* at age thirty? Wouldn't transiting Neptune square the Ascendant, transiting Saturn simultaneously conjunct the Ascendant, and SA Pluto simultaneously conjunct the Ascendant fit in? They do, as we shall see with a different Ascendant.

An apparently innocuous, self-aggrandizing—yet clearly self-delineating—brace of references caught my eye especially in my studies, and spoke volumes to put me on the track of Beethoven's Ascendant tonality: "From my earliest childhood my zeal to serve our poor suffering humanity in any way whatsoever by means of my art has made no compromise with any lower motive" ... "Since I was a child my greatest happiness and pleasure have been to be able to do something for others"... "Never, never will you find me dishonorable. Since my childhood I have learnt to love virtue—and everything beautiful and good."[25]

Beethoven had *no such sentiment* as a youth: he had no time away from music practice, he had severe home life problems, he was deeply withdrawn ("misanthrope," remember?) and, by his own

---

25 Solomon, 36.

description, he was "melancholic." Additionally, I have not uncovered *any* act of altruism and kindness at any time in his life.

In these thoughts of Beethoven, *we are hearing his Sagittarian love of virtue and Nature* (the latter so powerfully and frequently expressed throughout his life, and every afternoon when he took long, long walks, and practically every summer spent in the countryside; his reading of philosophy) built up by buttresses of the so-called Enlightened Thought prevalent in the socio-political climate of his late teenage years. Whenever Beethoven remembered back into his life, it was always with such *self-aggrandizing* twists as these thoughts reveal, to ennoble his being, his birth, i.e., to inflate and continue the defense organization of his Family Romance.

I have listed many keyword concepts that are repeatedly used to describe Beethoven in the biographical literature. These sentiments I have just quoted—indeed, sentiments of how *he wished he really was* (Ascendant?)—augment and self-consciously try to overcompensate for or balance this list most significantly: forceful of character, quarrelsome, outrageously fascinating, magnetic, impatient, dramatic, intense, eccentric, idiosyncratic, incoherent, radical and still more radical, demanding, heroic, titanic, turbulent, new and even newer, creating new forms, bewilderingly original, innovative, witty, untamed, mischievous, extreme, explosive, lunatic, sublimely mad.[26]

These describers are obviously, decidedly *Uranian*. His own aggrandizing sentiments about himself most definitely embrace the Aquarian sense as well, at a lofty level. Additionally—and remarkably, considering how difficult Beethoven was to be with and to deal with—Beethoven continuously had a large outreach of friends. Without trying, he fascinated and endeared himself to men and women of

---

26 Schindler wrote: "His head, which was unusually large, was covered with long, bushy gray hair, which, being always in a state of disorder, gave a certain wildness to his appearance. This wildness was not a little heightened when he suffered his beard to grow to a great length, as he frequently did."

The story of his arrest by the Wiener Neustadt (Vienna New-City) police in 1821 or 1822 on the grounds that he had been peering into windows and looked like a tramp was surely widely circulated.

"In the taverns and restaurants he would dicker with waiters about the price of each roll, or would ask for his bill without having eaten. On the street, his broad gestures, loud voice, and ringing laugh made Karl (his nephew) ashamed to walk with him, and caused passersby to take him for a madman. Street urchins mocked the stumpy and muscular figure, with his low top hat of uncertain shape, who walked Vienna's streets dressed in a long, dark-colored overcoat which reached nearly to his ankles, carrying a double lorgnette or a monocle and pausing repeatedly to make hieroglyphic entries in his notebook as he hummed and howled in an off-key voice." Solomon, 257, vignettes similarly reported in all sources.

many sorts. "Even when he was often wretchedly ill and his deafness was impenetrable, there was competition for the privilege of rendering him services, and devoted friends were never far off."[27]

Without any doubt or hesitancy whatsoever, the Uranian/Aquarian sense abounds in the study of indomitably Sagittarian Beethoven. What does this begin to suggest?

The word "beautiful" (a Taurus or Libra word, to be sure) is rarely encountered in relation to Beethoven's music, or, for that matter, to *anything* about Beethoven. The "Moonlight" Sonata was heralded for its avant-garde escape from the traditions of sonata form inherited from Mozart and Haydn more than it was for the romantic mood it established; and the sublime lyricism of the second movement of his "Grand Sonata Pathetique" is lost in the innovation of the sonata's whole idiosyncratic form.[28] We have to wait until one of his last string quartets to hear clear talk about *beauty*.

Beethoven would even *deride his audience for feeling emotion(!)*, another part of his denial to others of what was unreachable for him, as we shall see vividly in this chapter. The expert musician, pianist, and teacher Carl Czerny wrote of Beethoven's extraordinary effect upon audiences (indeed including one of the rare mentions of "beauty"):

> In whatever company he might chance to be, he knew how to produce such an effect upon every hearer that frequently not an eye remained dry, while many would break out into loud sobs; for there was something wonderful in his expression in addition to the beauty and originality of his ideas and his spirited style of rendering them. After ending an improvisation of this kind he would burst into loud laughter and banter his hearers on the emotion he had caused in them. "You are fools!" he would say ... "Who can live among such spoiled children!" he would cry.[29]

Beethoven was frequently criticized as being a poor melodist. Few of us can hum or whistle a Beethoven tune, if you will—except

---

27 The New Grove, 139.

28 These Sonatas became very, very popular immediately upon public presentation. According to music editor Joseph Banoweitz (in the General Words & Music Co. edition of the Pathetique), Beethoven regretted naming this work this way, "for he came to regard all his works as 'pathetic,' or having pathos and strong emotion."

29 Solomon, 58.

perhaps Da-Da-Da Da, which is a rhythmic motif used as a melody; and a flash of the frenetic "Ode to Joy" from the final movement of the Ninth Symphony—rather, one feels, senses, is aroused by, surrenders to the extraordinary, to the Beethoven style of dramatic statement. Through Beethoven's music, we become aware that there is another realm beyond our experience, that he has recreated it for us and that its gates are opening to reveal it magnificently.

What are we getting to feel here? Arch individualism, a rebel with the cause to create.

Beethoven was dedicated to the ethics (Sagittarius) of political liberty and personal excellence (Aquarius): "To do good whenever one can, to love liberty above all else, never to deny the truth, even though it be before the throne."

And yet, Beethoven could write: "The devil take you. I refuse to hear anything about your whole moral outlook. *Power* is the moral principle of those who excel others, and it is also mine." (Pluto leading the defensive structure.)

His *Eroica*, Symphony Number 3, was a personalization of political ideals. It was conceived as a tribute to the revolutionary hero of the age, Napoleon, and was dedicated to him. But when Napoleon proclaimed himself emperor, Beethoven flew into a rage and, according to Ferdinand Ries, Beethoven's friend (see Bibliography with Wegeler), cried out: "Is he [Napoleon] then, too, nothing more than an ordinary human being? Now he, too, will trample on all the rights of man and indulge only his ambition. He will exalt himself above all others, become a tyrant!" Beethoven then went to his desk, took the title page of the Symphony and tore it in two. He rewrote the first page as *Sinfonia Eroica*.[30] This is Beethoven's sense of individual ascendancy over tyranny; it is confused, volcanic, and repeated often in his life. In fact, the musically scholarly New Grove presentation of the story even suggests that the *Eroica* was conceived by Beethoven *as a tribute to Beethoven himself.*[31]

We see Beethoven as a powerhouse of Uranian impulse, eccentricity, and innovation. We see him fighting his way out of a household of rigor and misery, leaving it all behind, championing new ideas, and knowingly creating a new world of music. We see this

---

30 Ibid., 132, and most other sources.
31 New Grove, 109.

gigantic focus of individualism as a Plutonic defense function (empowerment) that was formidable. No one could bar the way. Here is the Grand Trine working among the outer planets, related by the Neptune square with the Moon (vision) into his inner ethical, truth-loving, Nature-worshipping Sagittarian core.

Wouldn't an *Aquarian* Ascendant *reinforce* all of this, align the parental axis to capture Beethoven's early realities and adjust the angles for the arcs and transits of development that etched Beethoven into world history? Wouldn't a birth near midday with an Aquarian Ascendant put Venus peregrine into the 12th to help us "see" his lifelong inability to find love, to yearn for the ideal, the private sense of beauty that seeded extraordinary creative upset of tradition? Wouldn't the Aquarian Ascendant establish nobility on the 7th through Leo, place Neptune there for public masking, put Saturn retrograde there as well, all again showing the consummate difficulty with relationship? Wouldn't the older archetypal rulership of Aquarius by Saturn loom important? Might the arcs of development then capture Beethoven's spiked footholds upon his private mountain?

All biographical sources point out that the years 1800–1802 marked extraordinary advance in Beethoven's career. It was the time of personal crisis as well. While each year brought forth a cluster of masterpieces and a "Beethoven fever" among connoisseurs, Beethoven at age thirty to thirty-two had to face *the appalling discovery that he who had already changed the history of music was going deaf.*

... Now let us pause ... that pause that always comes in the rectification hunt, just before important, conclusive decision.... In 1800–1802, Beethoven was thirty to thirty-two years old. Born in the winter month of December with a "fast Sun," his Solar Arc development would be very close to 1 degree for one year of life.[32] So, let's make a cursory test of the arc of 30–32 degrees, one sign and two more degrees. It is very easy. Put a pencil in your hand and look at Figure 1, the noon chart for December 16, 1770, repeated on page 324.

In rectification, it is always advisable to test the heaviest arcs and transits to angles and work from there to more subtle

---

32 Tyl, *Prediction*; Tyl, *Synthesis & Counseling*, sections beginning 204, 327, and 392.

measurements. If we advance natal Pluto by 32 degrees (Beethoven in 1800–02), we come to 18 Aquarius 34. If we advance Neptune 32 degrees, we come to 15 Libra 59. Note those positions carefully somewhere.

Now, let us imagine that Solar Arc Pluto actually did come to Beethoven's Ascendant at age thirty to thirty-two, i.e., to 18–19 Aquarius. At that *same* time, SA Neptune would have advanced to square with natal Pluto's position in 16 Capricorn. This is a very important confluence of arc measurements. We must always look

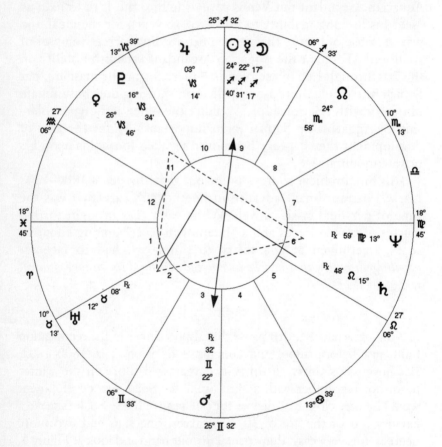

Figure 1
Beethoven/Planetary Orientation
Dec. 16, 1770, 12:00 P.M. LMT
Bonn, Germany
07E05 50N44
Placidus Houses

for this type of grouping in rectification tries, especially involving the angles. Simultaneity.

At that age, thirty to thirty-two, Beethoven would be coming out of his Saturn transit-return. With an Aquarian Ascendant, transiting Saturn would be just leaving natal Saturn and possibly be *opposing* the conjectured Ascendant at 18–19 Aquarius (i.e., Saturn in 18–19 Leo conjunct the imagined 7th cusp)! Think that through; let your mind anticipate that movement. See it.

We have established an important lead tying Beethoven's planetary arrangement at birth to a specifically timed development in his life. That lead is the axis 18–19 Aquarius-Leo.

Let's check *another* set of events against this lead. Look into your 1770–1827 Ephemeris with me.[33] When did *transiting* Pluto cross this new hypothetical Ascendant of 16–19 Aquarius (allowing for the strong orb of application)?[34] Pluto made that transit between *March 1787 and January 1791*, an enormously powerful transit as we know—and an extraordinarily important four-year time period in Beethoven's life. Here is what happened:

✦ In April 1787, at age sixteen and one-half, Beethoven journeyed for his first time to Vienna. He was sent there by the Elector as Bonn's extraordinary virtuoso pianist. He was to play for the consummate genius Mozart (born January 27, 1756 at 8:00 P.M. LMT in Salzburg, Austria[35]) and perhaps take some lessons.

Mozart biographer Woodford records that Mozart, though very busy with the composition of his opera *Don Giovanni*, did receive the "short, stocky, dark sixteen-year-old Beethoven." Mozart is said by sources to have been impressed, but, contrary to some romanticized interpretations, nothing lavishly romantic or

---

33 The Matrix Blue Star program generates any ephemeris for any length of time. Beethoven's lifetime ephemeris was ready within sixty seconds.

34 There is no doubt that the *application* of planets to aspects with angles (and, indeed, other planets) correlates with manifestation in real life very strongly, often more strongly than when the aspect is exact or separating. This is especially observable with the slower moving transiting planets (and the application of Solar Arcs); change takes time. Orb reflects that time. Astrology's measurements must encompass conception, build-up, action, and reorientation within change. Please see Tyl: *Synthesis and Counseling in Astrology*, section beginning 379, "Time Orbs."

35 Please see my analysis of Mozart's horoscope with reference to the outer planet alignment in Tyl-ed.: *How to Personalize the Outer Planets*, "When the Three were not There."

prophetic was said. Mozart and Beethoven never met again; Mozart died just four years later (December 5, 1791).[36]

But almost immediately after his arrival in Vienna, Beethoven learned by post from his father that his mother's consumptive condition had worsened; Beethoven was to return to Bonn at once. The young man brought back no success at all; nothing but debts.[37]

> ✦Beethoven's mother died July 17, 1787 (transiting Pluto still on the Aquarian Ascendant, *with Secondary Progressed Moon exactly at 17 Leo*, opposed the hypothetical Ascendant; SP Mars retrograde *exactly opposed the Moon*). This event critically affected Beethoven's entire life, not for any emotional reason, but because of his ensuing *ascendancy within the family*.

As Solomon points out strategically,[38] "after a parent's death, the child's relationship to the surviving parent usually undergoes a radical change, and often there is a desperate pathetic attempt by the survivors to put the child in the place of the missing parent. It was now Beethoven rather than Maria Magdalena who was in charge of the family finances."[39]

Young Ludwig, just sixteen and one-half, now took over from his mother the job of keeping together the family of an alcoholic father and two brothers. He who barely knew arithmetic was in charge of monies. He had to intervene with the police who wanted to put father Johann into custody. Beethoven became his father's guardian! Solomon says that this did Johann in and that he "largely gave up his grip upon reality, living a narcotized existence."

> ✦On November 20, 1789 (still with transiting Pluto on the Aquarian Ascendant), Beethoven audaciously petitioned the Elector that one-half the payments for his father be paid

---

36 And Beethoven's work was never compared with Mozart's. The two geniuses were so totally different. Mozart (and aging Hadyn, with whom Beethoven tried to study for one year upon his final arrival in Vienna in 1792–93) was the exemplar of the Classical form of the eighteenth century. Beethoven changed the form of music; he created the Romantic Period, not with lush loveliness, but with dramatic, heroic emotion and the expression of freedom. Comparison was almost impossible since the musical languages were so different.

37 Solomon, 29.

38 Maynard Solomon is reputedly one of the world's most renowned Beethoven scholars. He is also the editor of the book *Myth, Creativity, Psychoanalysis*.

39 Solomon, 29.

instead to him (transiting Saturn was precisely at 16 Leo!; Mars was conjoined as well one week earlier). Solomon points out that Beethoven knew this amounted to "patricide." Imagine the transformation of Beethoven's life perspective, the demoralization within the darkening family circle. Look at the empowerment of the young man which coincided with the Pluto transit of the Ascendant. Imagine the lessons he would learn.

✦ As well, a sudden sustained burst of creative work began late in 1789—with particularly glowing public notices as an improvisor at the piano—and continued for two years until his final departure from Bonn to Vienna three years later.

There simply is no doubt that our first tests with the arcs and transits involving extraordinary times in Beethoven's early life *bring the area of 18–19 Aquarius-Leo forward as a tenable Ascendant-Descendant axis.*

One very important life-observation and astrological insight seals the package in my opinion: in the eighteenth century, pianists (clavierists and harpsichordists originally) established their fame in two ways, through technique (the ability to play adroitly, acrobatically, communicatively) and through *improvisation* (the inspiration of playing spontaneously, "by ear" as we say, creating entire compositions "on the spot," creating original variations on established themes, much as jazz musicians do today).

Beethoven's earliest fame and, indeed, how he became celebrated in his first years in Vienna, was through his virtuoso piano playing and most dramatically *through his skill at improvisation.* It was simply overwhelming what new sounds and treatments of music Beethoven brought out of the piano. Such improvisation had never been heard. Special pianos were made for him to give even more sound and to sustain his fierce playing!

There were more than 300 accomplished pianists in Vienna when Beethoven arrived in the world's music capital, and it is estimated that there were some 6,000 students studying the piano there. Beethoven feared that other pianists might hear him extemporize and then copy down the "several peculiarities of my style and palm them off with pride as their own."[40]

---

40 Ibid., 58.

There is no way not to see Beethoven throughout more than the first half of his life as a pianist and improvisor first and a composer second, as even a "student of composition." He studied with Haydn and Salieri and others for little gain; his "mistakes" in the Classical way were continuous. But he was a consummate virtuoso performer of brilliance and power that the world had never heard. For contrast and ego aggrandizement, Beethoven would imitate the fashionably sweet and delicate style of earlier virtuosos, their "cloying and effeminate manner," and then profoundly change worlds for his listeners. When he played, he always brought the house down!

All of this is *Aquarian*, not Taurean. The archetype of Taurus has the unmistakable component of keeping things as they are, as they should be, to establish unchanging, secure, safe structures. Beethoven was consummately *the opposite:* daring, dramatic, rebellious, independent, changing, and inventive to the utmost! Uranus rising in *Taurus* is not enough to correlate with the veritable avalanche of idiosyncrasy one meets in Beethoven's life, in his every musical and spoken utterance.

Uranian *rulership* of an Aquarian Ascendant, on the other hand, fits like a glove: the Solar Arc Uranus moving on from birth to square the 18–19 Aquarius-Leo horizon with transiting Uranus *simultaneously* opposing his Midheaven at age seven when he gave his first concert; transiting Uranus opposing the Sun at age ten to eleven when he *outgrew* his father's teaching and began study with the most influential Gottlob Neefe, whom he succeeded as court organist a year and a half later(!); the transiting Uranus that traveled across the 7th cusp as Beethoven prepared his trip to Vienna, to the great public, to fame ... and so much more.

Uranus, Beethoven's patron planet: in his life positioned in Taurus, channeling the individualism of genius, creativity and improvisation *into* the newest structures conceivable, the structures that reframed the world of music differently than ever before. Uranus in Taurus, ruling the Aquarian Ascendant, *changing* form.

Figure 5 (page 330) shows Ludwig van Beethoven's horoscope born on December 16, 1770 at 11:03 A.M., LMT, in Bonn, Germany, establishing the tonality of Beethoven's life. The Ascendant at 19 Aquarius 08 now joins the Sun and the Moon to complete the chord.

Immediately we see the extraordinary tension axis of the triple conjunction opposed by Mars *within the parental axis*. We see the take-charge Moon in the 10th House; there is a focus on profession that is complete, except for the suggestion of psychodynamic counterpoint underneath it all, which we see in the retrogradation of Mars. And immediately we can suspect the bailiwick of this counterpoint, this anxiety: Mars rules the self-worth 2nd, tremendous anxiety about who he was as a person, his genius born not noble. Beethoven disruptively refused to play at so many parties and refused many, many gifts, because he wanted to be appreciated for himself, not as Beethoven the gifted pianist. He wrote: "Am I then nothing more than a music maker for yourself or others?"[41] But Beethoven did not have any other identity! So much self-worth anxiety smoldered in the depressing and punitive shadows of early childhood, was reconstructed through the Neptunian concept of the Family Romance (see page 306), and was volcanically discharged into the unfulfillable idealism that birthed his majestic art.

There is the Saturn retrograde on the Descendant, ruling the 12th, suggesting tremendous development difficulties on the relationship level, echoing the Mars counterpoint, pinpointing his interrelationships with his father, perhaps designating the Leonine nature of Beethoven's *inner* nobility. Its square from Uranus, ruler of the Ascendant, immediately suggests so powerfully that Beethoven would have to break with the old, leave the family dross behind and break into new forms of life experience in order to be free; holding the picture of his grandfather dear for an entire lifetime, erasing his painful father experience completely. His talent would break free from the limitations of the past.

The counterpoint of Uranus' retrogradation also links it to the substratum of Beethoven's psychological complex driving him up, up, and away to super freedom, independence, igniting the fires of the Family Romance. The retrograde Neptune in the 7th shows the public focus of the entire pretense of lineage, the essential mask of superiority feelings (motivated by and augmented through Saturn retrograde in Leo), and the identification of Beethoven as a "romantic" (certainly unreal on a personal level), as founder of the Romantic Era in music; Uranus, Neptune, and Pluto monumentally defending the identity through extraordinary power in terms of fantasy, imagination, creativity, presenting the self through the profession, *through the conduit of Neptune to the Moon, to Mercury, to Sun in the 10th.*

---

41 Ibid., 63–64.

Neptune always corresponds to something other than it seems, and here it is focused in public projection, within the center of Beethoven's sanity-saving Family Romance. Note that it is a co-ruler of Beethoven's Ascendant: Aquarius and Pisces, Uranus and Neptune. Through his nobility pretense in public projection (the 7th), Beethoven could identify with the mighty, share the insignia of supremacy and "conquer the nobility by pretending" to be so. Beethoven constantly assumed and asserted equality with the aristocrats. [Please recall the Egyptian wisdom so dear to Beethoven:

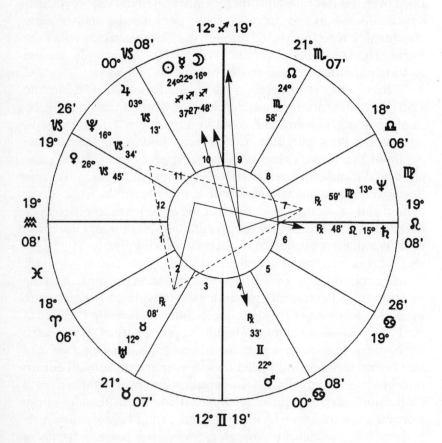

Figure 5
Beethoven
Dec. 16, 1770, 11:03 A.M. LMT
Bonn, Germany
07E05 50N44
Placidus Houses

"No Mortal Man has lifted my Veil," page 310]. Additionally, Neptune squares the Midheaven, a reliable, popular part of the signature of musicality.

The Sun and Mercury rule the 7th, holding Neptune retrograde, which squares these significators of the 7th. The extraordinary developmental tension among parental background, professional ascendancy, opinionation, social pretense, relationship difficulty, and psychological complex is symbolically and realistically undeniable.

There is Jupiter peregrine in the 11th, the admiring circle of friends who were always there in spite of Beethoven himself, the demand for recognition through publishing and payment for his works (the 11th is the second of the 10th); contrasting with the anxiety about finances that was eternally with Beethoven, suggested by Mars rulership of the 2nd, holding Uranus, and Mars tension with the core of Beethoven's personality.

As we can expect, Jupiter in Capricorn is easily manifested as exploitation, using others for one's personal good. I think this side of the expansive, opportunistically driven, self-administrating Jupiter in Capricorn is seen most openly when Jupiter is peregrine, when the need thrust is not modified by aspect contact with other need structures and energies. This particular Jupiter position in the 11th clearly suggests such an exploitation of friends, even a supercilious disdain for them. At age thirty-one, cresting in his popularity in Vienna, referring to two of his friends, Beethoven wrote: "[they are] merely instruments on which to play when I feel inclined ... I value them merely for what they do for me."[42] Solomon tends to excuse this attitude, i.e., not to take it literally, but to see in such utterances "the strengthening of a narcissistic tendency [the common foil for the Saturn retrograde phenomenon] which was, I believe, a necessary precondition for the formation of Beethoven's sense of mission and, consequently, of his 'heroic' style." Beethoven *needed* to see himself high and mighty, noble, above all others.

And there is Venus in Capricorn, peregrine in the 12th, echoing the absence of Water-family accent, symbolizing an all-too-private sense of beauty, a lost soul in terms of relationships with a beloved, an idealized infatuation with the unattainable. Every woman Beethoven pursued in his lifetime was either already married or so

---

42 Ibid., 86; additionally, Beethoven referred to his audience as "the rabble."

young as to be unattainable or absolutely not interested in him. He suffered. He sublimated. He discharged his pathos in the clenched fists, gnashed teeth, and burning eyes of his music.[43]

Beethoven wrote so much of this sentiment in May of 1810, with transiting Saturn exactly upon his Moon, with transiting Pluto exactly square his Moon, and Solar Arc Moon conjunct his pained Venus: "Thus I can only seek support in the deepest, the most intimate part of myself; as for the external world, there is absolutely nothing there for me. No, nothing but injuries for me in friendship and feelings of the same genre."[44]

Additionally, Venus is the ruler of the 3rd, and we shall see how Beethoven's idealistic Family Romance finally exploded in relation to his brother (3rd House) and *his* son, Karl (the 5th House of the 3rd, i.e., the 7th House once again!).

Venus rules Libra on the 8th, part of one's sexuality profile indeed, along with the 5th, suggesting again the unrequited love and unanswered overtures made by Beethoven to many women. But there was that one lady, *"die unsterbliche Geliebte,"* Beethoven's "Immortal Beloved," with a most surprising astrological link with the master! We will study this in detail.

The Aries Point of a horoscope is defined by the intersection and widest diversion points of two Great Circles, the Ecliptic and the Equator. The geometry of it all establishes 0 Libra as the cusp of the rising sign or Ascendant of the Earth.[45] When a planet is placed at 0 degree of any Cardinal Sign *it is conjunct or square or opposed the Aries Point*, and the planet's symbolism is given an undeniable *thrust into public view*. There is the potential of public projection for the person in terms of the planet, point, or midpoint configured with the Aries Point (see Midpoint table, page 333).

At this birth time, the midpoint of Uranus/Ascendant at 0 degrees 38' of a Cardinal Sign (Aries) is 38' of arc from exact conjunction with the Aries Point! This is an enormously strong statement of personal, Uranian, idiosyncratic public projection. It is further determination of what we know of Beethoven. Precisely.

---

43 We shall see that Venus, by Secondary Progression, assumed retrograde motion when Beethoven was three and a half (when his beloved grandfather died) and went direct in 1816, when Beethoven was forty-six, coincidental with the accumulated Solar Arc semi-square.

44 Autexier, 63.

45 Please see Tyl, *Synthesis & Counseling in Astrology*, section beginning 312.

LUDWIG VAN BEETHOVEN DEC 16, 1770

Midpoint Sort: 90° Dial

♅/Asc	000°38'	♀/♃	014°59'	♆/Mc	028°09'	♀/♆	050°22'	♆	073°59'	♃/Mc	082°46'
☽/♇	001°41'	Mc/Asc	015°44'	☽/♆	030°23'	☊	054°58'	♃/☊	074°05'	☉/☿	083°32'
♃	003°13'	☽/♄	016°18'	♄/♇	031°11'	♅/Mc	057°14'	♅/♇	074°21'	☉/♂	083°35'
☿/♇	004°31'	♇	016°34'	♇/Asc	032°51'	☽/♅	059°28'	☽/Mc	074°34'	☉	084°37'
♀/Mc	004°32'	☽/Asc	017°58'	☿/♆	033°13'	♄/♆	059°54'	☽	076°48'	☽/♃	085°00'
♂/♇	004°33'	☿/♄	019°08'	♂/♆	033°16'	♆/Asc	061°34'	☿/Mc	077°23'	♀/☊	085°51'
♄/☊	005°23'	♂/♄	019°10'	☉/♆	034°18'	☿/♅	062°18'	♂/Mc	077°26'	☿/♃	087°50'
☉/♇	005°36'	♆/☊	019°28'	♀/♄	036°17'	♂/♅	062°21'	☉/Mc	078°28'	♂/♃	087°53'
☽/♀	006°46'	☉/♄	020°13'	♀/Asc	037°57'	☉/♅	063°23'	♀/♅	079°27'	☉/♃	088°55'
☊/Asc	007°03'	☿/Asc	020°48'	♃/♆	038°36'	☊/Mc	063°39'	☽/☿	079°37'	♄/♅	088°58'
☿/♀	009°36'	♂/Asc	020°51'	♅	042°08'	☽/☊	065°53'	☽/♂	079°40'	♇/Mc	089°27'
♀/♂	009°39'	♀/♇	021°40'	♆/♇	045°17'	♃/♅	067°41'	☽/☉	080°42'		
♃/♇	009°53'	☉/Asc	021°53'	♄	045°48'	☿/☊	068°42'	♇/☊	080°46'		
☉/♀	010°41'	♃/♄	024°31'	♄/Asc	047°28'	♂/☊	068°45'	☿	082°27'		
♅/♆	013°04'	♃/Asc	026°11'	♅/☊	048°33'	☉/☊	069°47'	☿/♂	082°30'		
♄/Mc	014°04'	♀	026°45'	Asc	049°08'	Mc	072°19'	♂	082°33'		

The midpoint of Pluto/Midheaven, signifying reference to life's ultimate power position, is also related to the Aries Point from 29 Sagittarius 27 (i.e., 0 Capricorn), another corroboration of Beethoven's dominating professional posture, his fame.

Further midpoint pictures of importance include Saturn square the midpoint of Neptune/Pluto,[46] suggesting much grief, weakness, torment. By rulership, Neptune and Saturn bring relationships into this gloomy picture, and Pluto keys the 11th, love received, ruling the 9th, communication from others.

Beethoven's Pluto=Moon/Saturn suggests isolation, the repression of personal needs.

This horoscope clearly captures the planetary potentials within Beethoven's life reality. The Ascendant and Midheaven within Midpoint pictures are consonant with expectations as well. Now we must test the time of development through Solar Arcs, Secondary Moon Progressions, and major transits in relation most particularly to the angles of the horoscope, the determinators of the where and when in life, in parallel with the key experiences shaping Beethoven's life.

46 Any planet conjunct, opposed, square, semisquare or sesquiquadrate to the midpoint of any two planets or planet and point is said to equal (=) the other two reference points, i.e., Saturn=Neptune/Pluto. This equation is called a Midpoint Picture. Ibid., section beginning 303.

Beethoven's Development: His Fame and Pain

Biographers organize Beethoven's life work into three periods: the first one ending around 1802, the second ending about 1812, and a "transcendent" third period lasting from 1813 to 1827. They all agree—and so does this astrologer—that a very close relationship exists between Beethoven's creative energies and output and his emotional life and experience. In fact, they suggest that such enormous musical developments apparently *had to have parallel crises in the personal life*. Solomon begins his eleventh chapter with the heading "Crisis and Creativity—The years 1800 and 1801 marked an important advance in Beethoven's career."

Our astrology for this epic transition from his early years into the period of the hero revolves around prominent measurement groups that are very easy to see and analyze. These groups conspicuously involve the "new" angles we have determined in our rectification and, in parallel with dramatic manifestations of events in Beethoven's life, will work to prove our deductions.

Figure 6 (page 337) shows Beethoven's birth horoscope in the inner circle with the Solar Arcs for December 1802 in the outer ring. The year 1802 signifies *the end* of the first life-period. Noted in the 12th House is the Secondary Progressed New Moon for mid-1801 responding to SA Uranus opposed MC (Uranus=MC) which took place (along with SA Moon=Pluto) in July 1800, *at the beginning* of the transition time between periods. Stimulus, Vision, Change; one era ended, a new begun.[47]

Crossing the Descendant and leaving the 7th and 8th Houses are notations of the distance transited by Saturn, Uranus, and Neptune, respectively, during the two and one-half-year period of transition.

Finally, embracing all measurements, there is the gigantic Solar Arc of Pluto conjunct the Ascendant, applying powerfully throughout 1800–1801 and becoming exact in November–December 1802, at the same time that SA Neptune would square Pluto. All the other measurements take place within this enormous mark of time. All the measurements have come together in relation to one another at the time we have chosen for Beethoven's birth.

---

47 In the Secondary Progressed horoscope for Beethoven's birthday in 1800 (SP date January 15, 1771), Jupiter is tightly conjunct the Midheaven in 10 Capricorn, trined by Uranus, and the SP New Moon would take place six months later in June, 1801, from the 10th House square the SP Ascendant. This is even further corroboration of this epic success-time in Beethoven's career life, his coming of age, if you will.

Corroboration of this epic astrological period is obvious in Beethoven's life. Beethoven's vision, expression, medium, style, and posture in music changed dramatically and, at the same time, the torture within the Family Romance became exposed in shattering fashion. This period saw new energies of pain sublimated into creativity and fame (SP New Moon conjunct the problematic Venus in the 12th). There was tremendous "drive and determination toward success; a love of individual freedom; changing fortunes; dramatic adjustment of job status; sudden change of direction in every department of life; arch individuality; relocations"[48] (SA Uranus= MC with transiting Uranus square the Sun).

Beethoven gave his first concert "for his own benefit" on April 2, 1800, in Vienna's Burgtheater, a very important event signifying his "emergence as a major creative personality" in Vienna.[49] He was his own master, now clearly distanced from Haydn (with whom he had studied tempestuously and unappreciatively for a little over a year, the relationship ending in January 1794). Now, in 1800, Haydn was published as saying that Beethoven "writes [composes] more and more fantastically" all the time.[50] For such a Classical Period conservative as Haydn, the word "fantastically" is extraordinary indeed.

In this time period, Beethoven broke away, "was liberated" [note the Uranian term] from reliance upon the piano as the touchstone of his compositional style: he mastered the forms of string trios, quartets, and quintets (quartet with added viola).[51] This was very, very significant: this young virtuoso pianist—surely the finest the world knew at that time—now was instantly labeled master of new forms in the very music world he was transforming!

Beethoven changed his lodgings "almost as readily as his moods. The slightest provocation led him to pack his belongings, and at times it became difficult to find an apartment for so unreliable a lodger."[52] Biographers align his frequent moving at this time

---

48 Please see the "Solar Arc Directory," Tyl: *Synthesis & Counseling in Astrology*, Appendix; also Tyl: *Prediction in Astrology*.

49 Solomon, 111.

50 Solomon, 77.

51 Beethoven's String Quintet, op. 29, was written in 1800 and published in 1802. It is the acknowledged masterpiece in the genre, which medium he mastered in just two compositional efforts. Ibid., 101–102.

52 Ibid., 81.

with a peripatetic—and pathetic—search for home security and stability, for something in the external environment that would bring contentment to the inner spirit.

It is important to note, at this time, that Beethoven showed no signs of improved exterior polish, i.e., in contrast with his maturing professional style, Beethoven did *not* come of age socially in terms of proper clothing or manners. He was decidedly *un*mannerly in both appearance and behavior. He was rebelling in frustration of his unrequited loves; he appeared to flaunt his uniqueness; to claim exemption from the rules; changing the music world with every appearance and publication and yet never seeming to find an inner peace, to settle in, as it were. The Family Romance was manifested in this period of creativity and crisis as well (the New Moon, with the Sun upon the Venus time orb to partile was fifteen months, August 1802). Since he could not create his own family, he attempted to participate in the family life of others. This was the basic pattern of Beethoven's life almost all his years, attaching himself to a series of families as a surrogate son or brother, relying heavily on mother-figures in all situations and on all occasions. He searched constantly for an "ideal" family or a reasonable facsimile thereof,[53] and this quest became critical as we shall see, bordering upon dementia, in the four-year custody battle over his nephew, to make Karl *his son.*

In short, in this period musically, aged thirty to thirty-two, Beethoven took on the position of a mature master. The qualitative changes in his style of composition now illuminated what the sources call a "new path" (the measurements from Uranus). Also, in this period, on the level of personal well-being and satisfaction, Beethoven practically crumpled.

Note again in Figure 6 (page 337) that transiting Saturn crosses the Descendant (exact 5/1801) and, even more significantly and pervasively (since Neptune natally *squares* the Moon, Mercury and Sun), transiting Neptune squares the Ascendant January through April 1801 and again in November of that year and then, for the third, strongest time, between June and October 1802. As the Uranian and Plutonic Arcs establish Midheaven and Ascendant musically, these Saturnian and Neptunian transits *emphasize the rectified Ascendant on a personal level.* All these measurements operate within the

---

53 Ibid., 81.

background behemoth measurement of SA Pluto upon the Ascendant (exact 11/1802). Notice how these dates lead one into the other, like stepping stones across a stream. Time and development are punctuated in clusters of measurements and life activity.

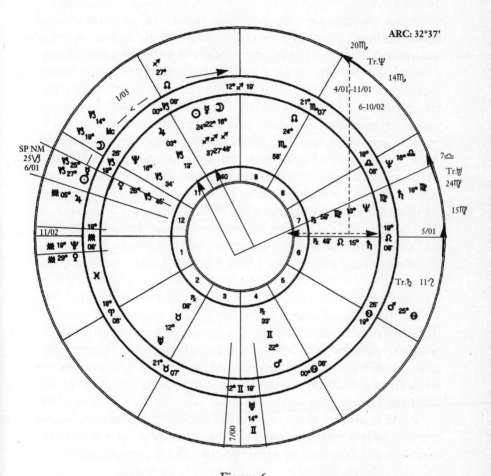

Figure 6

Inner Chart
Beethoven
Dec. 16, 1770, 11:03 A.M. LMT
Bonn, Germany
07E05   50N44

Outer Chart
Solar Arcs
Dec. 16, 1802

Placidus Houses

There is great upheaval and development suggested here. In correspondence to the Uranian emphases and the SP New Moon, we see great career advancement. Yet, with the accentuation of the Ascendant, we must ask about some deep, central weakness appearing within Beethoven, some personal debilitation as epic as his rise to fame.

Solomon records: "Beneath this surface of accomplishment, however, inner conflicts were converging to form a crisis of major proportions ... It is as though he were about to be destroyed by success itself."[54] We should see the enormity of this period also: here is Beethoven changing music history, near dementia with private torment, addressing the prospect of calamity as if fate and he were bartering together, *all at just thirty years of age!* Imagine that.

At this time, late in June 1801, exactly coincident with the SP New Moon, Beethoven wrote to his old friend Dr. Franz Wegeler (his eventual biographer) in Bonn a very famous letter. The letter is long, rambling, moody, and sick. He is asking his doctor friend for medical advice, and for the first time straight on and exposed, Beethoven speaks about his hearing becoming "weaker and weaker." He wrote, "For almost two years I have ceased to attend any social functions, just because I find it impossible to say to people: I am deaf."[55]

Beethoven mentions other symptoms that he refers to as chronic, involving his abdomen ("wretched") and diarrhea ("constantly afflicted") and more. He speaks poignantly and also angrily of doctors who have tried to help cure these ailments, the failures of all their remedies, all except the taking of tepid baths.[56] In these anomalous ill-health descriptions, we can see the Natal Neptune square with the Moon, ruler of the 6th, the difficulty with diagnosis, the stomach, intestines, the remedies, the sense of personal tragedy. We can see the planet of deafness, Saturn, looming painfully, eternally large upon the horizon at birth, opposing the Ascendant, again cor-

---

54 Beethoven wrote to Baron Nikolaus von Zmeskall, his most constant Viennese friend, "Sometimes I feel that I shall soon go mad in consequence of my unmerited fame (2nd House anxiety); fortune is seeking me out and for that very reason I almost dread some fresh calamity." The letter is dated July, 1801, coincident with the debilitating personal pressures of this period.

55 Solomon, 112–113.

56 Beethoven was dependent on these baths, frequently every day. He would spill so much water onto the floor in accomplishing the baths that lodging keepers simply didn't want him around; they literally turned Beethoven away.

roborating the angles we have established. We see natal Saturn emphasized by transit in this period (as co-ruler with Uranus and Neptune of the Ascendant). We see the Ascendant deeply done in, while at the same time the Midheaven is uplifted by Uranus and the Sun (SA Sun semisquare the MC, exact 1/1803).

Strangely, after this admission of deafness to Wegeler—really the central purpose of the letter—Beethoven's condition seems to have improved.[57] While all our test measurements are still operable, we have Beethoven's next letter to Wegeler on November 16, 1801, saying that the humming and buzzing in his ears is somewhat less, that while deafness continues to be present, life is more pleasant, and that "this change has been brought about by a dear, charming girl who loves me and whom I love. After two years I am again enjoying a few blissful moments; and for the first time I feel that marriage might bring me happiness."[58]

The "dear, charming girl" was one of Beethoven's piano students, just sixteen years old! Here was Beethoven's Venus in Capricorn, peregrine in the 12th, reilluminated by the Progressed New Moon, and the application of SP SA Sun to conjunction with Venus exact in June 1802 (just seven months into the future, an arc of 35', tantamountly already partile), again presenting the vision of ideal love within Beethoven's Family Romance. Tragic. Sad. So desperately lonely. So self-deceiving (Natal Neptune in the 7th and the square with Moon-Mercury-Sun).

Meanwhile in this period, his work output continued to be prodigious; his publishing income at an all-time high.

To close this first grand period of Beethoven's life—the arcing Plutonic dimension omnipresent as dictatorial background during this two and one-half-year time span, "an extremely important time of life with dramatic changes of perspective, identity transformation, a life milestone,"[59] we see Beethoven once again ailing with his "malaise" in the spring of 1802, *his deafness driving his intense discontent with life*. On doctor's orders, he repaired to the quiet village of Heiligenstadt (City of the Holy Ones) and remained there for six months.

---

57 So often this happens, it seems: admitting a condition frees up the energies so long used in denying it! There is a restorative release of tension; e.g., symptoms disappear (momentarily) as one enters the doctor's office!

58 Solomon, 114.

59 "Solar Arc Analysis Directory," Tyl, *Synthesis & Counseling*, Appendix; also Tyl, *Prediction*.

Beethoven's swings between manic and melancholic behavior were extreme [and this is constantly the manifestation of the riveting focal point of Mars in Gemini opposed Moon-Mercury-Sun, and, as well, the counterpoint of the Mars retrogradation, the core of Beethoven's critical family issues and the cerebrated reaction to defend himself through isolation and the psychodynamic Family Romance]; and intense as well were his thoughts of suicide (an attack upon the Ascendant, of course). This was revealed in the famous *Heiligenstadt Letter* that Beethoven wrote to his two brothers on October 6 and 10, 1802, (SA Saturn=Mercury/ Neptune; SA Uranus=Moon/MC; SA Saturn=Mars/Neptune), fulfilling SA Pluto conjunct the Ascendant and SA Neptune square Pluto (exact just two months later in December 1802, an application arc of 10'; see data, page 345).

The long, long letter is full of pathos and self-dramatizing theatricality: for example, "But what a humiliation for me when someone standing next to me heard a flute in the distance and *I heard nothing*, or someone heard a *shepherd singing* and again I heard nothing. Such incidents drove me almost to despair; a little more of that and I would have ended my life—it was only my art that held me back." And, "Yet it was impossible for me to say to people, 'Speak louder, shout, for I am deaf.' Ah, how could I possibly admit an infirmity in the *one sense* which ought to be more perfect in me than in others, a sense which I once possessed in the highest perfection, a perfection such as few in my profession enjoy or ever have enjoyed." Beethoven rationalizes that his deafness is the sole cause of his discontent, his anxiety that had been bordering on panic for several years.

Very importantly, we can see a *psychological* testament being presented here in this letter as well. In the salutation, very boldly, Beethoven wrote: "FOR MY BROTHERS CARL AND _____ BEETHOVEN," and later: "You, my brothers Carl and _____ , as soon as I am dead ..." And finally: "For my brothers Carl and _____ to be read and executed after my death." In these three places, Beethoven left blank spaces for one of his brothers' name. Even in hundreds of references to this brother in his Conversation Books (books in which Beethoven wrote his thoughts and people wrote messages to him, since he could not hear them speak), Solomon reports that there are only *two incidences* in which the brother's name is written! Beethoven avoided, avoided,

LUDWIG VAN BEETHOVEN		
Solar Arc Midpoint Pictures for Jun 1, 1802 to Jul 1, 1803		Page 1
Jun 1802	☿ □ ♃/♄	Studying one's philosophy of life; a long trip; speaking with great maturity; studying hard; asking the right questions.
	☉ ☌ ♀	Romance; love relationship; illumination of one's sense of beauty; aesthetics; marriage; birth.
Jul 1802	Asc ⚼ ♀/♄	Hiding one's light; withdrawing; fear of not being accepted.
	Mc ∠ ☽/♅	Much excitement about ambition, potential gains; sudden changes of plans.
	☊ ⚼ ♅	Shared experiences are particularly rewarding.
Aug 1802	♂ ⚼ ☉/☊	Vigorous drives with others to gain personal importance.
	♀ ⚼ ♄/Mc	Improvement in job situation; dryness in relationships.
	♆ ☌ ☽/♄	Feelings of inferiority; melancholy.
Sep 1802	☽ □ ☿/♄	Emotional quandary; emotional indecision because of fear of losing; frustration; taxing learning process.
	☿ ∠ ☉/☊	Communications with others; business contacts; news; commentary.
	☽ ☍ ♂/♄	Moodiness; possible depression; feelings about losing something.
Oct 1802	♄ ∠ ☿/♆	A gloomy reaction to real or imagined circumstances; looking at the down side of things, which may not be valid.
	♅ ☍ ☽/Mc	High degree of emotional excitement; nervousness in reaction to changes; the sense of vocational instability or the threat of pending upset; anxiety.
	♄ ∠ ♂/♆	Being taken advantage of; reticence; the sense of futility; persevering in spite of fear.
Nov 1802	♃ ∠ ☽/☉	Happy relationship; enthusiasm for life; success.
	♃ ∠ ♇/☊	Forcing oneself into a power position; self-promotion; attaining success through others.
Dec 1802	Mc ⚼ ♄/♆	Peculiar loss of ambition; moodiness; giving up or capitulating to demands of the environment totally.
	♇ ☌ Asc	Extremely important time of life: dramatic changes of perspective are possible; identity transformation; geographic relocation; taking command of things; a life milestone.
	♆ □ ♇	The supernatural; other realms seem to be involved with life's occurrences; unusual problems; peculiar experiences; possible concerns about death matters; creative enterprise.
Jan 1803	Mc ☌ ♀/♃	Wonderment at the feelings of love and/or success.
	♄ □ ☉/Mc	Maturation through sobering experiences; refinement of ambition; learning from apparent mistakes.
	☽ □ ♆/☊	High sensitivity; feeling ostracized; being misunderstood.
	☉ ∠ Mc	Ego recognition; potential glory; usually successful; fulfillment.
	♀ ☌ ☽/♅	Excitability of emotions; sudden sexual activities; artistic creativity.
Mar 1803	☊ ☌ ☿/♃	Sociability; the exchange of thoughts with others; meetings.
Apr 1803	☊ □ ♂/♃	Cooperation with others; getting their support.
	♇ ∠ ♀/Mc	Tremendous focus on an artistic career; cultural exposure; publicity; emotional expression; love relationship.
May 1803	♃ □ ♀/♄	Learning respect for the status quo; keeping to oneself.
Jun 1803	♀ ☍ ♄/♆	Deluded love feelings; inhibitions; diminished emotional expression, sexual activity; unrequited love; longing for attention; lack of popularity; appreciated more by senior people.

©1992 Matrix Software, Big Rapids, MI   Text ©1991 Noel Tyl

avoided use of this brother's name. His only use of it was when he was forced to do so by legal prescriptions. We certainly can corroborate this with Venus rulership of the brother's 3rd House, with Venus peregrine in the 12th, *central to the defensive psychic substratum of the Family Romance.* This Venus begins to run away with the entire horoscope, as suggested by its peregrine state.

Beethoven was loathe to use the name of *Johann*, the younger of his two brothers, his father's namesake.[60] He could not inscribe that name, even in the most emotional and poignant letter of his lifetime, "Farewell and do not wholly forget me when I am dead; I deserve this from you, for during my lifetime I was thinking of you often [!] and of ways to make you happy."

60 Actually, Nikolaus Johann; called "Johann."

We can just imagine how deep the pain of the early home life was within Beethoven *that his father's name upon his brother's life aroused such feelings of avoidance and dread.* We can appreciate how powerfully important the Family Romance—the change of birth-date (which was repeated in its two-year error within the *Heiligenstadt Letter*) and the imagined nobility—*how essential* all of this was to keeping Beethoven sane, to keeping his creative energy explosively cathartic. We can appreciate why marriage was unattainable, why the "chain of sorrows" his mother spoke of when he was five should not be repeated.

In the grip of Pluto, Neptune, and Saturn; in the light of the New Moon and the illumination by Uranus, we have the portrait of the artist not only as Olympic hero but hermit in a private Hades. And we have ever strengthening corroboration of the 11:03 late morning birth time.

— ✦ —

The "heroic" period of Beethoven's life, beginning around 1802–03—after the manifestation of SA Uranus=MC and then SA Pluto=ASC, and the powerful transits of Saturn and Neptune to contact with the Ascendant—and lasting through the summer of 1812 gives us several undeniably clear and powerful arcs and transits with which to work further, not only to test the birth time again and again through the angles of the horoscope but also to reveal the continuing dramatic dimensions of Beethoven's genius life.

Figure 7 (page 343) shows Beethoven's horoscope in the inner circle and the Solar Arcs for December, 1812 in the outer ring, *marking the end of this second historical period.* Written in also are key transit positions during that time period: Pluto conjunct Neptune and square the Midheaven for two years (1807–1808), transiting Saturn crossing the Midheaven in 1810 and then transiting Neptune following across the Midheaven for a protracted period, 1811–1813.

Please refer back to Figure 6 (page 337): look at the Solar Arc position of the Midheaven in the 11th House at 14 Capricorn 56. This position for December 1802 is approaching conjunction with natal Pluto; the conjunction will take place in approximately 1 degree 38 minutes, i.e., one and one-half years, July 1804.[61] Now, in

---

61 The arc to December 1802 is noted as 32° 37'; added to the natal MC, we have SA MC 14 Capricorn 56. Orb to conjunction with Pluto is 1°38', equating to 1 year (1 degree generality) and 7 months (5' per month). The conjunction is precisely exact in July 1804, indeed one year and seven months later.

Figure 7 (below), with Arcs noted for December 1812, we see the SA MC past the conjunction, of course, but that conjunction will mark the beginning of our discussion of this second historical period in Beethoven's life. *Since it involves a rectified angle,* it is very important to our proof of the birth time.

In Figure 7, note also how the SA MC, Moon, Mercury, Sun, and Jupiter have all entered deeply into Beethoven's 12th House. The Sun has been there for some eighteen years, entering just after the *Heiligenstadt Letter* and Beethoven's shattering acknowledgment

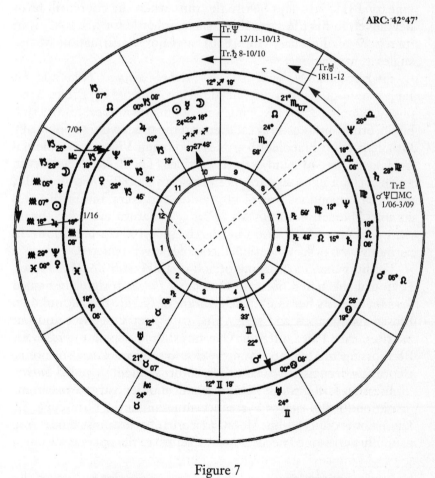

Figure 7

Inner Chart
Beethoven

Outer Chart
Solar Arcs
Dec. 16, 1812

of incipient total deafness. We can certainly expect a remarkable pulsation of the Venus-oriented Family Romance neurosis to twist the life painfully, especially with the Neptunian transit of the Midheaven, transiting Pluto's accentuation of the natal Neptune in the relationship 7th, the great tensions signified by SA Uranus conjunct Mars, opposing Mercury, and opposing the Sun, with SA Neptune semi-square the Midheaven. This second historical period promises to be a paroxysm, a convulsion of heroic pain.

We also can note SA Jupiter *nearing the Ascendant*, usually a tremendously positive measurement. This measurement is exact in January 1816, just days before the time when the court will favor Beethoven in his life-wrenching custody battle for his "son" Karl (precisely on February 16, 1816), a major confirmation of our angles as we shall see.

In July of 1804, with *SA MC precisely conjunct Pluto* and SA Jupiter semisquare Mercury, Beethoven completed his Eroica Symphony, Number 3.[62] This Symphony dominates musical history still, but its originality was so great then and the times were so politically turbulent (with Napoleon's armies occupying Vienna), people did not know where to stand in their reactions. The Eroica failed to win much acclaim upon its early performances in 1805. Astrologically, after the stupendous feat of inspiration and composition that was completed exactly with SA MC=Pluto, SA Saturn moved to square the midpoint of Sun/Moon in March-April 1805, a breakdown in harmony with others, the time the Eroica was premiered.

Additionally, in this time period of 1804 (still SA MC-Pluto), Beethoven sketched out his only opera, *Fidelio* (originally named *Leonore*, after its heroine). The creation of *Fidelio* (the faithful one) had so many stops and starts, fits, pains, revisions, out and out rewrites, even three different Overtures. In my opinion, *Fidelio* for Beethoven was a symbolic, unconsciously projected exposure vehicle for his deepest personal needs, showing them in veiled *human* forms instead of musical; *Fidelio* was still another extreme overcompensation for the lack of Water accentuation in the horoscope. SA Uranus was opposed his Moon, exacerbating his most tender and painfully imprisoned needs: Fidelio (Venus) in the opera is a woman

---

62 Actually, upon completion it was called the "Buonaparte" (Italian for Napoleon's last name). Beethoven formally changed the title to "Eroica" in October, 1806. Beethoven was all astew about Romanticism and Revolution, individual freedom and tyranny, upset with Napoleon's presumption to be Emperor. Solomon, 132–133.

disguised (Neptune) as a man (to become Beethoven himself?) conniving with the jailer of a prison to get to her husband, the political prisoner Florestan (Sun-ruled 7th) held in chains and alone deep in the dungeon (Neptune in the 7th). The enemy of the people, Don Pizarro (Saturn), compels the jailer to kill Florestan. Leonore unites with Florestan just before his planned death, and the benign Minister arrives (Uranus, the liberator), saves the day and frees Florestan, setting right a sorrowful human condition. Deepest darkness is conquered by brilliant light. Fidelio's faithfulness prevails; the virtuous wife's marriage to love, her loyalty to the ideal of freedom within that love, triumphs.

Only a few friends of Beethoven ventured to hear the opera at its premiere on November 20, 1805 (even with transiting Jupiter and Mars upon Beethoven's Sun, so insecure and stirred up were the political times).[63] Major rewrites took place, Fidelio was eventually reprieved, and became a success of granite-like, emotional heroics, greatly influencing Wagner.[64] That success took place in late May 1814 with *his SA MC just 15' of arc from exact conjunction with natal Venus!*

In January 1806 began the protracted transit of Pluto over Beethoven's Neptune and square to the Midheaven. Interestingly, Secondary Progressed Mars *assumed Direct motion* at 14 Gemini 45 and *SP Mercury conjoined Beethoven's Ascendant exactly*. We can anticipate the extension out of the *Fidelio* thrust (and symbolism) even more pressure on Beethoven's relationship problems, communicating perhaps a new freedom(!) in his idealizations, now

---

63 Reliable records of the first performances of *Fidelio* are chronicled: typically, "The story and plan of the piece are a miserable mixture of low manner and romantic situations; the airs, duets, and choruses equal to any praise ... intricacy is the character of Beethoven's music, and it requires a well-practiced ear, or a frequent repetition of the same piece to understand and distinguish its beauties ... it was much applauded ... Beethoven presided at the pianoforte and directed the performance himself ... Few people present, though the house would have been crowded in every part but for the present state of public affairs." Solomon, 144.

64 As an opera singer myself for some twenty years, I am very familiar with *Fidelio*; and I have sung the role of Don Pizarro often in Germany. *Fidelio* is among my handful of favorite operas because of its dramatic impact, its unique sweep of musical conception, its clear-cut interplay of human values, and because it is *emphatic*; you know exactly what the message is. The superb chorus *"Leb'wohl, du warmes Sonnenlicht"* (Farewell, thou warm sunshine) sung by the prisoners, later to return to that sunlight, is a great moment in operatic composition and drama. Because of the meaning of this chorus, its farewell to the light of freedom, and the plot itself, the hope for its return, the opera *Fidelio* was used by many opera houses of Germany and Austria to reopen their seasons in refurbished halls after the devastation of World War II.

clearly represented natally by Venus and Neptune. And indeed there *were* false reports published about supposed secret betrothals to Beethoven.

In addition, transiting Uranus squared natal Venus almost continuously from September 1806 to September 1807.

Intense Romance—There is a long list of real, imagined, and unattainable women—and a reliance upon them—throughout Beethoven's life. His pursuit of the unattainable is a dominant theme in all researchers' work (again a major statement about a 12th House Venus). We are understanding this as part of the Family Romance and the interplay of Venus and Neptune astrologically, related by the minor sesquiquadrate aspect (135 degrees; tension).

As I studied this enormous pain in Beethoven's life from our astrological point of view, I could grasp Neptune well—its musicality, its inspiration, the psychodynamic charade, the veil to the public, all that was other-than-it-seemed within Beethoven; its co-rulership of the Ascendant. I could grasp Venus, slow in development within Capricorn, idealized and martyred in the 12th House, alone, without support, and all-pervasive through peregrination. Always, I returned to Saturn: dominant, retrograde, the father-dysfunction symbolization at the Descendant marshalling the gate to relationships, administering the isolation (Pluto= Moon/Saturn; Saturn=Neptune/Pluto), inexplicably enforcing the relentless suffering of deafness, defining a Leonine ego aggrandizement that was truly epic. And I felt over and over again: *there must be a relationship here between Saturn and Venus*, between Saturn and Neptune, some geometry that synthesizes their positions further into Beethoven's undeniable, severe neurosis.

I suddenly saw it: while Saturn is semi-sextile to Neptune, Saturn—161 degrees from Venus (a quincunx, five signs, plus ten)—is *four noniles* (noviles) in its relation to Venus, i.e., 4 x (360/9 or 40)=160 degrees. *Here was synthesis in terms of the 9th harmonic*. I theorized the significance of this to give "the 160 aspect" the sense of Neptune. While I was pleased with my geometric paths to this conclusion (not presented here), I was happier still to have had this corroborated by two colleagues whom I telephoned immediately for consultation on the aspect—Michael Munkasey and John Townley, both specialists with harmonics and minor aspects.

Both agreed with me that the 160 was the nature of Neptune: Munkasey likened it to "Venus and Saturn on the telephone together, with Neptune paying for the call." Townley talked about the "bleeding heart liberal aspect" of the situation, "the helplessness of never getting what one wants, always wanting more." Of course, all of this is intensified by the lack of Water accentuation in Beethoven's horoscope.[65]

The synthesis of these interrelated planets, Venus, Saturn and Neptune (like the Midpoint Picture Venus=Saturn/Neptune), suggests "deluded love feelings, inhibitions, diminished emotional expression and sexual activity, unrequited love, and more."[66] Beethoven's Solar Arc Venus came to just this Midpoint picture (SA Venus=Saturn/Neptune, at 29 Leo 54) in June 1803 (romantic frustrations and his writing of the oratorio *Christ on the Mount of Olives*, just seven months after his *Heiligenstadt* crisis).

In the overview we are taking of Beethoven's life through the prism of astrology, we can not overlook that every major compositional zenith reached in Beethoven's career was paralleled by a tremendous nadir of emotional pain. Elliot Forbes, the distinguished Beethoven scholar who edited Thayer's monumental work in the Princeton edition, comments on Beethoven's frequent "decision to plunge into work when faced with the possibility of a permanent attachment with a woman."[67] This is a description of what I call Beethoven's escape valve, the sublimation of romance energies into work, the Neptune square to the Moon *and* to the rectified Midheaven.

It all came to a phantasmic climax with "Die unsterbliche Geliebte" (the *Immortal Beloved*), a mystery romance, an idealization, that begins strangely in 1806 (with transiting Pluto upon Neptune) and concludes mysteriously yet illuminated in the summer of 1812 (with SA Uranus opposed Sun, SA Neptune square Venus, and transiting Neptune conjunct the Midheaven), ending this Middle Period of Beethoven's life. Not only is this once again a test of our astrological angles but a stretching of Beethoven's neurotic yearning to the end of its limits.

---

65 It is helpful to recall Jacqueline Kennedy Onassis' horoscope (July 28, 1929 at 2:30 p.m. EDT in Southampton, NY): her dominant Saturn retrograde in 24 Sagittarius (exactly conjunct Beethoven's Sun!) in her 2nd House opposed her Venus in 21 Gemini (exactly conjunct Beethoven's Mars!) Here is powerful relationship between Saturn and Venus, ruler of her 7th, not a 160, but a registration of further understanding of the relationship between two planets in life manifestation.

66 See "Natal Midpoint Analysis Directory," Tyl: *Synthesis & Counseling*, Appendix.

67 Reported by Solomon, 158.

In respect for the length constraints of this presentation, we can cover only the bare outlines of this extraordinary idealistic quest. It is an intriguing mystery story. First the strange beginning in 1806:

✦ Beethoven wrote a letter dated only "July 6, Monday" to an unnamed woman in an unspecified location. He wrote morning, evening, and the next day, expressing intense passion, naming the lady only as his "Immortal Beloved." Copies of the letters were found among Beethoven's papers after his death.

✦ Initially, Alexander Thayer, the most respected Beethoven biographer (Berlin 1866), inserted 1806 *unknowingly wrongly* into the letter. But July 6 in 1806 was *not* a Monday—and so the mystery began. And so it was solved a century later by biographer Maynard Solomon.

✦ Solomon determined the date, the places, and the identity of the woman who fully reciprocated Beethoven's idealized, explosive, passionate love. "There was no tinge of amorous charade here; Beethoven, for the first and as far as we know the only time in his life, had found a woman whom he loved and who fully reciprocated his love." Solomon determined that the affair had climaxed in the summer of 1812 and that it had been between Beethoven and Antonie Brentano, a married woman in a family circle which often had Beethoven as guest.[68]

✦ Antonie Brentano was born on May 28, 1780, in Vienna. Her astrology with Beethoven's was remarkable: her Mars-Uranus conjunction in 23 Gemini conjoined his Mars, opposed his Mercury-Sun conjunction and trined his Ascendant tightly; her Venus (and I think, Ascendant) at 22 Cancer opposed his major Venus in Capricorn; her Lunar Nodal axis (always a key in synastric contacts) *was conjunct Beethoven's!* In 1812, transiting Uranus was conjunct those Nodal axes. She was the one, and we should note that from the list of possible women, astrology could have made the right selection and solved the mystery handily and conclusively!

---

68 Ibid., 159, Chapter 15 entirely.

✦ Worship of this woman from afar, through her family circle, turned into love sometime in the fall of 1811, according to Solomon, *with transiting Saturn—the emissary between Venus and Neptune, if you will—exactly conjunct Beethoven's Sun!* Here was the crystallization potential for his entire life, the immortality of the eternal love.

✦ *Transiting Neptune was upon Beethoven's Midheaven, and SA Neptune was semisquare the Midheaven as well, while transiting Uranus squared his Ascendant(!):* inspiration, yes; phantasm, yes; all senses heightened; but so easily, the ideal lost, the dissolution of personality, the identity destructured, the deepest life tension twisted again into pain and destroyed.

✦ Solomon analyzes, "the opportunity was at hand, therefore, to convert his conscious and professed desires for marriage and fatherhood into reality. Gratitude toward and love for Antonie, however, struggled against the ingrained patterns and habits of a lifetime [and an obsessive complex; his inability to relate, to be received; in this case, to believe it]." Beethoven did not want to bring break-up and sorrow to Antonie and her husband and children, to change the circumstances of their lives. He was decidedly and fearfully ambivalent, and close reading of his letter(s) shows that.

✦ There was a meeting and a platonic resolution into the future. Solomon feels that the failure of the affair "shattered" Beethoven's illusions that he could ever lead a normal sexual or family life. Solomon sees this as Beethoven's final renunciation of marriage and an acceptance of aloneness as his fate. In his diary, underlined, Beethoven wrote: *"Thou mayest no longer be a man,* not for thyself, only for others ..."

✦ Five years later, looking back, Beethoven told another family of friends his rationalization, certainly a paraphrase of his memory of his mother forty-three years earlier: that "he did not know a single married couple who on one side or the other did not repent the step he or she took in marrying; and that, for himself, he was excessively glad that not one of the girls whom he had passionately loved in former days had become his wife."[69]

---

69 Ibid., 188.

Venus, Neptune, Saturn

The final period of Beethoven's life spans from after the Period of the Eternal Beloved to his death in March 1827. The very respected, musically sophisticated New Grove biography refers to this last period as the "Transcendent" period. Is that because Beethoven was now over his love quest? While he was over the hurdle on the marriage level, he was not over it on the grand Family Romance level, and we shall see that drama in a moment. Was it that his works now took another turn: fewer, bigger, more final somehow? It seems so: Beethoven's output had been prodigious in the middle period of some twelve years, some thirty major works (including Symphonies 3 through 8), some thirty smaller works, and all of them personally guided through revisions, editing, copyist's corrections, proofreading, negotiations with publishers, etc. Age, emotional turmoil, the imponderably severe deafness now had all taken their extreme toll. In 1813, Beethoven was aged understandably and conspicuously well beyond his forty-three years.

Figure 8 (page 351) shows Beethoven's Solar Arc accumulation in December 1824, twelve and one-half years *after the Immortal Beloved* and two years and three months before his death. Look back to Figure 7 for a moment (page 343): most clearly, SP SA Sun is on its way out of the 12th House and will arrive exactly upon Beethoven's Ascendant in July 1824 (25' of arc back from the December 1824 position, i.e., five months) as shown in Figure 8. Beethoven should have a grand Hurrah then in 1823 and 1824!

Now, here in Figure 8 (page 351), note that transiting Saturn (in the 3rd House area) will square the Ascendant in March 1824 just as transiting Pluto squares Jupiter (simultaneity yet again), the latter transit to continue until Beethoven's death in March 1827. Transiting Saturn then goes on to cross the 4th cusp in June 1825. SA Pluto (see outer ring, Ascendant area) semisquares Venus and squares the Midheaven in 1825. And finally, SA Mars opposes the Ascendant—representing all of the formative tensions of Beethoven's life—in August 1826, when Beethoven is taken into his death illness. At his death, transiting Neptune was exactly conjunct his Pluto; fantasy and pretense, frustration and sublimation end.

After the Immortal Beloved affair that climaxed in failure in the summer of 1812, Beethoven's entire being went into shock. Transiting Neptune was constantly on his Midheaven from December 1811 through October 1813: he wrote to Archduke Rudolph (12/12), "I have been ailing, although mentally, it is true, more than physically." And further in January 1813, "As for my health, it is pretty much the same, the more so as moral causes are affecting it and these apparently are not very speedily removed." And then in May 1813 (with SA Neptune 10' of arc from exact semisquare with his Midheaven, and with transiting Saturn at his Mars/Saturn midpoint), "A number

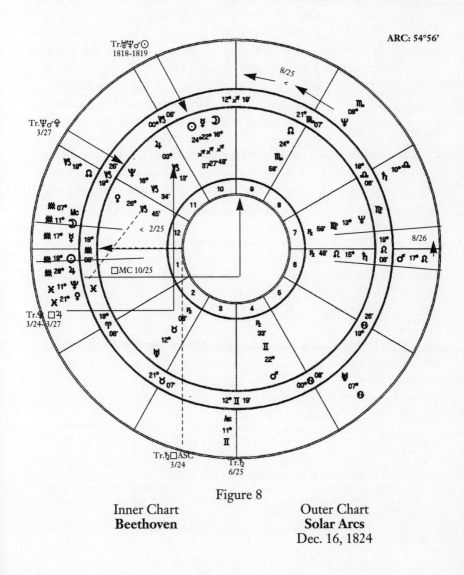

Figure 8

Inner Chart	Outer Chart
Beethoven	**Solar Arcs**
	Dec. 16, 1824

of unfortunate incidents occurring one after the other have really driven me into a state bordering on mental confusion."[70]

Solomon and Schindler suggest that Beethoven may have made an attempt to take his own life after the Immortal Beloved crisis, the attempt made the spring or summer of 1813 (see paragraph above). Suicidal thoughts were not uncommon to Beethoven (as we saw in the Heiligenstadt reference, "I was on the point of putting an end to my life ..." and in other letters to many friends).[71]

All sources report that Beethoven's mourning his Beloved had brought him into a mental and physical disorder that was unstable and also *brought his musical productivity to a halt.* The connoisseurs around him started to withdraw their allegiance. Here is the dissolution of the ego presented to us practically invariably by transit or arc contact between *Neptune* and the Midheaven (and other angles, but less publicly observable normally). Additionally and symbolically so poignant, the sources refer to this beginning of Beethoven's last period as "the dissolution of the heroic style."

The accumulation of 45 degrees by Solar Arc is an important time in everyone's life. The SA Semisquare[72] shows all natal planets arced uniformly to a strong tension point with their original positions at birth. It occurred in Beethoven's life, in 1815, precisely in February.

At this time, Beethoven was awarded honorary citizenship of Vienna (it appears like an end-of-career recognition), the revised *Fidelio* had been presented to great acclaim. What music writing he did was "for the public." Beethoven became a "rude materialist" as opposed to continuing as a monument for posterity.

The culmination of the Family Romance neurosis now took place, developing over a five-year period that began with this Solar Arc semisquare period: Beethoven's favored brother Carl Caspar became gravely ill with tuberculosis and then died on November 15, 1815. Carl's son Karl, Beethoven's nephew, immediately dominated Beethoven's mind and life.

---

70 Ibid., 219.

71 Curiously, this time of deep despondency was also a time when Beethoven made many references to prostitutes in his correspondence with a friend. They had a code word for the prostitutes, "fortresses." Soon Beethoven came out of the reaction formation (Neptune) to the horror of his crushed ideal and exhibited a sense of guilt and even revulsion concerning sexual activity, i.e., "bestial."

72 Bill Clinton precisely in election—November, 1991; O. J. Simpson precisely in double murder—June, 1994.

Beethoven detested Carl Caspar's wife (widow) who was named *Johanna* (we can note again Beethoven's extreme discomfort with an echo of his father's name, Johann, as we saw in the Heiligenstadt letter to Caspar and the younger brother also named Johann). On his deathbed, Caspar designated that Johanna and Ludwig were to be co-guardians of son Karl, who was nine at the time. Ludwig insisted *he* be made *sole* guardian. Then Caspar added a codicil to the will for emphasis: "I by no means desire that my son be taken away from his mother ... guardianship should be exercised equally by my wife and my brother."

Beethoven went to court, and in February 1816, precisely with Solar Arc Jupiter conjunct his Ascendant (see page 343), he was awarded favorable judgment to be Karl's sole guardian![73] Johanna then went continuously to court for almost five years, with Beethoven ultimately winning again, based upon his colossal reputation. The fight was bitter and scandalous.

Beethoven's ideal love had escaped him, his sexuality was gone, his hearing had abandoned him, his music had "failed" him (in terms of halted output indeed). He had to have family, a son. He had to gain that structure and security. This attachment to Karl overwhelmed Beethoven's personality. It raced into the vacuum of identity. Solomon states bluntly the consensus of all biographers that Beethoven apparently approached the borderline of irreversible pathology.[74]

Figure 9 (page 355) shows the tie between Ludwig and young Karl:[75] Ludwig's critical relationship trauma shown through Neptune is conjoined by Karl's exact Sun-Mercury opposition with Pluto which, in turn, tightly squares Ludwig's rectified Midheaven; Ludwig's awesomely pained Family Romance Venus is squared by Karl's Saturn-Uranus conjunction; and *Karl's Nodal axis is precisely*

---

73 Autexier, 80; Solomon, Chapter 18; and other sources.

74 So extreme was this attachment to work out his Family Romance neurosis, that books have been written solely about Ludwig and young Karl's relationship; deep psychoanalytic treatises that do not affect our astrology, but do delineate the pained vortex of Beethoven's emotional disintegration.

75 I have done a general rectification of Karl's horoscope, based upon details of his tortured early life and *his later suicide attempt* (two shots to the head) to rid himself of Ludwig's dominance.

conjunct the master's Sun![76] This is extraordinary corroboration of everything we have shared astrologically about Beethoven's neurotic life development and vulnerability to obsession.

Within Beethoven's horoscope alone, we see Venus rulership of the brother-3rd; we see the brother's child (fifth of the 3rd) bringing the 7th House forward, ruled by the Sun and Mercury, both so severely under stress, with Saturn retrograde upon the cusp and Neptune retrograde within the 7th referring to deepened pathology and contrapuntal themes.

It was during a high-court hearing about Karl on December 18, 1818 that Beethoven's tacit nobility pretense was finally completely shattered. In response to direct questioning, *he confessed that nobility was not his.* In exactly that month, transiting Pluto was exactly square Beethoven's Sun, transiting Uranus and Neptune in conjunction conjoined his Sun, transiting Saturn exactly squared his Midheaven on that day, transiting Jupiter conjoined his Pluto, and Mars was exactly conjunct his Moon ... two days after his birthday, the day before his mother's.

Johanna continued to fight.

On March 29, 1820, a final hearing on this issue began. "The magistrates, aware that political influence had been brought to bear,"[77] ruled on April 8 that Beethoven should be appointed guardian. Then, Johanna appealed the decision to the emperor(!), but to no avail. On July 24, 1820, the case was closed (Ludwig's SA Venus had come to the square with his Moon just 25 minutes of arc earlier, and his SP SA Sun was applying to opposition with his Saturn).

An extraordinary wrinkle in this story is that Karl's mother, Johanna became pregnant in the spring of 1820 (to replace her "stolen" child?). She then named her new daughter *Ludovica*, the feminine form of Ludwig.

After all of this and Beethoven's public demeanor on his walks and in his minimal social interaction, peering into people's windows, ranting and raving in the streets, Vienna thought Beethoven, its greatest composer, was a "sublime madman." Goethe was told

---

76 The Lunar Nodal axis tie with a planet or point in someone else's horoscope is extremely important and even obsessing; Hitler and Eva Braun, Prince Ranier and Grace Kelly, and so many more famous couples and tragic pairs. Recall the congruence of Nodal Axes with the "Immortal Beloved" (p. 207). Please see, Tyl: *Synthesis & Counseling*, sections One-C and Two-E beginning 207.

77 Solomon, 249.

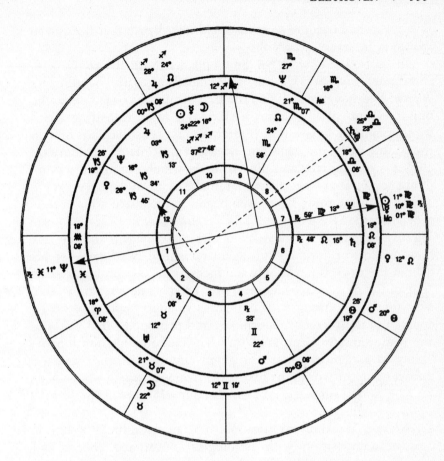

Figure 9

Inner Chart	Outer Chart

Ludwig Van Beethoven   Karl Van Beethoven (Rectification)

Dec. 16, 1770, 11:03 A.M. LMT   Sept. 4, 1806, 11:24 A.M. LMT

Bonn, Germany   Vienna, Austria

07E05   50N44   16E20   48N13

Placidus Houses

+ 0:00 UT		Geocentric Tropical Longitudes for DEC 1818										
Date	Sid.Time	Sun	Moon	Node	Mercury	Venus	Mars	Jupiter	Saturn	Uranus	Neptune	Pluto
15	5:32:12	22♐28 54	17♋43	26♈42	10♑41	10♑27℞	14♐55	17♑28	12×16	20♐30	26♐04	24×22
16	5:36:08	23 29 50	29 36	26 39	12 04	10 04	15 39	17 42	12 19	20 33	26 07	24 22
17	5:40:05	24 30 55	11♌31	26 36	13 25	09 39	16 23	17 55	12 22	20 37	26 09	24 22
18	5:44:02	25 32 00	23 33	26 32	14 44	09 12	17 07	18 09	12 25	20 40	26 11	24 22
19	5:47:58	26 33 06	05♍43	26 29	16 01	08 43	17 51	18 22	12 29	20 44	26 13	24 23
20	5:51:55	27 34 13	18 07	26 26	17 14	08 12	18 36	18 36	12 32	20 48	26 16	24 23

Copyright (C) 1987 Matrix Software, Big Rapids MI 49307

Beethoven had become a lunatic. Schindler wrote that Beethoven looked to be seventy years old.

In early 1821, with SA Sun opposed Saturn exactly, and, simultaneously, SA Uranus in opposition with Beethoven's *Jupiter*, Beethoven developed the first symptoms of jaundice, the ominous sign of liver disease (Jupiter). Also, transiting Pluto would begin to square that Jupiter, a most sensitive spot now in the ending of Beethoven's life. Beethoven ultimately did develop cirrhosis of the liver and died from it, which condition was no doubt accelerated by a substantial intake of alcoholic beverages.[78]

At the same time, Beethoven began to reconstruct his professional life, *the SP SA Sun applied to his Ascendant in 1822–1824* (see Figure 8, page 351). The volcano stirred once again and the lava flowed; the world would still again recognize Beethoven for his genius. He worked ploddingly and incessantly; he was described as "one of the most active men who ever lived";[79] he was rarely seen, even for meals. Along with numerous smaller works, Beethoven completed the tortuous, enormous, and profound *Missa Solemnis* and made substantial progress on what was to be his Ninth Symphony, a gargantuan mark of genius innovation and dramatic impact upon the world, the first performance of which was on May 7, 1824, *just 10 minutes of arc before SA Sun=ASC partile!*[80]

Special Note: We know rectification to be a most difficult task. It is creative composition with astrological notes and chords and themes, working within prescribed rhythms of time and forms of history. Our astrology emphatically fits Beethoven's life reality in the substance of analysis and the duration of time. Over and over again, we have seen transits and arcs to angles and to the Moon *coinciding naturally within life activity and psychological development.*

---

78 Ibid., 257.

79 According to Johann Sporschil, historian and publicist studying in Vienna at the time, reported by Solomon.

80 The Ninth Symphony utilizing vocal soloists and a massive chorus along with the orchestra in the final movement—an extraordinary break with form, style, tradition—was extremely influential on another genius, Richard Wagner. Wagner, who was only eleven years old at the time of the premiere, would credit the Ninth as inspiration for his own grand break from operatic traditions with his original form-concept of "Music Drama." Wagner himself conducted the Ninth Symphony in concert many times.

Additionally, Beethoven received a gold medal, weighing one-half pound (21 Louis d'or), from Louis XVIII of France. Schindler suggested that this medal was "the greatest distinction conferred upon the master during his lifetime." Schindler-MacArdle, 242.

The true test of birth time is indeed the orientation of the angles of the horoscope within time. When we *also* inspect the Secondary Progressed Moon in relation to the angles, we have a *triple-bind check* on the birth time, as it were, since the Moon and the two angular axes *all* are sensitive to the slightest change of birth time; each determines and depends on the others.

Within the three major periods of Beethoven's life, the following *angular contacts were made by the Secondary Progressed Moon:*

✦ *SP Moon conjunct Ascendant (19 Aquarius)* June 1804: this is precisely to the month when Beethoven completed the Eroica Symphony Number 3, the monumental, giant statement that established his personal position within music history and changed the course of that history forever.

✦ *SP Moon conjunct the 4th cusp, opposed MC (12 Gemini-Sagittarius)* July 1812: this is precisely to the month when Beethoven's rapture for the Immortal Beloved came to full development, realizing his enforced pattern of failure in relationships, ending the interpersonal romance charades of his life, the difficulties stemming from his early parental trauma.

✦*SP Moon conjunct the 7th cusp, opposed ASC (19 Leo-Aquarius)* November 1816: this time coincided with the Progressed Full Moon as well, the period when Beethoven neurotically completed his Family Romance relationship delusion, imagining *he actually was* Karl's (his nephew's) father, gaining custody of Karl, and, a bit later, succeeding in his demand that Karl call him "Father."[81]

✦*SP Moon conjunct the MC (12 Sagittarius)* February 1825: in this month exactly, Beethoven completed the first of the five great works that ended his compositional output, exclusively in the medium of the String Quartet (which he had begun in May 1822 and had put aside in favor of the Ninth Symphony). "The five late string quartets contain Beethoven's greatest music."[82]

---

81 "But Beethoven's central delusion in this pathological sequence was even more extraordinary: he began to imagine that he had become a father in reality. [There are many letters and diary entries to this effect throughout 1816.] 'I am now the real physical father (*wirklicher leiblicher Vater*) of my deceased brother's child.'" Solomon, 235.

82 New Grove, 133, and all sources.

At this time in 1825, Beethoven was experiencing as well the penultimate powerful arc to an angle in his horoscope: *SA Pluto square the Midheaven* (see Figure 8, page 351), exact in October 1825, certainly a milestone in one's life, yet for Beethoven, so grievously wounded, *also the beginning of his final breakdown and death.*

The greatness of the final Quartets is attributed to profundity of thought and feeling. Again, Beethoven changes the course of music history with his originality, always going beyond the bounds of tradition and accepted style. Finally, we see some mentions of lyrical beauty in the critical descriptions of his work. We also hear a dramatically dissonant fury in some movements of the works as if myriad ideas were scrambling to be heard at the same time. Some singular movements from the Quartets played by just four musicians have been compared in weight of impact with the Ninth Symphony finale, marshalled by forces usually 200 strong! To the Quartet in B-flat, op. 130 (citing the original last movement, the *Grosse Fuge*), Stravinsky responded: "this absolutely contemporary piece of music will be contemporary for ever."[83]

Look again, please, at Figure 8 (page 351). Note that Solar Arc Pluto (in the Ascendant area) when square the Midheaven is *simultaneously* semisquaring the problematic Venus. The musical inspiration and career power are clear, but so *is the painful revival of Beethoven's problematic ties to family/sexual neurosis.* At this time, all sources report that "Beethoven had now become obsessed with Karl's sexuality,"[84] (clearly a transference of his own). Beethoven exerted every effort to block his nephew from sexual opportunities of any sort; he spied upon the boy and continued to attempt to separate him from social interaction that could become intimate.

Finally, Karl could not take Beethoven's confinement any longer. On July 30, 1826, Karl wrote suicide notes, bought two pistols, went to Baden to the top of a mountain, and shot himself in the head. Miraculously, he failed to take his life. This suicide attempt occurred exactly coincidental with the *final* major Arc in Beethoven's life: SA Mars conjunct the 7th cusp, opposed the Ascendant.

It is most telling to recall that Beethoven's rectified Ascendant of 19 Aquarius 08 is almost precisely square the midpoint of

---

83 Ibid., 135.
84 Solomon, 280.

Venus/Neptune (ASC=Venus/Neptune). Here is the music thrust, yes, but also statement of the contrapuntal theme we have been following throughout this analysis, the love-relationship frustration and the Family Romance defense. At the time of Karl's suicide attempt, SA Mars arriving to opposition with Beethoven's rectified Ascendant *also conjoined its midpoint relationship to Beethoven's Venus and Neptune.*

At the same time, throughout the month of June 1826, thirty days before Karl's suicide attempt, transiting Saturn opposed Beethoven's Sun.[85] His health worsening for three months, Beethoven became gravely ill: inflammation of the lungs (Gemini, Mercury); his "respiration threatened suffocation" (Mercury); and his liver (Jupiter).

On December 7, 1826, Beethoven seemed to rally. He could sit up and correspond (SA Mercury conjunct Ascendant). He wrote to long-time friend, Dr. Wegeler about—above all things—a renunciation of the rumor about his royal birth, "being the natural son of the late King of Prussia!" While Beethoven had denied this fantasy in court during the custody proceedings about Karl, he had yet to bring the issue to personal closure on his own. Realizing his imminent death, this was the time. He asked Wegeler "to make known to the world the integrity of my parents and especially of my mother."[86]

On that day, Beethoven's SP Moon was precisely upon his peregrine Jupiter, dispositor of his Moon and ruler of his Midheaven.[87]

Following this short remission of his illnesses, Beethoven's condition once again rapidly deteriorated. He was trembling and shivering and was bent double because of the pains that raged in his liver (Jupiter) and intestines (Mercury, Virgo) and his terribly swollen feet (Jupiter, Neptune, Pisces). His abdomen was tapped to release enormous amounts of fluid, and he was given frozen alcoholic beverages to relieve discomfort. From December 20 on, Beethoven was confined to his bed.[88]

---

85 "Karl's suicide attempt thus bespoke his shattering rejection of Beethoven's presumed fatherhood. Beethoven wrote: 'all my hopes have vanished.'" Solomon, 285.

86 Ibid., 286.

87 And interestingly, the SP SA Sun was upon the Ascendant of the SP horoscope for that SP date (February 10, 1771, at birth time and location; i.e., symbolically Beethoven's birth year picture beginning in December, 1826).

88 The underlying pathology became evident on December 13 when Beethoven developed jaundice and ascites (dropsy). The abdominal taps to relieve the enormous amounts of fluid were done on December 20, January 8, February 2, and 27. Autexier, 88.

As Beethoven's end quickly approached, one lovely scene transpired in his chamber: two young singers, an engaged couple who "worshipped" Beethoven, came to pay their respects. Beethoven asked the tenor, Luigi Cramolini, to sing for him. Writing to Beethoven in his "Conversation Book," adoring pleasantries were exchanged and the little recital was arranged. Schindler (the biographer himself) who was regularly present, sat down at the piano, and Luigi tried to sing. However, he found that he was incapable of making a sound, so emotionally overwhelming was the situation. When Schindler explained (wrote) the situation to Beethoven, the master laughed heartily and said to them: "Sing, sing then, my dear Luigi; unfortunately I can't hear you, but I would like at least *to see* you sing!"

Finally, Luigi gathered himself and sang Beethoven's adored song *Adelaide*. Luigi's own report continues: "When I had finished, he called me to his bed and said, tightly squeezing my hand: 'I saw from your breathing that you sang it the way it should be, and I read on your face that you felt what you sang. You have given me great pleasure.'"[89]

Karl had been at Beethoven's bedside throughout December. Their conflicts were over. Karl, in the military and apart from Beethoven, then wrote: "My dear father[!] ... I am living in contentment and regret only that I am separated from you." On March 23 (1827), "Beethoven wrote his last testament, willing everything to 'My nephew Karl.' Beethoven put down his pen, saying, 'There! I won't write another word.'"[90] In the will, upon Karl's death, Johanna, his mother, would be the heir[!].

Schindler wrote a letter on March 24 saying that Beethoven "feels the end coming, for yesterday he said to me and H. v. Breuning, 'Plaudite, amici, comoedia finita est.'" (*Applaud, friends, the comedy is ended*, a well-known Latin epithet).[91]

On the wall of Beethoven's chamber was the oil painting of his beloved grandfather, the Kapellmeister Ludwig van Beethoven.

On the same day, some wines arrived that Beethoven had ordered some time before his critical illness, and Schindler brought

---

89 Autexier, 95, and other sources.
90 Solomon, 292.
91 Ibid., 292.

the bottles to Beethoven's bedside. Beethoven whispered, "Pity, pity—too late!" and spoke no more.

Beethoven fell into a coma that evening.

On March 26, 1827, there was a strange turn in the weather: snow was piled outside, it was very cold, and there were snow flurries, with thunder and lightning. This unusual weather was described as a "revolution in nature."[92]

Anselm Huettenbrenner, an esteemed composer and music lover, had come to pay his respects to Beethoven, the master, before his death. Although he was not personally known to Beethoven, Huettenbrenner was known to Beethoven's friends. They had given the comatose Beethoven up for dead and therefore allowed the devoted musician in to view Beethoven. Late in the afternoon of that final day, Huettenbrenner and a woman were alone with Beethoven. Huettenbrenner reported an enormous crack of thunder and bolt of lightning which illuminated the "death chamber" with a harsh light. "After this unexpected natural phenomenon, at about 5:45,"[93] Beethoven momentarily opened his eyes, lifted his right hand, and clenched it into a fist. When his hand fell back from this effort, Beethoven was dead.[94]

Figure 10 (page 362) is the chart for the moment of Beethoven's death, i.e., "at about 5:45 P.M." What is truly remarkable about this chart is that *all four angles are at the Aries Point*, almost precisely; if Beethoven indeed died at 5:46:40 P.M., one and one-half minutes later, the *four* angles would measure 0 degrees of the Cardinal signs precisely. Additionally, the Saturn in this chart "equals" the midpoints of Moon/Pluto and Sun/Moon; transiting Saturn had come to opposition with Beethoven's natal Pluto/*Midheaven* Midpoint, "circumstances of death." Finally, note the Sun-Pluto conjunction in Aries, projected to the world at the Descendant. At that moment in time in Vienna, indeed—with a bolt of lightning—an historic hero had died.

Figure 11 (page 362) shows the death chart in the outer ring of Beethoven's rectified horoscope. The remarkable conjunction of transiting Venus precisely upon Beethoven's Ascendant fulfills our wish that Beethoven died with inner peace.

---

92 Detailed person, on-the-scene reports; Landon, 232-234.

93 New Grove, 88; and other sources, from Huettenbrenner's description.

94 Solomon, 292; Robbins, 232.

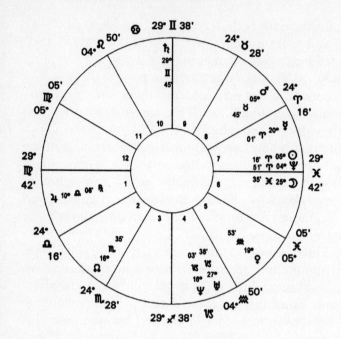

Figure 10
**Beethoven's
Death**
Mar. 26, 1827
5:45 P.M. LMT
Vienna, Austria
16E20   48N13
Placidus Houses

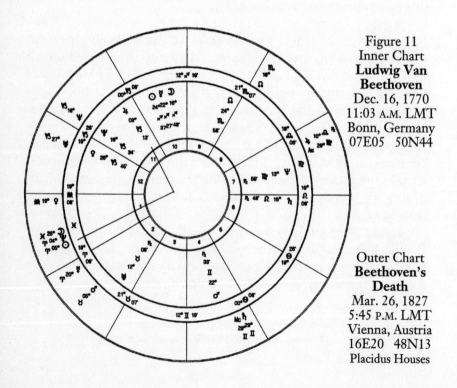

Figure 11
Inner Chart
**Ludwig Van
Beethoven**
Dec. 16, 1770
11:03 A.M. LMT
Bonn, Germany
07E05   50N44

Outer Chart
**Beethoven's
Death**
Mar. 26, 1827
5:45 P.M. LMT
Vienna, Austria
16E20   48N13
Placidus Houses

But note transiting Uranus and Neptune as well. Here are sharp, dramatic reiterations of the struggles of Beethoven's entire life: the triumph of the heroic rebel through the veils of Family Romance neurosis (tr. Uranus with Venus, 160° natal Saturn; tr. Neptune with Pluto quincunx natal Saturn). In the death chart's congruence with the potentials and actualities of life, we can see corroboration that Beethoven *did* come to grips with it all finally, recanting his noble-birth rumor, projecting his estate through Karl to Johanna.

Johanna is Beethoven's Pluto here, the ruler of his 9th, the seventh of his 3rd, i.e., his brother's wife, another embodiment of the unattainable woman and the final reference perspective of his life's dream of family. With transiting Neptune exactly upon his Pluto at his death, it is no surprise that "the woman in the room" at the moment of Beethoven's death—the identity suppressed by Schindler and unknown for almost fifty years until given correctly to Thayer—was indeed *Johanna* van Beethoven. Schindler had thought such a [an implicit?] reconciliation to have been impossible; he was antipathetic to Johanna and Karl because of the upset to Beethoven's life. In fact, Schindler urged Huettenbrenner, the only other witness to Beethoven's death, to reconsider the fact about Johanna being the woman in the room, and himself substituted the name of Therese van Beethoven, the younger brother Nikolaus Johann's wife, into the account of Beethoven's death.[95]

But it was indeed *Johanna* who cut a lock of Beethoven's hair and gave it to Huettenbrenner, the sole other witness, as a "sacred souvenir of Beethoven's last hour."

The crowd attending Beethoven's funeral on March 29 was formidable, estimated variously from 20,000 to 30,000 people—an enormous gathering in those times—including eight *Kapellmeister* as pallbearers. At the gate to the cemetery in the suburban village of Waehring, the actor Heinrich Anschuetz delivered a funeral oration written by Franz Gillparzer. At the grave site, a choral *Miserere* was sung to the somber accompaniment of four trombones.

Sixty-one years later in 1888, Beethoven's remains were moved to the Central Cemetery in Vienna.

---

95 Ibid., 293.

Beethoven was born at 11:03 in the morning, local mean time on Sunday, December 16, 1770 in Bonn, Germany. I must believe the details of biography, the confluence of astrological measurements, the analysis of life and astrological deductions, and how all these come together to sound the chord, to establish the tonality of Beethoven's being. My conviction must prevail in the respect I have for my craft, my work with it, the labor of love this research has commanded, and what the hunt has provided: the emphatic astrological sound of the master.

Bibliography

Listed in order of 1994 bookstore/library accessibility:

Autexier, Phillipe A. *Beethoven: The Composer as Hero.* New York: Harry N. Abrams, Inc., Discoveries, 1992.

Kerman, Joseph and Tyson, Alan. *The New Grove BEETHOVEN.* New York: W. W. Norton & Company, 1983.

Solomon, Maynard. *Beethoven.* New York: Schirmer Books, 1979, Paperback Edition.

Schindler, Anton Felix. *Beethoven as I Knew Him;* Editor. Donald W. MacArdle. New York: W. Norton & Company, 1966.

Landon, H. C. Robbins. *Beethoven: His Life, Work and World.* London: Thames and Hudson, 1992. [Particularly important for the thirty-seven pictures of sketches, paintings, and sculpture of Beethoven from age thirteen to his death.]

Wegeler, Franz and Ferdinand Ries. *Beethoven Remembered.* Arlington, VA: Great Ocean Publishers, 1987.

Thayer, Alexander W. *The Life of Ludwig van Beethoven,* Volumes I and II; Editor. Elliot Forbes. Princeton, New Jersey, 1964. [The master source, but hard to find, even in libraries.]

Elliot Forbes is the renowned Beethoven scholar and editor of this epic Thayer biography of Beethoven, in the Princeton Edition, 1964, 1967. I knew professor Forbes —"El"—at Harvard and reached out to him before preparing this rectification to see if there were any hidden birth details that would help my research.

In my telephone discussion with El about this astrological project, he was respectfully startled, momentarily bemused, and clearly delighted with the fresh approach. With great charm, he said, "Well, Noel, this won't be the first time that superior powers have been brought into the discussion about the Master!"

In his "review" letter to me after studying this astrological profile, El voiced a "Bravo!" and with my permission presented the chapter to the Edna Loeb Music Library at Harvard.

Kendall, Alan. *The Life of Beethoven.* London: Hamlyn Publishing Group Ltd., 1978.

Woodford, Peggy. *Mozart: his Life and Times.* Kent, England: Midas Books, 1977.

Recording Notes. *Beethoven/Bernstein 9 Symphonies.* Deutsche Grammophone, 1980.

Index

STAY IN TOUCH!

On the following pages you will find listed, with their current prices, some of the books now available on related subjects. Your book dealer stocks most of these and will stock new titles in the Llewellyn series as they become available. We urge your patronage.

TO GET A FREE CATALOG

You are invited to write for our bimonthly news magazine/catalog, *Llewellyn's New Worlds of Mind and Spirit*. A sample copy is free, and it will continue coming to you at no cost as long as you are an active mail customer. Or you may subscribe for just $10 in the United States and Canada ($20 overseas, first class mail). Many bookstores also have *New Worlds* available to their customers. Ask for it.

In *New Worlds* you will find news and features about new books, tapes and services; announcements of meetings and seminars; helpful articles; author interviews and much more. Write to:

Llewellyn's New Worlds of Mind and Spirit
P.O. Box 64383-735, St. Paul, MN 55164-0383, U.S.A.

TO ORDER BOOKS AND TAPES

If your book store does not carry the titles described on the following pages, you may order them directly from Llewellyn by sending the full price in U.S. funds, plus postage and handling (see below).

Credit card orders: VISA, MasterCard, American Express are accepted. Call us toll-free within the United States and Canada at 1-800-THE-MOON.

Special Group Discount: Because there is a great deal of interest in group discussion and study of the subject matter of this book, we offer a 20% quantity discount to group leaders or agents. Our Special Quantity Price for a minimum order of five copies of *Astrolgy of the Famed* is $87.80 cash-with-order. Include postage and handling charges noted below.

Postage and Handling: Include $4 postage and handling for orders $15 and under; $5 for orders *over* $15. There are no postage and handling charges for orders over $100. Postage and handling rates are subject to change. We ship UPS whenever possible within the continental United States; delivery is guaranteed. Please provide your street address as UPS does not deliver to P.O. boxes. Orders shipped to Alaska, Hawaii, Canada, Mexico and Puerto Rico will be sent via first class mail. Allow 4–6 weeks for delivery. **International orders:** Airmail – add retail price of each book and $5 for each non-book item (audiotapes, etc.); Surface mail – add $1 per item.

Minnesota residents add 7% sales tax.

Mail orders to:
Llewellyn Worldwide, P.O. Box 64383-735, St. Paul, MN 55164-0383, U.S.A.

For customer service, call (612) 291-1970.

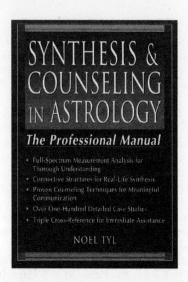

SYNTHESIS & COUNSELING IN ASTROLOGY
The Professional Manual
by Noel Tyl
One of the keys to a vital, comprehensive astrology is the art of synthesis, the capacity to take the parts of our knowledge and combine them into a coherent whole. Many times, the parts may be contradictory (the relationship between Mars and Saturn, for example), but the art of synthesis manages the unification of opposites. Now Noel Tyl presents ways astrological measurements—through creative synthesis—can be used to effectively counsel individuals. Discussion of these complex topics is grounded in concrete examples and in-depth analyses of the 122 horoscopes of celebrities, politicians, and private clients.

Tyl's objective in providing this vitally important material was to present everything he has learned and practiced over his distinguished career to provide a useful source to astrologers. He has succeeded in creating a landmark text destined to become a classic reference for professional astrologers.
1-56718-734-X, 924 pgs., 7 x 10, 115 charts, softcover $29.95

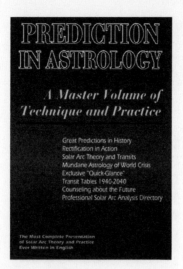

PREDICTION IN ASTROLOGY
A Master Volume of Technique and Practice
by Noel Tyl

No matter how much you know about astrology already, no matter how much experience you've had to date, you'll be fascinated by Prediction in Astrology, and you'll grow as an astrologer. Using the Solar Arc theory and methods he describes in this book, the author was able to accurately predict the Gulf War, including the actual date it would begin and the timetable of tactics, two months before it began. He also predicted the overturning of Communist rule in the Eastern bloc nations nine months in advance of its actual occurrence.

Tyl teaches through example. You learn by doing astrology, not just thinking about it. Tyl introduces Solar Arc theory in terms of "rapport" measurements, which you begin to do immediately, without paper, pencil, or computer, dials, or wheels. Just with your eyes! You will never look at a horoscope the same way again!

Tyl, in his well-known, very special way, also gets personal. He presents 30 Aphorisms, the keenest of maxims, the most practical of techniques, to create predictions from any horoscope. And as if this were not enough, Tyl then presents 20 Aphorisms for Counseling. Look for Tyl's "Quick-Glance" Transit Table, 1940-2040, to which you can refer more quickly than a computer. The busy astrologer will use this Appendix every day for many years to come.

0-87542-814-2, 360 pgs., 6 x 9, softcover   **$17.95**

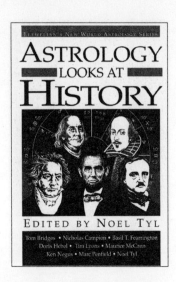

ASTROLOGY LOOKS AT HISTORY
edited by Noel Tyl

This book shows astrology performing at its very best through rectification (working backwards to determine someone's correct birthtime), capturing in astrological terms the fascinating lives of geniuses who have touched the development of the arts, sciences and government in Western history. *Astrology Looks at History* reveals the details of personal development in the lives of 10 notables, and illuminates their interactions with the world as they changed it.

- Scholars are one day off on Shakespeare's birth; astrology establishes that he was murdered! – Maurice McCann

- Why such a powerful man named Machiavelli was so withdrawn, reclusive, and realistic – Basil T. Fearrington

- Astrology studies with keen historical grounding the many times lightning struck in the life of Benjamin Franklin – Tim Lyons

- The meanings between the lines of Edgar Allen Poe's tortured life, sensitive spirit and wondrous imagination – Doris Hebel

- Historical detail about Slavery, Jamestown, and Lincoln reveals a country in the making – Marc Penfield

- What do the Creation of the World, the horoscope of astrology and Jack the Ripper have in common? – Nicholas Campion

- Astrology times Nelson Mandela's past and projects into the future – Noel Tyl

1-56718-868-0, 464 pgs., 6x9, 92 charts, softcover $16.95

Prices subject to change without notice.

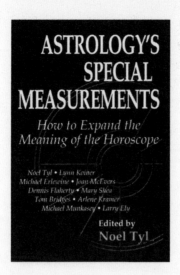

ASTROLOGY'S SPECIAL MEASUREMENTS
How to Expand the Meaning of the Horoscope
edited by Noel Tyl

Every new student of astrology looks with bewilderment at that first horoscope and asks, "What's it mean when there's nothing in my 7th house? Won't I ever get married?" The student feels the strong need to measure. He needs something to define the space in the house and give meaning to the picture. Measurements are the lenses that help us see nearer, farther, and with greater contrast and clarity. In the process of analysis, measurement becomes diagnosis.

In this volume, ten experts discuss the finer points of measurement and meaning, analysis and diagnosis. How many measurements do you need? How many should fortify you for meaningful conversations with clients? Not all measurements work in every horoscope or for every astrologer—and too many can present so much data that you lose confidence within the multiplicity of options. Furthermore, no matter how precise the measurements, they still rely on the astrologer to adapt them to the human condition. *Astrology's Special Measurements* will be a tremendous resource for putting those special measurements to work easily and without fear.

1-56718-864-8, 6 x 9, 352 pgs., charts, tables, softbound $12.00

Prices subject to change without notice.

Wendy Ashley ◆ *Christian Borup*
◆ *Susie Cox* ◆ *Donna Cunningham* ◆
Karen M. Hamaker-Zondag ◆ *Jeff Jawer*
◆ *Haloli Q. Richter* ◆ *Diana Stone*

Edited by Noel Tyl

COMMUNICATING THE HOROSCOPE
edited by Noel Tyl

Help your clients reach personal fulfillment through thoughtful counseling! Each person's unique point of view functions as a badge of identification that can alert you to what you should listen for during a consultation. The horoscope presents a portrait of each person's perspective, which the successful consultant will use to communicate and counsel clients more effectively.

Communicating the Horoscope presents the viewpoints of nine contributing astrologers on factors crucial to a client's successful analysis: the importance of the timing of the consultation for both client and astrologer; how to help clients explore major issues and how to use the insights of their charts to sort out problems; suggestions for reading the client's behavior and unspoken messages; ways to simplify chart interpretations for clients unfamiliar with astrology and translate the horoscope into terms they can grasp; techniques for empathetic listening; and how interpreting the chart in terms of its possibilities opens clients to making the changes necessary for their own growth. Includes many insightful chart examples.

1-56718-866-4, 6 x 9, 256 pp., charts, softcover　　　　**$12.00**

Prices subject to change without notice.

EXPLORING CONSCIOUSNESS IN THE HOROSCOPE
edited by Noel Tyl
When Llewellyn asked astrologers across the country which themes to include in its "New World Astrology Series," most specified at the top of their lists themes that explore consciousness! From shallow pipedreaming to ecstatic transcendence, "consciousness" has come to envelop realms of emotion, imagination, dreams, mystical experiences, previous lives and lives to come—aspects of the mind which defy scientific explanation. For most, consciousness means self-realization, the "having it all together" to function individualistically, freely, and confidently.

There are many ways to pursue consciousness, to "get it all together." Astrology is an exciting tool for finding the meaning of life and our part within it, to bring our inner selves together with our external realities, in appreciation of the spirit. Here, then, ten fine thinkers in astrology come together to share reflections on the elusive quicksilver of consciousness. They embrace the spiritual—and the practical. All are aware that consciousness feeds our awareness of existence; that, while it defies scientific method, it is vital for life.
0-87542-391-4, 256 pgs., 6 x 9, tables, charts, softcover $12.00

Prices subject to change without notice.

Be the Best Astrologer You Can Be!

NOEL TYL'S

Certification Correspondence Course for Astrologers

22 challenging lessons — for those who already know the basics of astrology — to build your analytical and counseling strengths; each written lesson accompanied by a test and followed by an evaluation! ■ That's 22 tests, one every step of the way to professionalism, with Noel Tyl's personal audiotape evaluation to help polish your performance on each one! ■ And then the Final Examination, 30 text-pages to fulfill Tyl's certification as "Practicing Professional Astrologer."

NOEL TYL'S Certification Correspondence Course for Astrologers is your opportunity to be the apprentice, associate, and colleague of one of the world's most skilled astrologers. This demanding course builds your strength at *your* pace, through 22 lessons and over 150 case studies, to the culmination of learning that certifies you as a practicing professional astrologer.

This is Your Chance of a Careertime!

For full details, call: (602) 816-0000. Or write:

TCC, 17005 PLAYER COURT, FOUNTAIN HILLS, AZ 85268-5721